PRACTICAL JAVA™ GAME PROGRAMMING

DUSTIN CLINGMAN

SHAWN KENDALL

SYRUS MESDAGHI

CHARLES RIVER MEDIA, INC.
Hingham, Massachusetts

Publisher: Jenifer Niles
Cover Design: The Printed Image

CHARLES RIVER MEDIA, INC.
10 Downer Avenue
Hingham, Massachusetts 02043
781-740-0400
781-740-8816 (FAX)
info@charlesriver.com
www.charlesriver.com

This book is printed on acid-free paper.

Dustin Clingman, Shawn Kendall, Syrus Mesdaghi. *Practical Java Game Programming*.
ISBN: 1-58450-326-2

Library of Congress Cataloging-in-Publication Data
Clingman, Dustin.
  Practical Java game programming / Dustin Clingman, Shawn Kendall, Syrus Mesdaghi.
     p. cm.
  ISBN 1-58450-326-2 (pbk. with cd-rom : alk. paper)
  1. Java (Computer program language) 2. Computer games—Programming. I. Kendall, Shawn. II. Mesdaghi, Syrus. III. Title.
  QA76.73.J38C56 2004
  794.8'1526—dc22

                              2004008478

Printed in the United States of America
04 7 6 5 4 3 2 First Edition

**Books are to be returned on or before
the last date below.**

7–DAY
LOAN

AME

LIBREX —

Contents

Acknowledgments

Many people contributed in a variety of ways to the creation of this book.

The authors would like to acknowledge the contributions of the following groups and individuals that have helped make it possible.

We would like to thank everyone at Charles River Media especially Jenifer Niles for her patience, guidance, and support from start to finish.

We would like to thank Rob Catto and everyone in the Full Sail Game Design and Development curriculum and management. Your encouragement and tolerance of our projects helps make us better educators and makes our jobs that much more professionally satisfying.

We would like to thank our fantastic art team. Chad Kendall has been Art Director on several of our projects leading to this book and has gathered a great team of artists for our examples, specifically Aaron "AirRun" Stahl, Ken Norman, and Jeff Parrott.

We would like to thank those who reviewed portions of this manuscript prior to publication including Troy "Enders" Humphreys, Mike "Papa Snuff" Fawcett, Josh "Sir Foxman" Fox, Brad "Schmeldy," and Iris Leffler.

We would like to thank Chris Melissinos and all the great developers in Sun's Game Technology Group as well as the excellent community support from the regulars at the *JavaGaming.org* forums. A special thanks goes to Gregory Pierce for various JOGL examples and support, particularly texture and image processing.

We would like to thank our loving families who had to endure countless rain checks during the writing process.

And finally, thanks to all the unnamed people whose inspiration and teachings have indirectly contributed to this book.

1 Java as a Game Platform

In This Chapter

- The Java Platform and Its Legacy
- Current Java Game Development
- Sports Games
- Puzzle Games
- Racing Games
- Massively Multiplayer Online Role-Playing Games
- Strategy Games
- Action/Adventure Games
- Looking Ahead
- Summary

Games are everywhere! Today, interactive entertainment can be found on cell phones, televisions, wristwatches, DVDs, and PCs. The process of developing games for platforms not originally intended to offer interactive entertainment can be difficult. Programmers have used creative ingenuity to overcome the hardware and software limitations for decades. This effort has often resulted in the creation of games on devices—such as an oscilloscope—not normally considered game machines. Many game developers enjoy making a computer or piece of technology perform in a manner that was not previously thought possible.

Time has passed, and game development continues as strong as ever. Game developers diligently seek the small adjustments and optimizations that will make games perform faster and create more dynamic and immersive worlds. Some aspects of technology have become more stratified while others continue to explore and push boundaries. Java™ has provided a powerful platform on which to develop interactive content.

Although this book is centered on Java and the platform technologies, its message is for programmers to maintain an open mind regarding new technologies as well as to keep creative ingenuity intact while implementing games on the Java platform. Sometimes it can take quite a bit of searching and effort to figure out the solution to a problem and the relevant implementation for the technology currently in use. In the past, the authors of this book have decompiled and modified SDK (software developer's kit) code to repair or modify an implementation and drilled down to the native functionality of a platform to get accurate timers and devices, as well as numerous other tasks specific to the implementation of the project at hand, all in the name of game development.

Some Java purists have criticized the use of "dirty Java" techniques as breaking the promise of platform independence; others have complained that it is the job of Sun Microsystems™ to make sure these tools exist for developers. Game developers are frequently called upon to create something completely new and untried. If the technology won't handle a required task, use creative ingenuity to get it working. If it can't be done for some reason, drop that technology as soon as possible and move on. Java is a great platform, but given its target user base, it is difficult to make everyone who uses the technology happy.

This chapter discusses the main advantages and disadvantages to be aware of when using Java, as well as game genres that exist in game development and some of the challenges of implementing them using Java. Each genre is defined and discussed with an emphasis on how Java can be used to create a game of that particular style. This chapter is not meant to be an exhaustive list of game genres because there is only so much space available, and many genres overlap or can be defined in more than one way. Toward the end of the chapter, the discussion covers the upcoming release of Java Development Kit (JDK) 1.5. This new technology presents some unique advantages for developers.

THE JAVA PLATFORM AND ITS LEGACY

Numerous texts document the benefits and advantages of using Java. This section identifies just those advantages that are helpful when developing games. Most of the advantages relate to the productivity boost gained from working with Java. This section also lists a few notorious disadvantages and possible solutions for them.

The Advantages of Java for Game Development

Platform independence: Java is a platform-independent language that allows users to write a program on the Windows®, Macintosh®, or Linux platforms without any serious localization requirements. This aspect is fundamental for development in Java and a key to its popularity. Platform independence means that a game written in 100 percent Java can immediately be shipped under all three platforms, thereby extending the potential market without incurring large porting fees to make the game available in traditional development. Several major Web providers have selected Java for the creation of Web-enabled games because of this fact. Being able to reach such a large potential market can make a major impact on a business's bottom line and directly affects when a given game will begin showing returns.

Improved object-oriented architecture: Java was designed to provide a more modernized look at object-oriented programming (OOP). With the benefits of code reuse, data encapsulation, polymorphism, and inheritance, the object-oriented paradigm has taken hold in a large segment of PC games. Even with the strengths associated with OOP, one of the major benefits to using Java is that it limits inheritance and allows for the usage of only a single child class. This might not seem to be an immediate benefit, particularly to a C++ programmer. Java explicitly states that any additional customization need for a child class requires the implementation of an interface class. This requirement creates a chain of responsibility that can be logically followed. Frequently, overzealous C++ coders have been found mired in the swamp of multiple inheritance. This situation can be overcome with careful programming practices in C++, but it is already built in as a standard mechanism in Java—just one of the OOP improvements that the Java platform offers.

Easy to learn: Java is easy for new programmers to learn. This fact doesn't necessarily benefit a seasoned programmer, but it eases the process of getting new programming hires acclimated to the development environment and code base. Because Java does not use pointers, the disadvantages (and advantages) associated with their use are gone. In some aspects of game development, this is a particular disadvantage, but as Moore's Law continues to hold true, performance-related issues continue to subside. Another benefit is that Java does not require the programmer to explicitly delete classes when finished with them. A garbage collector is maintained in the Java virtual machine that identifies when it needs to delete these variables and safely does so without the prodding of the programmer. These aspects of the Java language come together to make a quick entry for experienced and new developers.

Improved productivity: Applications developed using Java are typically completed much more quickly and have fewer bugs. Another of the best aspects relating to Java is reflection. Reflection is a built-in mechanism on the Java platform that allows the programmer to identify key information about a given object. For example, at a game's runtime, the programmer can query, modify, and dynamically create instances of classes that are not known until the game is actually running. This tool is particularly powerful, with its key benefit for game developers coming late in the development cycle when the product is approaching completion. Debugging is faster, and delivery of an on-time product is an easier task. This last part is, of course, directly related to the management of the team and not Java, but having solid backing from technology never hurts the ship date of any project.

The Disadvantages of Java for Game Development

Performance concerns: The old myths associated with Java relating to its performance, center on the fact that it is an interpreted language, meaning to some that it couldn't possibly work as quickly as native code. In some cases, this was absolutely true. Early on in Java's history, many people turned away from Java as a game development platform thinking that it could be used only within Web pages and had no real value for the commercial game market. In some situations Java is a bit slower than C++, but the inherent language benefits tend to outweigh losses due to performance. Current implementations of Java can use a Just-in-Time (JIT) compiler to overcome most of the speed issues, but when the JIT compiler is not deployed, noticeable slowdowns may occur while the code is interpreted. Recent benchmarks have pitted Java against all three of the major .NET languages and found Java's performance in arithmetic operations to be almost identical, excluding trigonometric calculations. This result represents a huge boost for Java, allowing it to demonstrate the improvements made by the development team.

The truth is that poorly written code will perform badly, regardless of the language in which it is implemented. Many of these apparent limitations regarding Java's performance can be overcome with a bit of tweaking and profiling, though optimizing a particular task in Java usually requires more knowledge of the platform to properly tweak than an equivalent optimization performed in C++. Many useful game-oriented optimizations for Java are discussed later in this book in Chapter 6, "Performance and the Java Virtual Machine."

The need to get "dirty" to get performance: As new technology is released, game developers usually try to take full advantage of the new advances in the hardware, particularly on graphics cards. The near annual revisions of Microsoft® DirectX® frequently present developers with the latest access to hardware- and performance-related features. When a particular hardware or software feature is not implemented on the Java platform, Java developers may be required to get "dirty" through the use of the Java Native Interface (JNI) to take advantage of some of the features that are openly available to C/C++ developers. The JNI allows the programmer to make native function links back to Java so that they can be explicitly used through a Java interface. Although the presence of this tool is great (and is really the foundation of the entire language), it does require time to become productive with it. It can also break the platform independence that was listed earlier as an advantage. Chapter 11, "Java Native Interface," discusses the methods for using this technology for typical gaming applications.

Lack of an accurate high-precision timer: Time calculation is critical in game programming. It controls how quickly the game should render, how frequently an object should animate, and numerous other game-play-related features. The lack of this timer has put many Java game developers at a distinct disadvantage. One common, partially successful solution was to tell the main execution thread to Sleep(). This solution is inaccurate and is not a real solution. Another workaround was to use the JNI to map a local timer such as QueryPerformanceCount, which uses 64-bit representations of time. This solution works but requires that developers "get dirty," as was mentioned in the previous section. This local timer solves only the problem local to the current implementation. Of all concerns related to programming games using Java, the lack of a supported high-precision timer is the largest single disadvantage.

Security Model for Java Classes

An additional disadvantage regarding the use of Java is the ease in which class files can be decompiled and the source code contents stolen. Java compiles code into a class file, which is really partially compiled byte code that will be finalized when the program is run on the platform of choice. This means that the .class file can be opened and its contents displayed or potentially modified. This has been a large concern among many developers who don't want to see their work lost or don't want to deal with client-side hacks that allow for cheating in multiplayer games. This disadvantage can be easily overcome with the use of code obfuscators. Code obfuscators take existing and functional code and make it unreadable to anyone. With regard to commercial games, code obfuscators are imperative to prevent the theft of source code.

Conclusion

This list of advantages and disadvantages relating to Java is by no means exhaustive. These issues tend to manifest themselves during the game production cycle and must be mentioned. Additional advantages and disadvantages are discussed in the next section for each genre; they are related to the process of creating a game of each given type while using Java. A prospective Java developer shouldn't let any myths influence his opinion of the technology until he has had a chance to explore the platform fully.

CURRENT JAVA GAME DEVELOPMENT

Developing games with the current Java platform can be a challenge. Though that might sound like a criticism of the technology, it can just as easily be said about any game-related technology or platform. Sooner or later, developers bump up against the limitations of the platform and want more resources, more control, and more power. This section identifies some of the specific challenges related to developing games on the Java platform through an analysis of some of the major genres popular in current game development. The discussion centers on some of the key elements that each genre needs to be able to execute to be considered successful. It then maps those elements against the current Java platform, identifying strengths and weaknesses that may be exposed.

SPORTS GAMES

The sports genre is currently one of the most popular in modern gaming. In early days, sports-related video games were limited to those shown on major television, such as baseball, football, and hockey. The sports genre has benefited significantly from increases in technology. When playing original sports titles such as *Atari Football* on the Atari 2600, viewers had to stretch their imagination to see the star quarterback as a tiny pixel. Although it was a fun game to play, almost everything was left to the imagination. Newer technology sparked an increase in overall complexity of sports titles, allowing for league play as well as trading and customized player creation. Current versions of sports titles are likely to have almost a perfect tie-in with the current season with regard to team rosters and player stats, as well as startlingly realistic depictions of the stadiums and the players' images.

Over time more niche sports such as the X-Games have become popular. Some have even achieved greater fame due to the video game adaptations of their events, such as *Tony Hawk: Pro Skater* by Neversoft. This game not only allows players to execute crazy tricks that defy the laws of physics completely but also defies the main characters in the game for their seemingly unlimited skateboarding skills.

Sports Genre and Java

From a purely developmental perspective, Java is a good development platform to use to create a sports title. One of the aspects that set most sports games apart is the cataloging of data related to plays and players. This data is particularly important for the hardcore fans and those who like to keep track of current players and team statistics. Some games allow players to play old all-star teams against the current player rosters. This feature requires strong organization and rapid access to the data during the game. Java is particularly strong when using database management, which can either hold this information locally or store it on a remote game server.

Another popular element in sporting games today is the multiplayer networked aspect. The ability to play head to head has significantly expanded the sports market as well as created great experiences for the throngs of fans. Sun Microsystems™ is a company that sells high-end servers and server technology. One of the important aspects of Java's development was that it needed to play well with Sun hardware. For this reason, Java is notoriously powerful in server-based applications and can handle databases containing sports data.

A key criticism related to Java is that the most successful implementations of sports games occur in the console space. Though PC ports of many sports games exist, they are usually afterthoughts for a successful console release. Java currently has no implementation with major console providers. It is important to note the console market dwarfs the PC market by an estimated factor of 10 to 1. Whereas this is a goal for the future, limited progress has been made in making Java available for console developers. Part of the delay is the lack of Java compliance on the current generation of hardware, particularly related to floating-point restrictions. From the commercial standpoint, this limitation continues to hurt Java's play for a larger acceptance from game developers working on sports titles as well as other typically successful console titles.

In summary, Table 1.1 lists the major benefits to using Java and the drawbacks for sports titles.

TABLE 1.1 Pros and Cons of Java in Sports Games

Pros	Cons
Offers strong network libraries	Lacks a standard performance timer
Provides a scalable database foundation for use in custom playbooks and rankings	Lacks Java ports to major console platforms

PUZZLE GAMES

People love to solve puzzles. Puzzle games appeal to a search for order in chaos and can also provide hours of fun. If the total number of hours a student spent playing *Tetris* were amortized over the total amount of time spent in class during a college year, the result would most likely show an amazing number of hours spent playing the game in contrast to studying. The puzzle genre is alive and well to this day. Many Web sites have implemented Java applets for popular games such as *Chess* and *Spades*, as well as a number of original puzzle titles. A recent game of note that was built in Java is the innovative massively multiplayer online (MMO) pirate role-playing game (RPG)/puzzle by Three Rings called *Puzzle Pirates* (see Figure 1.1). In *Puzzle Pirates*, players participate in pirate adventures in an online RPG, but when trouble breaks out, the players must use their powerful puzzle-solving skills to overcome adversity.

Puzzle Games and Java

Puzzle games leverage some of the best aspects of the Java platform. Games that don't require intense timing accuracy work incredibly well and provide a strong

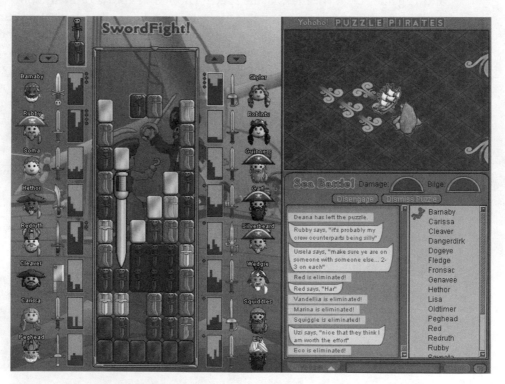

FIGURE 1.1 *Puzzle Pirates* by Three Rings.

productivity boost because of the wide range of graphic tools and multimedia libraries. Puzzle games can be distributed as applets or stand-alone applications, allowing them to work with multiple rendering pipelines (Abstract Window Toolkit [AWT] or Java OpenGL [JOGL] API/J3D). Java's strong networking and database support lend themselves to creating and storing a lot of information for the player, such as rankings or high-score tables.

On the downside, although puzzle games can be distributed through a range of methods, those that are run online through applets must contend with the fact that many Web browsers are not released with the most current Java Runtime Environments (JRE). Therefore, the applet developer must post new locations for players to download the latest JRE. Although this fact might not seem to be a major disadvantage, the fact that applets can't work as simply as they were designed could turn some players away from a game. Additionally, for games that require high-performance timers, developers could see the lack of timer support as a limitation to some types of game play that might require a high-resolution analysis of when input is received or a move is executed.

Generally speaking, the puzzle game genre represents one of the most ideal and immediate prospects for any new Java game programmer. In summary, Table 1.2 lists the major benefits and concerns when using Java to create puzzle games.

TABLE 1.2 Pros and Cons of Java for Puzzle Games

Pros	Cons
Offers a platform on which one can easily develop games for release as either an applet or as a stand-alone application	Timing concerns could affect certain types of game play
Provides a built-in application program interface (API) for rapid development boost	Many browsers ship with outdated Java Runtime Environments

RACING GAMES

The racing genre has been around for some time. Racing can be composed of space vehicles with less regard for a physics system or other vehicles in hostile environments, but the true test of a racing game comes from its implementation under circumstances to which we are all accustomed. Car racing is one of the most popular sports in the world. It is broken out into a separate section to identify some of the concerns that would come from creating a fairly accurate representation of the physical forces involved with racing.

Originally, games such as *Pole Position* challenged players to "Prepare to Qualify" as they drove on a winding track, avoiding other cars and oil slicks. Today, this genre has stepped out into a showcase for real-world simulation. Vehicle dynamics between restrictor-plate stock car racing and Formula 1 racing radically alter game play, but the fundamental forces involved are pretty similar. Though older than most games on the market, *Gran Prix Legends* is still hailed for its accuracy and maintains throngs of loyal players because of its startling realism. Fans are willing to deal with a lower graphic component if the game play holds up well.

Racing Games and Java

Java is well matched to produce commercial-quality racing games. The authors of this book developed a commissioned technology demo/game for Sun Microsystems called *Java Gran Prix* in 2002 (Figure 1.2). The spec required that it drive like a real Formula 1 race car in a networked environment, showcasing the strengths of Java3D and the Java platform overall. The game debuted at SIGGRAPH 2001 and maintained long lines of players who wanted to see just what was possible when people really pushed the Java platform.

FIGURE 1.2 *Java Gran Prix.*

The earlier description of racing games showed that the true test of these games is in the physics system. During the development cycle of *Java Gran Prix*, the physics system and vehicle dynamics were modeled far too well—so well, in fact, that only a driver with the skills of the great Mika Häkkinen could make it around the track. A new player needed more than 30 minutes to learn to drive the car. The conclusion was reached that the car was too hard to drive, so the physics system was curtailed for the entertainment value. One downside was the lack of a standardized input API that allowed for easy access to steering wheel controllers. When *Java Gran Prix* was written, a special linkage was required to allow the game to be played with a steering wheel. The actual implementation wasn't too difficult, but it required the use of native function calls to complete. The full implementation of devices is covered later in Chapter 11, "Java Native Interface." A fully networked Formula 1 simulation was created using dated technologies that were not as well suited for game production as the tools currently available and discussed later in this book.

In summary, Table 1.3 lists the major benefits and drawbacks to using Java for creating racing games.

TABLE 1.3   Pros and Cons of Java in Racing Games

Pros	Cons
Contains Java math libraries, which can be organized to create a satisfactory physics model for racing vehicles	Lacks a standard high-precision timer
Provides high-quality rendering tools through JOGL and LWJGL	Offers limited official support for nontraditional input devices

MASSIVELY MULTIPLAYER ONLINE ROLE-PLAYING GAMES

Saying this type of game aloud is always a mouthful, so these games are often referred to as MMORPGs or just MMOs. In recent years, the online role-playing genre has attracted hundreds of thousands of players, who spend incalculable hours taking their characters on numerous quests. As *Star Wars: Galaxies* by Sony, the upcoming *Worlds of Warcraft*, and the infamous *Everquest* show, the MMOs are here to stay and have been adapted to some of the most successful franchises in history. Currently, several commercial Java-based MMO games, including *Galactic Village* by Galactic Village Games, are available.

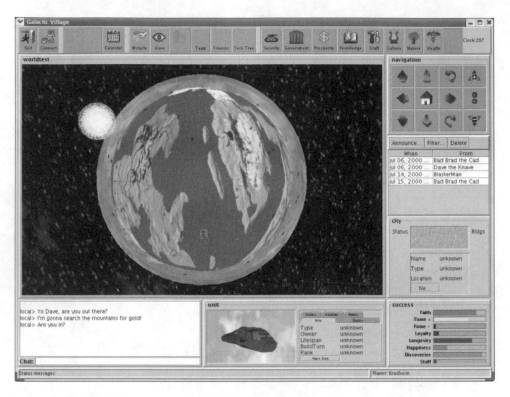

FIGURE 1.3   *Galactic Village* by Galactic Village Games.

Galactic Village (Figure 1.3) is a particularly fun game to play and gives a good indication of the growing possibilities for commercial development of MMO games using Java. The actual visualization of an online RPG varies based on the particular game, but some components are consistent in most instances of MMO games. First, an MMO game has a strong need for both reliable and secure networking on game servers. Nothing irks players more than to lose a battle due to unacceptable levels of latency or to have someone who is cheating beat them down and rob them. Second, as the characters improve in level, complete quests, and acquire items or create new items freely available to others in the world, a powerful database must be designed to scale alongside the popularity of the game. So much information is stored for *Star Wars Galaxies* characters that the cost of adding server space forced the developers to limit the number of characters a player could have on a single server.

MMOs and Java

MMO games are another area in which Java is a solid fit. Because Java was built to integrate seamlessly with servers, it is a straightforward fit with networked games. In addition, Java is also particularly powerful when used with databases that hold all the player and world data that the game generates. When the game has more than 20,000 players on a single server, stability becomes key. As was mentioned earlier, Sun Microsystems manufactures high-end servers, so it makes sense that Java was designed to scale well and is well suited to handle these tasks. Both networking and database programming are covered in detail later in this book. Another point of particular value is that *Star Wars Galaxies* utilized Java as a scripting language. This fact is of particular importance because it outlines a way that Java can be used for games in association with other external technologies. Any game that uses a scripting language is likely to see a heavy portion of the game play and game logic components written in that script. Java fits perfectly into this role and is also discussed as a scripting language in Chapter 10, "Java as a Scripting Language."

On the downside, Java hasn't been tested thoroughly for large commercial game projects such as an MMORPG beyond usage as a scripting language. The tools to create such a game exist on the platform, but it will take a major commercial success to convince developers that Java can handle implementation of a full-scale MMO game. Also, any optimizations made regarding graphics or other hardware must be re-implemented on all supported platforms, which is consistent with most development today and can be overcome with good design. Nevertheless, most Java developers are used to the "write once, run anywhere" paradigm and might take issue with having to re-implement features obtained from "dirty Java."

In summary, Table 1.4 lists the major benefits and drawbacks to using Java MMO games.

TABLE 1.4 Pros and Cons of Java in Massively Multiplayer Online Games

Pros	Cons
Contains scalable networking tools	Commercially unproven for large-scale games
Provides powerful database management	Requires "dirty" optimizations to be implemented on all platforms separately

STRATEGY GAMES

One genre still predominately handled on the PC is that of strategy. Strategy games may involve the player commanding a group of characters of units into some sort of conflict or in guiding a whole civilization through its history. Strategy games have been with computers since the first version of *Chess* was coded. Since then the games have become much more complex and require the player to develop deep strategies. Games such as *Warcraft 3* and *Command and Conquer* top the charts in the strategy realm and introduce a new level of competition in the form of the real-time strategy (RTS) games. The RTS requires the player to think and plan quickly, then execute and manage the units to a victory condition. These games have been particularly popular over the last few years. Currently a few commercial Java-based strategy games are on the market. One of the more creative and popular is the incredible *Kingdoms of War* by Abandoned Castle Studios (Figure 1.4). *Kingdoms of War* is a combination of online strategy game and RTS, in which players compete for three months in a persistent environment, pitting different medieval kingdoms against each other. This game illustrates some of the strengths of Java for games in this genre.

FIGURE 1.4 *Kingdoms of War* by Abandoned Castle Studios.

Strategy Games and Java

Strategy games developed with Java have similar concerns as the other genres that have already been discussed, but Java is perfectly suited to tackle one aspect of this genre. Most RTS games require a large number of specialized units that may be subclasses of a Unit class or some derivation thereof. Java's limitation on multiple inheritance attempts to enforce a good solid object hierarchy. In addition, when debugging a game using a wide range of similar classes, it is nice to have an easy way to find out about the information contained within a given class. This technique is called reflection. Reflection, which has been with Java since the 1.1 release, allows programmers to retrieve a myriad of information about specific classes, including the classic toString() method. Also, using reflection developers can find out what constructors and methods are declared for a given class and use them as they are identified. This feature is built into the language and is contained in any object created on the platform. Bugs happen all the time. The key is working with a tool that allows the programmer to best protect the code from the inevitable mistakes that creep in. Java supports dynamic class loading, which allows other developers to create new classes and load them into the game without touching the underlying engine. This ability is a powerful advantage and gives control back to the designers instead of requiring a programmer to implement even the most minor of changes.

In summary, Table 1.5 lists the major benefits and drawbacks to using Java for strategy titles.

TABLE 1.5   Pros and Cons of Java in Strategy Games

Pros	Cons
Offers reflection, which makes for easy debugging and flexibility when using objects	Lacks a precision performance timer
Allows for easy expansion without engine modification using Dynamic Class loading	Commercially unproven for high-quality strategy games

ACTION/ADVENTURE GAMES

The action/adventure genre can be considered a catchall for many types of games. Classics such as *Tomb Raider* have shown many gamers hours of fun. Other types of games fit into this classification as well. In general, action/adventure games center on a single character or ship that goes through numerous levels. Sound familiar? One of the best action games written in Java is *Alien Flux* by Puppy Games (Figure 1.5). This game encapsulates the classic feel of an action-based shooter.

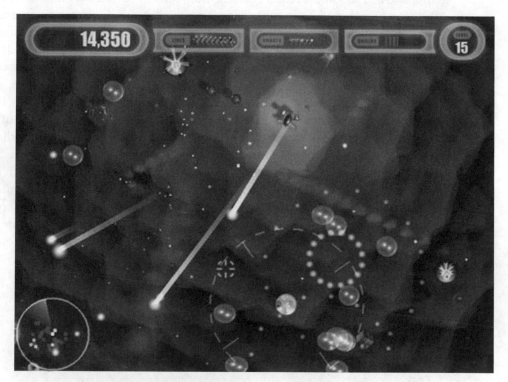

FIGURE 1.5   *Alien Flux* by Puppy Games.

One popular subset of the action/adventure genre is the platformer. Some of the most memorable games in history fall into this category. Platformer games require the player to maneuver through a set of obstacles and frequently involve jumping or some other type of movement to work through the world and achieve goals in the game. Traditionally, platformers generally bring to mind 2D classics such as *Super Mario Bros.*, but the genre isn't limited to two dimensions. A number of great 3D platformer games exist, including *Rayman 2* and the venerable *Sonic Adventures*. Platformer games require speed and good-looking graphics. In addition, many games of this type are centered on a solid character franchise and spectacular game play, which makes a strong animation system critical for the attitude of the character to come alive in the various situations.

Action/Adventure Games in Java

Action/adventure games are well suited for development in Java. Given that fully immersive 3D environments are completely possible to construct within Java, it is important to reference the character animation system as the keystone foundation of a character-driven action/adventure game. This problem is not related to the Java platform, though; in fact, the algorithms are consistent across platforms. Building a solid 3D animation systems take serious time and a good understanding of 3D programming, but it is completely possible with Java. With the right algorithms and use of the JOGL API, animation systems can be built in 2D or 3D environments.

On the downside, the lack of the solid timer constricts development of some types of action/adventure games. Also, the limitation of hardware devices makes Java a difficult choice for games that require specialized controllers or accessories that native platforms automatically support. This problem can be overcome by using the JNI, but it still represents a limitation regarding this genre.

In summary, Table 1.6 lists the major benefits and drawbacks to using Java for creating action/adventure games.

TABLE 1.6   Pros and Cons of Java in Action/Adventure Games

Pros	Cons
Offers high-quality graphics capabilities	Lacks a high-precision timer
Can create commercial-grade animation engines	Contains limitations on usable hardware devices

It is important to note that numerous other games and hybrid genres beyond those mentioned here have been successfully implemented using Java. One of the groups most notably missing in this chapter are games written for mobile devices. There has been incredible growth in the mobile sector for games on cell phones and PDAs. The Java2 Micro Edition gives mobile game developers tools to create content for these devices, which continue to rise in popularity as gaming platforms. The focus of this book is PC Java game development, and further discussion is beyond the scope of this book.

Although some criticisms about Java have been mentioned, you should not interpret temporary shortcomings as a reason to give up on the platform as a whole. Several of the main issues that must be corrected regarding language issues are currently in development and are slated for release later this year. That being said, let's look at some of the features in the near future of Java.

LOOKING AHEAD

Toward the end of 2004, Sun Microsystems is slated to release JDK 1.5. This section discusses some of the publicly announced improvements being implemented into the language and how they may impact game development. Some aspects of the actual language may be slightly different from those presented here, but the core philosophies are not likely to change. Be sure to double-check the information provided in this section against the most current documentation. This information is presented to show how Java continues to grow as a platform and will continue to provide solid resources for game developers. (Also visit the book's Web page at *www.charlesriver.com* for updates.)

One important note to make before continuing relates to the technology presented later in this book. Nothing that changes in JDK 1.5 should have any effect on the core game technology as it is presented in this book. This is a considerable strength of the book compared to similar texts. Don't worry about this book becoming obsolete before it gets back to your development station.

Accurate Native Timers

One of the most consistently mentioned weaknesses of Java has been the lack of a supported high-precision timer. The nanoTimer class is planned for implementation in JDK 1.5 and will hopefully completely remove this concern from Java game development. For more information on timers and the nanoTimer, see Chapter 2, "Fundamentals of Game Programming."

Generics

The concept of generics comes from one of the problems that has been observed over the lifespan of the language. In the current implementation of Java, games that use collections cannot check the type of object that enters the collection at compile time. Objects that are inserted into the collection must be cast back to the needed type at runtime. The problem with this model comes when someone adds an incorrect object to the collection. The game tries to cast the object as the expected type and throws a ClassCastException when the error is ultimately found. This behavior can certainly be a problem. JDK 1.5 will use the concept of generics to test the type of object being added to a given collection at compile time. This feature also removes the need to explicitly cast the object back while iterating the collection or accessing the data. A quick look at the old style follows:

```
List l = new LinkedList();
l.add = new Player();
Player p = (Player)l.iterator.next;
```

The new style of the same code using generics follows:

```
List<Player:l = new LinkedList<Player:();
l.add(new Player());
Player p = l.iterator.next;
```

The new style of code looks much cleaner and allows the program to type-check the information before the game gets out the door. The changes due to generics will not add any additional overhead due to code sizes, making them immediately useful.

Autoboxing

One of the interesting and unique aspects of the Java language is that it maintains two sets of basic types within the language—the standard primitive types, such as int, as well as a group of objects that serves as wrapper classes, such as class Integer. One of the elements lacking in the language is an easy way to convert these types back and forth, especially when they are used with collections. The new autoboxing feature removes this problem and is of particular use to games.

An example of the current way to set and retrieve one these objects follows:

```
List highScores = new LinkedList();
highScores.add(new Integer(5000));
int score = ((Integer)highScores.get(0).intValue());
```

With autoboxing this same code is reduced to the following:

```
List highScores = new LinkedList();
hiScores.add(5000);
int score = highScores.get(0);
```

This code is much cleaner and easier to manage. The autoboxing spec allows for conversions of these types for all similar primitives in the language.

The Enhanced for Loop

JDK 1.5 will also contain a newly enhanced for loop to use with collections. This idea stems from the fact that most iterators are used only to get access to a given element in the collection. Because this practice is common, why not let the compiler take care of the heavy lifting? An example of the current methodology follows:

```
void render(Collection c)
{
 for (Iterator I = c.iterators();i.hasNext();)
  {
    Actor a = (Actor)i.next()
    a.render();
  }
}
```

The same code using the new for loop follows:

```
void render(Collection c)
  {
        for( Object o:c)
           ((Actor)o).render();
  }
```

The colon in the for loop is to be read as "in". Therefore, the loop would be read as "Object o in Collection c". This feature is a nice addition that should be fairly easy to adopt.

Enumerations

A particularly powerful construct in C/C++ is the enumeration. The enumeration effectively acts as a numeric mask with highly legible values that can be passed through control mechanisms, most notably the switch statement. These types of enumeration are used in games for everything from controlling the current execution state of the game to monitoring various AI states of enemies. The closest thing Java has had in the past has been to implement something like the following code:

```
public class State
    {
        private final int currentState;

        public State(int state)
        {
        this.currentState = state;
        };

        public static final State GAME_PAUSED = new State(1);
        public static final State GAME_INIT   = new State(2);
    }
```

Although this code might seem fine to the average Java programmer, the one thing that can't be done with this class is to pass it through to a switch statement. JDK 1.5 has a solution for this problem.

A new keyword will be added to the JKD 1.5 in the form of the enum. The enum type will contain public, self-typed members for each enum constant. An example of the enum type using the previous State example follows:

```
public enum State
{
   GAME_INIT(1), GAME_MAIN(2), GAME_PAUSED(3);

   State(int state)
     {
       this.currentState = state;
     }
     private final int currentState;
}
```

An example of how this new enum type can be used with a switch statement follows:

```
Switch(state)
{
  case State.GAME_INIT: //execute game init method.
  Case State.GAME_MAIN: //execute game main method.
  Case State.GAME_PAUSED: //pause game
  Default: throw new AssertionError("Unknown state" +state);
}
```

This new type presents a number of new possibilities for control of execution programming and gives a lot more power than the private static int style enumerations of the past.

Static Importing

A problem that many programmers encounter when using constants related to a specific class is the need to fully qualify a constant before using it. For example, if a game needed to use a definition of PI, it would have to properly import the class and then use the value such as the following:

```
import java.lang.Math;

float degrees,radians;
degrees = radians *(180.00/Math.PI);
```

Using the new static importing feature, this same code can be reduced down to the following:

```
static import java.lang.Math;

float degrees,radians;
degrees = radians *(180.00/PI);
```

This might not seem like a massive improvement, but it does make the code much more readable, as well as remove the need to create customized interface classes that contain only constants for the sake of avoiding the default import statement.

These new additions to the Java platform should prove valuable to the continuing efforts of Java game developers. They are indicative of the responsive manner in which Java has been centered on the developer and the growth of the language.

SUMMARY

Much has been detailed in this chapter regarding the viability of Java and its use in game development. Change is usually not welcomed by many, particularly programmers who are accustomed to old methodologies. In some ways Java's best complement comes from the .NET transition. .NET has many similarities to Java and rightfully draws a number of the powerful aspects of the language into its own environment. For some game developers, Java will not represent the right fit in terms of performance goals. Despite some of Java's limitations, it is difficult to argue with the importance of third-party platforms continuing to provide new choices and delivery models for game developers. Java is alive and well, but it needs good commercial-quality games to reach the flash point of widespread acceptance. The remainder of this book identifies the technological path by which to achieve these goals and deliver outstanding games. This path may be rough at times, but it does indeed come to an end. By reading this book, you have already taken the first step in the journey to create great games using Java.

2 Fundamentals of Game Programming

In modern game development it is common to hear the designers and developers talking about the all-inclusive term *game engine*. What exactly is a game engine? Most people mistakenly think it relates only to the graphical rendering capabilities of a particular game. In truth, the game engine is really the game's guts, which are leveraged to complete a host of tasks in unison, thereby creating the interactive content most commonly viewed as a game. Thinking about a game as a machine is an excellent metaphor. A game has a set of specific tasks repeated in a dataset to deliver interactive entertainment.

This chapter is set up to provide programmers who are relatively new to Java or game programming a chance to get information regarding some of the most fundamental aspects of game programming across numerous topics. If you have programmed games in the past or feel that you have an understanding of how the basic components of a game work, you can probably skim this material or skip to the other portions of the book that fall in your domain of work. Most of the solutions presented here are organized for clear understanding and not necessarily for optimization.

BASIC GAME STRUCTURE

One of the most frustrating tasks for novice game programmers is organizing the execution of the tasks involved in programming a game. Sure, you can read all the tutorials on a particular API and then modify code snips and functional examples, but tutorials usually don't emphasize where to put those tools so they work inside of the guts of the game. The basic idea seems pretty straightforward from the start, but it continues to increase in difficulty as the game develops. In truth most games are programmed in a similar manner at the beginning. They all have the same fundamental jobs to complete to display the visual representation of the game world on the screen. At the highest level of organization, a game can be represented by the three main components required during its operation. These aspects can be called Game Initialization, Game Playing, and Game Shutdown. The individual responsibilities of these components are key to understanding the underlying layout of a game.

During Game Initialization, most of the required elements for game operation are loaded into memory. These elements include all images, sounds, and data files, as well as anything else the game specifically requires to operate. Any classes used for the operation of the game should be instantiated and prepared for usage. This method is called *caching* and is particularly common for games built with a narrow or limiting system bus, such as the PC. Loading the data from disk during the actual gameplay generates performance problems, so it's better to cache the needed components into memory for later consumption. Some systems, such as the Sony® Playstation®2, offer programmers a much wider bus that reduces the amount of information that requires caching.

Game Shutdown is designed to do the exact opposite of Game Initialization. Game Shutdown is responsible for releasing all information and memory to the operating system and making sure that the game is exited properly. On the Java platform, memory management is generally handled for the programmer, but a number of operations may be handled in this component, including writing out log files regarding game performance or verifying that the user's preferences have been stored for the next time the game is played.

Game Playing is a bit more complex, so it is listed last in the series. Game Playing internalizes a fundamental concept in game programming called the *game loop*. A *game loop* is nothing more than a standard looping mechanism that contains the tasks the game normally processes repeatedly until the game ends or the user indicates that he wants to quit playing. The programmers code the actual definitions of these tasks in the game as defined by the game documentation. Figure 2.1 shows the process of a single pass through the game loop.

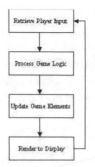

FIGURE 2.1   A single pass through the game loop.

The main tasks the game loop is required to code against are: getting the user's input, applying game logic, updating the game information, and rendering to the screen. The following code shows this process at the high level.

```
while(true)
{
 GetUserInput();
 ApplyGameLogic();
 Update();
 Render();
}
```

Each of these tasks involves many more steps to process and will be reviewed individually.

OBTAINING INPUT

Allowing for the player's input is arguably the single-most important aspect of the game. Without input, the game is just a dazzling implementation of a screen saver. Three main types of input devices can be used. These devices are the keyboard, mouse, and game controller or joystick. The most common of these devices is the keyboard, which along with the mouse come pretty commonly with all computers. The Java platform already contains several utilities that allow the user to capture input from the mouse and keyboard for applications and applets written on the platform in the form of *listeners*. If you are using the AWT event model in your game, the MouseListener, the KeyListener, or the more generic EventListener classes should be implemented.

These classes work just as they would normally be expected to in a typical Java application or applet. If the game in question requires joystick or gamepad input, a number of useful classes are handled by the Jinput API discussed in Chapter 11, "Java Native Interface." This section gives a quick overview of the classes most commonly used for obtaining keyboard and mouse input.

The *KeyListener* Interface

The *KeyListener* interface listens for keyboard input from the user. Depending on how the game is set up, this input might be the most common that comes into your game. Three methods are available when using the *KeyListener* interface— keyPressed, keyReleased, and keyTyped. Each of these methods takes a KeyEvent as its argument.

The KeyEvent class allows the program to analyze the actual key that was selected by using a set of virtual key (VK) codes. The VK codes cannot be generated on every keyboard, so be careful when determining input from them. The majority of them are available and listed in the Java documentation. If the program must know the actual character (for example, for a high-score table initial entry) use the getKeyChar method. This method returns the actual character pressed.

A quick code block indicating the basic use of the *KeyListener* interface follows:

```
public void keyPressed(KeyEvent e)
{
  int keyCode = e.getKeyCode():
  if(keycode == KeyEvent.VK_W)
  System.out.println("You pressed up!");
}
```

```
//This one is empty, but must be defined
public void keyReleased() {}
public void keyTyped(KeyEvent e)
{
char key = e.getKeyChar(),

  switch(char)
  {
    case'r':
    {
     System.out.println("You typed an R");
    break;
     }
  }
}
```

The *MouseListener* Interface

The mouse is also a great way to take input for a game. This listener is required to implement the following methods: `mouseClicked`, `mouseEntered`, `mouseExited`, `mousePressed`, and `mouseReleased`. These methods take a `MouseEvent` object to determine the result of the given input. When using listener interfaces, always remember to implement each of the methods unless the class is abstract, in which case you are just pushing the work to a later point in time.

A small code block of working with a `MouseListener` interface follows:

```
public void mouseClicked(MouseEvent e)
{
if(e.getModifiers()== MouseEvent.BUTTON1_MASK)
{
   //Fire the main weapons!
}
}

public void mousePressed(MouseEvent e)
{
System.out.println("The mouse is at "+e.getX()+" "+e.getY());
}
```

These are just two of the numerous types of listener classes. When working with an AWT model of input, you will find they are reliable and allow players to get more immersed in your game.

APPLYING THE GAME LOGIC AND UPDATING THE SYSTEM

Game logic is generally defined as the internal decision-making code that makes a game function normally along some predetermined specification. It is the programming equivalent of the paper rules that come with board games. Game logic encompasses a wide array of programming concepts and includes development of artificial intelligence (AI) routines, collision detection, and several other aspects of game programming. Some of these topics will be discussed later in the chapter.

One of the most important things to do regarding game logic is to ensure that the rest of the game can access the newly adjudicated situation. For example, if a collision detection routine determines that a dangerous rock has collided with a laser ray and been destroyed, it is important that the game understands this rock has been destroyed and reacts accordingly. This rock should no longer be drawn on the screen and is not eligible for further collision detection. This process is referred to as *updating* the system. Many of these techniques result in automatic updating of the game to reflect these changes, but this update will not be seen until the next phase of the game's operation has occurred.

RENDERING

Rendering is the portion of the game in which the information that has been determined to exist on the screen at the given time is drawn and made visible to the player. The visual feedback is a critical point of immersion, allowing the player to interact with the game. The quality of the graphics and the realism engendered by the rendering is of particular importance. This book contains discussions relating to rendering in 2D and 3D game applications later. It is important to note that these things occur in this manner so a basic architecture can be constructed with the understanding of where each piece will have its place when completed.

PULLING IT ALL TOGETHER

All of these components are used to compose and display what amounts to a single image on the screen. Each time the game renders to the screen, it is said to have rendered a *frame*. Frames are similar to a strip of developed movie film. Figure 2.2 analyzes each one of these frames over a short segment of a game.

You can see an illusion of movement is created by making subtle and small movements as each frame progresses. Interactive entertainment capitalizes on this measure of control. The illusion of movement in a game is based on the rapid display of each frame. Interactivity comes from the fact that a game passes through a

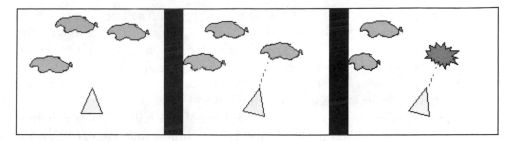

FIGURE 2.2   Transitions from frame to frame in a game.

set of rules that determines how the game looks each time you pass through the game loop. Because games tend to use all the resources that a given machine may have, there are differing philosophies regarding how to present the frames in a game. Should frames be shown as frequently as possible, or should they be limited in some regard?

BLOCKING VERSUS NON-BLOCKING LOOPS

One of the biggest challenges that game developers who work on the PC face is the myriad of possible configurations they may encounter while trying to develop applications. The game loop presented earlier executes only as quickly as the computer running it is capable. The computer tries to draw to the screen as often as it can. This practice would be perfect if everyone had the same configuration, but that is not the case. This situation forces the philosophical questions: Does the game being created require the use of all resources on the machine? Will this game still be expected to be played in five years? Depending on the answer to these questions, developers need to choose between blocking and nonblocking loop structures.

Blocking Loops

A blocking loop effectively limits the overall frame rate that can be displayed by an application by placing a timing mechanism at the end of the game loop. The timing mechanism forces a specific amount of time to pass before the game can return to the top of the loop. Regardless of the CPU speed of a given machine, the maximum number of times the game can be drawn to screen *correctly* is determined by the vertical sync (VSYNC) of the monitor used.

VSYNC refers to the number of vertical refreshes the monitor can process per second. There is no visual benefit to displaying more frames, and often anomalies will appear on the screen when a game tries to draw faster than the VSYNC. This method can also limit the resource consumption on a machine, but, in some cases, it shows better performance on a wider range of system configurations. This method gives you a wider potential audience for the game and could increase its acceptance and overall success from the commercial perspective.

When using a blocking loop in Java, you have several possible choices. In the following example, the decision to use the `Thread.sleep` mechanism was made due to a question of accuracy. The specific issue of time is discussed later in this chapter.

The following code details how to use a timing function in conjunction with a blocking loop:

```
public void gameMain()
{
  System.out.println("The Game Main is executing");
    while(playerlives>=0)
     {
       System.out.println("Darn, you died!");
       playerlives-=1;
       try
       {
       Thread.sleep(60);
       }
       catch(InterruptedException e)
       {
          System.out.println("Someone Interrupted my Thread!");
       }
     }
}
```

The actual amount by which the thread is put to sleep is determined by the acceptable frame rate for the game. To determine this number, divide the delay in milliseconds by the desired frame rate. If a game is to render 30 times per second, then each frame should take 1/30 of a second to display.

Nonblocking Loops

Nonblocking loops are generally used in games considered high-performance applications. These games do not use a timing mechanism to control the frame rate; they just allow things to run as quickly as possible. This method is seen mostly in 3D games that require the extra time to make their rendering passes. This technique has one drawback in the form of running on future machines. Because nothing slows down the progress of the game loop, this method will allow a 10-GHz processor to run through the loop in the same way it did a 2-Ghz processor. The performance will be much better in terms of rendered frames, but this jump will make the game unplayable for future gamers. The choice between these methods should be based on the type of game that you are planning to implement.

THE ROLE OF TIMING IN GAMES

Timing in games is a critical and important mechanism. The illusion of movement and interaction with a game world is founded on the ability to rapidly progress through the game loop and display the outcome of those interactions to the player. Games are atypical applications and are often intrusive into the various platforms on which they exist. These efforts require accurate timers that can report things such as frame rate or the length of time an enemy has exhibited a particular AI behavior. Without a reliable timing mechanism, developing games is a particularly difficult task. Some games often go to the actual hardware to get the performance they need. Lack of a standardized high-resolution timing routine in Java has been an issue for quite some time and has caused game developers to seek new and more accurate timing mechanisms in games. Some of these methods actually cause the portability of Java to be broken to some degree by binding Java functions to the local system; you can take advantage of more accurate system timers. This method is discussed more fully in Chapter 11: "Java Native Interface."

Programmers who cannot allow for system-level timing must rely on the old tried-and-true techniques that have been developed over the years. One of these options is to use the method `System.currentTimeMillis()`. This method returns a value in milliseconds but has a resolution of approximately 50–55 milliseconds on Windows machines. This resolution is decent, but it may cause certain elements of a game to act jerky or prevent them from responding to updates quickly. This method is useful but may quickly show its limitations. A quick example of using `currentTimeMillis` follows:

```
long begintime = System.currentTimeMillis();
//time something out in between
long endtime = System.currentTimeMillis() — begintime;
```

Another useful method is to tell the executing thread to sleep using the method of the same name. This method can have a resolution of closer to 5 milliseconds and is much more precise than the `currentTimeMillis()`. A call to `sleep()` tells the executing thread to stop for a specified number of milliseconds. With a resolution of 5 milliseconds, this method is a decent but an admittedly sloppy way to control the time for a game. An example of how to use the `Thread.sleep()` method from earlier in this chapter follows:

```
public void gameMain()
{
System.out.println("The Game Main is executing");
 while(playerlives>=0)
  {
    playerlives-=1;
    try
    {
     Thread.sleep(60);
    }
    catch(InterruptedException e)
    {
     System.out.println("Someone Interrupted my Thread!");
    }
  }
}
```

One final and currently experimental method of tracking time is using a little documented class on the Java platform as of the time of this writing. Fortunately, this class, or one close to it in performance, is planned for the next major release of the JDK and will be implemented as the nanoTimer class, according to the Java Specification Request (JSR) 166. Unless JDK 1.5 has been released by the time you are reading this book (which means a second edition must be written), this class is the most precise way to obtain a high-resolution time. Each version is implemented for the various platforms for which Java is available. Some tests have yielded a 1-millisecond resolution. Remember that this code should be considered experimental and that it should not be relied upon completely until the finalized version of the class is included as part of the standard JDK. If you use this code, be sure to test for its availability before distributing mission-critical code that uses the following code segment:

```
import sun.misc.Perf;

public class Timer
{
  Perf Timer;
  long freq;

  public Timer()
  {
   Timer = Perf.getPerf();
   freq = hiResTimer.highResFrequency();
  }
```

```
public long currentTimeMillis()
{
 return Timer.highResCounter() * 1000 / freq;
}
}
```

This `timer` class will allow for precise resolutions for timing of many operations in games. You should ensure you have it available on any systems with which you use it.

Timing is used everywhere in game programming. Some of the more common uses in games include:

- Updating the state of the game by the duration of the previous frame
- Locking the frame rate of a renderer
- Maintaining and evaluating proper transition of AI states
- Correctly identifying times to change frames in an animation
- Testing for the proper amount of time to pass before adding additional input from a device

These are just a few uses of timing in games that require accurate timer controls to deliver consistent performance. Make sure that you know how accurate the timer on your system is before you depend on it.

CORE ARCHITECTURE USING STATE CONTROLS

Earlier in this chapter we used a `Game` class to organize the relevant parts of the games core functions. As the complexity of a given game increases, so should its underlying architecture. Creating a state-driven `Game` class is a way that allows for much better control within the application and allows the relatively seamless integration of additional possibilities, such as pausing the game or displaying a menu system.

The concept of a *state machine* is used first to identify the discrete components of a particular system or machine. Each state has some change applied to it to cause a *state* change. For example, ice has heat applied to it to cause a change from a frozen state to a liquid state. Each state in a system is linked by a series of valid causes for transition from one state to another. Consider the ice example again; if the ice has no additional heat applied, it remains in the current frozen state. The change to a liquid form can occur only when heat is applied. If too much heat is applied to the liquid form, it continues its transition into a gaseous state until the gas becomes cool again and returns to a liquid state.

You can use this same structure and apply it to the `Game` class that will handle the overall execution of the game. For the sake of this example, we will identify four major states: Game Init, Game Main, Game Menu, and Game Shutdown. Each of these states is completely separate from the others in its functions. Figure 2.3 shows the current state system:

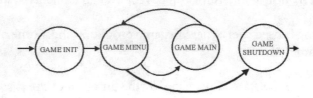

FIGURE 2.3 A basic game state machine.

For the most part, transitions in the game are driven by player input. When the player starts the game, he is sent to the main system menu. From there he makes selections and is forwarded to the relevant components of the game. At this point it becomes important to note that these functions themselves define the game that is ultimately playable. The actual definitions of these functions are defined in the remaining components of this book and vary greatly based on how the game is developed. For now we are just laying the blueprint of what is yet to come. The state-driven model is completely flexible and can be adapted to much more complicated models, as needed. Let's look at a state-driven `Game` class.

The first thing that must be done is to identify the key states that will be available.

```
static final int GAME_INIT          = 1;
static final int GAME_MAIN          = 2;
static final int GAME_SHUTDOWN      = 3;
static final int GAME_MENU          = 4;
```

We have decided on four possible states for now. At any given time, the current game state is held by a member integer in the class. When this class is created, the state initially is set to `GAME_MENU` by the constructor. The two major functions of importance in this class are the `setState()` method and the `update()` method. Let's look at those now.

```
public void setState(int state)
{
  gamestate = state;
 update();
}
```

This method automatically adjusts the state with one of the existing classes and then calls the update method to process .

```
/*This function will process the current game state and call the
*underlying functions until the execution is terminated by input or
*breaking the game state.
*/
public void update()
{
  switch(gamestate)
  {
    case GAME_INIT:
        gameInit();
      break;
    case GAME_MAIN:
      gameMain();
      break;
    case GAME_SHUTDOWN:
      gameShutdown();
      break;
    case GAME_MENU:
      displayGameMenu();
      break;
    default:
      System.out.println("Could not ID Gamestate");
  }
}
```

The local definitions for each function are defined as needed. At the completion of each one, a decision is made about the next state. When the gameMain() method returns, it immediately sets the state to GAME_MENU and presents the player with choices to continue with his game, to start over, or to stay at the menu. Although no graphics are on the screen, this method is one way to control the execution of the core game structure.

Note that this example is a simple implementation of this idea. Many additional possibilities exist, including maintaining specialized listener classes that focus on discussion between the running game and the infrastructure. This implementation is designed only to display this concept at work and should be a good starting point for making a game application.

CONSTRUCTION OF BASIC ENTITIES

When first deciding on a game's premise, designers usually have visions of the eventual gameplay in their minds. They envision large starships hurling energy blasts at nearby rocks to avoid a destructive collision, or small amphibians trying desperately to avoid being crushed by traffic. Regardless of the genre or implementation of the game, certain common attributes of the game world are needed for representation of items in game. For example, a player-controlled frog will always have at a bare minimum a current position with an x- and y-representation, as well as a height and width. If we decide to take our game into the world of graphics, we need some way to show the frog on the screen. When these core elements can be pulled from a game, they compose the set of attributes needed when developing game entities.

An entity is an object that has attributes needed for playing the game, without regard to whether the game is 2D or 3D. Some of the most basic components an object could hold follow:

- A position represented by an x-, y-, and, z-coordinate system
- A height and width value for representing bounds of the particular object
- A state that indicates at minimum ALIVE or DEAD
- The current frame of an animation sequence
- Information relating to current velocity and current levels of heath or armor
- An image or generalized access to relevant content for the game (such as models or textures)

This list could easily go on and on until we cover an entire book on the subject (or at least a good portion of one). This section identifies these basic components in a fundamental implementation. Do not consider this discussion anything more than a starting point for developing game entities. A great many implementations, ideas, and opinions on the subject are available—and this is just to get a new game programmer started.

Building the Basic Entity

Now that a general idea of what an entity is has been established, let's take the steps to construct one. Immediately, a number of important questions come to mind, and there is much to be decided. Should entity be a class? An interface? How should the internal methods for accessing attributes be handled? Although these questions are important, it is even more important to take a second to contemplate the ideas of game programming. Developing games is a process not a solution. When a programmer (even a skilled one) begins programming in a new medium, a certain amount of time is required to transfer the existing skill set that may exist to the new problem domain. We are trying to learn to program games; the coding process might seem similar, but it is not always directly transferable. For the sake of providing a common platform from which to begin, the entities for this basic system will be implemented as a class with a set of interfaces that will allow us to extend those basic attributes as needed.

Let's look at a sample entity class called Actor. The Actor class takes its name from a long line of simulation programs and other nomenclature. Its name defines that an Actor will be responsible for exhibiting some sort of prescribed behavior, either from a player-controlled instance or any of the numerous baddies that are bound to make their evil presence known. A sample version of the Actor class follows:

```
class Actor implements Updater,Drawable,Loggable{
    static final int ALIVE = 1;
    static final int DEAD  = 2;
    private int state;
    private int x;
    private int y;
private int height;
private int width;
//default constructor.
Actor(){}

//accessor functions for updating the entity
public void setState(int curr_state){
    state = curr_state;
}
public int getState(){
    return state;
}
public void setX(int curr_x){
    x= curr_x;
}
public int getX(){
    return x;
}
public void setY(int curr_y){
    y = curr_y;
```

```java
    }
    public int getY(){
        return y;
    }
    public void setHeight(int curr_height){
        height = curr_height;
    }
    public int getHeight(){
        return height;
    }
    public void setWidth(int curr_width){
        width = curr_width;
    }
    public int getWidth(){
        return width;
    }
    //update ourselves properly
    public void update(){}
    //can we collide with you?
    public boolean collidesWith(Updateable other)
    {
        boolean bool = true;
        return  bool;
    }
    //If we can collide, then lets do so if needed.
    public void handleCollisions(){}
    //can I be seen this frame?
    public boolean isVisible()
    {
        boolean bool = true;
        return  bool;
    }
    //Local definition of drawing routines as needed.
    public void Draw(){}
    //Make sure we can write out debug and major event info.
    public void logDebugString(Object s){}
    public void logString(Object s){}
```

This class gives us straightforward access to all the major attributes and functions that might be needed in a 2D game. With extended definitions of the functions and a few added members, this code could be converted and extended into a 3D game. Though certainly not the only way to tackle this problem, this solution is a great place to begin from an architectural perspective.

One of the things that probably jumps quickly to mind are the three main interfaces that `Actor` is responsible for implementing. Each of these interfaces is responsible for taking care of certain aspects of the gameplay and the execution of the game logic. Let's look at each of them individually.

```
public interface Updater{
  public boolean collidesWith(Updateable other);
  public void handleCollisions();
  public void update();
}
```

The `Updater` interface is responsible for defining the core collision routines for this particular `Actor`, as well as specifying how he will update himself when the time comes. Each `Actor` that is alive during a pass in the game loop must know how it is to process its updates. Generally, updates are directly related to the physics model that is implemented into the game. If the `Player` `Actor` has a speed of 4 milliseconds, the coordinates should be updated to reflect this change in position in each frame. The actual implementation of the `update()` method is left to the domain of the game in question. The `collidesWith()` method will be implemented to identify if this `Actor` can collide with another `Updateable` object. It will return `true` if an `Actor` can collide with a specified other. This feature allows us to define specific collisions for specific interactions rather than one main solution for every object in the world. The `handleCollision()` method will process the selected collision routine once the need to do so has been identified.

The `Drawable` interface is listed as follows:

```
public interface Drawable{
    public boolean isVisible();
public void draw();+
 }
```

In the `Drawable` interface, each Actor class knows whether it should be drawn to the screen through the `isVisible()` method. This method can be used as a control mechanism and a built-in optimization for a game. If most of the `Actor` classes in a game don't need to be drawn, they can short-circuit the code that would normally trigger the group to draw, or process collisions, for example. This characteristic allows the game to do less work with respect to the current situation in the game. The `draw()` method is ultimately what games are all about. This method allows for the local implementation of the display as needed by the given entity. This implementation could be rendering code for a 2D or 3D game and is defined based on the overall usage of graphics in a given game. The `draw()` method is left mostly for conceptual purposes. Actual games may find limited use for the localized implementation of rendering beyond specifying a particular style of rendering, such as drawing an object reversed from its normal facing or causing some other special coloring effect to be used on the Actor. Many games choose to work with a construct called DisplayManager.

DisplayManager is responsible for dealing directly with the drawing of the objects and pulls information from the Actor classes present in the game to create the actual display. These methods will be further discussed in Chapter 3, "2D Graphics Programming."

The Loggable interface may seem the least obvious with regard for the need to implement this interface at the base entity level. The definition of the interface follows:

```
public interface Loggable
{
  public void logDebugString(String s);
  public void logString(String s);
}
```

Many games that are written in Java are window-based applications or applets that allow the developers to use the standard output on the machine to print and display messages regarding input or execution. This is one of the coolest features in Java. The concern does arise as Java games have a more full-screen implementation. When an application takes over responsibility for a full-screen application, the debugging results may be limited. Creating a basic control that allows the Actor or its subclasses to write to the screen or to a text or HTML file is a particularly valuable tool. The specific implementations of these methods are not particularly difficult to imagine. One thing that should be noted is the argument list could be modified to take objects instead of just strings. This modification allows for a much more open-ended and robust implementation. Some developers prefer to work with a system-wide logger that can retrieve the information needed from the Actor classes and any other objects within the system. Either method works equivalently.

At this point this core concept has been outlined, and now the overall implementation should be a bit more thoroughly explained. Any number of Actor classes can exist in a game. Some of them will be mobile, some of them can be animated, some modify others when they interact, and some of them are controlled by AI. They can be created and extended as far and wide as you need, but they still can lay claim to that core characteristic that an object must be displayable in a game world.

Although this idea isn't a big step for programmers who use object-oriented programming on a daily basis, consider the alternative by which many early games were coded. So many global variables floating around made debugging incredibly difficult. Everything was customized to the application itself, meaning a lot of rework was required to get a basic game framework in place to run on the next project. Many game programmers ditch a lot of their previous work anyway, but that's another story.

Now that the discussion has further detailed the concept of the Actor class, progress can continue. Remember, this is a rudimentary discussion of these classes, and the concepts are intended to be expanded on as needed. This chapter is by no means the final word on game entities. So, what comes next? Now this family of objects needs management.

Actor MANAGEMENT

ActorManager is a class responsible for all of the activities of the Actor classes in the game. This manager must make sure that all of the key functions of the objects can be accessed and presented to the game logic. The class is also responsible for ensuring that entities are properly updated, logged, and drawn to screen in games that don't have a specific display list or separate control mechanism for rendering. This class uses a LinkedList and implements a series of methods designed to handle the various components in each segment. Let's look at the ActorManager class:

```java
import java.util.*;
public class ActorManager
{
  LinkedList actorList;
  ActorManager()
 {
  //make a linked list to hold all the actors.
   actorList = new LinkedList();
  }
  public void createEntity(String s, int number)
  {
    for (int i = 0; i<number; i++)
    {
    actorList.add(entityFactory(s));
  }
 }
  Object entityFactory(String name)
  {
   Class temp;
  Object targetClass =null;
   try
   {
```

```
        //Find the class in question
        temp = Class.forName(name);
        // Make an instance of the desired class
        targetClass = temp.newInstance();
        }
        catch (Exception e)
        {
         System.out.println("Cannot create insance of" +name);
        }
        System.out.println("Created the " +name+ "!");
        return targetClass;
    }
public void clearEntities()
{
    for (int i = 0; i<actorList.size(); i++)
    {
        actorList.remove(i);
    }
System.out.println("The entity list has been cleared");
}
public void updateAll()
{
    Updater u;
 for (int i = 0; i<actorList.size(); i++)
 {
    u = (Updater)actorList.get(i);
    u.update();
 }
}
 public void drawAll()
 {
    Drawable d;
  boolean  b;
  for (int i = 0; i<actorList.size(); i++)
  {
        d = (Drawable)actorList.get(i);
        if(d.isVisible() == true)
        d.draw();
  }
 }
}//end ActorManager.java
```

This class is designed around the precepts of a Factory pattern. In the method createEntity(), the string and number of specified types of object are passed through. The call to the `entityFactory()` method is made and resolved based on string comparison with available classes that will result in the creation of the listed number of entities based on type. These new objects are then immediately added to an internal `LinkedList` that will hold them for processing.

One advantage to this method is that redefinition isn't needed to use new classes. A check can be made to see if the class is available and then the creation process occurs. This is an example of one of the most powerful aspects of the Java language. New classes need only to be added into the project to be included in this step. The largest disadvantage to using the `Class.newInstance()` method is that it calls only the default constructor on the given objects. Objects that need nondefault constructor calls must be created separately or redefined to map within this methodology.

The converse method to `createEntity()` is `clearEntities()`, in which the entire list of elements in the game is removed from the list. This method is required when making transitions from level to level or when the eventual completion of the game is over. Java handles the garbage collection on its own, but this is a good methodology to follow, nevertheless.

Looking at the functional calls to both `updateAll()` and `drawAll()`, we can see how we are leveraging the earlier definitions of `Actor` and its interfaces. Regardless of the individual implementation in subclasses of `Actor`, the `LinkedList` still processes those methods as they are defined in one sweeping task. One particular note on the `drawAll()` method is that it makes a minor optimization on the draw routines when it checks to see if the class is actually visible before processing the actual `draw()` method. This optimization prevents unwanted calls to draw objects that are outside the boundaries of the particular screen or situation in the game.

A sample program that uses the ActorManager follows:

```
public static void main(String args[])
{
    ActorManager am = new ActorManager();
    am.createEntity("Player",1);
    am.createEntity("Enemy",10);
    am.updateAll();
    am.drawAll();
}
```

As you can see, this code cleans up the implementation of the process a bit. If this class were to be implemented in the earlier mentioned game class, the `Actor-Manager` would have been constructed with the preparation of the `Actor` classes and the list in the `GAME_INIT`. The calls to update and draw would be made in the `GAME_MAIN` method.

Looking forward a bit, it's not too hard to envision scripted files that can parse out the string names of entities and the number needed for a particular level, and then have them automatically set up by the game itself. Remember the engine metaphor at the beginning of this chapter. The key is to create structures that process this work in a way that allows for the designers to focus on making great gameplay. These are just the first few steps of that process. The `ActorManager` class is an attempt to control and limit access to the entities in the game. Other more extensive implementations exist, and experimentation with this methodology is encouraged.

COLLISION DETECTION

After a group of entities has been created for the game, it's time to define the fundamental ways in which they can interact with the game world. The algorithmic process of determining where two game objects have intersected with each other or with the environment is called collision detection. The concept of collision detection is a fundamental premise in almost every game.

Fundamentally, two types of collisions exist.

Collisions with environments: Collisions with environments represent objects that are overlapping segments of the game world that offer some sort of response. Consider the outlines of the court in the basic game of *Pong*. When the ball reaches the top of the screen, the ball finds the upper-most border of the game world and determines that a collision has occurred. Look at Figure 2.4.

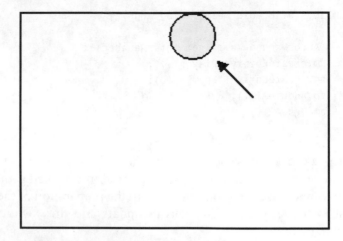

FIGURE 2.4   Collision is detected between the ball and the wall.

The incoming ball determines that collision has happened when the outline of the ball equals or overlaps the boundary. Most of the time, programming basic outlines such as this can be done using points. Some sample code for detecting collisions against environments follows:

```
if(Ball.getX()<=0) //Test the left wall
    return true;
if(Ball.getY()+Ball.getWidth()>= SCREEN_WIDTH) //Test right wall
    return true;
if(Ball.GetY()<=0) //Test Top;
    return true;
if(Ball.getY()+Ball.getHeight()>=SCREEN_HEIGHT)//test bottom wall
    return true;
```

If any one of these statements is evaluated to be true, the function returns properly.

Collisions with objects: Let's look at object-to-object collisions.

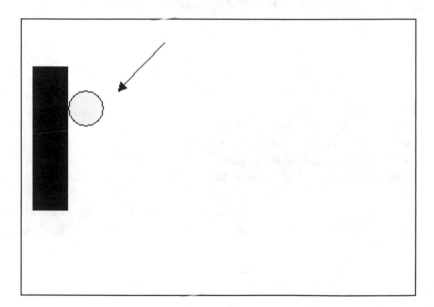

FIGURE 2.5   Collision is detected between the ball and a paddle.

Figure 2.5 sets up the most common type of collision detection in the form of object-to-object collision. A basic collision detection algorithm used in games is called the *bounding box*. The basic idea is that a box surrounds an object on all four sides. During a game, collision is checked on all four sides of the box. The collision check returns true when any two collidable objects overlap.

Figure 2.6 shows the bounding box algorithm on a typical game-styled sprite.

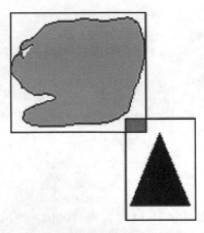

FIGURE 2.6   Collision is detected between a ship and a meteor.

The small overlap between the outlined boxes represents the point where these boxes overlap. It is important to carefully bound objects based on how accurate the collision needs to be.

Testing for bounding box collision is particularly simple when using the `Rectangle2D` class. The `Rectangle2D` class is abstract, so it must be created with one of the subclasses. In this case, the choices are either `Rectangle2D.Double` or `Rectangle2D.Float`. The float version will be more than enough for the basic algorithm used here.

When the rectangle has been initialized with a given `Actor` class's height and width, the process of detecting collisions between `Rectangle2D.Float` objects works as follows:

```
rectangle1.intersects(rectangle2.getBounds2D());
```

This call returns a Boolean as to whether the intersection was found given the current coordinates in both of these rectangles. This is a good addition to the `Actor` class and will be presented for the remainder of the chapter. Check the sample code on the CD-ROM for further implementation details.

ON THE CD

Detecting collisions is only part of the process. When a collision has been found, the game must then specify how it plans to react. In some cases, a collision causes the player's lives count to drop by one. Other games might determine that the game is over when collision happens. Whatever the response chosen, the reaction walks hand-in-hand with the detection.

Let's take another look at the collision detected by the ball against the wall in Figure 2.4. Those who remember the original *Pong* game know that the ball reflects off in what appears to be a fairly accurate collision by reversing the vector on which the collision is first detected. It is completely possible to program axis-aligned and non-axis-aligned vector reflections to maintain a reasonably accurate reflection in all cases. For this example, let's distill out the vector math and get to the point.

When the ball intersects with the wall, the vector is multiplied by –1. Figure 2.7 demonstrates the resulting vector of the collision based on this method.

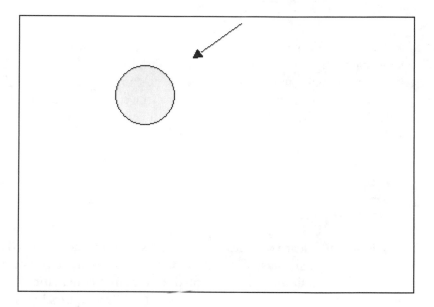

FIGURE 2.7 Vector reflection off the wall after collision.

With this new information, we can modify the collision-detection code to include the reaction as follows:

```
if(Ball.getX()<=0) //Test the left wall
    Ball.setVectorX(-1*Ball.getVectorX);
...
```

Using a method like this incorporates the result immediately into gameplay without requiring an additional infrastructure.

The same process is also possible for object-to-object collisions, but it is much more common to take an iterative approach to working through the object collisions. Remember the `ActorManager` from earlier in this chapter? There already exists an `Updater` interface that is capable of handling the collision detection for us. All that is needed is a list of collidable objects. Thankfully, courtesy of the `ActorManager`, all of the collidable objects in the game are in one place. Our collision pass ends up looking something like the following code:

```
for (int i = 0; i<actorList.size(); i++)
{
    u = (Updater)actorList.get(i);
    if(u.collidesWith((Actor)actorList.get(i))
        handleCollision();
}
```

This check goes through each of the `Actor` classes in the list, testing collision against each other. The actual implementation of the `handleCollision` function is left to the actual game implementation. It's important that the `collidesWith` method tests for equality to avoid returning true collisions against the `Actor` classes in the list when they test collisions against themselves. The easiest way to do this follows:

```
if(actor1 == actor2)
return false;
else
return actor1.getRect().intersects(actor2.getRect());
```

The art and science of collision detection is wide and varied, based on the needs of a given game. 3D collision detection requires the ability to perform quickly determined test conditions. These calculations require mathematics that are beyond the scope of this chapter. Check out Chapter 12, "3D Graphics Foundations," for a more in-depth discussion regarding 3D collision.

ARTIFICIAL INTELLIGENCE

Now that a foundation exists with regard to object creation and the game world, let's discuss briefly some of the behaviors that players might encounter in the form of artificial intelligence. The main purpose of AI is to present the player with competition or companionship during the game. The AI routines discussed in this section draw lineage from the classic coin-operated games of the '70s and '80s but remain remarkably valid even today for certain types of games. As the complexity of game projects increase, so too will the expectation of challenge to the players. Let's look at a few basic ways to get enemy actors moving around in Java.

Before getting started, it's a good idea to note that the algorithms presented here are designed to function within the Actor class's Update method. This will allow the Actor to automatically know where to be positioned based on the outcome of the algorithm.

> **Deterministic AI:** This is the most basic form of AI in games. There really isn't a lot to it. Actor classes equipped with this AI update their positions in the world based on a preset increment and continue to do so as long as they are on screen. Certain games such as *Asteroids* fit this model perfectly. The player is in an asteroid belt, and the big rocks just float by due to gravity or other force. As the player shoots at these asteroids, they exhibit the results of the force, breaking into smaller pieces and taking new vectors. Figure 2.8 shows an image and vector of an object using deterministic AI.

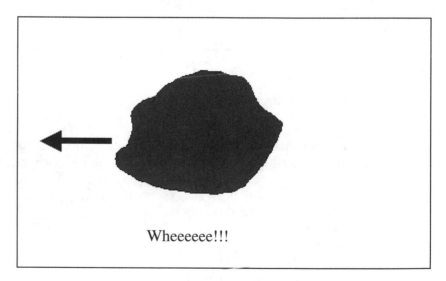

Wheeeeee!!!

FIGURE 2.8 Deterministic AI.

Coding this out is pretty straightforward:

```
Enemy.setX(Enemy.getX()+Enemy.getXVector());
```

This code takes the values stored in the class and updates this object in relation to its Vector's X component only.

Tracking: The tracking algorithm is a much more recognizable algorithm for games that hail from the old days. The fundamental idea behind this algorithm is that the enemy can always ask for the current position of the player, which allows the AI to "see" the player mathematically, then adjust his position based on the player's current position. As long as the player is skilled and a bit faster than the AI, he should be able to stay away from him. Figure 2.9 shows before and after shots from one frame to the next as the tracking AI updates according to the player's position.

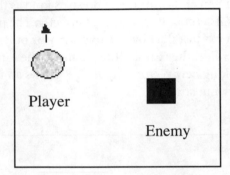
Before Tracking Applied

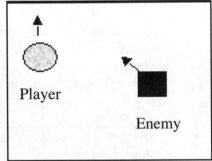
After Tracking Pass

FIGURE 2.9   Tracking AI.

To program a tracking AI, the player's coordinates must be accessible to the AI that is doing the tracking. An example of how to do this in code follows:

```
If(player.GetX()>enemy.GetX())
    Enemy.setX(enemy.GetX()+=2);
If(player.GetX()>enemy.GetX())
    Enemy.setX(enemy.GetX()-=2);
If(player.GetY()>enemy.GetY())
    Enemy.setY(enemy.GetY()+=2);
If(player.GetY()>enemy.GetY())
    Enemy.setY(enemy.GetY()-=2);
```

As you can see, the enemy updates his position by 2 in whatever direction needed to move toward the player. This algorithm is particularly useful to motivate a player by chasing him.

Evasion: The evasion algorithm is the opposite of the tracking algorithm just discussed. It takes the current position of the player and uses it to increase the distance between the player and the enemy or target. The basic code structure for this algorithm follows:

```
If(player.GetX()>enemy.GetX())
   Enemy.setX(enemy.GetX()-=2);
If(player.GetX()>enemy.GetX())
   Enemy.setX(enemy.GetX()+=2);
If(player.GetY()>enemy.GetY())
   Enemy.setY(enemy.GetY()-=2);
If(player.GetY()>enemy.GetY())
   Enemy.setY(enemy.GetY()+=2);
```

Figure 2.10 shows this algorithm in a before-and-after format.

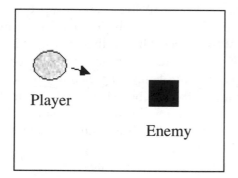
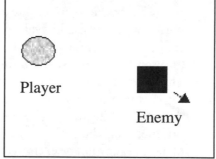

Before Evasion Applied   After Evasion Algo

FIGURE 2.10   Evasion AI.

The basic idea here is that the enemy tries to keep the maximum distance between himself and the player. A careful player can corner this algorithm, so be careful not to let that happen.

These basic AI algorithms don't even begin to touch the tip of the iceberg that is game AI. The reader is encouraged to continue algorithmic research to find the best AI algorithms for a current game. Always remember that the game AI has a radical impact on the player's expectations of the game and the game's ability to function in a cohesive and fun manner.

PULLING IT ALL TOGETHER

At this point, we have seen the general game structure, including the game loop and its support methods. We have also looked over the use of timers in games with an analysis of the performance of each one. We have identified the importance of base `Actor` classes and looked at ways to manage them, as well as ways to bring them to life using AI and collision-detection algorithms, which ultimately brings us to the next question:

WHERE ARE MY GRAPHICS?

Being completely honest, this is the ugliest way to discuss architecture. There haven't been any pretty pictures or sounds, no cool animations or input schemes—nothing that indicates that what we have discussed is much more than a bunch of `println` statements. The main reason this material is presented without all the flash relates back to the car metaphor once again. When buying a car, most people look at the color, check the interior, take a test drive, and maybe listen to the radio. The true power of the car is undervalued. What is meant here is that most people assume the engine works behind the scenes without interaction, beyond providing fuel for those thousands and thousands of tiny explosions happening right in front of the driver. The engine usually isn't as flashy as the renderer, but when building something from the ground up, building it properly pays off in the long run. Taking this road with the core architectures allows us to break down those components, look them over, put them together, and then build all the pretty stuff on top. The core architecture of a game may not be exciting, but it makes all the rest possible.

SUMMARY

At this point you have seen one of the basic architectures that can be used when programming games in Java. Remember that this is a starting point that will be referenced later in the book. Experiment to discover more robust architectures that can be implemented in your own games.

3 | 2D Graphics Programming

In This Chapter

When video games were just coming into existence, programmers found all sorts of interesting ways to get rudimentary images drawn to the screen to represent the player and his obstacles. These "graphics" were often just single pixels that would change color or position to indicate some form of interaction. As time progressed and computers gained more processing power and memory, game developers quickly found ways to consume the extra resources and to use them for gaming. Although these resources allowed for more color and immersion in games, they still had the biting limitation of being almost exclusively two-dimensional. With that sort of limitation, most of the games focused almost exclusively on developing compelling gameplay through innovative use of the system's capabilities.

Today, the hardcore gamer usually finds most games set in a three-dimensional environment complete will all sorts of special effects and lighting tricks. This is certainly a natural progression in the development of games, but a couple of important points should be noted. First, most people who play games are not hard-core gamers and tend to play a lot more less-graphically intense genres of games such as puzzles or card games. Second, the most-played game in the world on a daily basis is *Solitaire*. 2D games are still just as popular as ever, just with a different audience than the past. Every game today still maintains 2D elements, even if they form only the heads-up display or the menu system. To cut to the chase, 2D is not even close to being dead!

The Java platform has a number of tools to enable game development in 2D. This chapter will discuss and provide an overview of the basic concepts and techniques that game developers need to create full-screen 2D games using Java.

QUICK 2D OVERVIEW

Before getting deeper into the concepts behind using Java for 2D games, a quick overview is in order. Each 2D game uses images that it draws to the screen. Given that the display and the images are the two major components of a 2D game from a graphical view, a general overview should get everyone on the same page. For most readers, this will be a quick review.

Display Overview

The display in 2D games is ordered in an inverted coordinate system with the starting point of the grid being set to the upper-left corner.

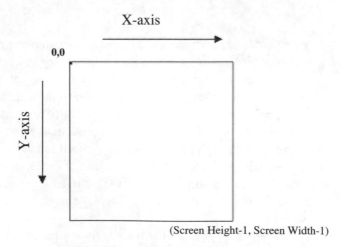

FIGURE 3.1 The 2D coordinate system.

The screen is composed of picture elements (pixels) that store a color value used to display images and background during the game. A screen has the additional properties of height, width, and bit depth. The bit depth indicates how much memory is used to store each pixel. Common depths are 8, 16, and 32 bits per pixel. The amount of memory needed to store any image or background can be determined by multiplying the height, width, and bit depth. The combined attributes are referred to as the screen's *resolution*. Some particularly high resolutions require megabytes of memory to store and can affect performance during the execution of the game.

Each time a frame is ready to be drawn, the computer renders it to the screen. To understand how to get smooth animation with no artifacts, it is important to understand a little bit about how the computer draws images to the monitor.

Monitors draw the screen image based on the image in video RAM from the upper-left corner to the lower-right corner. As an electron beam moves in a zigzag pattern, as shown in Figure 3.2, the dark lines are the beam drawing to the screen and the lighter lines are the beam moving back to the left side of the screen to draw the next raster line. The movement from the right side back to the left side is called the horizontal retrace.

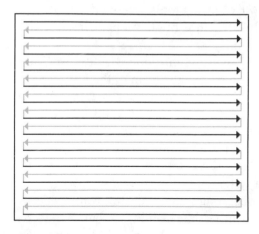

FIGURE 3.2 The order in which a monitor displays the screen.

The length of time it takes the monitor to draw a complete frame to the screen is called the *refresh rate* for the video mode. A refresh rate of 60 Hz means the monitor is redrawing the screen 60 times per second. Generally speaking, higher refresh rates are better, but not always, as will be seen later. When the electron beam reaches the lower-right corner of the screen, it moves back to the upper-left corner to begin drawing a new frame.

Image Overview

The ships, bullets, and enemies that are drawn in a starship combat game are classified as images. Much like screens, each image has a height, width, and bit depth. When selecting the resolution for images, be careful to consider the total memory being used when storing images. A number of image file formats are supported on the Java platform. Some of the more common ones are .gif and .png. Review the Java documentation to find other supported formats.

When images are linked to Actor classes, they become *sprites*. Sprites contain the x- and y-coordinates for the location where the image will be drawn. When the time to render comes, the coordinates are retrieved from the sprite and copied into the screen memory. This topic will be discussed more fully later in the chapter.

Screen Modes

Games that are built using applets and AWT windows are limited because they are rendered the same basic way as GUI components for any typical application. This methodology is less consistent and less useful for applications that require performance. Games that are turn-based or have infrequent updates can be built using the standard AWT or Swing tools presented without issue. Puzzle and card games are perfect for this structure, but to get performance, developers need full control over the screen memory.

The Java 2 SDK 1.4 introduced an exciting new feature of special interest to Java game developers in the form of the full-screen exclusive mode API. This new feature allows developers to create games that can take control of the entire screen memory. Until full-screen mode was introduced, developers were constrained to a small section of the screen in a window or perhaps an applet in a Web browser. It was possible to create a window and maximize it so the entire screen would be encompassed. Such presentations retained the ugly window decorations such as the title bar and system buttons. There aren't many triple-A game titles on the market that use the operating system's default window decorations as part of the interface.

Another issue was the inability to change the screen resolution to match the desired resolution for games. If a game is designed that needs a display area of only 320 pixels by 200 pixels at a bit depth of 16 bits per pixel ($320 \times 200 \times 16$ bpp) and the only choice is a window, then there are some real problems to face. What if the person playing the game has the desktop display set to $1024 \times 768 \times 8$ bpp? The game is going to show up as a tiny window on the display and may be hard to see, making it impossible to play. The opposite situation causes even more trouble—if the game needs a display area of 1024×768 and the player has the display set to a lower resolution, the player won't be able to see the entire window on screen.

The second problem is the display color depth. If a game is to use a color depth of 16 bpp but the user has the display set to 8 bpp, the graphics that took months to render at 16 bpp will look horrible. The system has to dither the colors because the user's display has only 256 colors available for the game to use, causing a frustrating loss of quality.

Thankfully, these issues have been solved primarily through the use of the full-screen API. The majority of this chapter will use the full-screen techniques to render 2D images to the screen.

The Full-Screen API

The full screen API provides direct access to the screen memory to speed rendering for applications that need this performance. Most games want access to the direct memory so that they are not burdened with other events or delays that might cause slowdowns in the game's execution. This section discusses at length how to use the full-screen API to render.

The GraphicsEnvironment Class

The first step required to set up the desired display for a game is to understand what video resolutions the computer on which the game is running is capable of. For instance, the game may be set to run on a display resolution higher than the computer's video card is capable of using. The GraphicsEnvironment class can determine what modes are available. This class provides access to the collection of GraphicsDevice objects available on the computer. The GraphicsDevice class is described a bit later.

To create an instance of the GraphicsEnvironment class, do the following:

```
GraphicsEnvironment gfxEnv
=GraphicsEnvironment.getLocalGraphicsEnvironment();
```

Now the GraphicsEnvironment object can be queried as to what devices are available for the game to use.

The GraphicsDevice Class

A GraphicsDevice object can describe many devices types, such as display screens, printers, and image buffers. It is key to know what screen devices are available. Use the GraphicsEnvironment object obtained in the previous code to request a list of the display devices.

```
GraphicsDevice[] screenDevList = gfxEnv.getScreenDevices();
```

The getScreenDevices method returns an array of GraphicsDevice objects that describe display screens on the system. On a computer with a single display, this array will contain only a single element; however, it is becoming more common for computers to have multiple display screens. If the game will use only the default display screen, the getDefaultScreenDevice() method can be used.

```
GraphicsDevice defaultDevice = gfxEnv.getDefaultScreenDevice();
```

The rest of this chapter assumes the use of only the default display screen device.

The DisplayMode Class

The next step is to request the capabilities of the display device. The DisplayMode class contains the information for the bit depth, width, height, and refresh rate of a GraphicsDevice object for a given video mode. It may become necessary to adjust a game to the capabilities of the current computer. To do this, the display modes available are needed for the current display device. Use the getDisplayModes() method of the GraphicsDevice object.

```
DisplayMode[] displayModes
        = defaultScreenDevice.getDisplayModes();
```

This method returns an array of the display modes available for the specified display device, in this case, the default display.

ADJUSTING TO THE ENVIRONMENT

Most games are written with a target display mode in mind. Unless it is a low resolution with a color depth of 8 bpp, no assumptions can be made on the end user's system. It is important to have a minimum set of requirements that will serve as the lower bounds for the execution of the game. If a better mode is found to be available, the application can select it.

How can an acceptable video mode be determined? The simplest method would be to compare a list of acceptable modes against the list of available modes for the device. If the system doesn't support any of the modes, the game can be set to run in windowed mode instead of full-screen mode. First, let's define the list of acceptable modes. Note that this list can continue through the full list of desired display modes; just add it to the existing list.

```
DisplayMode[] requestedDisplayModes = new DisplayMode[]
{
new DisplayMode(1280, 1024,32, DisplayMode.REFRESH_RATE_UNKNOWN),
new DisplayMode(1024, 768, 32, DisplayMode.REFRESH_RATE_UNKNOWN),
new DisplayMode(800,  600, 16, DisplayMode.REFRESH_RATE_UNKNOWN),
new DisplayMode(640,  480, 16, DisplayMode.REFRESH_RATE_UNKNOWN)
};
```

Now let's create a method to compare the video mode "wish list" with the available list of modes. Let's call this method findRequestedMode(). This method searches through the returned values in the displayModes array trying to find a match for the height, width, and bit depth of the display. It returns the highest possible match for all three of these factors.

```
public static DisplayMode findRequestedMode()
{
    DisplayMode best = null;
// loop through each of our requested modes
for(int rIndex=0; rIndex #### requestedDisplayModes.length; rIndex++)
{
   // loop through each of the available modes
      for(int mIndex=0; mIndex #### displayModes.length; mIndex++)
      {
        if(displayModes[mIndex].getWidth() ==
        requestedDisplayModes[rIndex].getWidth()
        &&
        displayModes[mIndex].getHeight()
        ==requestedDisplayModes[rIndex].getHeight()
           &&
           displayModes[mIndex].getBitDepth() ==
           requestedDisplayModes[rIndex].getBitDepth()){
   // We found a resolution match
      if(best==null)
      {
      // if the refresh rate was specified try to match that as well
           if(requestedDisplayModes[rIndex].getRefreshRate() !=
           DisplayMode.REFRESH_RATE_UNKNOWN)
   {
    if(displayModes[mIndex].getRefreshRate() $$$$=
      requestedDisplayModes[rIndex].getRefreshRate())
        {
```

```
                              best = displayModes[mIndex];
                              return best;
                          }
                      }
                  else
                  {
                   best = displayModes[mIndex];
                   return best;
                  }
               }
             }
           }
         }
    // no matching modes so we return null
    return best;
    }
```

When the determination has been made as to the available display modes and the resolution, the game can begin. In the source code provided for this chapter, the FullScreenFrame1 example uses the basic structures that have been discussed so far to create a full-screen window with the best resolution available on the monitor. If the system doesn't support full-screen mode, or if it does but none of the desired modes is available, the program will run in windowed mode. It is possible to set the windowed mode by default by passing the string windowed from the command line. This code is abbreviated to conserve space. Please refer to the actual provided code for the full implementation.

```
public static void main(String[] args)
{
  DisplayMode newMode = null;
    // we need to make sure the system default display can
    // support full screen mode, if it can't we will run
    // in windowed mode
    boolean fullScreenMode = false;
    if(defaultScreenDevice.isFullScreenSupported())
    {
        fullScreenMode = true;
        // try to get one of the modes we really want
        newMode = findRequestedMode();
      // if the mode doesn't exist then go into windowed mode
        if(newMode==null)
          fullScreenMode = false;
```

```
      }
      else
      System.out.println("full screen mode unsupported.");
      FullScreenFrame1 myFrame = null;
      if(fullScreenMode && !forceWindowedMode)
  myFrame = new FullScreenFrame1("FullScreenFrame1 Full Screen
  Mode", newMode);
      else
  myFrame = new FullScreenFrame1("FullScreenFrame1 Windowed Mode",
  false);
      myFrame.initToScreen();
    }
}
```

When the program starts, it first determines if the system on which it is running supports full-screen exclusive mode by calling the isFullScreenSupported() method on the default screen device. If this method returns true, the program prints a list of all available display modes for the device to the console, so you can get an idea of what is available. Next, the findRequestedMode() method attempts to get a display mode that matches one of the preferred modes. If the system doesn't support one of these modes or if full-screen mode isn't supported, the fullScreenMode variable is set to false.

If full-screen mode is supported and the system can use the desired video mode, a new FullScreenFrame1 object is constructed by passing it the new video mode. The constructor first saves the current video mode so it can be restored when the program ends.

Next, using the Frame class's method setUndecorated, it turns off window decorations such as the title bar. If this isn't done, the video mode will be set and the window will be a normal window positioned in the upper-left corner of the screen with the width and height of the screen. The user will be able to drag it around, just like any other window. The constructor also calls the Frame class's method setIgnoreRepaint, passing it a value of true. This setting makes sure that the windowing system won't send repaint events to the window. The reason for this will be explained a bit later.

Finally, the constructor calls the method setWindowListener to make sure the program gets the closing, iconified, deiconified, activated, and deactivated events. The reason these events are needed will be explained a little later in this chapter.

The constructor for the FullScreenFrame1 class follows:

```
public FullScreenFrame1(String title, DisplayMode mode) throws
HeadlessException
    {
        super(title);

        // this is the video mode we will run in
        newDisplayMode = mode;
// assume window decorations are not desired
    setUndecorated(true);
    // make sure the windowing system doesn't send repaint events
    setIgnoreRepaint(true);
    // make sure we get the window events
    setupWindowListener();
    }
```

If full-screen mode is not supported, a new `FullScreenFrame1` object will be constructed that will run in windowed mode. The main difference between this constructor and the previous one is the window is set so that it can't be resized, and the caller has the choice of whether or not the window is undecorated.

The last action the main method performs is calling the `initToScreen` method, which puts the window on the screen. If the `windowedMode` variable is `false`, this method calls the methods needed to get the window on the screen in full-screen mode and set the video mode. If the `windowedMode` variable is `true`, the size of the window is set and the `show` method is called.

```
public void initToScreen()
{
 pack();
 if(!windowedMode)
 {
    // set this Frame as a full screen window
    defaultScreenDevice.setFullScreenWindow(this);
    // change the video mode to the one we wanted
    defaultScreenDevice.setDisplayMode(newDisplayMode);
 }
  else
  {
    setSize(windowedWidth,windowedHeight);
    show();
  }
}
```

If this program runs properly, the screen should be cleared and set to white. If the modes of choice are not available or windowed mode is selected, the window will look like that shown in Figure 3.3.

FIGURE 3.3   Results of running the FullScreenFrame1.

RENDERING TO THE DISPLAY

At this point the foundation has been created to get a game running in full-screen or windowed mode, allowing drawing to the screen. Although the program can take full advantage of exclusive control over the display memory, a few concerns still need to be reconciled before the issue can be put to rest. Depending on how the images are drawn to the screen, some visible anomalies may cause confusion or disrupt gameplay. These problems must be alleviated.

THE RENDER LOOP

At its simplest, the algorithm for rendering objects on the screen requires the creation of a rendering loop, such as the following:

```
while(doRender)
{
clear the screen
update object (sprite) positions
draw all objects
}
```

Fundamentally, this code is sound, but a few problems exist with this algorithm. Because image updates are happening directly, the updates will be visible and will result in a strobe effect, sometimes called *flashing*. Flashing occurs because of direct updates and because the entire screen image is being cleared before the sprites are redrawn. The diagram depicted in Figure 3.4 shows the sequence of draw events. The flashing occurs each time the screen is cleared.

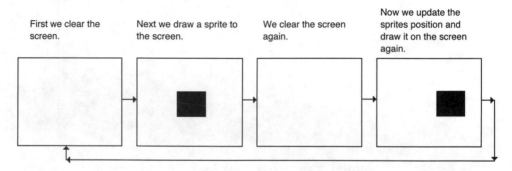

FIGURE 3.4   The drawing process.

The second problem with this rendering method is called image *tearing. Tearing* occurs when an object is moving on the screen and the direct updating of the screen image allows the user to see part of the new frame and part of the old frame. This situation is illustrated in Figure 3.5.

The main technique to correct image tearing is using a buffering algorithm. The most common buffering technique is called *double buffering*.

Double Buffering

Double buffering helps to remove the flashing problem and, with some slight adjustments, can fix the tearing issue as well. When you use double buffering, the direct updates of the video RAM that the monitor is currently displaying are avoided.

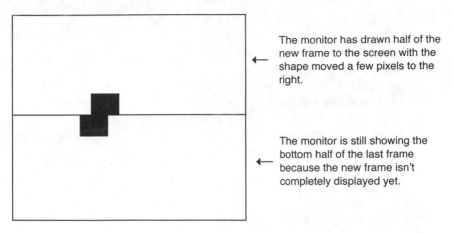

The monitor has drawn half of the new frame to the screen with the shape moved a few pixels to the right.

The monitor is still showing the bottom half of the last frame because the new frame isn't completely displayed yet.

FIGURE 3.5   Image tearing.

To enable this technique the application must first render to a chunk of memory called a *buffer*, and then display that buffer on screen after the entire image has been rendered. This buffer is called the *back buffer*, or *secondary buffer*. The buffer that contains the image currently displayed on the screen is called the *front buffer*, or *primary buffer*. An updated version of the rendering algorithm that includes changes to accommodate the double-buffering technique follows:

```
while(doRender)
{
clear back buffer
update object (sprite) positions
draw all objects to the back buffer
copy the back buffer to the front buffer
display the front buffer
}
```

When this algorithm is implemented, the flashing will be gone. When the back buffer is moved onto the screen, however, the tearing effect may still be present because a direct update to the video RAM being displayed by the monitor is still being performed. To remove the tearing effect, the back buffer must be moved onto the screen only when the monitor is not actually drawing a frame and only after a frame has been completely displayed. This means that the back buffer must be moved onto the screen during the monitor's vertical retrace. Another update to the existing rendering illustrates this concept as follows:

```
while(doRender)
{
clear back buffer
update object (sprite) positions
draw all objects to the back buffer
wait for the vertical retrace
copy the back buffer to the front buffer
display the front buffer
}
```

After doing all the work to remove the flashing and the tearing problem, there is still one last concern. During each vertical retrace, the entire back buffer image is being copied to the front buffer. This wholesale copy is very slow and to be avoided if possible.

The current version of the rendering loop is set up to wait for the vertical retrace of each frame before continuing with the loop. With this structure, all of the game logic and rendering is being attempted in the time it takes the monitor to draw a single frame to the screen. The faster the refresh rate of the video mode, the shorter this period will be and the less time left to perform the game logic.

If the video mode's refresh rate is 60Hz, the monitor is redrawing the screen 60 times every second. Given that there are 1,000 milliseconds in a second, the amount of time to process everything can be surmised by dividing 1,000 by 60. This evaluates to around 16.7 milliseconds to do everything between frames. A large amount of time is being used to copy the back buffer to the front buffer, leaving less time to run the game logic and rendering. If this slow copying of the buffers were removed, more time would be available for game logic.

Page Flipping

The solution to the slow copying of the back buffer to the front buffer is to use a method called page flipping. With page flipping the pointer to the video RAM that is to be displayed by the monitor is changed to a new location in the video RAM (Figure 3.6). This solution is far faster than copying an entire screen image. For example:

```
while(doRender)
{
clear back buffer
update object (sprite) positions
draw all objects to the back buffer
wait for the vertical retrace
move the video pointer to the back buffer to make it the front buffer
display the front buffer
}
```

The video pointer always points at the image to
be displayed on the screen. By making it point
to a new location in the video RAM we can
instantaneously change the screen image.

On each vertical retrace the pointer is moved
from the left to the right frame and then back
again on the next retrace.

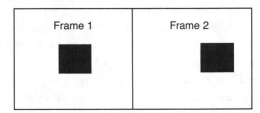

FIGURE 3.6   Page flipping.

Page flipping is not always available on all systems. If page flipping is not available, the game code must be structured so as to respond accordingly in this event. Page flipping is also not a choice when the program is running in windowed mode.

An interesting side effect of page flipping is that the frame rate of the game is capped, meaning that the game can't display more frames per second than the refresh rate of the video mode you are using, in a similar fashion to the blocking loop referenced in Chapter 2. Because windowed mode isn't using page flipping, frame rates are generally extremely high because the game doesn't have to wait for the vertical refresh to display a new frame each time through the loop. In windowed mode, the tearing effects seen earlier will likely return. The amount of time the render method sleeps in each loop should be adjusted up, using the `setRenderLoopSpeed` method, to slow the frame rate and prevent tearing. You may wonder how the game can know when to use page flipping and when not to. This information comes from the `BufferStrategy` class, which handles all of the details.

THE BUFFERSTRATEGY CLASS

This class makes it easy to implement the correct rendering techniques mentioned previously without having to do much work. The method `createBufferStrategy()`, which is inherited from the `java.awt.Window` class, is called to create the appropriate buffering method. Let's override the `initToScreen` method to include the creation of the BufferStrategy.

```
public void initToScreen(int numBuffers)
{
super.initToScreen();
// create a BufferStrategy with a number of buffers
// the window must be on screen before this call is made
createBufferStrategy(numBuffers);
}
```

You can now pass in the number of buffers you want to use. The strategy will be created after the window is placed on the screen. (Double buffering uses two buffers, triple buffering uses three, and so on.) If the number of buffers requested is greater than the number that can fit into video memory, the extra buffers are placed into system memory. This slows down everything, so don't do it. Use the getAvailableAcceleratedMemory() method of the GraphicsDevice class to determine how much accelerated memory is on the video card.

THE RENDERING LOOP

It's finally time to create the rendering loop mentioned previously. A new class will be created that implements the Runnable interface, and the rendering loop will be controlled by a thread. The startRenderThread() method starts the rendering loop and stopRenderThread() causes it to stop and the thread to die. The thread can be temporarily paused by calling the pauseRenderThread() method.

The run method contains the rendering loop. The loop is just as discussed previously, with a few extras—stopping and pausing the rendering thread as well as handling the possibility of corruption of our rendered frames. The corruption issue will be discussed in the section on volatile images. The doRender() method, which is called each time through the loop, simply gets the Graphics object handle from the buffer strategy and passes it to the render method. The default render() method clears the back buffer to the background color and then returns. This method is overridden to call all the game logic and to perform the game rendering.

```
public void run()
{
boolean contentsLost = false;
try
{
// get the buffer strategy that we set up
BufferStrategy bs = getBufferStrategy();
 // Stay in the render thread until it is stopped
 while(doRender)
```

```
    {
    // if paused then don't do anything
      if(!pauseRender)
      {
      // perform the rendering for the new frame
          doRender();
// Because the buffer strategy may have used volatile
// images to speed things up make sure that
// the frame buffer just rendered has not
// been corrupted or lost
          if(bs.contentsLost())
              contentsLost=true;
     // If the buffer has been corrupted or lost then we
// don't want to show the contents of it yet. We
// will go through the loop again and redraw the frame.
      if(contentsLost)
      {
        if(bs.contentsRestored())
          contentsLost=false;
      }
      else
      {
      // Things are okay,swap the buffers to show the frame
          bs.show();
      }
    }
//Sleep for a bit and keep the frame rate static.
      Thread.sleep(renderLoopSpeed);
    }
    }
    catch(Exception x)
    {
      x.printStackTrace();
    }
    }
    public boolean doRender()
    {
        boolean shouldSwap =
        render(getBufferStrategy().getDrawGraphics());
    return shouldSwap;
    }
```

ON THE CD
In the code provided, the FullScreenFrame2 renders using the page-flipping technique. It was adjusted to draw random-size rectangles of random color at slow

intervals. When it's running properly, it will look something like that shown in Figure 3.7.

FIGURE 3.7   Page flipping some color rectangles of random color. (See color version on companion CD-ROM.)

HANDLING WINDOW EVENTS

Earlier it was mentioned that the constructor for `FullScreenFrame1` calls the `set-WindowListener()` method to ensure the program gets the `closing`, `iconified`, `de-iconified`, `activated`, and `deactivated` events. In the `FullScreenFrame1` class, the methods that handle these events were empty, except for the `exitForm` method. This method is called when the window-closing event is detected. The game window is removed from the screen, the video mode is restored, and the program exits. In `FullScreenFrame2`, code is introduced to handle the other events.

Basically, when the game's window is deactivated or minimized, the rendering thread is paused so the player won't get killed by the thousands of enemies that are constantly bearing down on him. When the window is reactivated or restored, the thread is unpaused so the player can continue the game.

IMAGES

Up to this point the focus has been on building a small framework to use for getting into full-screen mode. The Java2D API contains many classes and methods that support loading and manipulating image files of various formats. Typically, a game has to deal with only one type of image class. Fundamentally, three basic types of image classes exist: buffered, volatile, and managed. Each of these image types has its advantages and disadvantages. This section identifies how to load game images into the different types of image classes and how to draw them to the screen.

The BufferedImage Class

The BufferedImage class is particularly good at giving the programmer direct access to an image's actual data. With this access, a programmer can change the color, add image filtering, or just modify a single pixel. This access could be thought of as free reign to change or modify any desired aspect of the image. Although this mechanism is great, the downside is that images must be held in system memory, which greatly reduces the computer's performance.

The BufferedImage and ImageIO Classes

Let's figure out how to get an image loaded and drawn to the screen. The Buffered-Example class in the provided source code shows how to load an image into a BufferedImage object and use that object to display the image on the screen. One required variable is an imageResourceName, which will hold the name of the image file to load. The second is an image, which will be the handle to the image after is has been loaded. The loadImage method uses the read method of the javax.im-ageio.ImageIO class to load the image from disk. Multiple versions of the read method are available. The sample code uses the parameter list that takes a URL object as the location of the image to load.

```
// The resource location of the image to display
private static final String imageResourceName = "/rock.png";
// The handle to the buffered image we will load and display
private BufferedImage image = null;
//Read in the image to display and put it in a BufferedImage
private void loadImage()
{
try
{
  URL imageURL = getClass().getResource(imageResourceName);
    if(imageURL==null)
```

```
        {
        System.out.println("Can't load"+imageResourceName);
        return;
        }
        image = ImageIO.read(imageURL);
    }
    catch(IOException x)
     {
        x.printStackTrace();
     }
    }
```

Now that the image is loaded, it can be displayed. Putting an image on the screen is extremely simple using the Java `Graphics` class method `drawImage()`. Simply pass in the image object to be drawn, upper-left x-pixel coordinate, upper-left y-pixel coordinate, and a handle to an `ImageObserver` object. The `ImageObserver` object is used in circumstances where the image may not yet be completely loaded. Because this application used the `ImageIO` class to read in the image, this isn't going to be a concern, and the `this` object is passed in the current window. Let's draw something to the screen using this method.

```
public boolean render(Graphics g)
{
super.render(g);
if(image!=null)
{
    g.drawImage(image,200,200,this);
}
return true;
}
```

When the source code for the `SimpleBuffer` example is executed, it should look something like the image shown in Figure 3.8.

Now that one can be drawn, let's draw 100 in random locations on the screen, as seen in the following `BufferedExample` source code:

```
public boolean render(Graphics g)
{
super.render(g);
Random rand = new Random();
if(image!=null)
{
    for(int loop=0; loop<100; loop++)
    g.drawImage(image,
```

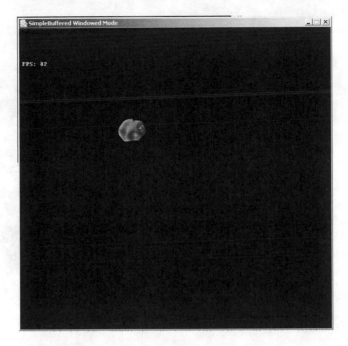

FIGURE 3.8   A SimpleBuffer in action.

```
      rand.nextInt(getWidth()),
      rand.nextInt(getHeight()),
      this);
   }
   return true;
   }
```

This example will be only a slightly more exciting one because of the limitations of the BufferedImage class. When the BufferedExample is run, it should look something like the image shown in Figure 3.9.

Running the BufferedExample program on the development machine gives a whopping performance of four frames per second in the video mode 1280×1024× 32<60. This rate is extremely slow, given that the image is drawing only 100 times each frame. For a video game, this would be totally unacceptable. Luckily, there are ways to speed up things using the VolatileImage class.

The VolatileImage Class

The VolatileImage class gives the potential for hardware acceleration of image-drawing operations. It does this by storing the image data in the video card memory

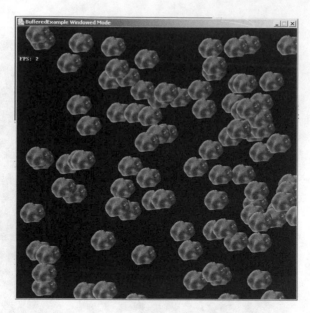

FIGURE 3.9 Results of running the BufferedExample code.

(VRAM) instead of on the computer's main system memory. Therefore, when the image is drawn to the screen it can be retrieved directly by the video card from its own memory instead of having to be transferred to the card from the main memory. The BufferStrategy class uses volatile images behind the scenes whenever hardware acceleration is available. To load a volatile image use the same ImageIO method used previously, first loading the image into a BufferedImage. After the image is loaded, use the GraphicsConfiguration class's method createCompatibleVolatileImage() to create a VolatileImage object that is compatible with the graphics device on which the game is running. The last step is to copy the contents of the BufferedImage object to the VolatileImage object.

```
// Read in the image,Put it in a VolatileImage object.
private void loadImage()
{
try
{
URL imageURL = getClass().getResource(imageResourceName);
if(imageURL==null)
{
  System.out.println("Unable to locate the resource "+
  imageResourceName);
return;
}
```

```
bufferedImage = ImageIO.read(imageURL);
image =   getGraphicsConfiguration().createCompatibleVolatileImage(
bufferedImage.getWidth(),
bufferedImage.getHeight());
image.getGraphics().drawImage(bufferedImage,0,0,this);
}
catch(IOException x)
{
    x.printStackTrace();
}
}
```

The VolatileImage class was aptly named. The downside of using this class is that under certain situations the image can be lost or invalidated. Unfortunately, the invalidation can't be determined until after the game tries to draw to the screen. When using VolatileImage, check the image after it has been drawn to the back buffer. If it has been corrupted, completely redraw the frame. This step complicates the render method code a little bit, but not much. The new changes are shown in the following code:

```
public boolean render(Graphics g)
{
super.render(g);
Random rand = new Random();
if(image!=null)
{
   for(int loop=0; loop<100; loop++)
 {
int returnCode =
image.validate(getGraphicsConfiguration());
     if (returnCode == VolatileImage.IMAGE_RESTORED){
     // the contents need to be restored
     image.getGraphics().drawImage(bufferedImage,0,0,this);
     }
else if (returnCode ==  VolatileImage.IMAGE_INCOMPATIBLE){
// the old volatile image is incompatible
image = getGraphicsConfiguration().createCompatibleVolatileImage(
bufferedImage.getWidth(),bufferedImage.getHeight());
     image.getGraphics().drawImage(bufferedImage,0,0,this);
     }
         g.drawImage(image,
             rand.nextInt(getWidth()),
             rand.nextInt(getHeight()),
             this);
     }
```

```
}
return true;
}
```

The VolatileImage class's validate method is called at the top of the loop each time through to determine if the image surface has been lost and to make sure the graphics configuration for the window is compatible with the image. If the image surface has been lost, it is restored so that it can be used again. This restoration causes the image to be corrupted, so the game will have to draw the BufferedImage back into the VolatileImage.

The graphics configuration can become incompatible with the image surface if, for example, it was created on one graphics device and now the user is trying to use it on a different device. In this case, create a new VolatileImage to match the graphics configuration and again draw the BufferedImage into the new VolatileImage.

On the development machine, running the VolatileExample program gives 60 frames per second in the video mode 1280×1024×32<60. This speed is a substantial improvement over the buffered image example. You may have noticed that the rock image being drawn now has a large white area around it every time it is drawn. This white area results because volatile images do not support transparency, and the rock image contains large transparent areas. Figure 3.10 shows a picture from the VolatileExample program.

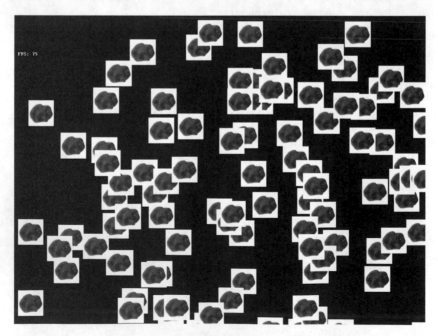

FIGURE 3.10   Results of running the VolatileExample code.

Unless you are writing programs that need graphics that are only rectangular, volatile images aren't going to help you much. However, you can use them to draw only the rectangular portions of the display. Those portions would then be hardware accelerated.

At this point the discussion on images has revealed two techniques. The game can use slow, buffered images or fast, nontransparent, volatile images. Neither seems to fill the needs of a game programmer. This is where *managed images* come into the picture.

Managed Images

Managed images aren't an official type of image in the API; they are images that can be accelerated behind the scenes by the API. You don't have to do anything special to use them, which makes them easier to deal with than volatile images. Managed images also support transparency, which allows us to have nonrectangular objects drawn to the screen.

The ManagedExample class demonstrates how to use five methods of creating a managed image. These five methods are named loadImageN where N is 1 to 5. You can change the call in the constructor to call the one you want to try. The first three methods load and create a managed image in a single call.

```
//Read in the image to display using swing ImageIcon class
private void loadImage1(URL imageURL)
{
image = new ImageIcon(imageURL).getImage();
}
/*
* Read in an image Toolkit's createImage(URL) method
*/
private void loadImage2(URL imageURL)
{
image = Toolkit.getDefaultToolkit().createImage(imageURL);
}
/*
Read in an image using Toolkit class's method getImage(URL)
*/
private void loadImage3(URL imageURL)
{
image = Toolkit.getDefaultToolkit().getImage(imageURL);
}
```

The image-loading methods shown in the previous code all give about 20 frames per second with transparency, which is better than using the `BufferedImage` class. This performance still isn't very good, and we would be hard-pressed to create a good game at these speeds. The last two methods give us a full 60 frames per second at a refresh rate of 60Hz. They both first use the `loadBufferedImage` method to load the rock image into a `BufferedImage` object, and then draw the image into a managed image that supports transparency.

```
/**
 * Read in the image to display using the
 * Component class's method createImage(width,height)
 */
private void loadImage4(URL imageURL)
{
pack(); // component must be displayable
image = createImage(bufferedImage.getWidth(),
        bufferedImage.getHeight());
Graphics2D g2d = (Graphics2D)image.getGraphics();
g2d.setComposite(AlphaComposite.Src);
g2d.drawImage(bufferedImage,0,0,this);
}
/**
  * Read in the image to using GraphicsConfiguration
  *createCompatibleImage(width,height,transparency)method
  */
private void loadImage5(URL imageURL)
{
image = getGraphicsConfiguration().createCompatibleImage(
    bufferedImage.getWidth(),
    bufferedImage.getHeight(),
    Transparency.BITMASK);
image.getGraphics().drawImage(bufferedImage,0,0,this);
}
```

When the code from the ManagedExample is run, it should appear as shown in Figure 3.11.

Using managed images is a good general choice for most games.

BRINGING IT ALL TOGETHER

Now it's time to tie all this information together with the previous chapter. You remember that the Game class was designed to contain all the relevant components

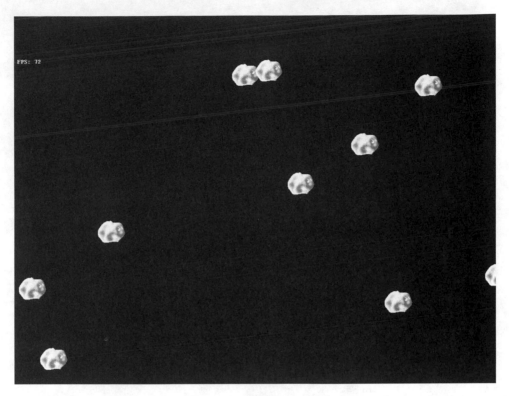

FIGURE 3.11   Looking good with managed images.

of a game in a nice, orderly manner. In addition, the Actor class was created to allow for the creation of flexible game pieces that could be drawn during the game and respond to input from the player. The Actor class contains all the relevant information that a playable component in the game should know, including position and velocity. The ActorManager class allowed for dynamic class loading and contained a LinkedList of Actor classes used in the game. Now it's time to take one of Actor class's child classes and link it together in the Game class, as well as getting it drawn to the screen.

Actor Input Management

Before getting deeply into the reorganization of the Game class, let's make a connection with the keyboard. In Chapter 2, the KeyListener interface was briefly discussed. Let's make a class that will allow all of the input for an Actor to be contained in one easy-to-use class called `PlayerAdapter`.

```java
import java.awt.event.*;
class PlayerAdapter extends KeyAdapter
{
 private Player player;
 public PlayerAdapter(Player p)
 {
   player = p;
 }
 public void keyPressed(KeyEvent e)
  {
   switch(e.getKeyCode())
   {
       case KeyEvent.VK_UP:
       player.setY(player.getY()-5);
       break;
       case KeyEvent.VK_DOWN:
       player.setY(player.getY()+5);
       break;
       case KeyEvent.VK_LEFT:
       player.setX(player.getX()-5);
       break;
       case KeyEvent.VK_RIGHT:
       player.setX(player.getX()+5);
       break;
       default:
        break;
   }
 }
}
```

PlayerAdapter allows for easy modification and extension of a given Actor class's movement. This adapter is registered with the object or objects that must take input. When something needs tweaking, it's all stored here in one place.

UPDATES TO THE GAME CLASS

You remember that the Game class is composed of three main methods controlled by a state machine: GAME_INIT, GAME_MAIN, and GAME_SHUTDOWN. These states are also mapped to methods of the same name. The fundamental strategy at this point is to make the Game class capable of organizing the full-screen and image components discussed so far in this chapter as well as link Actor classes to the actual display. Let's look at the updates for each method in turn.

The code samples referenced here are contained in the `SimpleGame` example in the provided source code. `SimpleGame` extends from the `FullScreen3` class used earlier in this chapter.

```
public SimpleGame(String title, DisplayMode mode) throws
HeadlessException
    {
        super(title,mode);
        am = new ActorManager();
        setState(GAME_INIT);
    }
```

The constructor is updated so that it instantiates the ActorManager and immediately sets the gamestate to GAME_INIT.

```
public void gameInit()
{
  URL imageURL = getClass().getResource(imageResourceName);
  if(imageURL==null){
   System.out.println("Unable to locate resource   return;
    }
loadBufferedImage(imageURL);
loadImage5(imageURL);
initToScreen(2);
// start the rendering thread
startRenderThread();
am.createEntity("Player",1);
  //add some input to update the player position on screen.
addKeyListener(
new PlayerAdapter((Player)am.actorList.getFirst()));
setState(GAME_MAIN);
}
```

First, the gameInit method loads the images and prepares them to be rendered. The second step is to create the buffers used for the rendering, and subsequently to begin the renderThread. At this point, the game attempts to draw information to the screen. The `ActorManager` uses the factory method `createEntity` to create a single instance of the Player class. Then, using the newly created `PlayerAdapter`, the Player class is linked up to take input from the keyboard. Finally, the gamestate is set to move on to GAME_MAIN.

```
public void gameMain()
{
```

```
        while(gamestate == GAME_MAIN)
        {
         //Perform game logic here.


         }
        setState(GAME_SHUTDOWN);
    }
```

Not much new information is added to gameMain at this point. At the correct time, all the game logic will be performed inside the code. Because the rendering for the game is being handled in a separate thread, the rendering call isn't made inside each gameMain call. As code is added to the gameMain method, the frame rate begins to drop a bit as the application time slices the processing power.

```
public void gameShutdown()
{
  System.out.println("The game is shutting down.");
  am.clearEntities();
  System.exit(0);
}
```

The gameShutdown() method has the added responsibility of cleaning up the entity list before exiting. Because of its parent classes, SimpleGame has Listener classes designed to handle exiting methods. This method must still be defined for internal state changes to the game that do not include exiting the game.

Finally, let's look at the changes to the render method. The render method is structured to be overloaded as needed. In this case, it displays the Actor classes in turn, based on their internal positions.

```
public boolean render(Graphics g)
{
    super.render(g);
    Player a;
    if(image!=null)
    {
      for (int i = 0; i<am.actorList.size(); i++)
        {
                a = (Player)am.actorList.get(i);
                g.drawImage(image,a.getX(),a.getY(),this);
            }
    }
    return true;
}
```

The render method now traverses the actorList, requesting the coordinates of the actors and displaying them using the loaded Image from the gameInit() method.

When the SimpleGame example is compiled, it should look like the image featured in Figure 3.12.

FIGURE 3.12   Looking good with managed images.

SUMMARY

This chapter is full of information, but it can't begin to cover the far-reaching scope of 2D graphics on the Java platform. A great number of topics are still open and to be discussed. This architecture is by no means optimal for all applications and, in most cases, is presented in a format that is structured to promote familiarity for ease of explanation. Once you feel comfortable with the mechanics of the rendering thread, begin to tinker around and look for more applicable solutions to the games you are creating. If you come up with something that you think is particularly impressive, please send it along. The authors are always looking for cool solutions to game-related problems.

4 Creating Game Audio Using Java

In This Chapter

- An Overview of Java Audio Components
- JavaSound
- OpenAL Basics
- Getting Started
- Tinkering with Source and Listener Properties
- JOAL Error Handling
- The AL Context API
- Sound Rendering Contexts
- Looking Ahead
- Summary

A udio has historically been one of the most overlooked aspects of game development with good reason. In the early days of video games, simple bleeps and bloops were the only sound tools available to the game programmer. Whereas the emergence of digital audio gave new resources to game developers, consumer sound card sales were not driven by games to the same degree that graphics cards were. High-end audio cards existed for the connoisseur, but most consumers stuck with older audio cards, not realizing what they were missing. As the forward progress on graphic cards begins to slow, more attention is being paid to the audio component of games. The importance of quality audio in games continues to grow each year. Audio is a key element in maintaining cohesiveness and improving immersion in games and other forms of interactive entertainment.

A number of key technologies have come to the forefront in recent years that allow developers reasonable flexibility when developing the audio component of a game's core engine. One such technology developed by Creative Labs, the Open Audio Library (OpenAL), can be reasonably thought of as the audio equivalent of the Open Graphics Library, better known as OpenGL. Where OpenGL provides extreme flexibility for rendering 3D graphics, OpenAL seeks to create flexible controls for audio programmers to use sound in three dimensions. OpenAL is currently implemented on all major PC platforms, including Windows, Macintosh, and Linux and has been featured as an audio component in games such as *Unreal Tournament 2003* and *Star Wars: Jedi Knight 2, Jedi Outcast.*

This chapter gives a basic overview to the different options available to Java game developers regarding sound. The primary discussion will center on the fundamental usage of the new core game API sound component known as Java OpenAL Library (JOAL).

AN OVERVIEW OF JAVA AUDIO COMPONENTS

Applets

Developers who create games using applets have some limited but effective options for using sound in games. The primary interface designed to handle all applet-related audio work is the AudioClip(). This interface class is found in the standard applet toolkit. The AudioClip has the basic controls to play, loop, and stop a sound. If multiple sounds are played, the applet mixes them together to form a composite sound. The AudioClip can play audio clips stored in the .au format. This format is fairly low quality but is usually capable for most applets.

Loading and playing a sound with this class is as easy as passing a string to the class constructor. An example of how to load a sample into an AudioClip follows:

```
AudioClip sound;
sound = getAudioClip(getCodeBase(), "sound.au");
```

To then control the audio clip, the user must only make calls to the AudioClip as follows:

```
sound.play();
```

For games that require more complete tools, there is also the option of using JavaSound in applets. This tool thoroughly extends the capabilities for games distributed as applets. An overview of JavaSound will be discussed in the next section.

JAVASOUND

JavaSound represents the built-in libraries that accompany the JDK. JavaSound is still listed as an extension to the JDK and is included in the Java extension packages. Before the release of JOAL, JavaSound represented the game programmer's best chance of working with audio.

The core classes of JavaSound are found in the `javax.sound.sampled` and the `javax.sound.midi` packages. These packages each offer a range of options for sound-related programming for use in both applications and applets.

> **javax.sound.midi:** Contains everything a programmer needs to load and play back MIDI files in an application. The capabilities of the MIDI library go way beyond the needs of the typical game. The standard loading and playback mechanisms as well as a complete MIDI synthesizer can be found. Most PC games would not have obvious use for full MIDI synthesis, but the imagination is the only limitation. Historically, MIDI synthesis formed the backbone of game audio until memory prices dropped to allow the average machine to have more than 32MG of RAM. As long as there are embedded game systems, MIDI synthesis will be an integral part of game development.

> **javax.sound.sampled:** Handles all aspects of digital audio in JavaSound. The fundamental architecture of this package views the use of audio in the same manner as a physical mixer. Full support exists for audio mixing, filtering, recording, and streaming. This package contains the basic utilities to process playback in a number of audio formats and is capable of handling custom formats through the service provider classes. Frankly, JavaSound provides far too much for basic game playback. JavaSound is designed to handle professional-quality sound recordings and to give the Java platform a robust group of tools to process audio for a number of types of applications.

The general downside to JavaSound is the real-time performance drawbacks. Most of the basic functionality cannot process looping quickly enough to be implemented in games requiring quick repeating sounds. You can circumvent these limitations in code, but they tend not to be preferred against the group of other available options.

Light Weight Java Game Library (LWJGL)

This project stems from a group of game developers taking the initiative to create powerful game libraries centered on OpenGL and OpenAL. This is not an official Java release, but several games have been created using it. The LWJGL OpenAL bindings are more mature than the official libraries in many cases, but they require a different style of programming to achieve their power. One of the core premises of the project is that the APIs are stripped to the bare minimum of functionality, hence the name "Light Weight." The LWJGL goes so far as to expose pointers to Java programmers to reduce additional overhead created by working with the JNI. The LWJGL continues to evolve and can be found at *www.lwjgl.org*.

Java OpenAL Library (JOAL)

The Java OpenAL Library (JOAL) represents a binding of Java functions to the native OpenAL implementations through the use of the Java Native Interface (JNI). Effectively, the set of Java functions are mapped directly through to the native C calls made in the actual OpenAL library. JOAL is one of the three core game technologies available on the Java platform. JOAL is designed to present game developers using the Java platform with high-performance audio capabilities and, in doing so, replace JavaSound for most game audio requirements.

JOAL is still a young library and will no doubt go through a number of revisions until it implements all expected functionality of OpenAL. JOAL is a great step forward for audio programming on the Java platform.

This chapter is designed to give an overview of JOAL and introduce you to the basic concepts regarding its usage. Per the authors' knowledge, this book is the first to catalog this new Java gaming technology. Be sure to check for an updated implementation before working with JOAL. Although it is certainly the intent of this chapter to be thorough, technology is ever changing and improving itself.

This section has shown a number of existing technologies available to Java game developers regarding sound. Additional options exist beyond those listed here. Be sure to evaluate each one to find the best fit for your next project.

With that technology overview, the remainder of the chapter emphasizes the Java games core library JOAL, demonstrating the capabilities and limitations of the API.

OPENAL BASICS

Let's begin the discussion of JOAL by looking at the core classes that compose the basic structure of the OpenAL API. Given that the JOAL implementation is designed around the actual OpenAL spec, it is no surprise that the key objects used in OpenAL are also available in JOAL. These core classes are the Buffer, Source, and Listener.

Buffer holds the audio data that the user wants to play. It is capable of being set to handle 8- or 16-bit audio data in mono or stereo formats. OpenAL currently supports pulse code modulation (PCM) file formats such as WAV or AIFF. To use any other format requires decoding to a PCM format. Work is currently in progress to extend OpenAL to support the popular Ogg Vorbis format in the near future. When this work is complete, future versions of JOAL may support it. In addition, there is no current mechanism in JOAL to allow for streaming from a CD-ROM source, though future versions may support this feature.

Source holds all the information related to the sound slated for use in JOAL that is not directly related to the actual original audio data. The Buffer is attached to the Source so that they can be positioned in the world and updated as a result of changes during a game. The Source contains no audio itself. The Source class also contains the controls for starting, stopping, and looping, as well as volume.

The Listener class represents an actual person or location that is potentially able to hear audio in the game. Depending on the Buffer and the Source positions, OpenAL interpolates and renders the audio based on how the Listener should hear it in the world. The term *renders* might sound strange when applied to audio. That idea most likely comes from the OpenGL mindset of rendering graphics to a screen. Despite the strangeness of the term, rendering is the preferred way to reference the audio output that a Listener can hear. Listener classes can move and can also modify the volume based on position. Only one Listener can exist at any given time, though there may be multiple Buffer and Source classes, each with unique data and settings.

GETTING STARTED

To begin programming with JOAL, the application must first gain a context to a sound device. When a JOAL application begins, it finds a sound device residing on the system through the process of creating or acquiring a context to that device. JOAL supports the ability to create multiple contexts for systems that have more than one sound card, but only one context can be active at any given time. Later, the process for creating and setting up a nondefault audio device context will be discussed more thoroughly.

In general, most users maintain only a single audio card in their computers. To simplify the initialization process for systems needing to work only with the user's default audio card, the creators of OpenAL created a utility called the `Alut`. The `Alut` class allows developers to simplify the initialization and file loading. It creates a single OpenAL context and uses the default settings for the primary device.

The `Alut` utility is summarily implemented in JOAL. Most applications can initialize access to the default sound card with just a single line of code such as the following:

```
Alut.alutInit();
```

The next major utility provided through the Alut class is the `Alut.alutLoad-WavFile()` method. This method allows the user to specify a short set of parameters and automatically loads the audio data and allows it to be set into a Buffer.

The method's signature follows:

```
alutLoadWAVFile(String fileName, int format[], ByteBuffer data[],
int size[], int freq[], int loop[])
```

A quick explanation of the parameters follows:

String fileName: A string that represents the file to be loaded and may include relative paths.

int format: The OpenAL format specifier that tells what the resolution is and whether the sound is in mono or stereo. Available formats are 8- and 16-bit resolution, stereo or mono.

ByteBuffer data: A storage place for the actual sound data.

int size: The size of the buffer in bytes.

int freq: Holds the actual frequency of the audio data.

int loop: Indicates whether the sample will loop.

When ready to load a sample, declare the needed variables as follows:

```
int[] format = new int[1];
int[] size   = new int[1];
int[] freq   = new int[1];
int[] loop   = new int[1];
ByteBuffer[] audioData = new ByteBuffer[1];
```

Then make the actual call to the WAV loader as follows:

```
ALut.alutLoadWAVFile("bleep.wav", format, data, size, freq, loop);
```

The application should keep this file in memory only for a long enough period to copy the information into a Buffer. It should then be let go as follows:

```
ALut.alutLoadWAVFile(format[0], data[0], size[0], freq[0]);
```

This process is simple compared to the early versions of DirectSound that required the user to eat the data a chunk at a time to fill out WAVEFORMATEX structs that were used to fill the DSound buffers on the DirectX platform. If you have ever had to write a loader that ate memory a bite at a time (no pun intended, though arguably they all do this), you will recognize the almost overwhelming simplicity provided in this method.

When the application is completed, OpenAL must be uninitialized. This process is just as easy as the process of setting it up. Make the following call, and OpenAL is shut down:

```
Alut.alutExit();
```

The only things left to do here are to set up the basic Buffer, Source, and Listener classes, bind the audio to Buffers, and then push the play button.

In the JOAL implementation, the AL interface contains all the methods for controlling Listeners, Buffers, and Sources. When setting the properties for the three core classes, use this interface's methods to get everything going. To give an example, let's set up the Listener for an application.

The first thing to do is specify how the application will hold the information relating to the Listener. They key things that must be defined are the Listener class's position, velocity, and orientation.

A Listener class's position is represented as a single three-dimensional point in space. To keep things simple, let's start the Listener class's position at the origin. Use float arrays to keep the coordinates straight.

```
float[] listenerPosition = {0.0f,0.0f,0.0f};
```

Setting a Listener class's velocity is also fairly straightforward. The main reason this value is needed references how OpenAL implements the Doppler effect. A Doppler shift occurs when apparent movement occurs between one or more sources that receive or transmit sounds. Imagine driving quickly past a honking horn. The sound of the horn emits in a forward direction. How you hear the sound changes, based on your changing position. Consider the example shown in Figure 4.1.

The sound of the object at point A varies in contrast to that at point B. OpenAL calculates the Doppler shift using the following formula, referenced from the *OpenAL Programmer's Guide*:

```
sif' = f * (DV - DF * vl) / (DV + DF * vs)
where
DV = AL_DOPPLER_VELOCITY
DF = AL_DOPPLER_FACTOR
vl = listener velocity (scalar value along source-to-listener vector)
vs = source velocity (scalar value along source-to-listener vector)
f = frequency of sample
f' = Doppler shifted frequency
```

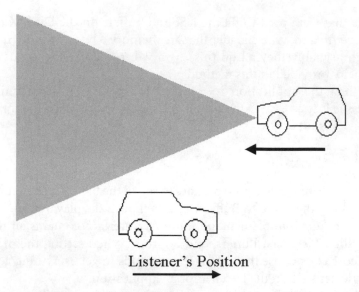

Listener's Position

FIGURE 4.1 The sound of the horn is Doppler shifting.

JOAL provides a couple of functions to help process the Doppler shift that will be discussed later in the chapter.

Setting the Listener class's velocity is just as straightforward as setting the position. Let's set it up.

```
float[] listenerVelocity = {0.0f,0.0f,0.0f};
```

A Listener class's orientation describes the current facing in three dimensions. Setting up the orientation requires six parameters to describe the precise facing of the Listener. The main reason all this description is needed relates to how sounds are spatially organized. Accurate data is needed to make correct audio renderings relative to the Listener. The Listener class's orientation is set as follows:

```
float[] listenerOrientation = {0.0f,0.0f,-1.0f,0.0f,0.0f,0.0f};
```

The first three parameters specify the current x-, y-, and z-vectors, which represent what the Listener is currently looking at. The second three parameters specify the x-, y-, and z-vectors that lead straight out of the top of the Listener. These parameters are sometimes referred to as the "at" and "up" vectors, or the "forward" and "world-up" vectors, respectively. When a game is running, the Listener class's orientation and position are frequently updated through the game loop. Figure 4.2 shows a graphical representation of the "at" and "up" vectors.

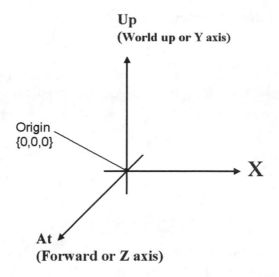

FIGURE 4.2   The Listener class's "up" and "at" vectors.

After the initial setup process, accessing and changing the Listener class's properties must come through one of the alListener[3f,fv,i] methods. The values in the brackets represent the specified types of properties that are being set for the Listener. Each one of them is implemented as a separate method that takes data of the listed type. Some of the control methods accept three floating-point values and are appended with a "3f" at the end of the method's name. Others accept floating-point vectors as valid parameters. These methods are appended with an "fv" to indicate that they can accept data in this format. The final and simplest data type is the straightforward integer. Methods that can accept an integer value are appended with an "i". This convention is consistent when working with OpenAL and JOAL.

As the player moves through the world, the sounds are going to be modified based on the current position that he occupies. These methods will be used many times to update the player's position based upon direct input from a device or as a result of some physical effect, such as a spring pad or an explosion that hurls the player back, that might cause the player's position to change. Table 4.1 shows the complete list of properties that are associated with the Listener class as well as the data types that can be applied to them for adjustment.

A more detailed discussion of how these properties can be used in a game as well as the process for adjusting them occurs later in the chapter.

TABLE 4.1 Listener Properties

Property	Data Type	Description
AL_GAIN	f	Gain control; should be set to a positive value
AL_POSITION	3f, fv	x- y-, and z-position
AL_VELOCITY	3f, fv	velocity vector
AL_ORIENTATION	fv	orientation expressed as "at" and "up" vectors

Now let's set up the required Buffer classes. JOAL requires an application to specify the number of Buffer classes it plans to use, then to generate those Buffer classes before moving on. Let's get started with these points before moving on.

```
int[] buffer = new int[1];
```

This line identifies where the Buffer will be held and referenced later.

```
al.alGenBuffers(1,buffer);
```

This line creates a single Buffer to hold audio data referencing it from the first Buffer declared previously.

Now we must copy information from an audio file and move it into the Buffer. Remember the alutLoadWaveFile() method? Now it's time to link the loading of the file and copy the data obtained into the Buffer. This step is done with the method alBufferData() and references some file format variables that were identified and described earlier. Information is copied into the Buffer in the following way:

```
ALut.alutLoadWAVFile("bleep.wav", format, data, size, freq,loop);
Al.alBufferData(buffer[0],format[0],data[0],size[0],freq[0]);
```

Once the data is copied over, the file is closed out.

```
ALut.alutLoadWAVFile(format[0], data[0], size[0], freq[0]);
```

At the end of the application, all the allocated Buffer classes must be deleted using the alDeleteBuffers() method as follows:

```
Al.alDeleteBuffers(1,buffer);
```

So far so good. Now the only thing remaining is to set up a Source. Remember that a Source object is bound with a Buffer and contains much of the processing and positioning capabilities of the system. Note that the Buffer classes do not contain or hold any location or velocity data. This data is all controlled by the Source that is bound to it. The first steps are to create a holding place for the Source and get its position and velocity set up.

```
int[] source = new int[1];
float[] sourcePosition = {0.0f,0.0f,0.0f};
float[] sourceVelocity = {0.0f,0.0f,0.0f};
```

The next step is to bind the Source with a Buffer. The first step in this process is to generate a Source in a manner similar to generating a Buffer.

```
al.a.GenSources(1,source);
```

Now the individual properties of the Source must be set up through the use of a set of functions based on the type of property that needs to be set. All of the properties for Source classes are controlled through the alSource[3f,fv,i] methods. These methods accept the same types of parameters but are capable of modifying a different set of values as they relate to the Source. Some of the properties are only used to identify.

Table 4.2 shows the different integer-based Source properties that can be set through these methods.

TABLE 4.2 Source Integer Properties

Property	Data Type	Description
AL_SOURCE_RELATIVE	i	Source position is determined by listener's position
AL_LOOPING	i	Looping for a Source (boolean)
AL_BUFFER	i	Indicates Buffer to provide samples
AL_SOURCE_STATE	i	Used to control and identify current state of a Source
AL_BUFFERS_QUEUED	i	Number of Buffer classes in line on the Source (read only)
AL_BUFFERS_PROCESSED	i	Number of buffer classes process by Source (read only)

Although the use of most of these properties will be discussed later, it's a good time to discuss what each of them does to a Source.

AL_SOURCE_RELATIVE: Source relative coordinates refer to the distance or orientation of a Source relative to the Listener. If a particular Source is set to AL_SOURCE_RELATIVE and given coordinates of (0,0,0), it will be set to the position of the Listener at all times. It is common to use a Source in this way to play background audio or other constant sounds for the player to hear. A 2D game that wanted to "lock" the positioning of a Source so that it didn't move could avoid updates to the positioning but could also use the AL_SOURCE_RELATIVE property to ensure that the sound would always be oriented in the current location of the Listener. This setting would be useful for almost all sounds in a 2D game.

AL_LOOPING: This is a state set to AL_TRUE or AL_FALSE. To indicate that a given Source is going to loop, a call must be made to set the property. From that point on, the sample will loop whenever it is played and can be stopped only using the standard stopping mechanisms. The downside of this state is that once this property is set, it can't be modified. If an application needs to imitate looping for a particular number of times, it can be done through the use of queued Buffer classes that are discussed later in the chapter.

AL_BUFFER: This property is used to indicate the particular Buffer that will be bound to the Source so that the audio data can be properly rendered.

AL_SOURCE_STATE: The Source state is normally used to evaluate the current activity of a given source. Typical states for Sources are AL_PLAYING, AL_STOPPED, and AL_INITIAL. These state transitions are controlled by methods, but it is common to query the state of a Source before taking action. For example, if a Source is currently in the state of AL_PLAYING, calling the play method results in it being set to AL_INITIAL, putting the position of the play cursor back at the beginning of the Buffer and potentially limiting the completion of the currently playing sound. Although it is common for gun or laser sounds in a 2D shooter-styled game to be replayed frequently, a dialog segment might be interrupted at a crucial point if this check isn't made first.

AL_BUFFERS_QUEUED: This property allows the user to find out the total number of Buffer classes in line to be played through the given Source. The process of lining up multiple Buffer classes to a single Source is discussed more thoroughly later in this chapter. One important note regarding this property is that the value is read only and cannot be set. The value is retrieved using the alGetSourcei() method.

AL_BUFFERS_PROCESSED: This property allows the user to identify the number of Buffer classes that have been processed through the given Source. This property is read only and its value can be retrieved using the alGetSourcei() method.

Sets of Source properties are also controlled through the use of single-float primitives, a floating-point vector, or a group of three plain floating-point values. Table 4.3 identifies each property as well as the proper data type used in conjunction with modifying the relevant property.

TABLE 4.3 Source Floating-Point-Based Properties

Property	Data Type	Description
AL_PITCH	f	Increases a source's pitch
AL_GAIN	f	Increases/decreases a source's gain
AL_MAX_DISTANCE	f	Sets the maximum distance for a source's gain to be adjusted
AL_ROLLOFF_FACTOR	f	Adjusts the speed of sound reduction once it reaches a max distance
AL_REFERENCE_DISTANCE	f	Represents the distance for a sound to drop by one half its normal volume
AL_MAX_GAIN	f	Represents the maximum gain for a given source
AL_MIN_GAIN	f	Represents the minimum gain for a given source
AL_CONE_OUTER_GAIN	f	Represents the gain outside an oriented cone
AL_CONE_INNER_ANGLE	f	Represents the gain inside an oriented cone
AL_CONE_OUTER_ANGLE	f,i	Represents the outer angle of a sound cone in degrees
AL_POSITION	fv,3f	Sets the x-, y-, z-position
AL_VELOCITY	fv,3f	Sets the velocity vector
AL_DIRECTION	fv,3f	Sets the direction vector

This list of properties is long, so let's review the most frequently used properties.

AL_POSITION: This value is one of the more frequently used properties of Source classes. The position value of a Source might be updated frequently to represent the current location of the object in the world. The value is described in the x-, y-, z-coordinates of the Source. This value may remain static in a game if it were positioned around an immobile particle effect. It would be mobile to represent the maneuvering of a level boss maintaining its position with the updating coordinates of the boss enemy.

AL_VELOCITY: This property represents the speed and direction of an object that exists in the game world. The velocity of an object is important to the correct calculation of the Doppler effect, as used by OpenAL. To make an object update by its current velocity, the AL_POSITION property must be updated accordingly. JOAL does not automatically process updates related to velocity.

AL_PITCH, AL_GAIN, AL_MAX_GAIN, AL_MIN_GAIN: This group of properties is fairly straightforward. These values should be positive when applied to a Source. Generally speaking, a value of 1.0 is considered to be the default setting for the given audio.

Distance Model Properties: JOAL provides the ability to render sounds in a realistic fashion through attenuation of a sound over a given distance through the use of Distance Models. In the real world, the attenuation of a sound is governed by the Inverse Square Law, which states that a sound will drop in intensity proportionally to the inverse square of the distance from the source. JOAL provides functionality to calculate and render a sound for a Listener based upon these natural acoustic phenomenons through the implementation of the AL_INVERSE_DISTANCE and AL_INVERSE_DISTANCE_CLAMPED Distance Models.

These Distance Models are fundamentally the same, with one chief difference. The AL_INVERSE_DISTANCE_CLAMPED model uses the AL_REFERENCE_DISTANCE property to clamp down sounds that are below that distance's threshold. This means that sounds using this distance method can have a minimum distance from the Source by which they can be audibly rendered. Any distance set at less than the reference distance will be clamped accordingly. AL_INVERSE_DISTANCE processes the attenuation of a sound without the limitation of the reference distance. It should also be noted that AL_INVERSE_DISTANCE is the default Distance Model for JOAL, though it can be modified through the alDistanceModel() method.

With that little discussion, let's review the actual properties in question. The properties AL_MAX_DISTANCE, AL_REFERENCE_DISTANCE, and AL_ROLLOFF_FACTOR are used to calculate how a sound's gain should be modified as it travels over a given distance away from the Source per the applied Distance Model.

In the real world, sound reflects off many surfaces as it travels through a given medium (usually air) on its way to someone's ears. A sound heard from a distance may be loud and discernable at certain distances from the originating point but will decay as the sound travels and ultimately dissipates. In JOAL, using the AL_MAX_DISTANCE property allows a given Source to have a specific distance at which the sound will no longer be subject to attenuation. The actual value set is used in the calculations to determine how the sound would appear at the Listener class's position. A sound that would normally travel beyond the maximum distance is clamped at the actual maximum distance value.

The use of the AL_ROLLOFF_FACTOR allows for the calculation of a scale by which the sound decays up to the AL_MAX_DISTANCE. This is the amount by which the sound's gain will be reduced in an amortized fashion over the valid distance from the Source. The rolloff factor can be set to 0, which marks individual sources that are not to be attenuated through the Distance Model.

Depending on the Distance Model in use, the AL_REFERENCE_DISTANCE can be defined as the point where a sound will have lost half of its intensity, or, in the case of its use in the AL_INVERSE_DISTANCE_CLAMPED Distance Model, the reference distance specifies the effective minimum distance a Listener must be from a sound to hear it.

One additional note regarding calculations related to distance in OpenAL: JOAL allows developers to process the natural attenuation of a sound based on distance but does not identify standard units of measurement. All calculations related to distance are scale invariant. This means that the application in question must create this standard on its own and maintain consistency. It's completely fine to use meters, feet, or whatever other measurement necessary; just make sure that the measurements are consistent to save some annoying headaches later.

After that lengthy discussion relating to Source properties, let's go through and set some of these values based on our loading example up to this point.

```
al.alSourcei (source[0], AL.AL_BUFFER,   buffer[0]);
al.alSourcef (source[0], AL.AL_PITCH,    1.0f     );
al.alSourcef (source[0], AL.AL_GAIN,     1.0f     );
al.alSourcefv(source[0], AL.AL_POSITION, sourcePosition);
al.alSourcefv(source[0], AL.AL_VELOCITY, sourceVelocity);
al.alSourcei (source[0], AL.AL_LOOPING,  loop[0]  );
```

This source is now bound to use the Buffer created with the *bleep.wav* file. It uses normal pitch and gain. The position and velocity are mapped to the settings in the appropriate float vectors created earlier. The sound is set not to loop by default. This is a pretty straightforward controlling mechanism.

Quick Recap

Let's review what has been covered so far. OpenAL is initialized and shut down using the ALut class. PCM-encoded files can be loaded into the Buffer using the Alut WAV-loading method. Three main classes help render the audio in the form of Buffers, Sources, and Listeners. Buffers contain the actual sound data and are bound to Sources. There can be only one Listener at any given time. Source and Listener classes need to be described with position and velocity but also have other properties that can be modified as well. Listener and Source classes can set their attributes (such as current position and velocity) using descriptor methods and by specifying a particular property to set. JOAL is also capable of handling natural sound attenuation over distances by automatically using one of the provided Distance Models. Finally, JOAL doesn't specify any particular units of measurement for processing calculations related to distance. It is the developer's responsibility to organize positions and distances in a consistent measurement.

After all that, what's left?

Player Controls

The most important part of an audio library is the playback controls that it provides. JOAL lets the user play, pause, stop, and rewind a single source or a group of sources. The control methods are contained in the AL interface. Each method takes the Source or group of Sources as arguments. One important thing to note is that a sound will play as long as you decide it should. Should a sound get interrupted or the Alut shut down, the playing of the samples will stop immediately, sometimes without playing at all. Getting a sound to play is as easy as using the following code:

```
al.alSourcePlay(source[0]);
```

Stopping is also easy.

```
al.alSourceStop(source[0]);
```

It is also easy to perform the playback methods on a group of Sources at a single time. Each playback method has an alternate form that takes a number of samples and the integer array that holds the Sources. An example that pauses an entire group of Sources follows:

```
alSourcePausev(3,sources);
```

It is also useful to identify a Source class's current state before making calls to stop or to play errantly. To find out the current state of a given Source, we can make a query as follows:

```
if(al.alGetSourcei(source[0],AL.AL_SOURCE_STATE)== AL.AL_PLAYING)
System.out.println("The sound is playing!");
```

The alGetSourcei() method returns an integer to be stored and queried later as needed. The previous code sample is a more direct technique for smaller examples.

The `SimplePlayer` class in the provided Source code shows how to combine all the topics discussed so far to get a single sound playing. Compile it and tinker around with modifying the attributes of the Source and Listener. One note when compiling JOAL applications—be sure to place the *joal.jar* file and the library in the appropriate files so that it can be seen in your classpath; otherwise, the application will have no idea what an `Alut` is.

Loading More Than One Sound

Now that one file can be loaded and played, the next logical step is to increase the number of sounds that can be played in a given application. The process of loading more than one sound is also easy. Making that the next step on the JOAL to do list, let's get started.

At the high level, the first step is to create additional Buffers and Sources in the same manner as described earlier. The number of Sources must be at least as large as the number of Buffers. It might be good to make a `final int` of the size needed.

```
final int MAX_SIZE 2;
int[] buffers = new int[MAX_SIZE];
int[] sources = new int[MAX_SIZE];
```

The next step is to sequentially generate Buffers and load the files in incrementing positions in the `Buffers` and `Sources` arrays. It is easy to make a mistake in this segment, so make sure that the Buffer and Source are bound correctly to each other or the application will exhibit unexpected results.

```
al.alGenBuffers(MAX_SIZE, buffers);
    if (al.alGetError() != AL.AL_NO_ERROR) {
        return AL.AL_FALSE;
    }
```

```
ALut.alutLoadWAVFile("bleep.wav",format,data,size,freq,loop);
al.alBufferData(buffers[0],format[0],data[0],size[0],freq[0]);
ALut.alutUnloadWAV(format[0], data[0], size[0], freq[0]);
ALut.alutLoadWAVFile("blorp.wav",format,data,size,freq,loop);
al.alBufferData(buffers[1],format[0],data[0],size[0],freq[0]);
ALut.alutUnloadWAV(format[0], data[0], size[0], freq[0]);
```

When the sounds have been correctly loaded into Buffers, the next step in the process is to generate the correct number of Sources and then fill out the Buffers, each with its own set of properties.

```
al.alGenSources(MAX_SIZE,sources);
al.alSourcei(sources[0], AL.AL_BUFFER, buffer[0] );
al.alSourcef(sources[0], AL.AL_PITCH,  1.0f);
al.alSourcef(sources[0], AL.AL_GAIN,   1.0f);
al.alSourcefv(sources[0], AL.AL_POSITION, sourcePosition[0]);
al.alSourcefv(sources[0], AL.AL_VELOCITY, sourceVelocity[0]);
al.alSourcei(sources[0], AL.AL_LOOPING, AL.AL_FALSE);
al.alSourcei(sources[1], AL.AL_BUFFER, buffer[1] );
al.alSourcef(sources[1], AL.AL_PITCH,  1.5f);
al.alSourcef(sources[1], AL.AL_GAIN,   1.0f);
al.alSourcefv(sources[1], AL.AL_POSITION, sourcePosition[1]);
al.alSourcefv(sources[1], AL.AL_VELOCITY, sourceVelocity[1]);
al.alSourcei(sources[1], AL.AL_LOOPING, AL.AL_TRUE);
```

Each source can be modified based on whatever properties are needed. It is possible to link multiple sources to the same Buffers to avoid needing to load multiple copies of a given audio file. Just make sure that the correct values are set for each source. In most 3D games, the audio will be statically placed in the world to represent audio effect. For example, imagine walking through a jungle and hearing environmental sounds of monkeys and macaws that occasionally recur throughout a given level. The Sources used all have different positions in the world but are using the same set of Buffer information.

Once the Sources and Buffers are set up, it's time to play back the audio. Triggering the audio effect to play is identical to working with a single Source, but make sure that the application adjusts the parameters based on the actual Source desired. Also watch out for off-by-one errors.

```
al.alSourcePlay(source[1]);
```

When a finalized sound engine is implemented in a game, it might function similarly to an actual audio mixer based in software. Channels can be muted, grouped, and processed. Keep that image in mind when building audio libraries for a game.

When the application is complete, and it's time to clean up the mess, a couple of minor adjustments must be made to removes all Buffers and Sources:

```
al.alDeleteBuffers(MAX_SIZE, buffer);
al.alDeleteSources(MAX_SIZE, source);
ALut.alutExit();
```

Make sure that all of the Buffers and Sources are deleted when the application ends, then follow up with a call to alutExit().

ON THE CD

Most of this code should look familiar. It's mostly a repeated version of the SimplePlayer example used to process and load a single sound for playback. The sample program MultiSounds in the provided Source code shows this process in effect. This code is used for demonstration purposes and for that reason seems a bit less robust than might be desired. We will investigate some cleaner ways to work with multiple Sources and Buffers later. One more thing about the samples provided—they are the vocal styling of the author and are some of the few samples that could be made available with full permission. They are a bit quirky, but they work like a charm.

TINKERING WITH SOURCE AND LISTENER PROPERTIES

Now that basic playback capabilities are understood, let's venture further. Often in a game, a sound may be too modified in some ways from its raw, normal format. JOAL provides the basic functionality internally to modify these properties. Let's look first at the changes that can be applied to the Listener.

Listener Properties

Earlier on, the list of properties were given but not implemented. Let's look at how some of these properties can be adjusted for use within a game.

In most games, the Listener is going to be at the same point as the character. Because most players tend to move around in games, the Listener should update its position with accordance to the player's current movement. JOAL is capable of processing and rendering the audio based on the Distance Models described earlier in this chapter. This ability is important because it takes the work away from the programmer of determining how a sound will be received at the Listener. Consider a game that uses the Actor class presented in Chapter 2. Updating the position of the

Listener based on the current position of the class is a fairly trivial adjustment. This function takes three floating-point values to set the new location of the Listener.

```
void setListenerPosition(int x, int y, int z)
  {
    al.alListener3f(AL.AL_POSITION,x,y,z);
  }
```

We can easily plug in the current position of the Actor to move the Listener, as follows:

```
setListenerPosition(Actor.getX(),Actor.getY(),Actor.getZ();
```

Using this method, we can automatically update the position of the Listener based on the position of the Actor. Using this function in this manner is most likely to set the Listener to the center of the mass of the object. Given that a player is likely to move each frame, this method should be called frequently enough to keep up with the player. Feel free to modify the parameters if the camera system or other game requirements are needed to properly position the Listener.

The other main position-oriented Listener attribute is the orientation. The orientation is expressed as the "at" and "up" vectors that describe the facing of the object. The OpenAL specification expects these vectors to be orthogonal to each other. When making a linkage to a 3D rendering, these vectors are usually the same as the camera view when set at the player's perspective as in a First-Person Shooter (FPS) game.

A quick function that can set the orientation of the Listener follows:

```
void setListenerOrientation(float[] orientation)
  {
    al.alListenerfv(AL.AL_ORIENTATION,orientation);
  }
```

This function takes a float array that holds the current vectors in a single location. Some applications may need to use separate values in these spaces, then combine them when passing through to the actual setting method. Make sure that the vectors are properly calculated for the game in question. For a quick refresher on 3D transformations, see Chapter 12, "3D Graphics Foundations."

Additional controls for the Listener include setting gain and velocity. Velocity is identical to setting the position, but with one clear distinction. The term *velocity* is used here to determine how the rendering context will process the Doppler effects to give the Listener a correct view of the sound from an arbitrary position.

Velocity does not involve updating the position of a Listener or other object. Make sure to keep this distinction clear when using JOAL.

The last Listener control remaining is the gain. To set the gain at the Listener, use one of the float methods to modify the gain value, as shown in the following code:

```
void setGain(float gain)
    {
        al.alListenerf(AL.AL_GAIN, gain);
    }
```

This method allows the sounds at the Listener to be increased or reduced by a floating-point value. Passing a value of 1.0 will result in a sound that is not modified. Remember that only one valid Listener class per rendering context exists, so modifying the gain changes the value for all sounds being rendered for the Listener in question.

Now let's look at the modification of Source properties. Because any number of Sources can be in a game, the functions available to them are fairly extensive. This section discusses the most functions that can be used for game development.

Source Properties

Several properties of particular importance regarding Source control are available. One of the most important is the distinction about how the Source will be rendered in relation to the player. If a game needs a sound to always play at a fixed distance from the Listener, it should be set to AL_SOURCE_RELATIVE, as follows:

```
al.alSourcei (source[0], AL.AL_SOURCE_RELATIVE, buffer[0]);
```

Sounds that are generated from a sidekick or a weapon are likely candidates for being rendered with respect to the Listener at all times.

In most games, Sources often represent enemies or other environmental audio components. Many of these Sources never move in the world and await the appearance of the Listener before ever doing any real work. When setting up the game world or applying sounds to mobile Actors and Object, it is important to be able to quickly update the positional properties related to a given Source. The AL_SOURCE_RELATIVE property has already been discussed, so let's move on to the particulars of setting object positions that are not to be immediately relative to the Listener.

To set the position of a source using Cartesian coordinates, plug in the following code:

```
al.alSource3f(source[0], AL.AL_DIRECTION,0,0,0);
```

This property must be set for each additional sound that is loaded and prepared for play in a game. Remember that the last three parameters of this method are the x-, y-, and z-locations within the world. Look at Figure 4.3 to see how the Sources may be positioned in relation to the Listeners sitting at the origin.

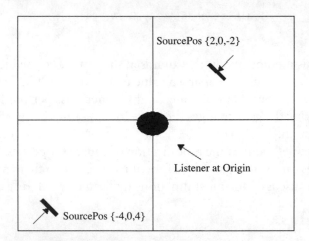

FIGURE 4.3 Sample Source positions with respect to the origin.

As Figure 4.3 shows, the position behind the player is considered to be a positive z-value, whereas the Source in the front right of the Listener is at the −2 z-position. The 3D coordinate system might take some time to get used to for newcomers. Tinker around with positions and values until this process becomes rote. To properly position sounds in 3D, knowledge of the coordinate system is imperative.

Numerous additional Source properties can be used. Several of these have been discussed earlier in the chapter. Now let's look at a few quick code samples to demonstrate the use of the controls that were not yet discussed.

To set the pitch of a Source:

```
al.alSourcef (source[0], AL.AL_PITCH,1.0f);
```

When setting the pitch, 1.0 causes no adjustment to the pitch. Remember that 0 is not a valid argument for this function call.

To set the gain of a Source:

```
al.alSourcef (source[0], AL.AL_GAIN,1.0f);
```

A value of 1.0 represents no change in the gain of the Source. This value is ultimately capped by the gain values of the Listener, so bear that in mind while muting or increasing the gain of the Source.

To apply a direction to a Source:

```
al.alSourcefv(source[0],AL.AL_DIRECTION,direction);
```

where direction is defined as an array of three floating-point values. When this property is set to the 0 vector, the direction is considered to be symmetric about the vector. To restore the Source to nondirectional, just pass back the 0 vector as follows:

```
al.alSource3f(source[0], AL.AL_DIRECTION,0,0,0);
```

It's a good idea to carefully organize Sources in the game so they aren't accidentally muted or set incorrectly.

Tinkering with the Doppler Effect

There is one more point of interest with regard to sound rendering in JOAL—the Doppler effect. The Doppler effect describes how auditory perception is changed when objects move relative to a sound source. JOAL and OpenAL try to emulate the real-world rendering of sound by including the Doppler effect as a parameter that can be manipulated by programmers.

JOAL provides two functions that allow the user to modify the Doppler values used to calculate the audio rendering described previously. These functions are alDopplerFactor() and alDopplerVelocity(). The alDopplerFactor() allows the user to modify how great the Doppler effect is presented within the game. Any positive value from 0.1 to 1.0 adjusts the way sound is rendered but also has the side effect of modifying the reality of how the sound is rendered to the Listener. The default Doppler value is 1.0. To turn the Doppler effect off completely, pass a 0 to this method.

When creating sounds in a strictly 2D environment, the Doppler effect is not likely to be needed. Processing the Doppler effect may affect performance on low-power systems as well as in games where the rendering thread has a high priority.

The second method is alDopplerVelocity(), which modifies the effective speed of sound within the application. This method requires a nonnegative, nonzero value; otherwise, the call is ignored. The default value is set to 343 and was designed to give the same speed that sound has in the real world. OpenAL does not maintain a sense of units, so if this value is modified, make sure that all the related values in the world are consistent. To use these methods, simply call the following:

```
al.alDopplerFactor(.99);
al.alDopplerVelocity(500);
```

Tinkering around with these methods is good for countless hours of enjoyment.

JOAL ERROR HANDLING

Error handling is of particular importance to game programming—or any programming, for that matter. It is important that the API in use is able to indicate where errors or other types of unstable events are occurring.

One nice feature that OpenAL and JOAL provide is a single method that returns an error state in the application. Whenever an application wants to make a check for an error, it makes a call to the al.alGetError() method. This method returns any of the valid error enumerations used for OpenAL when an error is discovered within the current rendering context. The current list of error messages that OpenAL and JOAL can return is shown in Table 4.4.

Table 4.4 Valid Error Returns and Descriptions

Error Name	Description
AL_NO_ERROR	There is not currently an error
AL_INVALID_NAME	A bad name (ID) was passed to an OpenAL function
AL_INVALID_ENUM	An invalid enum value was passed to an OpenAL function
AL_INVALID_VALUE	An invalid value was passed to an OpenAL function
AL_INVALID_OPERATION	The requested operation is not valid
AL_OUT_OF_MEMORY	The requested operation resulted in OpenAL running out of memory

These error enums can be used with the OpenAL defined AL_TRUE and AL_FALSE, which serve as direct Boolean enumerations. Most of the error messages are self-explanatory. An example of how the alGetError() method can be used to check the status when generating a Buffer follows:

```
al.alGenBuffers(1, buffer);
if(al.alGetError() != AL.AL_NO_ERROR)
    return AL.AL_FALSE;
```

Good programs check for errors immediately after the creation of Buffers and Sources or loading audio data, as demonstrated in the previous code.

One other note—the most recently released version of JOAL also implements a new Exception class named the OpenALException that is designed to catch initialization errors regarding the AL and ALC objects. Creation of the Alut and ALC classes require the setting of try/catch blocks to initialize.

THE AL CONTEXT API

Up to this point, all the sample applications have relied heavily on the Alut class. The Alut class is a valuable resource that lets new developers get acclimated with the API quickly without being mired in minutia from the start. That being said, at some point in time it may become necessary to be more specific in the setup and structure of JOAL's initialization or with controlling how OpenAL interacts with the operating system on which it is deployed. This section discusses AL Contexts and how an application can manage them using the AL Context API.

Fundamentally, the AL Context API works through the use of the ALC class. This class is structured to allow the user to gain access to hardware by presenting it as a resource. Through the AL Context API, the audio resources are presented in the form of *devices*. A device can be thought of as a handle to the actual physical audio card used, which is exposed through the local implementation. At this point, it is not possible to enumerate the list of available sound cards through the use of the ALC. It is possible, however, to identify a particular implementation or to use the implementation's default device.

JOAL provides an ALFactory class to work with the generation of AL and ALC classes. The ALFactory has already been used to create the AL objects earlier in the chapter. When creating a context, the first step is to initialize the ALFactory, then to retrieve an ALC object for use in the application. Let's set up this basic step.

```
ALFactory.initialize();
ALC alc = ALFactory.getALC();
```

Now that the application has access to an ALC object, it is time to create the device instance that will be used by this application. When creating one of the device objects, the application can be set to use the default device by passing null through to the alcOpenDevice() method, or it can specify a particular string to work with a valid implementation. Be sure to reference the platform-specific documentation to verify that the desired implementation is valid before using it.

Let's set up a device for the Window's platform using the DirextX Direct-Sound3D implementation.

```
ALC.Device device = alc.alcOpenDevice("DirectSound3D");
```

This method will return null if it is unable to find a device on the system. When this call correctly returns, the application holds a handle to the specified device. When the application is completed, we must destroy the context and then close the device before exiting, as follows:

```
alc.DestroyContext(context);
alc.alcCloseDevice(device);
```

SOUND RENDERING CONTEXTS

OpenAL uses contexts to organize and control rendering of audio according to the spec that has been detailed so far. The term *sound-rendering context* is used to identify the core operation of OpenAL and its ability to manage and process spatialized audio. Readers who are familiar with OpenGL will probably recognize the use of rendering contexts. Although there can be multiple contexts for OpenGL rendering, there can be only one active context at any given time. OpenAL and JOAL follow this standard as well. When the AL class is used to make a change of some sort within the application, the effect is applied to the current context for the game in question. For most applications, a single AL Context is used throughout the entire execution.

Because the device has already been created and opened, let's specify a context and set it to be the current context.

```
ALC.Context context = alc.alcCreateContext(device, null);
alc.alcMakeContextCurrent(context);
```

The alcCreateContext() method accepts an opened device as well as a flag. If the flag is set to null, as in the example, the default values for the chosen implementation will be used. Currently supported flags for context creation include:

ALC_FREQUENCY: Allows the context to set its output Buffer frequency (in Hz).

ALC_REFRESH: The context's refresh interval. Can be used to set the timing for state changes to the same as in OpenGL (in Hz).

ALC_SYNC: A Boolean flag that indicates that the context is synchronous.

To set one or more of these values, use an integer array and pass the whole thing through the method that creates the context, as follows:

```
int[] attribs = {ALC.ALC_SYNC, AL.AL_TRUE, ALC.ALC_FREQUENCY, 9600};
ALC.Context context = alc.alcCreateContext(device,attribs);
alc.alcMakeContextCurrent(context);
```

At this point a new context is created and ready for use. These calls can be used to make a custom initialization routine for JOAL and summarily replace the Alut.alutExit and Alut.alutInit calls. All calls related to the destruction of Sources and Buffers remain. Additionally, applications can still use the file loading routines of Alut that have been demonstrated so far.

After a context is created, it can be managed through a set of methods designed to report information and control the activities of a context. As mentioned before, it is completely possible to maintain and manage more than one context, even if it is not currently selected. Let's look at a few of the more immediately useful methods available to the developer who creates and manages contexts.

alcSuspendContext: This method is one of the more useful control mechanisms available when working directly through contexts. This method allows the current context to be suspended. Whenever a context is suspended, all processing is stopped. This control could be useful as a way of maintaining the state in a game when the user decides to pause the game. The same effect could be handled if the gain on a source was set to 0, but the context would continue to process the audio. The combination of suspending a context and reducing the gain results in a true pause for the current context.

alcProcessContext: This method allows a context to return to the normal processing state. Call this method to remove suspension from a selected context. It is also possible to process a context, even while it is not the current selected context.

alcIsExtensionPresent: One of the best aspects of both OpenGL and OpenAL is that vendors or anyone else with access to the source tree can create customized extensions for the API and include them into the implementation. At this time, JOAL implements the EAX extension, which allows for customized audio processing. In the future other extensions are planned for integration, including Ogg Vorbis support. Using this method allows you to check before using an extension so that the application can set internal switches accordingly to avoid errors or performance degradation.

alcGetString: This method allows the device to return information based on the current device. The attribute parameters can be one of the following attributes:

ALC_DEFAULT_DEVICE_SPECIFIER: When using this attribute, the method returns information about the device that the current implementation prefers the application to use. This information can be helpful when attempting to provide support for multiple implementations.

ALC_DEVICE_SPECIFIER: This attribute returns a string that contains the current device specifiers for the version of OpenAL in use.

ALC_EXTENSIONS: This attribute is designed to return a list of ALC extensions. None of these are currently implemented, making this parameter a placeholder of sorts.

AlcGetError(): This method allows the user to retrieve error messages from the ALC. Table 4.5 shows the list of valid error messages and descriptions for each.

TABLE 4.5 ALC Error Codes

Name	Description
ALC_NO_ERROR	The device handle or specifier name is inaccessible
ALC_INVALID_DEVICE	The context argument does not name a valid device
ALC_INVALID_CONTEXT	The context argument does not name a valid context
ALC_INVALID_ENUM	A token used is not valid or not applicable
ALC_INVALID_VALUE	An invalid or inapplicable value/attribute was passed

That wraps up coverage on the AL Context API. Double-check the most recent JOAL documentation to verify support, and check for any updates that might affect the implementation of any of these routines.

LOOKING AHEAD

As JOAL continues to grow it will continue to implement new features and extensions that are available for the OpenAL platform. The two major extension inclusions for the near future include Creative's EAX processing and the open format Ogg Vorbis. This section takes a brief look at both of these and their potential impact on JOAL.

> **EAX:** Created by Creative Labs, the Environmental Audio Extensions (EAX) began as a way to improve the audio-rendering models for both Direct-Sound3D and OpenAL. Whereas both APIs contain powerful rendering tools that have been discussed in this chapter, they are limited with regard to their ability to properly process reverberation or objects that might block a sound, causing its rendering to be changed. EAX was created to extend the capabilities of these APIs to further enrich the immersion of the player through audio.

These effects are introduced into OpenAL through the use of Listener- and Source-based property effects. Each class has its own set of possible parameters regarding the effects. EAX gives developers the freedom to work at a high level of abstraction by setting environmental effects that provide a general algorithm for how a sound will be processed. One example of an environmental effect is EAX_ENVIRONMENT_AUDITORIUM. This environment gives an immediate idea of how sounds should be rendered with regard to the Listener. EAX also provides much lower-level abilities to manipulate the audible environment. Many current games use EAX, including *Call of Duty* and *Tron 2.0*. Look for a fully functioning implementation of EAX on the JOAL platform in the near future.

> **Ogg Vorbis:** In recent times, the need for high rates of audio compression introduced the MP3 format to the world. Although MP3 is a popular and high-quality format, a group of developers decided it wasn't good enough. Thus, the Ogg Vorbis format was born. These newly compressed files, seen with the .ogg extension, offer a royalty-free, high-quality format for use with audio. The most likely use for games comes in the form of streaming background music.

A beta version of the Ogg Vorbis extension to OpenAL was recently released. The streaming capabilities of OpenAL are limited, but it is highly likely that this feature will be adopted through JOAL and made available to game developers. For those who can't wait and need to make Ogg Vorbis work in games immediately, check out the Jorbis project that offers a Java-based Ogg Vorbis decoder and the libraries to use them.

SUMMARY

This chapter has tried to serve as a basic introduction to JOAL and OpenAL. JOAL is a fairly straightforward library to use and can easily fill most needs in any game. As with all new technologies, JOAL is still working to get into a finalized and perpetually stable state. This process has indeed taken some time but will likely be resolved in short order. Make sure to check for updates to take full advantage of this growing toolkit. Now there is no excuse for having lackluster audio on the Java game platform.

5   Java IO and NIO

In This Chapter

- Introduction
- Flow of Data between an Application and the Disk
- The Java IO Package (`java.io`)
- Java New IO (`java.nio`)
- Performance
- Summary

INTRODUCTION

Reading from and writing to a stream of data is essential to every game. Streams have been part of Java since it was introduced. Over the years, the standard IO package (`java.io`) has matured and a new IO package (`java.nio`) has been introduced to meet the demand for an efficient and high-performance IO API. In this chapter, we will discuss the `java.io` and `java.nio` packages. More specifically, we will discuss streams and the new IO-related objects such as `Channels` and `Byte-Buffers`. This chapter also covers the process of storing and restoring the state of Java objects, known as serialization. We will also provide benchmarks that compare the different IO approaches in Java as well as native IO. Native IO refers to IO performed in a native language, such as C or C++. We will show how you can achieve IO performance that is up to par with native IO.

115

FLOW OF DATA BETWEEN AN APPLICATION AND THE DISK

Before we start talking about streams, let's look at what happens when a file is accessed. This information is crucial to understand how to achieve optimal IO performance. The remainder of this chapter will refer to the process explained here. Figure 5.1 shows the path that some data must take to make it from the disk drive to an application.

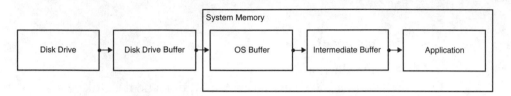

FIGURE 5.1 Flow of data when read request occurs.

The journey starts from the disk drive and ends in the application. When writing to a file, as opposed to reading from a file, the flow of data is in the reverse order. Some applications may read a single byte at a time, whereas others may read multiple bytes at a time.

The cost of transferring data from the disk to the application is very expensive when compared to transferring data in memory. By using caching or buffer techniques, the overall cost of reading data from the disk can be significantly reduced. The general goal behind caching data is to reduce the number of times expensive operations must be performed. As you can see from Figure 5.1, multiple caches exist between the disk drive and the application. The drive buffer, OS buffer, and intermediate buffer each play a part in reducing the cost of reading from the disk.

The drive buffer is the first attempt to reduce the overall cost of reading from or writing to the drive and can result in a noticeable performance gain. The drive buffer, shown in Figure 5.1, is built in to every hard drive and is a form of RAM. The larger the drive buffer, the better overall behavior can be expected, and the more you can expect to pay for the drive. The cost of getting the data from the disk surface to the drive buffer is by far the most expensive step in the pipeline. This high cost is because reading data from the disk surface involves physical movement of the heads among other things, which depends on the RPM of the drive.

The drive buffer is actually composed of a separate read cache and write cache. When reading from the drive, the read cache allows a chunk of data to be read at once. If a request to read a single byte is made to the drive, the drive also reads the data near the requested byte and makes it available to the operating system (OS). By doing so, if some data must be re-retrieved from the disk, if the data has already been read, the disk surface does not have to be accessed. This is a form of investment with some risk. There is no guarantee that reading more data than has been requested will end up paying off because a later request may want to read from an entirely different location on the disk. However, on average it is an investment worth making.

When writing to the drive, the data that must be physically written to the drive is simply written to the drive buffer instead. The drive can then write the data to the disk when it gets the chance to do so. Without a write buffer, a request to write some data would have to block the system until every byte is physically written to the drive. When a write buffer exists, if the data that needs to be written to the disk fits in the drive's cache, the request can return immediately and let the drive write the data in its cache whenever it gets the chance to do so.

Besides the caching that is performed at the drive level, the OS does its own buffering because the OS can cache more data than the drive and can manage the data elegantly. In addition, the OS can perform optimizations that are not possible at the drive level. Unlike the drive, the OS is quite aware of the state of the system. For example, the OS knows which applications are trying to read from a file. If multiple applications are reading from the same file, the OS can eliminate redundant requests to the device altogether.

In addition to the drive-level and OS-level caching of file data, most applications do their own buffering. Accessing the OS buffer can be more expensive than accessing data local to the application. Note that this buffering is optional and is not performed by every application. This buffer has been labeled as the intermediate buffer in Figure 5.1. The decision as to whether it is worth caching data at the application level depends on the total amount of data and the size of data that needs to be used by the specific application. Some applications need to read very small chunks of data, whereas others may need to read very large chunks or even copy an entire file. If the application needs to read or write a few bytes at a time, using the intermediate buffer can pay off tremendously. However, if an application reads and writes data in chunks that are optimal in size, using an intermediate buffer will become strictly an overhead.

To get a better feel for what happens when data is read from the disk, let's consider the process of duplicating a file. A file can be duplicated by opening the source file, opening a destination file, reading data from the source file, and writing the data to the destination file. Even though the procedure is generally the same, the details of how much data is copied at a time and how far the data has to make it in the chain of buffers shown in Figure 5.1 can make a substantial difference.

If a single byte is read at a time but an intermediate buffer exists, the first time a single byte is read, the intermediate buffer is filled. Depending on the size of the intermediate buffer, the implementation details of the OS buffering, and the size of the drive buffer, enough accesses are carried out at OS and disk level to fill the intermediate buffer. Thereafter, single-byte reads will simply read from the intermediate buffer instead of accessing the disk. This process continues until some data that is not in the intermediate buffer must be read, in which case the process repeats and the intermediate buffer is filled again.

If a single byte is read at a time and no intermediate buffer exists, the OS will still read a chunk of data from the disk. Because the OS deals with memory in terms of pages, it reads at least one page, or 4K, of data at a time. After that point, single-byte reads end up reading the cached data at the OS level until there is a cache miss, in which case the process repeats.

It is better to read data from the file in, say, 4K chunks and not use an intermediate buffer as opposed to reading data one or a few bytes at a time and using an intermediate buffer. If data is already read in optimal chunks, there is no need to use an intermediate buffer. In fact, in such a scenario, using an intermediate buffer can slow down the process because it forces an unnecessary copying of data. We will come back to this point in the performance section of this chapter.

An even better approach to duplicating a file would be to ask the OS to duplicate the file instead of having the application duplicate the file. If the OS is responsible for duplicating the file, the data of the file will not even have to make it to the intermediate buffer or the application. The OS can directly duplicate a file by reading the data of the file into its buffer and copying the data from its buffer back to the disk. Note that this process can allow the application to stay out of the loop and leave all the work to the OS. Because this approach is OS dependent and there already are alternative ways to duplicate a file, Java does not expose such OS-level functions. If, and only if, your game needs to perform a reasonable amount of copying or moving of files, you may want to consider writing a simple native function that calls the corresponding OS functions. For more information on wrapping native functions, refer to Chapter 11, "Java Native Interface."

Prior to JDK 1.4, every IO operation—including operations that sent data to a device, such as the video card or the sound card—resulted in extra copying of the data. With the introduction of direct-byte buffers in JDK 1.4, the extra copy can be avoided, which can result in a substantial performance gain. We will discuss this topic in detail in an upcoming section.

Memory-mapped files were also introduced in JDK 1.4. Memory-mapped files are files that are dealt with entirely at the OS level. In other words, they can be used to expose the OS buffer directly. When used appropriately, they can result in substantial performance gain. A specific section in this chapter is dedicated to discussing mapped byte buffers.

THE JAVA IO PACKAGE (`java.io`)

The `java.io` package contains interfaces and classes that deal with byte streams, character streams, and object streams. Some streams can be read from, some can be written to, and others may support both read and write operations.

In this chapter, we will focus on streams that use files as the source and destination. The `java.io.File` class is just an abstract representation of a file or directory name and should not be thought of as a file handle. Some of the methods of the class do deal with actual files. For example, the `delete` method can be used to delete a file denoted by the abstract pathname. The `java.io.FileDescriptor` class, on the other hand, is equivalent to a C/C++ file pointer. `FileDescriptor` objects are opaque file handles and are manipulated internally by the virtual machine (VM) and certain classes. When there is a need for Java to interact with the hardware or operating system, some native code must be executed. Fortunately, Java comes with many classes and packages that cross over to the native world when necessary, and you do not have to deal with native code directly. Therefore, our code is abstracted from the underlying hardware and OS so that it can be independent of the underlying platform.

Streams

Streams in Java are in many ways similar to C++ streams. One of the biggest distinctions is that entirely different classes deal with bytes and characters. Because in C/C++ a char is exactly one byte in length, a file stream object can work perfectly for both text and binary files. In fact, to distinguish between the two, you would only have to pass in a different flag when creating a stream object. A char is two bytes long in Java, so a character stream must be dealt with differently. Java uses Unicode characters, which make internationalization of a game or application easier. A character can be from any language and does not have to be a typical English character. This may not seem like a benefit until you have to translate the strings in your game to another language.

Byte Streams

Byte streams are used to read and write binary data serially. As shown in Figure 5.2, the IO package contains many classes that can deal with binary data.

The `InputStream` and `OutputStream` classes are abstract or incomplete classes that provide read and write methods, respectively. Because their methods are incomplete, they must be defined in their subclasses. For example, the `InputStream` class declares the following abstract read methods:

```
int read()
int read(byte bytes[])
int read(byte bytes[], int offset, int length)
```

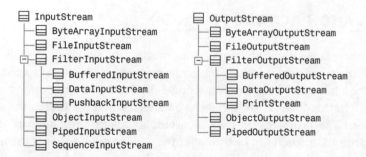

FIGURE 5.2 Byte stream classes.

The read methods that take an array as a parameter provide an interface for reading chunks of data at once. For example, read(byte bytes[]) specifies that a subclass must define a method that attempts to read bytes.length number of bytes and returns the number of bytes that are actually read. FileInputStream is one of the subclasses of InputStream. In addition to overwriting the read methods, it is capable of opening and closing files. The following code segment shows how to use a FileInputStream and a FileOutputStream to copy a file:

```
File inFile = new File(inputFilename);
File outFile = new File(outputFilename);
FileInputStream fis = new FileInputStream(inFile);
FileOutputStream fos = new FileOutputStream(outFile);
//— copy a single byte at a time
int aByte;
while((aByte = fis.read()) $$$$ -1){
    fos.write(aByte);
}
```

If the section of the code that does the copying is replaced by the following, the file is copied as a chunk instead of one byte at a time. Neither one of these code segments uses the buffer denoted as the intermediate buffer in Figure 5.1. The following segment uses a buffer local to the application that is bufferSize in length.

```
//— copy a chunk of length bufferSize at a time
byte[] bytes = new byte[bufferSize];
while (true){
    int count = fis.read(bytes);
    if (count <= 0)
        break;
    fos.write(bytes, 0, count);
}
```

Operations such as opening, closing, reading, and writing to a file rely on native code. When the corresponding methods of `FileInputStream` are called, some native code is executed to communicate with the operating system. Besides IO operations being fundamentally expensive, calling native methods from Java have some additional cost. Minimizing IO requests from the application reduces not only requests from the OS but also the overhead involved in calling native methods.

`BufferedInputStream` and `BufferedOutputStream` are forms of *filtered* streams. A `BufferedInputStream` can sit on top of an `InputStream` and act as a buffer, which is denoted as the intermediate buffer in Figure 5.1. Reading too few bytes at a time can be very inefficient, so you should either read data in chunks or use a `Buffered-InputStream`. By doing so, even if you try to call the read method that returns a single byte, the buffer object tries to minimize requests to the OS and the device by maintaining an array internally. We will look at some important benchmarks in the performance section of this chapter. The following code segment shows how to use a `BuferedInputStream` and a `BufferedOutputStream` to copy a file:

```
FileInputStream fis = new FileInputStream(inputFilename);
FileOutputStream fos = new FileOutputStream(outputFilename);
BufferedInputStream bis = new BufferedInputStream(fis, bufferSize);
BufferedOutputStream bos = new BufferedOutputStream(fos, bufferSize);
int aByte;
while((aByte = bis.read()) >= 0){
    bos.write(aByte);
}
// must be called to ensure data is not left in the buffer
bos.flush();
```

Note that streams are opened automatically, and if they have not been closed already, their `close` method is called by their *finalizer*. Even though it is not necessary, it is not a bad idea to explicitly close streams because their resources will be reclaimed immediately instead of staying around until the garbage collector gets the chance to call their finalizers. Objects that overwrite the `finalize` method of `java.lang.Object` can take reasonably longer to reclaim because of some additional management that is involved. If you are dealing with many different files in a specific part of your game, you should explicitly close each file as soon as you are done with it.

In addition, output streams have a `flush` method that input streams do not have. The flush method is responsible for making sure that any data held by the object or another object chained to this object is propagated through. If a `Buffered-OutputStream` is chained to `FileOutputStream`, calling the flush method of the `BufferedOutputStream` first causes its data to be passed on to the `FileOutputStream`, and then calls the `flush` method of the `FileOutputStream`. When objects are chained together so that one forwards its data to another object, and one of the objects in the chain is capable of buffering some or all of the data, it is important to explicitly call the `flush` method of the last object in the chain that has the potential of buffering some data. If this is not done, data may be lost.

Many of the classes in the IO packages are meant to make programming easier. `DataInputStreams` and `DataOutputStreams` sit on top of other streams and allow for convenient reading and writing of multibyte primitive types, which is a functionality also provided by the NIO package's `ByteBuffers`. `ByteArrayInputStream` and `ByteArrayOutputStream` use byte arrays as the source and destination for their read and write operations. `PushbackInputStreams`, as their name implies, allow bytes to be "unread" so subsequent reads retrieve the same data. `SequenceInputStream` allows a sequence of input streams to be treated as a single source of data. The `ObjectsOutputStream` and `ObjectsInputStream` are used for serializing Java objects and extracting them from a stream. We will cover these in the serialization section of this chapter.

Character Streams (Readers and Writers)

`java.io.Reader` and `java.io.Writer` serve as the abstract base class of character streams. They are, in fact, equivalent to `java.io.InputStream` and `java.in.Output-Stream` in the sense that they provide abstract read and write methods. The main difference is that their read and write methods deal with characters instead of bytes. Figure 5.3 shows the class hierarchy of Reader and Writer.

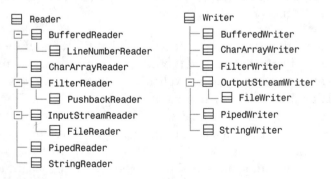

FIGURE 5.3 `char` stream classes.

`InputStreamReader` uses an `InputStream` as its source for bytes that must be converted to characters. In C/C++, converting a byte to a `char` is not necessary because a byte is exactly an `unsigned char`. On the other hand, because Java uses two bytes to represent a character, an extra step is involved. `InputStreamReader` and `OutputStreamWriter` can be viewed as objects that convert between bytes and characters. They use `charsets` to map bytes to characters and vice versa. `FileReader`, `FileWriter`, `BufferedReader`, and `BufferedWriter` are equivalent to `FileInputStream`, `FileOutputStream`, `BufferedInputStream`, and `BufferedOutputStream`. A convenient addition to `BufferedReader` and `BufferedWriter` is their ability to read and write lines. The following code segment shows how to duplicate a text file while converting its characters from one charset to a different charset.

```
File inFile = new File("input.txt");
File outFile = new File("output.txt");
FileInputStream fis = new FileInputStream(inFile);
FileOutputStream fos = new FileOutputStream(outFile);
InputStreamReader isr =
    new InputStreamReader(fis, Charset.forName("UTF-8"));
OutputStreamWriter osw =
    new OutputStreamWriter(fos, Charset.forName("UTF-16"));
char[] chars = new char[8*1024];
while (true){
    int count = isr.read(chars);
    if (count <= 0)
        break;
    osw.write(chars, 0, count);
}
osw.flush();
```

A Reader can be used to create an instance of `StreamTokenizer` that can be used to simplify the parsing of a character stream. A token can be a number or a word. The following code segment shows how to count the number of word tokens in a file:

```
FileInputStream fis = new FileInputStream("input.txt");
InputStreamReader inputStreamReader = new InputStreamReader(fis);
StreamTokenizer tokenizer= new
StreamTokenizer(inputStreamReader);
int wordCount = 0;
while(tokenizer.nextToken() != StreamTokenizer.TT_EOF){
    if (tokenizer.ttype == StreamTokenizer.TT_WORD){
        wordCount++;
    }
}
```

Serialization (`ObjectStream`)

Object serialization is the storing and loading of objects to and from a series of bytes. Serialization can be used to save and load a program's state, or send and receive objects over a network. Loading and storing a game state is significant to just about any game. Sending and receiving objects is important for a multiplayer game. In either case, the significant and relevant data of objects must be converted to a stream or series of bytes.

For those who are used to native languages such as C/C++ where the data of objects is readily available and directly accessible, the need for serialization support may seem odd. In Java, because direct access to an object's binary representation is not permitted, object serialization support is fundamental to the language. Even when direct access to memory content is possible, other issues, such as separating significant and relevant data of an object as well as versioning of objects, can promote the use of APIs similar to the Java Object Serialization API.

Another issue that may seem odd to a C/C++ developer is that arbitrary objects cannot be serialized. Only objects whose class implements `Serializable` or `Externalizable` can be serialized. This characteristic is mainly due to safety and security concerns. For example, classes that store sensitive information should not be serializable by default. Without this restriction, any object would be able to serialize a sensitive object and then read its information, including its private fields. As another example, consider the scenario where an object contains fragile data, such as the memory address of a native object that it uses internally. If the object is serialized and then restored, the memory address is no longer valid and attempting to use the services provided by the object can result in memory access violations.

A Simple Example

Serialization allows for the convenient and safe conversion of graphs of objects to a stream of bytes. Note that if you want to store an object that refers to another object, the second object also needs to be serialized so that the state of the first object can be restored properly. This is why the definition given earlier contained the word *graph*. Serializing an object is simple and does not require much work from the developer. In fact, most of the work is automatic. The serialization and deserialization process can be highly customized to give the developer full control over just about every byte written to the stream. Let's look at an example to see how easy it is to store and load objects to and from a file. Consider the following two classes:

```
class Actor implements Serializable{
    int     id;
    String  name;
    Point   position;
}
```

```
class Point implements Serializable{
    float x;
    float y;
    float z;

    Point(float x,float y,float z){
        this.x = x;
        this.y = y;
        this.z = z;
    }
}
```

The following example creates an array of Actor objects, writes them to a file, and then restores their state.

 The following code can be found on the book's companion CD-ROM in Code/Chapter 5/Serialization/Serialization:

```
class Sample{

    Actor[] actors;

    public void initialize(){
        actors = new Actor[3];

        // initialize actors
        for(int i=0; i<actors.length; i++){
            actors[i] = new Actor();
            actors[i].name   = "actor" + i;
            actors[i].id     = i;
            actors[i].position = new Point( Math.random()... );
        }
    }

    public void test() throws Exception{
        initialize();
        printActors();

        System.out.println("---- writing");
        FileOutputStream fos = new FileOutputStream("actors");
        ObjectOutputStream oos = new ObjectOutputStream (fos);
        oos.writeObject(actors);
        oos.close(); // flush, clear, close

        actors = null;
```

```
                System.out.println("---- reading");
                FileInputStream fis = new FileInputStream("actors");
                ObjectInputStream ois = new ObjectInputStream(fis);
                actors = (Actor[])ois.readObject();

                printActors();
        }

        public static void main(String args[]){
            Sample sample = new Sample();
            try{
                sample.test();
            }catch(Exception e){
                e.printStackTrace();
            }
        }
    }
```

Both the Actor and Point classes implement the java.io.Serializable interface. Any serializable class should implement either java.io.Serializable or java.io.Externalizable. The test method uses instances of ObjecOutputStream and ObjectInputStream classes. Their corresponding writeObject and readObject methods conveniently do all the work for us. It is a good idea to understand what happens behind the scene so that we get a better idea of the cost and overhead.

The ObjectOutputStream implements two interfaces, namely DataOutput and ObjectOutput. DataOutput is an interface for writing primitive Java types as well as strings, and ObjectOutput is for writing objects. Some of the more important details of the process follow. If you want to see all the details, you can look at the Java Object Serialization Specification or the source code of the corresponding classes.

The writeObject method is responsible for storing complete serialized representation of the graph that starts at the object passed to the method. To store the complete state of the object, the writeObject method must be recursively called for objects referred to by the object that is being serialized. Note that the default behavior of the method does not write redundant objects. That is, if both object A and object B are serialized and they each have a reference to object C, only one copy of object C is written to the stream. If object A is serialized first, when object B is serialized, only a handle to object C is written to the stream because object C has already been serialized when object A was written to the stream.

It is important to note that some information about the class of every serialized object is written to the stream. This includes information such as the name of the serializable fields of the corresponding class. Such information is written as instances of `java.io.ObjectStreamClass` and `java.io.ObjectStreamField` classes, which are also referred to as class and field *descriptors*.

In the example shown earlier, the `writeObject` method first writes the array object to the stream. This means that it writes a descriptor for the array object. Then the length of the array is written to the stream, and `writeObject` is called for each of the references of the array object. Because the descriptor for the `Actor` class has not yet been written, an instance of `ObjectStreamClass` is made to represent the name of the class and serializable fields of the class. After the descriptor is written to the stream, the data of the `Actor` instance is written. An `Actor` object has a reference to a `Point` object, so `writeObject` is recursively called for the point object. This action results in the creation and serialization of a descriptor for the `Point` class. The data of the point object is then written to the stream. The `ObjectOutputStream` maintains a list of objects that have been written to the stream. Therefore, the serialization of the remaining `Actor` objects will no longer result in the creation or serialization of descriptors for the `Actor` and `Point` classes. If the `Point` class did not implement `Serializable` or `Externalizable`, the serialization of the array object would eventually result in an exception being thrown.

The `writeObject` obtains a list of the fields of a serializable class and writes their corresponding values to the stream. Fields that are `transient` or `static` are skipped. Instead of having to flag which fields should be ignored, it is sometimes more convenient to list which fields should not be ignored. The following code provides a behavior equivalent to the original `Actor` class:

```
class Actor implements Serializable{
    int     id;
    String  name;
    Point   position;
    // Alternative approach can be used instead of having to
    // explicitly use the transient keyword to skip a field.
    private static final ObjectStreamField[]
        serialPersistentFields = {
            new ObjectStreamField("id", int.class),
            new ObjectStreamField("name", String.class),
            new ObjectStreamField("position", Point.class)
    };
}
```

Creating instances of `ObjectStreamField` and storing them in the private and static member named `serialPersistentFields` is safer than assuming nontransient members should be serialized. This is in part because when a member is added to the class, it is not automatically considered serializable. It also makes the job of the writeObject method easier because it can forward these instances to the class descriptor of the Actor class.

Objects that implement the Serializable interface automatically support versioning of classes. This means if the class of an object that is written to a stream changes, the object can still be restored and represented as an instance of the newer class. The symbolic names of fields are written to the stream as part of the class descriptor, so the serialization mechanism knows how to interpret the data in the stream, even if the class of an object in the stream has evolved. Every class is assigned a unique serialVersionUID, which is written to the stream. A class can explicitly indicate that it is compatible with the older version by identifying itself with the serialVersionUID of the older class, as long as the changes made to the class are considered compatible, as described by the serialization documentation. This identifier can be retrieved using the serialver program, which is included with JDK. The serialization documentation specifies the list of compatible and incompatible changes.

Controlling the Serialization of Objects

Classes that implement the Serializable interface can perform custom writes and reads by defining the writeObject and readObject methods that have the following exact signatures:

```
private void writeObject(java.io.ObjectOutputStream out)
    throws IOException;
private void readObject(java.io.ObjectInputStream in)
    throws IOException, ClassNotFoundException;
```

These methods are intended for appending data to the stream and not necessarily taking full control of the serialization process. Even though they can be used to gain full control of the serialization of an object, doing so will increase the likelihood of the incompatibility of two classes with different versions. A typical implementation of the readObject and writeObject should call the default-WriteObject and defaultReadObject of the ObjectOutputStream and ObjectInput-Stream. They can then perform special handling of a specific field of the class.

The Externalizable interface is a subinterface of the Serializable interface. If you want to have total control over the serialization of an object, you may choose to use the Externalizable interface instead of the Serializable interface. Only the identity of the class of an Externalizable object is written to the stream, and it is the responsibility of the class to save and restore the contents of its corresponding objects. It is imperative to note that using the Externalizable interface stops not only the default writing of the content of a class but also the default writing of any parent classes' datum. However, using the Externalizable interface allows for efficient serialization in terms of both CPU and space. The CPU advantage comes from the fact that the system will not do much for you anymore. The space advantage comes from the fact that only the descriptor of the current class is written to the stream, and the metadata of the super classes are excluded. In addition, field descriptors are not written to the stream. The exclusion of the metadata can add up to a significant amount if many objects are serialized.

The following example accomplishes what the previous example accomplished but instead uses the Externalizable interface:

```java
class Actor implements Externalizable{
    int     id;
    String  name;
    Point   position;

    // must be public
    public Actor(){}

    public void writeExternal(ObjectOutput out) throws
        IOException{
        out.writeInt(id);
        out.writeUTF(name);
        out.writeObject(position);
    }

    public void readExternal(ObjectInput in) throws
        IOException, ClassNotFoundException{
        id = in.readInt();
        name = in.readUTF();
        position = (Point)in.readObject();
    }

}

class Point implements Externalizable{
    float x;
    float y;
    float z;

    // must be public
    public Point(){}

    Point(float x,float y,float z){ ... }
```

```
public void writeExternal(ObjectOutput out) throws
    IOException{
    out.writeFloat(x);
    out.writeFloat(y);
    out.writeFloat(z);
}

public void readExternal(ObjectInput in) throws
    IOException, ClassNotFoundException{
    x = in.readFloat();
    y = in.readFloat();
    z = in.readFloat();
}
}
```

The Sample class, including its test method, remains unchanged. So, what is so different here? A noticeable difference is that writeExternal and readExternal give the class complete control over the format and content of the stream.

When the writeObject method of ObjectOutputStream is called from the test method, the writeExternal method is called indirectly. The method then writes the value of any relevant primitive or string fields of the object to the stream and causes the writeExternal method of another object to be called indirectly. Note that classes that implement the Externalizable interface must have a public constructor that has no parameters. This is because when an object of, say, type Actor is restored, an instance of the class is made first, and then its readExternal method is called. This behavior is unlike a class that implements the Serializable interface. In fact, when a Serializable object is restored, its constructors and field initializers are not executed at all.

Because the writeExternal and readExternal are public, they can be called directly. The following code segment shows the changes necessary to the test method:

```
public void test() throws Exception{
    initialize();
    printActors();

    System.out.println("---- writing");
    FileOutputStream fos = new FileOutputStream("actors");
    ObjectOutputStream oos = new ObjectOutputStream (fos);

    oos.writeInt(actors.length);
    for(int i=0; i<actors.length; i++){
        actors[i].writeExternal(oos);
    }
```

```
        oos.flush();
        oos.close();

        actors = null;

        System.out.println("---- reading");
        FileInputStream fis = new FileInputStream("actors");
        ObjectInputStream ois = new ObjectInputStream(fis);

        actors = new Actor[ois.readInt()];
        for(int i=0; i<actors.length; i++){
            actors[i]= new Actor();
            actors[i].readExternal(ois);
        }

        printActors();
    }
```

As you can see, the test method writes the length of the array and each reference directly. Therefore, the class descriptor is not written to the stream and the readObject cannot be called. Instead, the size of the array has to be read directly, an array object and Actor objects have to be created, and then the readExternal method has to be called for each one of them. It is also possible to modify the read and write methods of the Actor class so that it deals with the Point object directly.

```
public void writeExternal(ObjectOutput out) throws IOException{
    out.writeInt(id);
    out.writeUTF(name);
    position.writeExternal(out);
}
public void readExternal(ObjectInput in) throws IOException,
    ClassNotFoundException{
    id = in.readInt();
    name = in.readUTF();
    position = new Point();
    position.readExternal(in);
}
```

The extra code we had to insert is part of what the writeObject and readObject of what the OutputObjectStream and InputObjectStream automatically do for us. The default serialization mechanism conveniently does many things automatically at the cost of having some extra overhead. If you want full control, implement the Externalizable interface instead. Serializing objects through the Externalization interface is significantly more efficient than using the default mechanism. The second approach to externalization is also significantly faster than the former approach.

JAVA NEW IO (JAVA.NIO)

The java.nio package was introduced with JDK 1.4 to provide more powerful IO and accommodate for some of the shortcomings of the existing java.io package and other IO-related packages. It is important to note that NIO does not replace the standard IO package but serves as a new approach to some IO problems. The NIO package was designed to provide the following:

- Character sets
- Scalable network IO
- High-performance file IO

As explained in the Character Stream section, character streams use charsets, which are comprehensive mechanisms for converting between bytes and characters. Asynchronous or nonblocking network IO has been a long-standing problem for Java. Prior to NIO, an application could run into severe limitations if it needed to establish and maintain thousands of connections. The typical approach had been to create a thread for every connection. This approach is not a problem for a few dozen connections, but resource consumption becomes an issue when dealing with hundreds of threads, which is typical for server-side code. High-performance file IO is also important, and by providing a new approach to file IO, it has become possible to make many other performance improvements in other areas. java.nio introduced Buffers, which are one of the best additions ever made to Java, and in fact, games are one of the biggest beneficiaries of them. A significant benefit of Buffers is that they allow for efficient sharing of data between Java and native code. Because data such as textures, geometry, sound, and files is passed between Java and native code and is in turn passed to the corresponding device, Buffers can result in a noticeable performance gain. Before getting to Buffers, let's look at channels, which are NIO's version of streams.

Channels

Channels are used to represent a connection to an entity such as a file, network socket, or even a program component. They are in many ways comparable to streams and can be arguably referred to as more platform-dependent versions of streams. Because they have closer ties to the underlying platform, in conjunction with NIO buffers, they have the potential for achieving very efficient IO. Different types of channels such as `DatagramChannel`, `FileChannel`, and `SocketChannel` exist. Each of them provides a new way of dealing with IO. A `DatagramChannel` is a selectable channel for datagram-oriented sockets. A `FileChannel` is a channel for reading, writing, mapping, and manipulating a file. A `SocketChannel` is a selectable channel for stream-oriented connecting sockets and supports nonblocking connections.

A Channel object can be obtained by calling the `getChannel` methods of classes such as:

```
java.io.FileInputStream
java.io.FileOutputStream
java.io.RandomAccessFile
java.net.Socket
java.net.ServerSocket
java.net.DatagramSocket
java.net.MulticastSocket
```

For example, a `FileChannel` can simply be obtained by using the following code:

```
File inFile = new File(inputFilename);
FileInputStream fis = new FileInputStream(inFile);
FileChannel ifc = fis.getChannel();
```

A `FileChannel` is tightly bound to the object from which it is obtained. For example, reading a byte from the `FileChannel` updates the current position of the `FileInputStream`. A `FileChannel` can be obtained from a `FileInputStream`, `FileOutputStream`, or a `RandomAccessFile`. Note that if a `FileChannel` is obtained from a `FileInputStream`, you can only read from it; you cannot write to it. Similarly, if a channel is obtained from a `FileOutputStream`, it can only be written to and not read from. File channels can be used to duplicate a file in much the same way that file stream objects can be used to duplicate a file. One distinction is that file streams are typically read from and written to using an array of bytes, whereas channels are read from and written to using `ByteBuffer` objects A `FileChannel` can also be used to map a file into memory, which we will look at in an upcoming section.

```
// using ByteBuffer
void test(String inputFilename, String outputFilename){
    File inFile = new File(inputFilename);
    File outFile = new File(outputFilename);
    FileInputStream fis = new FileInputStream(inFile);
    FileOutputStream fos = new FileOutputStream(outFile);
    FileChannel ifc = fis.getChannel();
    FileChannel ofc = fos.getChannel();
```

```
        ByteBuffer bytes = ByteBuffer.allocate(bufferSize);

    while (true){
        bytes.clear();
        int count = ifc.read(bytes);

        if (count <= 0)
            break;

        bytes.flip();
        ofc.write(bytes);
    }
}
```

Buffers

Buffers can result in substantial performance gains for tasks that involve getting a rather large chunk of data to the operating system or the hardware. This gain is not specific to file IO. Figure 5.4 shows the different buffer types in the NIO package.

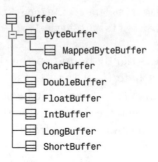

FIGURE 5.4 Buffer classes.

As you can see in Figure 5.4, a different buffer is available for every primitive type. A buffer is in many ways similar to an array. It represents a contiguous chunk of data and has a capacity that is fixed during its life. One of the fundamental differences between an array and a buffer is that a buffer can be *direct*, whereas arrays are always *nondirect*. A buffer can be thought of as an object that contains a reference to an array. A nondirect buffer's array is a typical Java array that resides in the Java heap, but a direct buffer's array resides in system memory, as shown in Figure 5.5.

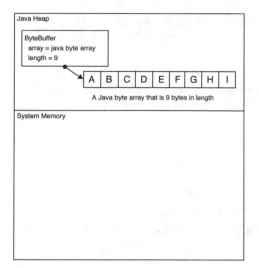
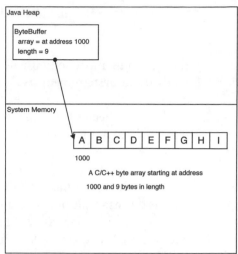

FIGURE 5.5   Direct versus nondirect buffers.

It is important to understand the difference between the Java heap and the system memory. Here we define the Java heap as the memory maintained by the garbage collector and system memory as all the memory on the host machine minus the Java heap. Typical native APIs including the OS API take the memory address of (or a pointer to) the data that needs to be manipulated. Because the data in the Java heap is managed by the garbage collector, direct access to data in the Java heap cannot be safely granted to native APIs without serious implications. This means that Java applications or the VM have an extra problem to deal with.

Note that the garbage collector may decide to move objects around in the heap when performing housekeeping. If some data in the Java heap must be passed to, say, the hard drive or the video card, the data in the heap is not guaranteed to stay where it is until the transfer is completed. One workaround would be to disable the garbage collector when any data in the heap must be passed to native APIs, such as the operating system. However, this action can result in serious problems. For example, if the garbage collector is disabled and a data transfer to a device is time consuming, the VM may run out of memory, even if there is a substantial amount of dead objects that could have been collected to free up some space. The other option would be to pin or lock the object so that the garbage collector knows not to move it. This technique would require less efficient and more complicated collection algorithms and has other side effects. Because of this, the VM does not allow direct access to the data in the Java heap.

Before the introduction of direct byte buffers, the solution to dealing with this problem was to copy the data from the Java heap to the system memory before it could be passed to a native function. Direct byte buffers allow the data to reside in the system memory so that when it needs to be passed to a native function, it is already in the system memory. This is the main idea behind why direct byte buffers can improve the performance of an application.

The overhead of copying the data may not be a bottleneck for small chunks of data that are not time critical and are rarely passed to native functions. However, the copy overhead can prove to be a bottleneck in many situations in different applications, especially games. Games rely heavily on the manipulation of data that is passed to the OS or the hardware. Geometry that needs to be manipulated by Java code is one example of where direct buffers can result in considerable performance gains. Refer to Chapter 12, "Java Native Interface," for additional information about using Java direct buffers from native code and additional details about direct byte buffers.

A `ByteBuffer` is for storing any binary data. The `CharBuffer`, `DoubleBuffer`, `FloatBuffer`, `IntBuffer`, and `ShortBuffer` classes, however, are for dealing with data of a specific type. There are different ways to allocate the array that stores the content of a buffer. The following code segment results in a creation of a nondirect buffer:

```
ByteBuffer byteBuffer = ByteBuffer.allocate(bufferSize);
IntBuffer intBuffer = IntBuffer.allocate(bufferSize);
```

In addition, a buffer can simply wrap an existing array of appropriate type using its wrap method. Because Java arrays reside in the Java heap, the following buffer is implicitly a nondirect buffer:

```
int myArray[] = new int[8];
IntBuffer intBuffer = IntBuffer.wrap(myArray);
```

ByteBuffer objects provide the `allocateDirect` method that can be used to explicitly ask the array to reside in the system memory as opposed to the Java heap. The following call is used to create a direct byte buffer:

```
ByteBuffer byteBuffer = ByteBuffer.allocateDirect(bufferSize);
```

Direct buffers can also be created by wrapping any region of the system memory through the `NewDirectByteBuffer` function, which is provided by JNI. In addition, a `MappedbyteBuffer`, which is a form of direct byte buffer, can be used to access memory in the OS buffer that was shown in Figure 5.1.

A byte buffer also provides methods that create other buffers to view its content as other primitive types. A *view buffer* is a buffer whose array is the same as the array of the byte buffer that was used to create it. A view buffer is not indexed in bytes but in corresponding primitive type. The only way to create a direct, say, float buffer would be to first create a direct byte buffer and then call its asFloatBuffer method to create a view. Because a byte buffer provides an interface for reading and writing primitive types, when dealing with multibyte data, the order of the bytes matters. The byte order can be either big-endian or little-endian. In the big-endian byte order, the most significant byte is stored at the lowest storage address (that is, the first address). In a little-endian byte order, the least significant byte is stored first (see Figure 5.6). Note that if you put an integer that occupies four bytes as little-endian and get it back as big-endian, the result will be entirely different. This is not a concern specific to Java but has to be dealt with in any language, especially when different applications share data through means such as a file or network packets.

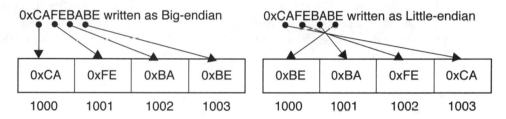

FIGURE 5.6 Little-endian versus big-endian byte order.

The default byte order is big-endian, but it can be set by calling order (Byte-Order newOrder). Note that different hardware uses different byte order. For example, Intel hardware uses little-endian byte order. The method ByteOrder.nativeOrder can be used to obtain the byte order of the underlying hardware.

A Buffer is allocated once and is typically reused. A Buffer contains member variables such as capacity, limit, and position. It also contains methods such as clear, rewind, flip, and reset that manipulate these members. Once allocated, the capacity of a buffer cannot be changed. When the clear method of a buffer is called, its position is 0 and its limit is set to its capacity. This is shown in Figure 5.7.

The position indicates the next index of the array where data can be written to or read from. As data is written to the buffer, the position is updated. The position of a buffer can be retrieved and set using the position() and position(int newPosition) accessors. Subclasses of the Buffer class can choose to use position to provide relative put and get methods. The limit of a buffer is used to keep track of

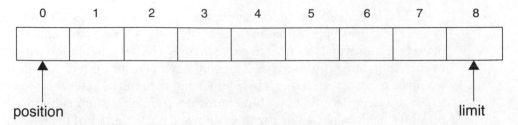

FIGURE 5.7 A buffer whose `clear` method has been called.

the segment of the buffer that contains valid data. For example, when a buffer is filled only half way, it is important to know the index up to where valid data has been filled. As with position, the limit can be retrieved and set using the `limit()` and `limit(int newPosition)` accessors. If a relative put operation tries to write past the limit, a `BufferOverflowException` is thrown and if the get operation tries to read past the limit, a `BufferUnderflowException` is thrown. The remaining method simply returns the difference between position and limit. Figure 5.8 shows a buffer that has some data in it.

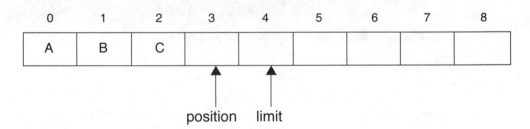

FIGURE 5.8 A buffer that contains some data.

The `flip` method is one of the most important. Once all the data of interest has been written to a buffer, the limit of the buffer must be set to the end of the new or relevant data in the buffer so that an object that reads the data knows when it has reached the end of relevant data. It is important to note that reading until the capacity is reached is not correct because the buffer might not be full. The `flip` method sets the limit to position and position to 0. By doing so, a reading object can start reading from position and stop when position has reached the limit. Figure 5.9 shows a buffer whose flip method has been called.

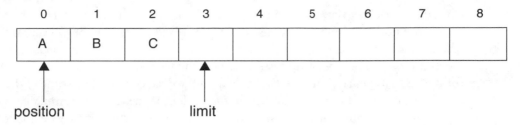

FIGURE 5.9 A buffer whose flip method has been called.

As the data in a buffer is read, the position is updated accordingly. If you want to reread the same data, you can invoke the reset method. Buffers also allow an index to be marked using the mark method. If you care to set the position back to a marked index, the reset method can be used. The rewind method simply sets the position to 0. In general, it is correct to say that the mark can be greater or equal to 0, the position can be greater or equal to the limit, and the limit can be greater or equal to the capacity.

$$0 <= mark <= position <= limit <= capacity$$

MappedByteBuffers

MappedByteBuffers are a form of direct byte buffer that were also introduced with JDK 1.4. They are rather complicated to understand compared to typical buffers, and if you want to use them to improve the performance of your game, you really must understand how they work. They can be rather mysterious if you do not understand what happens behind the scenes. They can bring efficiency if they are used properly but can also decrease performance, increase memory consumption, and reduce available disk space if they are not used properly. It is important to note that MappedByteBuffers are one of the most OS-dependent objects that have been added to Java. Some exact specifics of their behavior are not defined in the JDK documentation, and you are advised to check the OS-specific documentation. When necessary, this section assumes the behavior of MappedByteBuffers under the Windows operating system.

A MappedByteBuffer is a direct byte buffer whose content corresponds to a region of a file, and is managed by the operating system. In fact, the content of a MappedByteBuffer resides in the buffer or cache labeled as the OS buffer in Figure 5.1. In other words, a MappedbyteBuffer can be used to wrap a region of the OS buffer. This means that an application can manipulate the data in the OS buffer without having to use an intermediate buffer, or a buffer managed by the application. By being able to access the OS buffer, an application does not have to endure the cost of copying data from the OS buffer to the application buffer. However, this is not the main advantage. The main advantage is that because the OS is managing the data, it can do certain things that would not be possible if the application managed the data. The operating system can decide to update some of the data in the buffer so that it corresponds with the data on the disk, or to update some of the data on the disk to correspond to the data in the buffer that has been manipulated by the application. Because the OS is aware of the state of the system, it may decide to unload parts of the file data from the OS buffer if it is low on memory. It can also avoid reloading the content of the file until it knows for a fact that an application needs to use a specific portion of a file. In addition, because the data is maintained at the OS level, if multiple applications need to access a certain file, they can simply gain access to the same region of the OS buffer. In fact, this technique is sometimes used to share data between multiple applications. The shared part of the OS buffer can be looked at as a form of shared memory backed by a file. All of this can happen without the application having to know about what happens behind the scenes. In fact, once the buffer is retrieved, it is used as a typical direct byte buffer.

Figure 5.10 shows a region of a file that resides in the OS buffer. The region is visible to two different processes. Each process, represented by a block, stands for the memory local to the process. Each view in a process indicates a different Mapped-ByteBuffer object. The diagram shows three different MappedByteBuffers of which one belongs to Process 1 and two belong to Process 2. The memory addresses wrapped by each byte buffer is actually local to its corresponding process. That is, as far as the process is concerned, it thinks that it is accessing local data. The OS, however, knows that the memory region mapped by each view really refers to the memory pages in the OS buffer. Therefore, even though each process thinks that it is using some chunk of memory to represent the file region, the data is strictly resident in the OS buffer.

Process 1 has a view that can see the entire memory mapped region. Process 2 has two different views that see parts of the region visible to Process 1. As you can see, the content of the byte buffers are overlapping. Therefore, if Process 2 modifies the content of the buffer denoted by View 2, both View 1 of Process 2 and View 1 of Process 1 would be able to access the updated data. When the content of Region 1 is modified through any of the byte buffers, the OS does not immediately update the content of the file. It updates the file only when it finds it necessary.

Region 1 is only part of the actual file on the disk. Therefore, to modify a region of the file, the entire file does not have to be loaded. Furthermore, the amount of memory occupied in the OS buffer is not as much as the size of the region. If the three views are created but none of them is accessed, no memory is committed in the OS buffer. However, when the first byte of the byte buffer of Process 1 is accessed, one page of memory is committed in the OS buffer and updated to reflect

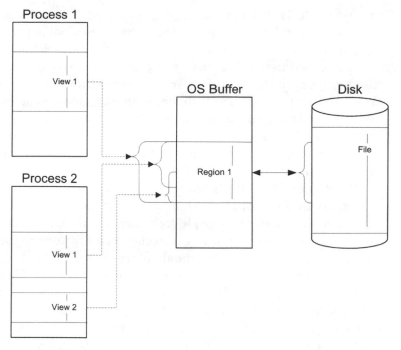

FIGURE 5.10   Memory mapped file region.

the data of the corresponding section of the file. If the second byte of the same byte buffer is accessed, no IO will occur and no additional memory is committed. If the first byte of the byte buffer corresponding to View 1 of Process 2 is accessed, the data is available and already up to date. In fact, 4K of consecutive bytes can be read without any need for the disk to be accessed. If the last byte of the second byte buffer of Process 2 is accessed, another page is committed, which would mean that only two pages have actually been allocated.

Now that you see when the OS actually reads data from the disk, let's see when it decides to unload them. There is no direct way to force the OS to unload the committed pages because that would intervene with the management strategy of the OS. Additionally, the memory can be uncommitted only if no other views of the region exist. To decrease the time it takes before the OS uncommits the pages, you can unmap the buffers and close any streams or channels that refer to the file. A mapped byte buffer is unmapped when its finalizer is called, which is some time after the object is no longer reachable.

The OS may decide to release a page if it needs to make room for other purposes. For example, if the game starts to perform some memory-intensive computations, the OS may decide to unload some of the pages. Whether the pages are written back to the disk depends on whether the pages have been modified. If the pages have not been modified, the memory is simply freed. In fact, when a buffer is mapped, a parameter is used to specify its mode. A `MappedByteBuffer` can be either read-only, read-write, or private. If a buffer is read-only, it slightly helps the unloading process. When a buffer that is in private mode is written to, the OS copies any of the necessary pages and modifies only the copies. The advantage of this approach over making a local copy of the file content and storing it locally to the process is that the OS will still manage the pages. If the OS needs to make more room, a modified copy is saved to the system page file instead of the original file.

It is important to note that the use of a `MappedByteBuffer` can affect the amount of memory used as well as the amount of space used on the disk. If, for example, many sections of a rather large file are loaded into the OS buffer, the virtual memory manager may consider saving out other memory pages to the system page file, which can in turn increase the amount of space used on the drive.

The data maintained in the OS buffer is not saved to the file immediately, so it is crucial to have a way of forcing an update. This is exactly what the `force` method of `MappedByteBuffer` does. Note that forcing the changes to be written to the file is different from trying to make the OS uncommit or free some of the pages that it has allocated to store sections of the file. As mentioned already, the latter is not possible. The `MappedByteBuffer` object also has a `load` method that forces the entire mapped region to be loaded into the OS buffer. The `load` method simply walks the direct buffer at 4K (or page size) intervals and touches each page to achieve the desired result. Keep in mind, however, that loading an entire mapped region causes the application to use a significant amount of memory if the mapped region is large.

A `MappedByteBuffer` can be retrieved from a file channel. As mentioned earlier, a file channel can be retrieved from a `FileInputStream`, `FileOutputStream`, or `RandomAccessFile`. The following example uses a `MappedByteBuffer` to copy a file:

```
File inFile = new File(inputFilename);
File outFile = new File(outputFilename);
FileInputStream fis = new FileInputStream(inFile);
RandomAccessFile fos = new RandomAccessFile(outFile, "rw");
FileChannel ifc = fis.getChannel();
FileChannel ofc = fos.getChannel();

long sourceSize = ifc.size();
```

```
MappedByteBuffer bytes1 = ifc.map(
    FileChannel.MapMode.READ_ONLY, 0, sourceSize);
bytes1.load();
MappedByteBuffer bytes2 = ofc.map(
    FileChannel.MapMode.READ_WRITE, 0, sourceSize);
bytes2.load();
// finally, copy the data
bytes2.put(bytes1);
```

How expensive do you think executing the put method is? Note that because the mapped regions have been loaded already through the load method, the put method results only in copying of data from one part of the OS buffer to another. This is a memory copy and the disk is not even accessed, so the put method alone is extremely fast. However, if the buffer's load method is not called before the put method is invoked, the put method would end up being very expensive because the entire source file would have to first be loaded into the OS buffer. Also, note that when the put method is done, the destination file has not been literally updated yet. To have the data written to the file, you can call the force method of the buffer. Note that closing the channel does not affect the mapped buffer. Once the file is mapped into memory, it has nothing to do with the channel from which it was created. As a side note, the behavior of the map method of Channel is unspecified and OS dependent when the requested region is not completely contained within the corresponding channel's file. The example just shown assumes that the source and destination files of the given size exist already and the intention is to overwrite the content of the destination file.

PERFORMANCE

In this section we will compare the performance of Java IO and NIO with native IO and consider different methods. We will see how to use direct byte buffers to achieve file IO just as fast as the fastest native file IO with benchmarks to support the claim. We will also see that to achieve fast file IO you must be careful and not make many assumptions. In fact, we will show that using NIO without making appropriate considerations can result in much slower IO than the regular IO package, and that using the standard IO package can result in very reasonable performance.

When a Java application reads a sequence of bytes from a file, the data retrieved from the file can incur an additional copy, which would not be necessary if a native application read the same data from the file. In fact, this is true for any form of IO. For example, if a chunk of data is passed from the Java heap to the sound card, written to a file, or sent to the video card, an extra copying operation has to be performed. This extra copying can have an adverse effect on the performance of the game, depending on how much data is involved and how often it needs to be retrieved from or sent to a device.

When the OS retrieves the data from the file but before it passes it to the application, the data is copied to a temporary buffer in the system memory and then copied from the system memory to the Java heap. This extra step is because the Java heap is managed by the garbage collector and should not be written to directly. On the other hand, when a native application reads a sequence of bytes, the data can be made available without the use of a temporary buffer (see Figure 5.11).

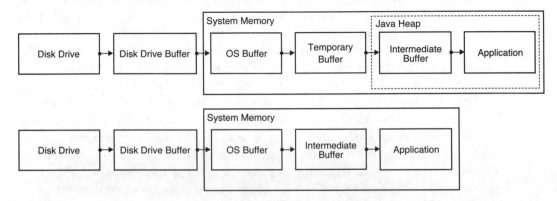

FIGURE 5.11 The flow of data when reading from a file in Java versus in a native application.

The following code segment shows how to duplicate a file in Java and the equivalent native code that we will use for our benchmarks.

 The following code can be found on the book's companion CD-ROM in Code/Chapter 5/ IO Performance Test:

```
public void test(String inputFilename, String outputFilename){
    File inFile = new File(inputFilename);
    File outFile = new File(outputFilename);
    FileInputStream fis = new FileInputStream(inFile);
    FileOutputStream fos = new FileOutputStream(outFile);

    byte[] bytes = new byte[bufferSize];

    while (true){
        int count = fis.read(bytes);
```

```
            if (count <= 0)
                break;

            fos.write(bytes, 0, count);
        }
    }
    void nativeTest(char* inputFilename, char* outputFilename){
        FILE *streamIn = fopen( inputFilename, "rb" );
        FILE *streamOut = fopen( outputFilename, "wb" );
        // disable stdio buffer
        setvbuf( streamIn, NULL, _IONBF, 0);
        setvbuf( streamOut, NULL, _IONBF, 0);
        bytes = (unsigned char*)malloc(bufferSize);
        while(true){
            readCount = fread(bytes, 1, bufferSize, streamIn);
            if(readCount <= 0)
                break;
            fwrite(bytes, 1, readCount, streamOut);
        }
        fclose( streamIn );
        fclose( streamOut );
        free( bytes );
    }
```

Java `FileInputStream` and `FileOutputStream` have a few private native methods that provide functionality for opening, reading, writing, and closing a file. They actually store a file handle internally that is used by these native methods, and call fread, fwrite, fopen, and fclose.

The native equivalent uses the functionality provided by `stdio.h`. Note that stdio by default creates a buffer for each stream. Here we explicitly disable the `stdio` buffering. The codes are otherwise similar. Table 5.1 shows the performance of the code segments with different sizes passed to their `read`/`fread` function. The tests were performed on a file over 16MB, and the timings were collected using a high-resolution timer. The Java tests were performed carefully to ensure that no house-keeping was performed while the tests ran. In addition, the VM was allowed to warm up and perform necessary compilation.

Even though some of the tests were performed sequentially in the same instance of the VM, care was taken to ensure that one test did not affect another. For additional details, you may view the test application provided on the companion CD-ROM at Code/Chapter 5/ IO Performance Test. Table 5.1 shows the performance of Java file IO using file input and output streams against the equivalent C code that was presented earlier. The data in the table has been normalized with respect to the optimal buffer size for the Java test.

TABLE 5.1 Java File IO versus Standard C File IO

Buffer Size	Java	Native
1B	80530%	65880%
1K	280%	230%
4K	180%	150%
8K	125%	110%
16K	100%	78%
32K	168%	60%
64K	158%	59%
128K	183%	64%
File Size	750%	600%

The best buffer size for the Java method was 16K, and 64K for the native function. Note that 16K buffer size did allow Java to run quite reasonably. In fact, it performed better than the native function that used an 8K buffer size, and it was only about 40 percent slower than the fastest native benchmark. The performance difference is because the Java code results in the invocation of native methods by the VM, which have some additional overhead. Additionally, the VM has to copy the data between the Java heap and system memory. Even though both the native and the Java benchmarks do depend on the drive and the implementation details of the underlying operating system, they are sufficient for relative comparisons.

Note that single-byte reads result in extremely poor performance for both the Java and native code. In fact, the one-byte Java test was more than 800 times slower than the Java test that used a 16K byte array. If you write a large file one byte at a time, you will be able to see the file slowly grow on the drive. When possible you should read and write data to a slow medium, such as a hard drive, in chunks. Multiples of 4K chunks are typically preferred in Java because they can be page aligned and allow the VM (and the OS) to transfer data more efficiently. Loading the entire file in a buffer and then writing it out not only results in a poor performance but also assumes that the system has enough free memory. It is important to know that when the VM needs to copy data from the Java heap to system memory, it uses a static temporary buffer (see Figure 5.11) for data up to 8K but must dynamically allocate a larger buffer so that it can copy larger amounts of data between the Java heap and system memory. Keep in mind that a larger buffer does not necessarily result in better performance and can, in fact, result in both more CPU usage and system heap fragmentation.

Table 5.2 shows the performance of different techniques. The first three listings are from Table 5.1 and are provided for easier comparison. The new tests in this table include a test that uses 16-K `BufferedInputStream` and `BufferOutputStream` objects, four tests that use direct and nondirect byte buffers, and a test that uses the `transferTo` method of `FileChannel`.

TABLE 5.2   The Performance of Different Java File IO Methods

Method	Performance
One byte	80530%
Array with the same size as the file	750%
Array with the size of 16K	100%
One-byte read with buffered streams of 16K	1600%
Nondirect buffer with the same size as the file	700%
Direct buffer with the same size as the file	690%
Direct buffer with the size of 64K	60%
Nondirect buffer with the size of 16K	110%
File channel transfer	700%

Table 5.2 shows that using `BufferedInputStream` and `BufferOutputStream` results in 16 times slower performance. This is because buffering results in an extra level of copying, which is the buffer labeled as intermediate buffer in Figure 5.11.

So, does this mean that buffering is not good? Note that even though using buffered streams is not the fastest possible approach, it performed more than 50 times faster than reading the data one byte at a time. The idea is that if you need to read bytes in small segments, you should use a buffer such as `InputStreamBuffer` or `OutputStreamBuffer`. If you can read data in chunks, you should definitely use an array and manage it in your own code. If you are reading data in optimal chucks, then there is no reason to use the Java buffer stream objects.

Note that the native and Java tests that read and write data in chunks (byte array, direct buffer, nondirect buffer, and channel transfer) and are as large as the file, perform similarly and just as poorly as each other do. This result is because when the overly large chunk is written, the primary bottleneck becomes the OS and the device. In general, the buffer of the device can be compared to a funnel. If a relatively small burst of data is written to the device, the buffer can hold the burst and let the device write out the data as soon as it gets the chance. However, if an excessive amount of data must be written to the drive, the buffer will not be able to hold all the data, and new data can be written into the buffer only as fast as it can be written to the device.

The direct buffer test does not perform much better for the very large buffer. On the other hand, you have probably noticed that a direct buffer of 64K in length performed very well. In fact, it performed exactly as the most optimal native operation. Because the buffer (or array) of a direct buffer resides in system memory, the VM does not have to copy the data.

The last entry, labeled as file channel transfer, does the following:

```
// channel to channel transfer
void test(String inputFilename, String outputFilename){
    File inFile = new File(inputFilename);
    File outFile = new File(outputFilename);
    FileInputStream fis = new FileInputStream(inFile);
    FileOutputStream fos = new FileOutputStream(outFile);
    FileChannel ifc = fis.getChannel();
    FileChannel ofc = fos.getChannel();

    ifc.transferTo(0, ifc.size(), ofc);
}
```

A `FileChannel` has `TransferFrom` and `TransferTo` methods that try to perform optimal transfers. They attempt to perform OS-level transfer and fall back to direct byte buffer transfer if lower-level transfers are not supported. The test performed here fell back to byte buffer transfer. A point that you should be aware of is that accessing the elements of a direct buffer and byte buffers in general is much more expensive (about 12 times) than accessing the elements of an array through accessors (see Table 5.3).

TABLE 5.3 Access Overhead of Byte Buffers

Structure	Performance
Byte array access (through accessors)	100%
Nondirect Byte Buffer	1187%
Direct Byte Buffer	1286%

As a last note in regard to direct buffers, you should know that because they are page aligned, they are created in 4K chunks. You should avoid making many small direct buffers, because 100 direct buffers that each have capacity of one byte will take up almost half a megabyte. In other words, creating 100 direct buffers with the capacity of one is as costly as creating 100 direct buffers with capacity of 4K.

When it comes to parsing text files, it does not make much difference whether you read one byte at a time, read an array of bytes, or wrap a `FileReader` or `InputStreamReader` with a `BufferedReader`. This is because they already use a buffer internally so that they can convert the characters in chunks. In fact, wrapping them with a BufferedReader can only slow down the parsing. If you want optimal text parsing, you should read the file as bytes and, if needed, use a charset to convert the bytes yourself. A custom reader can result in a significant performance gain. If you are sure that the input file contains only ASCII characters, you can simply cast each byte to a character without having to use charsets and paying the additional conversion costs.

SUMMARY

As you have seen in this chapter, it is possible to substantially improve serial reading and writing. Random file accesses are inefficient in comparison to serial access because the drive has to do a lot of seeking. In addition, buffering techniques do not pay off as much for random access. In fact, most games use resource files to pack many files together to reduce the overhead of locating, opening, and closing files. Some games even go as far as ordering the data in a resource file to match the order in which the files must be loaded in an attempt to reduce the load time. This is particularly important when data has to be read from a CD-ROM or DVD.

In this chapter, we have looked at the more important classes of the java.io and java.nio packages and seen how to use them. Perhaps the most important thing to take away from this chapter is the knowledge of what happens behind the scenes when IO, and particularly file IO, are performed. In addition, understanding of buffers and how they can be used to improve the performance of your game is important. Also, when it comes to performance, never make any assumptions about the performance of a task. Even if you find documentation that suggests certain results, if you need optimal performance, you have to find out for yourself. Much of the documentation that comes with JDK has to be generic and cannot provide VM-specific details. Keep in mind that changes to a version of VM, VMs implemented by different vendors, API changes, the underlying OS, and the hardware being used can result in significant performance changes.

6 Performance and the Java Virtual Machine

In This Chapter

- Introduction
- The Structure of the Virtual Machine
- Representation of Java Classes
- The Java Bytecode
- Runtime Execution Optimizations
- The Garbage Collector
- Measuring Performance
- Performance Tips
- Summary

INTRODUCTION

To make a Java game that has optimal performance, it is vital to understand some of the inner workings of the Java virtual machine (VM). The topics discussed in this chapter help you to understand how the Java VM (JVM) works so that you can get the most out of it for your games. The majority of this chapter focuses on the inner workings of the VM, which includes topics such as the optimizations performed by the HotSpot VM and the garbage collector (GC). A specific section of this chapter discusses benchmarking and profiling of a Java program. This chapter also has a dedicated performance tips section that offers numerous general game-programming performance tips as well as Java-specific performance tips.

THE STRUCTURE OF THE VIRTUAL MACHINE

The Java VM is in many ways similar to a typical machine or computer. It has a set of opcodes that perform operations such as loading and storing data. It has opcodes that can perform arithmetic computations and manipulate data. It distinguishes between floating-point and integer types. It has a *program counter* (PC) register that keeps track of the current instruction being executed. It also has registers for storing the operand and the result of an instruction.

Many computers use special-purpose registers for some of their instructions. Instead of using special-purpose registers, a stack machine uses a stack that serves as a list of registers. This approach significantly simplifies the design of the machine. The machine instructions simply pop their operands from the stack and push their result back onto the stack. Because a stack can be as large as necessary, a computation can use as many registers as it needs without having to worry about the number of registers available on the machine. Many of the Texas Instruments™ calculators are stack machines. The Java VM is a stack machine. It is actually a virtual stack machine because it is not physical hardware but a machine that is implemented in software.

Threads are structures used by the JVM to keep track of an execution state. Every thread has a program counter that keeps track of the current instruction (or bytecode) being executed. This is, in a way similar, to the PC register of a typical machine. A *frame* is a structure that represents the state of a method that has not completed or returned. Every thread has a stack of frames. The top frame corresponds to the current method being executed. This stack is typically referred to as a *call stack*. Every Java frame has an array that stores the values of all local variables. The local variables array is allocated when a frame is created. In Java, every frame also has its own *operand stack*, which should not be confused with the frame stack (or call stack) of a thread. The operand stack is the stack that acts as a list of registers for the VM instructions and is what makes the VM a stack machine.

The VM allocates a chunk of the system memory when it is launched. This chunk of memory is referred to as the Java heap. The memory consumed by Java objects is allocated from the Java heap. When the new operator is used, it essentially asks the VM to allocate a chunk of memory from the Java heap and return a reference to it. In addition to typical Java objects used in a program, frames (and, hence, local variables) can be allocated from the heap. Depending on the implementation of a VM, the heap may also contain the code (or bytecodes) of the methods of an application. Keep in mind that anyone can implement a JVM as long as it follows the specifications defined by Sun Microsystems.

The JVM has a GC that manages the data created during the lifetime of the VM. In Java, we do not have direct control over the heap, and the reclamation of objects is the responsibility of the GC. The GC is also responsible for compacting the Java heap to reduce memory fragmentation. We will discuss the GC in detail in this chapter.

An implementation of the JVM may choose to have a runtime-optimizing compiler. The compiler can optimize the bytecodes of a method and compile them to the language of the underlying hardware to increase the execution efficiency of an application. The HotSpot VM has this capability. We will have an in-depth discussion of some of the optimizations performed by the HotSpot VM.

REPRESENTATION OF JAVA CLASSES

In this section, we will look at both the compiled and runtime representation of a Java class. The compiled representation is the binary data outputted by a compiler. The runtime representation is the representation derived from the compiled version, which is used during runtime.

Compiled Representation

A Java class file stores information about its corresponding class. It stores information such as the type of the class, the type of its superclass, the fields, and the bytecodes of its methods. The following is a C-like structure that describes the general layout of a class file. The types u2 and u4 represent two- and four-byte values, respectively.

```
ClassFile {
    u4 magic;
    u2 minor_version;
    u2 major_version;
    u2 constant_pool_count;
    cp_info constant_pool[];
    u2 access_flags;
    u2 this_class;
    u2 super_class;
    u2 interfaces_count;
    u2 interfaces[];
    u2 fields_count;
    field_info fields[];
    u2 methods_count;
    method_info methods[];
    u2 attributes_count;
    attribute_info attributes[];
}
```

The item labeled magic stores the value 0xCAFEBABE, which is used to check whether the file is a Java class file. The items minor_version and major_version are used for keeping track of the version of the file to ensure that the compiled representation is compatible with a specific version of the VM. For example, if an opcode specific to newer VMs is used in the class file, an older VM that does not understand the opcode should know that the class file is incompatible.

The constant_pool table contains many different types of information. The information includes string constants and structures that are used to represent references to classes, methods, and fields of other classes. The constant pool table is in many ways similar to a symbol table used by C/C++ compilers. C/C++ files are compiled to intermediate object files, which are then linked together to generate an executable or library file. Each C/C++ file is compiled to an object file that uses a symbol table to keep track of its unresolved symbols. During the link stage, symbolic references are resolved and replaced by actual offsets. Because Java files are linked during runtime, as opposed to at compile time, symbolic references are needed during runtime. Therefore, they are stored in class files.

The access_flags item is a mask that indicates whether the class is public, final, and so forth. this_class and super_class are indices into the constant_pool table where information on the fully qualified name of the corresponding classes can be found. Similarly, the interfaces array stores indices into the constant_pool table where information on the direct interfaces of the class can be found.

The fields and methods tables represent the information about the fields and methods of the class. Each element in the fields table contains the following information:

```
field_info {
    u2 access_flags;
    u2 name_index;
    u2 descriptor_index;
    u2 attributes_count;
    attribute_info attributes[attributes_count];
}
```

The access_flags contains masks that indicate whether the field is private, static, and so forth. The name_index indicates where the name of the field can be found in the constant pool table. The descriptor_index is a string that describes the type of the field and is also stored in the constant pool table. If a field is constant, an entry in its attributes table provides information such as the length of the value and the index at which the value can be found.

Each element in the methods table contains the following information:

```
method_info {
    u2 access_flags;
    u2 name_index;
    u2 descriptor_index;
    u2 attributes_count;
    attribute_info attributes[attributes_count];
}
```

The descriptor of a method is a string that describes the type of its arguments as well as its return type. For example, `"(I)V"` describes a method that takes an `int` and returns `void`. The `descriptor_index` stores the index in the constant pool table where the descriptor of the method can be found. There are many different types of `attribute_info` of which some correspond to methods, some to classes, and others to fields. The `attributes` table of a method can indicate, for example, whether a method is deprecated and what exceptions it can throw. More important, the `attributes` table of a method contains a `code_attribute` element that stores the bytecodes of a method and looks like the following:

```
code_attribute {
    u2 attribute_name_index;
    u4 attribute_length;
    u2 max_stack;
    u2 max_locals;
    u4 code_length;
    u1 code[code_length];
    u2 exception_table_length;
    exc_info    exception_table[];
    u2 attributes_count;
    attribute_info attributes[attributes_count];
}
```

The `max_stack` item indicates the maximum depth of the operand stack required for executing the method. `max_locals` indicates the number of local variables in the method, which is used to allocate the local variables array when a frame is allocated. The `code` array stores the bytecodes of the method. The elements in the `attributes` table of a `code_attribute` do not have to be populated.

Runtime Representation

A Java class file must be represented during runtime so that it can be used by the VM as well as by a Java program. The VM has to understand classes for many tasks.

For example, when the new operator is used, the VM has to know how many bytes of memory must be allocated to represent an object of a specific type. The VM also has to understand different Java types so that it can perform runtime type checking or even access the members of a class or invoke its methods.

There are also times when a Java program must understand Java classes during runtime. For example, the following code segment uses a string to retrieve an arbitrary class and make an instance of it. The output of the segment is MonsterEntity's toString.

```java
class MonsterEntity{
    public String toString(){
        return "MonsterEntity's toString";
    }
}

class Sample{

    public static void main(String args[]){

        Object object = null;
        String name = "MonsterEntity";

        try{
            Class entityType = Class.forName(name);
            object = entityType.newInstance();
        }catch (Exception e){}

        System.out.println(object.toString());
    }
}
```

As far as a Java program is concerned, Java classes are represented as instances of the java.lang.Class class. The Java primitive types such as boolean, int, and float are also represented as instances of the Class class. The same holds for arrays and even the void keyword. A Class object can contain information such as the name, superclass, fields, and methods of a class. Such information is useful for obtaining information about a class during runtime, a process known as reflection.

The Java VM specifications do not give a specific internal representation that must be used by every VM implementation. This is because the specifications try not to impose unnecessary restrictions so that the implementers of a VM can make their design decisions based on what is appropriate for the target platform. The internal representation is typically a C struct. Some VMs, such as the Sun HotSpot

VMs, use multiple internal representations to track different information that corresponds to a class. By using different data structures, the more complicated VMs can track various data, such as the optimized version of a class, more efficiently. On the other hand, simpler VMs such as the KVM keep track of only a small set of data that is necessary. The KVM is an extremely lean implementation of the Java virtual machine, which has been designed for use in devices that have little available memory. In general, the internal runtime representation of a class is in many ways similar to the compiled representation. For example, it has a constant pool table, which is used to resolve unresolved symbolic references. The runtime version of the constant pool table of a class may store other information as well. For example, it may store information that can allow for direct (or nonsymbolic) access to methods and fields of other objects. The internal representation also needs to keep track of the bytecodes of the methods of a class.

The Loading Process

A *class loader* is responsible for taking the compiled representation of a class and constructing an instance of java.lang.Class. Most applications simply use the class loader that is already included with the VM, which is also known as the bootstrap loader or system class loader. It is possible to write a custom class loader by extending the java.lang.ClassLoader class. A custom class loader can be used to load a class from a source other than a class file. For example, if an application wants to load a class that is stored in memory as an array of bytes, it must use a custom class loader.

When a class is being loaded, it must be verified and prepared. The verification of a class is extensive. The verification process includes checking the entries of the constant pool table to ensure that they are proper. Some entries in the table refer to data at some other index of the table. Because, for example, a symbolic reference to a field needs to indicate the name of the class as well as the name and type of the field to which it refers, it contains additional indices that specify where such information can be found. The verification process will make sure that the indices are valid and refer to data of the appropriate type. In addition to verifying the integrity of the constant pool table, every single bytecode of the methods of a class is examined to make sure that it has legal operands. This may seem odd because such verifications are the job of the compiler that generated the bytecodes. Even though the compiler does perform these tests, they must be performed again when a class is loaded. These checks are important for the VM because it needs to prevent incorrect bytecodes from being executed. The VM does not assume that some Java compiler has outputted correct bytecodes. This rechecking is also important because a program may choose to generate code during runtime and ask the VM to execute it. Examples of other checks include making sure jump instructions jump to valid locations, array accesses are valid, and symbolic links are legitimate. As you can guess, these verifications directly affect the startup time of an application.

After a class has been loaded and verified, an implementation of a VM may choose to resolve its symbolic references. Sun HotSpot VMs do not resolve symbolic references at load time. They put off the resolution of the references as long as possible, a process known as late binding. Let's consider the case where class A calls a method in class B. When the VM invokes the method of class B, it first makes sure that the class has been loaded and then looks for the corresponding method in class B. If class B has not been loaded already, the VM loads and verifies it. The other option would have been to resolve all symbols when a class is loaded. Such an approach would cause all the classes used by an application to get loaded when the VM launches. This approach would, of course, substantially increase the startup time of the application. However, loading and verification would not be necessary once the application is ready to run. When a symbolic reference is resolved, a VM may choose to store a direct reference to the method so that it does not have to resolve the symbolic reference every time it needs to invoke a method. In fact, this is what Sun HotSpot VMs do. After a reference is resolved, the direct reference is stored in the constant pool table, and the bytecodes of the invoking method is changed to take advantage of the direct reference instead of using the symbolic reference.

As a side note, if the need to run more than one Java application at the same time arises, it is possible to run all of them in a single instance of the VM. To do so, the VM must guarantee that the classes of the different applications (that may have the same name) are not mistaken for one another. Because of this, the VM recognizes classes by their name along with the class loader that loaded the class.

THE JAVA BYTECODE

A Java compiler such as javac.exe is responsible for translating source files written in the Java language to a machine language, or, more specifically, the Java VM's language. The instructions or bytecodes outputted by the compiler are not dependent on the Java language. In fact, many compilers can translate source files written in other languages to Java VM's language. The VM's language is essentially an assembly language for a stack machine.

Every JVM instruction contains an opcode that specifies the operation that must be performed. The 8-bit opcode can be any of the predefined opcodes recognized by the VM. The JVM has more than 200 but less than 256 opcodes, which means that a bytecode needs only 8 bits to store the opcode. Most opcodes either read from or write to the operand stack. Some manipulate local variables, and others rely on the constant pool table to accomplish a task.

Bytecode Examples

The following are the bytecodes of a simple method that simply adds the value of two variables:

```
public static void arithmetic(){
    int var1 = 10;
    int var2 = var1;
    var1 = var1 + var2;
}

0:   bipush  10
2:   istore_0
3:   iload_0
4:   istore_1
5:   iload_0
6:   iload_1
7:   iadd
8:   istore_0
9:   return
```

The bytecodes of the method are rather straightforward. Before we go over the details, recall that every Java frame has a local variables array that stores the values of all the local variables. If a method has two local variables, the local variables array will have the length of two. If the method is nonstatic, the length of the array will be three and the entry at index zero will be the reference to the object whose method was invoked. The reference corresponds to the this keyword. The length of the array is determined at compile time and stored in the max_locals field of the code_attribute structure shown earlier.

The instruction or bytecode at address zero pushes the constant 10 onto the stack using bipush. Then istore_0 pops an integer from the stack and stores it in local variable at index zero, which corresponds to var1. Then the value of var1 is loaded onto the stack. Instruction istore_1, which is at address four, pops the value from the stack and saves it in var2. iload_0 and iload_1 push the values of var1 and var2 onto the stack, respectively. iadd pops two integers from the stack, adds them, and pushes the result back onto the stack. The value is then popped from the stack using the istore_0 instruction, which is the instruction at address eight, and stored in var1. The return instruction tells the VM that we are done in this method. Note that throughout this method the depth of the operand stack does not grow beyond two.

As you might have noticed, iload, istore, and iadd instructions all perform integer operations. If you want to add two longs together, you must use lload, lstore, and ladd instead. Similar instructions are available for other types, such as floats and doubles. If you have played with any assembly code before, you may find the redundancy of some of the instructions to be odd. Because the operand stack must store values of different lengths, the VM has to have type-specific opcodes so that it knows how many bytes to pop off the stack. For example, an integer occupies four bytes in the stack whereas a long needs eight. Therefore, each instruction must know how many bytes of the operand stack are occupied by its operand. It is important to note that integer values are the VM's favorite type. For example, a number of conditional branch opcodes are specific to integers and not available for other types. Another example is the iinc opcode, which increments a local variable of type integer without having to explicitly load the value onto the stack, add a value to it, and then store the result. Such operations are more efficient in terms of both memory and speed because the length of a method is reduced. The boolean type is arguably the VM's least favorite type. In fact, the VM does not even recognize the boolean type. The Java compilers are responsible for converting booleans to integers. The same is partially true for bytes, chars, and shorts. They are converted to integers and treated as integers. This behavior is in part because if every type had its own instruction sets, there would be over 256 different opcodes. This means that the opcodes would have to be two bytes long, which would have a significant effect on memory consumption. Instructions such as bipush and sipush push byte and short values onto the stack while at the same time converting them to integers. Note that in the example shown earlier, the first line pushed the constant 10 using the opcode bipush. This is because the compiler realized that the number 10 fits in one byte. Even though 10 is recognized as a byte, it is pushed onto the stack such that it occupies four bytes as an integer would. Again, this allows the VM to avoid having to explicitly understand the byte type.

Another example that it is a little more involved follows. You can view the bytecodes of a method by executing javap.exe on a class that contains the method of interest.

```
public int factorial(int number){
    int result = 1;

    for(int i=2; i<=number; i++)
        result *= i;

    return result;
}

0:    iconst_1
1:    istore_2
2:    iconst_2
3:    istore_3
4:    iload_3
5:    iload_1
```

```
6:    if_icmpgt 19
9:    iload_2
10:   iload_3
11:   imul
12:   istore_2
13:   iinc 3, 1
16:   goto 4
19:   iload_2
20:   ireturn
```

The first instruction loads the constant 1 onto the stack. istore_2 pops the value off the stack and stores it in the local variable at index two of the local variables array. Note that the variable at index one is number, and because the method is an instance method, the variable at index zero is initialized to store the this pointer. if_icmple at address six compares the top two integers on the stack, which are the values of the loop counter and the constant 1. If the value of the loop counter is less than or equal to 1, the program counter of the current thread will be set to 19. Note that the numbers next to each instruction are not line numbers but the address of the instructions. Because the opcode if_icmple is always followed by a short representing the target address, the instruction immediately after it is three bytes over. That is one byte used to store the opcode and two to store the short value. The following code segment is the recursive version of the factorial method, which demonstrates how method invocations work:

```
public int factorialRecursive(int number){
    if(number == 2)
        return 2;

    return number * factorialRecursive(number-1);
}
```

```
0:    iload_1
1:    iconst_2
2:    if_icmpne 7
5:    iconst_2
6:    ireturn
7:    iload_1
8:    aload_0
9:    iload_1
10:   iconst_1
11:   isub
12:   invokevirtual #9
15:   imul
16:   ireturn
```

The instruction `aload_0` loads a reference from local variable zero onto the stack, which is the `this` pointer. Because the method is an instance method, a reference to the object whose method is being called must be pushed onto the stack before the method is invoked. The `invokevirtual` opcode takes the index into the constant pool entry that contains the symbolic reference to the method that should be called.

As mentioned already, some bytecodes rely on the content of the constant pool table. The constant pool table must support types such as integers, longs, floats, and doubles, as well as strings. In addition to these basic types, data such as `MethodeRef_info` and `FieldRef_info` are used to represent symbolic references to fields and methods. They both provide information about the class name and the corresponding field or method. Opcodes such as `new`, `getfield`, `invokespecial`, and `instanceof` are just a few examples of opcodes that rely on the constant pool table. When an instruction such as `invokespecial` is executed, the symbolic reference must be resolved before the method is invoked. That is, the symbolic reference must be validated to ensure that it is appropriate, and if it is, a reference to the method can be retrieved. After the method is resolved, a VM may choose to replace the opcode with one that uses the resolved reference thereafter.

RUNTIME EXECUTION OPTIMIZATIONS

Interpreted languages generally have significant disadvantage when it comes to execution performance. This shortcoming is because the code is executed by a VM instead of directly running on the physical machine. The VM is an emulator that allows code written for a stack machine to run on a specific hardware. This also means that Java bytecodes do not take advantage of the capabilities of the underlying machine. This is, of course, what allows the code to be platform independent. One way to speed up the execution of Java bytecodes is to make actual hardware that understands Java opcodes so that it can execute the bytecodes directly. The disadvantage would be that the code would run fast only on such machines and would still have to be emulated on other hardware.

Another option is to compile the bytecodes to instructions that are native to the underlying machine, so that the bytecodes do not have to be interpreted by the VM. This approach raises the following question: when should the bytecodes be converted to native CPU instructions? Should they be compiled before runtime or during runtime? Compiling Java source code or bytecodes directly to the language of the underlying machine would cause the resulting code to be platform dependent. On the other hand, compiling bytecodes to machine code during runtime allows for code that is platform independent and efficient. This is exactly the job of a just-in-time (JIT) compiler. The JIT compiler is obviously platform dependent because it has to understand the instructions of the underlying machine. This means if a VM is implemented for a specific platform and comes with a JIT compiler, Java bytecodes can be executed as efficiently as code that is specifically written for that platform.

JIT compilers were shipped with JRE 1.2. The first versions of Sun VMs that came with a JIT compiler used to aggressively load and compile the methods of all classes to, say, Intel 586 instructions. Before compiling bytecodes to native instructions, the symbolic references would have to be resolved. As mentioned in a previous section, to resolve symbolic references, classes that are referred to have to be loaded first. Consequently, when the VM was launched, all classes were loaded and compiled. This approach resulted in significant startup time. Besides the additional startup time needed to load all classes, additional memory was also required. Even worse, extra memory was required to store all the additional native CPU instructions that were generated from the compiled bytecodes. In other words, the use of JIT compilers by older VMs caused faster code to be produced by consuming significant amount of memory.

The HotSpot VMs are the latest generation of VMs. They are designed to allow for even better performance while reducing the amount of required memory. The HotSpot VMs are designed based on the idea that most of the execution time of a program is spent in a small segment of the code. The 90-10 rule proposes that 90 percent of the execution time is spent in 10 percent of the code. Instead of trying to load, optimize, and compile the entire code of an application, HotSpot VMs load classes only when needed and try to locate the hot spot of the applications and perform substantial optimizations on that segment. This strategy has proven to be very successful.

In addition to compiling bytecodes to native code, making sure that the produced native code is well optimized can result in significant performance gains. Many C/C++ compilers perform optimizations such as loop unrolling, inlining, and data rearrangement to produce more optimized code. The same holds for Java code. More optimized Java bytecodes can result in better performance when the code is interpreted, as well as better native code when the bytecodes are compiled to native code. Static Java compilers (such as javac.exe) can perform optimizations similar to C/C++ optimizing compilers. Older JDK compilers supported the -0 option, which would signal the compiler to perform additional optimizations and generate optimized bytecodes. The optimizations included inlining and many other typical optimizations. The compiler that comes with JDK 1.4 does not perform any special optimizations. In fact, it does less than the older compilers. The few simple optimizations include constant folding and inlining of final fields. Constant folding means to compute constants at compile time, such as the following values:

```
final int MASK_A = 1<<1;
final int MASK_B = 1<<2;
final int MASK_DEFAULT = MASK_A | MASK_B;
```

Inlining of final values means that if someone refers to these members, instead of a symbolic reference, the actual value would be embedded in the code.

The more sophisticated optimizations are left for HotSpot, which can perform aggressive optimizations on the hot spots of the code. HotSpot keeps track of how many times each method is invoked. Once the counter breaches a threshold, the method is considered to be hot and is optimized and compiled to native code. This approach has a problem,—it does not promote a method that has a critical loop so that it can be compiled earlier than a typical method. This issue has been resolved by allowing loop iterations to increment the hotness of a method. Therefore, if a method that has a lengthy loop is called, the VM may decide to compile the method to native code, even if the method is called only once.

Do you think that it is okay for the VM to compile a hot method but wait until the method is invoked again before it can replace the method with its compiled version? The first version of HotSpot simply waited for the next invocation of the method so that it could start using the compiled version. Note that if the method has a loop that runs indefinitely, the bytecodes may never get replaced by the compiled code. This issue can cause unexpected results when developers write micro-benchmarks to time-specific operations. Benchmarking is discussed in a later section of this chapter.

Newer versions of HotSpot perform on-stack replacement (OSR). OSR allows the VM to switch from executing bytecodes to native code while it is interpreting the bytecodes. This process is by no means a trivial task, because a custom version of the compiled code must be used so that the execution state of the native code is equivalent to that of the interpreted code. Therefore, certain instructions must be added to, for example, load values already computed by the interpreted code into the registers of the machine.

Because the VM can collect information about the runtime behavior of an application, it has a great advantage over static compilers. First, it can perform traditional optimizations in a manner that typical optimizing static compilers do not. Because the VM can locate the hot spots of the application, it can perform aggressive optimizations that are not worth doing to the entire code of an application. Note that many optimizations can result in lengthier code. For example, inlining and loop unrolling can cause a method to be much longer that its original version. This means that the code will take up more memory during runtime. HotSpot can avoid bloating the entire code by focusing on the more important parts. Second, HotSpot can perform optimizations that traditional static compilers cannot perform. For example, devirtualization is an optimization that cannot always be resolved at compile time. In addition, because at runtime the VM has values of variables available, it can perform additional dead-code eliminations that are not possible at compile time.

Devirtualization is one of the fundamental optimizations for object-oriented languages such as C++ and Java. Optimizations that allow virtual calls to be replaced by direct (or statically bound) calls are known as devirtualization. Let's take the time to go into details of the process. Virtual methods are the basis of object-oriented languages, the idea being that the functionality of a method is chosen based on the actual type of the object. In Java, all nonstatic and nonfinal methods are virtual. In other words, unlike C++, all methods are by default virtual. Note that even iterators and read methods are typically virtual. The following code segment shows the method print, which has been defined in ClassA and ClassB. Note that ClassB extends ClassA.

```
class ClassA{
    public void print(){
        System.out.println("ClassA.print()");
    }
}

class ClassB extends ClassA{
    public void print(){
        System.out.println("ClassB.print()");
    }
}
```

The following code segment should print out ClassA.print() and then ClassB.print(), despite the fact that both object1 and object2 are referred to by references of type ClassA.

```
class Sample{

    public static void main(String args[]){

        ClassA object1 = new ClassA();
        ClassA object2 = new ClassB();

        object1.print();
        object2.print();
    }
}
```

Because at compile time the actual type of a reference is not known (that is, whether a reference of type ClassA refers to an instance of ClassA or ClassB), some runtime checks must determine which method should be called. Even though this check its not extremely expensive, the bad news is that if the compiler cannot tell which method needs to be called, it will not be able to inline it. Inlining is one of the most important optimization techniques that cannot be disregarded. Why is inlining so extremely important? The more important reasons are method invocations in general are not cheap, and when many small methods are concatenated into one, much better global optimizations can be performed.

You might have noticed that technically, a compiler can figure out the actual type of the object in the code segment shown earlier. That is correct. A compiler can figure out that object2 points to an instance of ClassB, even though it is declared as a reference of type ClassA. By tracing back to where the object is created, the compiler can determine its real type. Even though this is possible, the segment provided earlier is one of the most straightforward scenarios. If a method, for example, receives a parameter of type Object, the compiler would have quite a challenge trying to trace back to figure out its real type. Besides, even the most sophisticated compilers cannot resolve the following:

```
ClassA object3;
String name = "ClassB";
try{
    object3 = (ClassA)Class.forName(name).newInstance();
}catch (Exception e){}
```

As a side note, if you look at the bytecode that corresponds to invoking a final method, you might be surprised. The bytecode for invoking a virtual and final (nonvirtual) method are identical. Only constructors, private methods, methods invoked with the super keyword, and static methods are statically bound. This is because the Java language specifications explicitly note that removing the final keyword from a method should not break compatibility with existing binaries. That is, if ClassB invokes methodA in ClassA, and methodA is final, if methodA is changed so that it is no longer final, there should not be the need to recompile ClassB. This rule, which is designed to promote binary compatibility, indirectly implies that final methods should not be resolved at compile time. This makes devirtualization during runtime an even more important optimization.

Dead-code elimination is another optimization that static compilers cannot do beyond basic measures. Even though removing dead-code does not sound like an important optimization and is even the requirement for Java compilers as defined in the language specifications, it can have great rewards when performed at runtime. Consider the case where a method is called and the value of a local variable is passed as one of its parameters. As far as that particular invocation is concerned, the passed-in parameters can be considered constant. In other words, if the method is inlined, significant chunks of code as well as checks can be potentially removed. This can make the inlining of nontrivial methods a bit more appealing.

It is important to mention that some runtime optimizations can be performed only based on certain assumptions. For example, devirtualization may assume that no other types are dynamically loaded. Dead-code elimination may assume that the value of certain variables will not change. Such optimistic or speculative assumptions can obviously prove to be wrong at a later point during runtime. If every optimization keeps tracks of its assumptions, when an assumption no longer holds, optimizations can be undone. This process is also known as deoptimization, which requires a form of OSR. Deoptimization is OSR performed in reverse, where native code is replaced with bytecodes.

Some of the other optimizations include array-bounds-check elimination and null-check elimination. Note that the more extensive the optimization performed by a compiler, the more CPU cycles it is likely to consume to generate optimized code. Optimizations that require little CPU time can be performed immediately; others can be performed in the background and replaced when the compilation is complete.

It is also important to note that the Sun VM has two different variations. The Client VM, which is the default, has a faster startup time and requires less memory. This is in part because it does not perform the more complex optimizations. On the other hand, the Server VM assumes that the host machine has a reasonable amount of resources and that the application will be running long enough to make more complex optimizations worth performing.

THE GARBAGE COLLECTOR

Many developers who are not used to automatic memory management tend to be very skeptical about the performance of the garbage collector (GC). Memory management is an issue that has to be dealt with for just about any application. Many games come with custom memory managers that perform compaction to minimize fragmentation of the heap. In addition to performing memory compaction, the GC is responsible for allocating and reclaiming objects during runtime. This task is especially important because unlike C/C++, all Java objects are allocated from the heap. In Java, all objects are allocated using the new operator, which returns a reference to the allocated object. The only data that is allocated on the stack (in a frame) is primitive data types as well as object references. Nevertheless, even the frames are allocated on the heap.

Over the years, many improvements have been made to the GC. JDK 1.4.2 comes with four collection algorithms, each of which is designed for applications with different requirements. The one-size-fits-all approach to garbage collection does not work well for the wide variety of applications written in Java. For example, a Java program that runs on a server may not be concerned about pauses. On the other hand, even the slightest pauses in a real-time program such as a game can be noticeable. Fortunately, different algorithms can meet the needs of different applications. In addition to different algorithms, the behavior of the GC is highly tunable through different parameters.

The Default Collector

A garbage collector must determine which objects are garbage so that it can collect them. A simple approach would be to traverse the entire object graph. Any object that cannot be reached can be safely flagged as garbage. Though possible, this approach is extremely inefficient. Instead, the memory is divided into three partitions. Each partition corresponds to objects of a specific generation. The first partition stores young objects. Young objects are those that have recently been created. The second partition stores tenured objects. The third partition stores objects that are considered permanent, such as instances of `java.lang.Class`. A newly created object is part of the young generation. Young objects are assumed to die soon; however, if a young object survives through enough collection passes and shows that it was not used only for a brief computation, it is promoted to the tenure partition.

By separating objects that are likely to die from those that are likely to stay around for a while, the overall cost of garbage collection can be reduced. By using separate partitions, the GC will not have to traverse the entire object graph when it wants to reclaim dead objects. In addition, it can perform housekeeping on each partition at different intervals. Generally, when a partition becomes full, housekeeping is performed on it to reclaim dead objects and compact the live objects. The garbage collection of the young generation is referred to as a minor collection, and the collection of the tenured generation is referred to as a major collection. A minor collection is generally much faster than a major collection, primarily because the size of the young generation is typically much smaller than the tenured generation. In addition, because it is likely that most of the objects in the young generation are dead, its compaction requires even less time. The fewer objects survive, the less copying and updating has to occur. Note that when a minor collection is performed, not all dead objects can be collected because some of them may be referred to by dead objects in the tenured generation that have not been collected yet.

When dead objects are collected, the corresponding partition becomes fragmented. To defragment or compact the live objects in a partition, the objects in the partition have to be moved. Even though Java objects are moved during garbage collection, references to Java objects remain valid. That is, as far as a code segment is concerned, it should still be able to access the objects that were moved. To deal with this problem, the VM can represent references as handles. A handle is an identifier that can be used to retrieve a direct pointer to an object in the heap. By using a handle, when the location of an object is changed, the identifier that is used to retrieve the direct pointer can still be used and does not have to change. This approach was taken by older VMs, but newer VMs use handleless objects because accessing an object through a handle requires an extra level of indirection, which is more expensive than using direct pointers in a typical C/C++ program. Instead of referring to objects indirectly, newer VMs allow Java code to use the actual memory address of the objects. This approach significantly increases the time required to access an object. On the other hand, using actual pointers means that if an object has multiple references to it, when it is relocated by the GC, every single reference must be updated so that it stores the new memory address. Note that even though the VMs that use handles pay a greater cost to access an object, when they perform housekeeping, they have to update only a single item. Despite this fact, handleless objects have proven to allow for better overall performance.

The behavior of a collection algorithm can be described in terms of *footprint*, *pauses*, *promptness*, and *throughput*. Footprint and pauses are rather obvious from their names. Promptness refers to how promptly dead objects are reclaimed. Throughput is the amount of time that a running program does not spend on garbage collection. There are four collection algorithms available. The default and incremental collectors are beneficial for most applications that run on single CPU machines. The throughput and concurrent collectors are intended for multiprocessor machines. The default collector is often the best choice for games. It is highly tunable and worthy of fully understanding.

As mentioned earlier, a minor collection occurs when the young generation is full, and a major collection occurs when the tenured generation is full. The size of the heap and each of its partitions directly affects the behavior of the garbage collector. The size of the heap can be set using the -Xmx option. Even though a larger heap reduces the major collection intervals, you should note that the collection cost of a larger heap is higher. This means that even though the GC will not run as often, when it does perform housekeeping it has more work to do. The -Xms option can be used to set the initial size of the heap so that even with a large maximum heap size, the collection intervals can occur more often and, therefore, have smaller pauses. When the VM launches, the entire space is reserved, but if the -Xms is smaller than the -Xmx, only a portion of each partition is actually used. Setting both the initial size and the maximum size to the same value indicates that the heap should always be used in its entirety. If the initial size is smaller than the maximum size, at each collection, the size of the heap is changed so that a certain ratio of free space to used space is maintained. When the size of the heap is changed, it will not exceed the boundaries set by the -Xmx and -Xms options. The parameters -XX:MinHeapFreeRatio and -XX:MaxHeapFreeRatio are used by the VM to compute the appropriate size of the heap. The -XX:MinHeapFreeRatio parameter is used to grow the heap size to make sure that enough free space is available. Similarly, -XX:MaxHeapFreeRatio is used to shrink the heap size.

Note that changing the size of the heap means that the size of each partition can be affected. Because the size of the young generation is an important factor for just about every application, additional parameters are available for tweaking its size. The -XX:NewRatio allows you to declare the ratio of the heap that should be used for the young (or new) generation. So setting -XX:NewRatio=2 means there should be one unit allotted for the young generation for every two units allotted to the tenured generation. This parameter is used to compute the maximum size of the young generation. Because of the importance of the size of the young generation, the parameters -XX:NewSize and -XX:MaxNewSize can be used to bound its size. Similarly, -XX:PermSize and -XX:MaxPermSize can be used to bound the size of the permanent generation.

Other Collectors

The incremental garbage collector, also known as the train collector, is another collector that can be beneficial for a game because it is not necessarily intended for multiprocessor machines. The tenured generation is typically larger than the young generation and does not have many dead objects, so its housekeeping is far more expensive than the housekeeping of the young generation. The incremental collector tries to reduce pauses by breaking up the housekeeping of the tenured generation over multiple, smaller steps. At every minor collection, part of the tenured generation is collected as well. Because this algorithm only cleans part of the tenured generation, some complications arise. For example, the collector has to keep track of how much work is left. This means that the throughput is lower. In addition, because collecting only part of the tenured generation at a time can cause the overall collection of the tenured generation to take longer, the promptness of this collector cannot be as good as the promptness of the default collector. In other words, dead objects can stay around longer. Having a smaller young generation can help the collection of the tenured generation to occur more often for this specific collection algorithm. Using the incremental collector can also mean that the tenured generation is likely to become fragmented. To work around this issue, using a larger tenured generation can help reduce the fragmentation related concerns. In essence, the incremental collector reduces pauses at the cost of additional bookkeeping, as well as longer and more frequent minor collection. You should generally avoid using the incremental collector. If the default GC results in noticeable pauses and tweaking it does not rectify the problem, you can then consider the incremental collector. The command-line option -Xincgc can be specified to use the incremental collector.

The remaining two collectors are the throughput and concurrent collectors. They can pay off substantially on multiprocessor machines. The throughput collector is similar to the default collector but uses multiple threads to collect the young generation. This approach causes the minor collections to be very smooth. The overhead of multiple threads will be minuscule if the machine has more than one processor. On a single-processor machine, this collector is likely not to perform as well as the default collector.

The concurrent collector is also similar to the default collector but instead uses a separate thread that runs concurrent with the application threads and collects the tenured generation. The thread should be able to collect the tenured generation before it becomes full. If it does not, a full collection is forced. A full collection means that all the application threads will be paused and then resumed after the tenured generation is fully collected. Even though it is possible to have some improvement on a single-processor machine, the concurrent collector often results in poor performance on a single-processor machine. The command-line option -XX:+Use-ConcMarkSweepGC can be specified to use the concurrent collector.

MEASURING PERFORMANCE

To improve the performance of your game, you must be able to measure its performance. Benchmarking is a technique used to measure the performance of specific routines or even the overall performance of an application. In contrast, instead of computing a performance score for a specific task or a performance score for the game, profiling is a technique that tries to gather a lot of information about different tasks so that their performances can be compared with one another. By doing so, a profiler can help identify performance bottlenecks of a game. In the following sections, we will discuss benchmarking and profiling.

Benchmarking

There are two types of benchmarks. Micro-benchmarks are used to measure the performance of a specific part of the application, whereas macro-benchmarks are used to measure the overall performance of an application.

The idea behind micro-benchmarks is straightforward. If you want to measure the amount of time required to run a specific segment of code, you need a time stamp immediately before the segment is executed and another time stamp immediately after it completes executing. Subtracting the former time stamp from the latter one gives you the execution time of the segment. Once you know how long it took to execute the segment, you can modify its implementation and see whether the modified version performs better. Even though writing a micro-benchmark is conceptually straightforward, writing a micro-benchmark that benchmarks what you really want to benchmark is not a trivial task. Compilers such as Javac.exe and dynamic compilers such as HotSpot can perform optimizations that heavily affect the code you are trying to benchmark. The modifications can be significant enough to give you entirely misleading conclusions when you look at the results of the benchmark.

For example, if you want to measure the cost of invoking a method by measuring the time it takes to call an empty method, you may reach the conclusion that it is practically free. This is because the HotSpot may inline the method. When inlining occurs, the invocation will be replaced with the body of the method. In the case of an empty method, the invocation will be removed and nothing will be inserted. This means the only thing your micro-benchmark will measure is the time it takes to execute the method that retrieves the time stamps. This exact example can happen with a loop. If the runtime compiler decides to unroll a loop that does not have any code in its body, the loop may be entirely removed. Keep in mind that as newer VMs become available, more sophisticated optimizations may be performed on your code. In fact, an exact benchmark that you have used in the past may become useless. A runtime optimizing compiler may be sophisticated enough to realize that the result of some expensive computation is not used in the program and decide to remove an entire section of code.

If it were possible to disable specific optimizations when benchmarking an application, then writing benchmarks would be easier. Unfortunately, even though some compilers do provide some general options for controlling the optimizations, not all of them give total control over every single optimization. To write effective micro-benchmarks you should use the result of your computations. Even if you simply print a value computed by a method to the console, a compiler would not be able to remove the method. If you do not want a method to be inlined, pass a parameter to the method and add it to a public local variable in the object.

It is important to note that optimizing compilers love constant values. If it is guaranteed that a value will not be changed, compilers can use the value to perform optimizations such as pre-computing other values, loop unrolling, and dead-code elimination. You should try to use variables instead of constants when appropriate. For example, if you want to benchmark a loop that runs 10 times, you can store the value 10 in a variable and use the variable in the loop condition. The only problem with this approach is that a compiler can detect that a variable was initialized to a constant value but never modified. Therefore, it can still unroll the loop. A better approach is to use Integer.parseInt("10") as the terminating condition of the loop. Even the most sophisticated compilers cannot guarantee that the result of the computation is always the same value.

Keep in mind that an aggressive compiler may still be able to, say, unroll a loop if it really wants to. Recall from a previous section that a compiler can make opportunistic assumptions to perform additional optimization. As long as it keeps track of the assumptions that it makes and is capable of undoing an optimization, it can revert to the original code if an assumption is violated. In other words, the compiler can choose to use an arbitrary value as a constant so that it can perform some optimizations. However, it must be able to detect any changes to the variable so that it can deoptimize or undo the optimizations it made.

Executing a small segment of code may take fractions of a second, so you must make sure your measurements are useful. Note that the `System.currentMillies()` can have a very low resolution, depending on the underlying platform. If you use it to benchmark a segment that takes fewer than 10 milliseconds to execute, the time may not even be measurable. There are two ways of dealing with this issue. One is to use a timer that has higher resolution. This can work, but a better approach is to repeat the test numerous times and divide the overall time by the number of times the test was run. Repeating a test many times in a single run of the VM is also important because the VM will have the chance to start up and perform appropriate optimizations.

You should always check the latest VM options for interesting features. Options such as `-XX:CompileThreshold` and `-XX:MaxInlineSize` can give you a little control over what the HotSpot does. For example, setting `CompileThreshold` to a very low value ensures that HotSpot does its optimizations almost immediately. `MaxInlineSize` can be set to a low value to prevent the VM from inlining methods. `-XX:+PrintCompilation` can be used to find out which parts of the code are dynamically compiled. Note that the `x` and `xx` options change often, and you should read through the options of corresponding VM.

Unlike micro-benchmarks, macro-benchmarks try to measure the overall performance of an application with real-world data. They try to see how well an application will run in actual scenarios that the user may encounter. For example, an automated program can fly though the world and collect data to generate an overall score for how well the game ran. Some games test the capability of a machine by running the game with different settings. After performing a few tests, the score computed by the macro-benchmark can determine the highest settings that still allow the game to run well. Macro-benchmarks take much more effort to create, but a good macro-benchmark can be used throughout the development process to see how changes to the game affect the overall performance.

Profiling

The most fundamental step before optimizing a game is finding the performance bottlenecks. Many programmers try to optimize computations that are just not important enough. One can spend days trying to gain fractions of a percent when rather straightforward changes can result in substantial performance increase. Profilers are effective in locating the bottlenecks. Profilers are more accessible and easier to use than you may think. Many commercial and free profilers are available. If you have not used one already, you should definitely try them. Even JDK comes with a powerful profiler called hprof. It collects profiling information during runtime and writes them to an output file. You can open the output file in a text editor and look for specific tags. There are also free tools that read the outputted file to generate visual representation of the data. HPJmeter is one example of such a tool that is both free and well maintained. Even working with the text output is not too difficult. Commercial profilers such as Jprofiler, JProbe, and Optimizeit are valuable tools that are in many ways similar to hprof. They all use the JVM profiler interface (JVMPI) to collect information while a program executes. They also have additional powerful features that make them worth their price tag.

Execution

Here we will look at some general concepts and terminologies important to profiling. These concepts and terms are common to different profilers, even those written for a specific hardware and platform such as the Intel® VTune™. hprof enables you to collect information about CPU utilization as well as the state of the Java heap. hprof is a simple profiler agent that provides the base functionality provided by many commercial profilers. In addition, as mentioned earlier, tools such as HPJmeter use the data file outputted by hprof as their input and produce visual representation.

You can get the different possible options of hprof by executing the following command:

```
Java -Xrunhprof:help
```

The following lines are the more important option:

```
Option Name and Value    Description              Default
----                     ----                     ----
heap=dump|sites|all      heap profiling           all
cpu=samples|times|old    CPU usage                off
depth=<size>             stack trace depth        4
cutoff=<value>           output cutoff point      0.0001
```

The usage of the command-line parameter is as follows:

```
Java ... -Xrunhprof[:help]|[:<option>=<value>, ...]
    ApplicationClassName
```

The following line is a usage example:

```
Java -Xrunhprof:cpu=samples,depth=10,cutoff=0 MyGame
```

By default, the output of hprof is written to java.hprof.txt. The output file contains different tags such as TRACE, HEAP DUMP, SITES, CPU SAMPLES, and CPU TIME. Traces are *call stack* dumps that specify the locations of interest such as the location of where objects are allocated or the location of frequently called methods.

A *call graph* shows the relationship between different methods. It can be constructed from the traces outputted by hprof. For example, the following traces can be used to construct the call graph shown in Figure 6.1.

```
TRACE 1:
    ClassA.method1
    ClassA.main
TRACE 2:
    ClassA.method2
    ClassA.method1
    ClassA.main
TRACE 3:
    ClassA.method3
    ClassA.method1
    ClassA.main
```

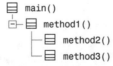

FIGURE 6.1   A simple call graph.

The main method is the root of the call graph because method1, method2, and method3 were called indirectly through the main method. Tools such as HPJmeter can easily construct the call graph from these traces. The depth option can be used to specify the depth of the traces saved by hprof. The larger the value, the deeper the traces can be. Note that if the depth is not deep enough, a complete call graph cannot be built. In addition, the cutoff option is used by the profiler to decide whether a trace should be excluded because it is insignificant. It is generally better to set the cutoff=0 so that no traces are left out. By doing so, a complete call graph can be constructed.

There are two common approaches to collecting information about the execution duration of different methods. One way is to actually time each method, and the other is to sample the running program every so often and take a brief peek at which methods are active. Even though measuring the exact execution time of different methods is useful, doing so can result in significant performance problems. To obtain exact times, every single method call has to be intercepted. The overhead can cause a program to perform disappointingly, which can in turn significantly skew the timing information. In contrast, sampling is a nonintrusive and statistical approach to estimating the execution time of different methods. The idea is to sample the running program at specific intervals and record the active methods. An active method is one that corresponds to the topmost frame in a call stack. The longer a method takes to execute and the more often a method is called, the more likely it is to be active when a sample is collected. Note that by doing so, we are not counting the number of times a method is invoked but simply estimating how much time is spent in a method. If enough samples are collected, a relatively accurate model of the program can be created.

hprof supports both the sampling and the timing approach. If you need to know the number of times a method is actually called, you cannot run the profiler in sampling mode. In addition, because the sampling approach finds out only about methods that happened to be active when the samples were taken, the call graph generated from its traces is usually incomplete.

The following lines are the profiling data collected by running the same application using cpu=times and then cpu=samples. Both tests were run for the same amount of time.

```
CPU TIME (ms) BEGIN (total = 210)
rank   self  accum   count trace method
   1 23.81% 23.81%     108     2 ClassA.method2
   2 14.29% 38.10%      24     1 ClassA.method1
   ...
CPU SAMPLES BEGIN (total = 4)
rank   self  accum   count trace method
   1 50.00% 50.00%       2     2 java.util.zip.ZipFile.open
   2 25.00% 75.00%       1     5 ClassA.method2
   ...
```

The output tagged with CPU TIME indicates that method2 ranked number one and constituted 23.81 percent of the execution time of the program. It also indicates that method2 was called 108 times. method2 showed up as significant in the sampling approach as well, but of course, the data from the two approaches is not identical because the latter is just an estimation.

As a side note, the time does not have to be actual time units and any abstract ticks can be sufficient to generate relative data. In addition, the runtime of a method is the accumulation of all the ticks spent in the method during all the calls to it.

When it comes to interpreting the timing information, there are two views of timing data, namely exclusive and inclusive times. Exclusive time is the time spent in the actual method without taking into account the amount of time spent in the methods it called. Inclusive time is the time spent in a method along with all the methods it called. Inclusive times are a practical and useful way of associating times with tasks. For example, they can help you realize that updating the AI of a character is taking a considerable amount of time, even though the task consists of many small computations that are not significant by themselves. Inclusive times of the methods, along with a decent call graph, can be used to compute their exclusive times. On the other hand, computing inclusive results from exclusive times is problematic and can yield only estimations. For example, if multiple traces lead to `method1`, simply accumulating the exclusive time of `method1` will cause problems when the traces have the same root. On the other hand, inclusive times are misleading when dealing with recursive methods. Using `cpu=times` or `cpu=samples` implicitly uses exclusive times. If you wish to look at inclusive times, you can run the profiler with `cpu=old`.

JDK comes with another tool that can give you an alternative way of looking at your application. By using the `-Xprof`, as opposed to `-Xrunhprof`, you can find out how much time is spent in interpreted versus compiled code. When providing information about the amount of time spent in interpreted code, it also notes how much of the time was spent in native code that was called from interpreted code. `Xprof` has a section labeled "Stub," which lists methods that were called through JNI. The interpreted column under that section specifies the amount of work it took before the native method was called, and the native column shows how much time was spent in the native function.

Memory

To solve memory-related problems and bottlenecks, you need to obtain information about the state and activities of the GC. The standard option `-verbose:gc` can be used to view the activities of the GC. Using `-verbose:gc` will print information such as the following to the console window. You can use `-Xloggc:log.txt` to have the GC activities written to a log file.

```
[GC 16952K->16916K(19640K), 0.0009694 secs]
[Full GC 17268K->100K(19640K), 0.0173905 secs]
```

Each line indicates whether the collection was performed on the young generation. The first line shows that a minor collection was performed, which dropped the amount of memory used from 16952K to 16916K. The number in parentheses shows that the total available memory in heap is 19640K, which is about 2MB. The time at the end of each line indicates how long it took to complete the collection. The second line indicates that a major collection was performed that was able to reclaim reasonable amount of memory and, of course, took longer than the minor collection.

The nonstandard option `-XX:+PrintGCDetails` provides more detailed information. For example, the following output indicates that both the young and tenured generations were collected:

```
0.299: [GC 0.299: [DefNew: 145K->5K(384K), 0.0016798 secs]0.300:
    [Tenured: 366K->221K(1600K), 0.0273660 secs] 511K
    ->221K(1984K),0.0312235 secs]
```

Note that the numbers in parentheses indicate the available heap for each generation. As mentioned earlier, the size of each generation may change when a collection occurs. If you want to fix the size of the generations, you can use `Xms`, `Xmx`, `NewSize`, `MaxNewSize`, `PermSize`, and `MaxPermSize`.

Programs such as HPjtune can read the activities of the GC and generate diagrams. They can also compute useful statistics such as heap usage, duration, cumulative allocation, and creation rate diagrams. In addition, they can point out the times at which the entire heap was collected. When minor and major collections have the same time stamps, it is an indication that the entire heap was collected.

To collect information about the content of the heap, you can use `hprof` and specify a value for its heap option. The `heap=sites` option allows you to collect information about the total count and type of allocated objects, live objects, and their site. This option can help you find out if a suspicious amount of objects of certain types are being created.

The parameter `heap=dump` can be used to obtain a full dump of the heap. Pressing Ctrl + Break in the console window will signal `hprof` to write a memory dump. By default, a heap dump is performed before the VM exits. A heap dump can be used to find out what objects are in the heap at specific times. For example, after your game has loaded, you can perform a heap dump to find out whether temporary load objects are kept around by mistake. In such scenarios, you must make sure that references to unwanted objects are set to `null`, or the references fall out of scope.

PERFORMANCE TIPS

This section offers generic and Java-specific performance tips that are presented as two separate sections. You should keep them in mind while designing, implementing, and tuning your game. Some may seem more intuitive than others. Nevertheless, they have been overlooked in many professional games and applications.

It is also crucial to know that a good design is generally more important than optimized code in the long run. Keep in mind that optimizations require more development and testing time. They can also make the code harder to maintain. You should not always give up good design for better performance, or vice versa. You should consider each design and optimization decision on a case-by-case basis.

General Tips

Focus on the Right Problem

Every computation requires some amount of CPU time to complete. Some take a large portion of the overall execution time of a game, whereas others take a negligible amount. Just because a single instance of a computation requires many CPU cycles does not mean it is a performance bottleneck. Similarly, just because a single instance of a computation requires very few CPU cycles does not mean it cannot be a performance bottleneck. To find out whether a method or computation is a bottleneck, it is extremely helpful to know what percentage of the game's execution time is spent performing it. Profile your game to find the bottlenecks so you can spend your time fixing the right problem and not waste your time on problems that are simply not important.

Some computations have a lot more room for optimization than others. For example, changing a computation so that it uses optimal data structures and algorithms that are more efficient can pay off far better than trying to optimize, say, the square root method. Once the algorithms and data structure are optimal, only if a computation is still a bottleneck should you consider desperate optimizations that can significantly reduce readability and increase maintenance cost.

Perceived Performance Is More Important Than Actual Performance

Keep in mind that in the end, your game is as fast as the user perceives it to be. The user judges only what he can detect. The user does not count CPU cycles to judge how fast a game runs. If some computations in the game execute much faster than can be detected, but others execute slow enough to be detected, most users will conclude that the game is slow. When putting the game together, you should be more concerned about the overall performance of the game, as opposed to the performance of, say, the collision-detection algorithms.

Take Advantage of the Strengths and Avoid the Weaknesses

Every design and framework has strengths and weaknesses. This is true of Java, your code, and existing APIs written for any language or platform. By understanding the strengths and weaknesses of a framework, you can take advantage of its strengths and, more important, avoid its weaknesses. If a task that must perform often exploits the weakness of a framework, you should try to find workarounds. Even if there is no obvious workaround, it is much better to know that a task is exploiting a weakness of the framework than to do so blindly.

Don't Assume All Optimizations Improve Performance

Optimizations are like investments. The same way an investment may not be worth making, an optimization may not be worth performing. Just like an investment, every optimization has a cost associated with it that must be paid. There is generally a crossing point where an investment starts to pay off. If that point is not reached, the investment will be a loss. Similarly, an optimization can in fact slow down your game. This is especially true for optimizations that are performed during runtime because CPU cycles are much more valuable during runtime than when the game code and content are being compiled.

The reason why the HotSpot VMs have two configurations is that they want to avoid optimizations that are likely to be losses. The client configuration does not perform optimizations that are simply not worth making because their overhead is too much to justify. On the other hand, the server configuration assumes that an application will run for a while. Therefore, it performs additional sophisticated optimizations that require more CPU cycles to perform but are still likely to pay off.

As another example, consider the following question: is it better to have an unsorted list and perform an exhaustive search when an element needs be removed, or is it better to pay the cost of keeping a list sorted so that the remove operations can be performed efficiently? The answer is not that simple. If there are many insertions, only a few removes, and the list is small, it is actually better to have an unsorted list and perform an exhaustive search for every remove operation.

Another example is visibility culling. A form of visibility testing known as occlusion culling is performed to remove geometries that are not visible because they are behind other geometries. Detecting geometries that fall behind others is an expensive task, but if on average it culls a significant chunk of the scene, it can be an investment well worth making.

To make sure optimizations pay off, you need to benchmark your code. It is also important to test your code with data that represents scenarios common in the game. This is one of the reasons why it is good to use macro-benchmarks in addition to micro-benchmarks.

Avoid Redundant and Unnecessary Computations

You can greatly improve the performance of your game by finding ways to perform a computation fewer times. Halving the number of times a computation is performed is even better than optimizing the computation by 100 percent or doubling its speed. You should be especially cautious about redundant computations in critical loops.

Sometimes, you can guarantee the result of a computation has not changed. In such situations, it is often beneficial to save the result of the computation and reuse it. For example, when a vehicle moves around on a terrain, its orientation has to be updated so that it is aligned to the terrain. If the vehicle has not moved since the last time it was rendered, there is no need to recompute its orientation. Even simpler computations such as recomputing the length of a vector multiple times can cause performance problems.

Other times, even if there is no guarantee that the result of a computation has not changed, you may be able to use slightly outdated data without any observable impact. For example, a non-player character (NPC) may be able to use some perceptual information that is tens of frames old without the player detecting it.

There are also scenarios where not ignoring redundant data can cause significant performance problems. Such problems are common in event-based applications that queue up events to make sure every single one is handled. For example, if a scrollbar forwards 15 scroll messages to a panel that has an expensive paint method, if the panel tries to process each event one at a time, a substantial delay will result from the time the user drags the scrollbar until the panel catches up. Similar problems can arise if an NPC receives multiple events about seeing the same enemy, or a client game that receives multiple network packets notifying about similar events. In such circumstances, it can be advantageous to ignore some of the older events when newer ones are received.

Precompute Expensive or Common Calculations

Precomputation is a technique that is heavily used in numerous games. Many computations can be performed before a game is even shipped. The results can be stored in a file, which can be loaded and used during runtime. Precomputation is essentially a tradeoff between memory consumption and CPU utilization during runtime.

For example, many games precompute the best path between every interesting location in a level and store them in a table. Some games precompute the best path between every pair of triangles that represents a walkable region in an entire level. By doing so, when the NPCs want to move around the level, they can simply look up a precomputed path based on the triangle they are on and the triangle they want to reach. As you can probably imagine, a table that stores the best path between every two triangles in a level can require a significant amount of memory during runtime. On the other hand, if multiple NPCs want to move around in a level, they do not have to perform individual searches every time they pick a new destination. Even the faster path-planning algorithms such as A* (A-Star) can be resource intensive when performed during runtime.

As another example, many games use binary space-partitioning (BSP) trees to divide a scene into volumes. When the level is being exported, an algorithm determines which other volumes can be visible from any point within a given volume. The visibility results are then stored in each volume. By doing so, the renderer can use the precomputed visibility list to determine which other volumes do not have to be rendered when the camera is in a specific volume.

Compress and Decompress Data During Runtime

Almost every game developed for a console desperately needs more memory than it has available to it. Because even modern-day consoles have as little as 32MB of RAM to store all code, data, and intermediate data, memory is very valuable. Because of this, many console games compress and decompress data in memory to make more room.

This technique can be used on PCs as well. Maintaining compressed data is particularly popular when a significant amount of precomputed data must be managed during runtime. To free up some memory, you can also write out large chunks of temporary data to the hard drive. To keep data more accessible, you may choose to use memory-mapped files. Memory-mapped files can take advantage of the underlying operating system's virtual memory manager. Because the OS is managing the data, you can typically get better performance than if you were to directly read and write from a file. Memory-mapped files have been added to Java as part of the new IO (NIO) package and are discussed in Chapter 5, "Java IO and NIO." Alternatively, you can write a few native methods to gain direct access to the virtual memory manager functions. Please refer to Chapter 11, "Java Native Interface," for more information on writing native methods.

Cull Expensive Computations and Try to Use Multiple Levels of Detail

Culling and multiple levels of details (LODs) are typically thought of as techniques specific to geometry rendering. Nevertheless, the same concepts can be used for any expensive computation. Geometry culling is the process of eliminating geometry that does not have to be rendered. For example, geometry that is not in front of the camera should not be rendered. Culling can be performed on sound sources or NPCs that are not close enough to the player so that their corresponding computations can be eliminated.

Geometry can have multiple LODs, so that when the camera is far away, a version of the geometry that has less detail can be rendered. This is because objects that are in the distance are less noticeable because they take up less space on the screen. Hence, rendering a simpler version can be undetectable by the user. LODs can be used for other computations, such as the physics of a flying airplane. If an opponent plane is far away, simpler flight models can be used.

Anticipate Upcoming Computations

When the likelihood of an action is relatively high, some of the computations corresponding to the action can be performed in the background. By anticipating upcoming computations, some computations can be performed ahead of time to lessen the sudden need to perform expensive computations in a short period of time.

For example, when the player is reaching the end of a level, the next level can start to be processed because it is likely that the player will leave the current level soon. Anticipation is fundamental for continuous worlds where there are no clear breaks between levels. Even when there are clear separations between levels, many games try to lessen the transition by preloading and preinitializing necessary data. To buy some extra time, many games have levels that are linked by rather empty hallways or even additional cut scenes.

When the game is on the main menu, you can start doing some of the inevitable computations that must be performed. Similarly, when a game has been launched and an active campaign is in progress, the player is far more likely to continue the campaign as opposed to exiting the game.

Approximate Instead of Computing Exact Values

Approximation is a technique that is used by many computations. Many times, by simply approximating some data, a reasonable amount of CPU cycles can be saved. In fact, many tasks performed in games would be computationally impractical to perform accurately.

Consider the task of determining which opponents are visible to an NPC. How expensive do you think it is to precisely determine which opponents are visible? Well, to precisely conclude whether an NPC can see the player or another NPC, the entire scene must be rendered from the perspective of the NPC, and then, if any of the pixels of the opponent end up in the final image, the NPC has the potential of seeing that opponent. This is, of course, not done in actual games. Instead, a single ray is cast from the eye of the NPC to, say, the head of another NPC. If nothing intersects with the ray, the NPC can potentially see the opponent. If only a single ray is tested, if a single branch of a tree happens to intersect with the ray, the NPC is not able to see the opponent, even if 99 percent of the opponent's body is visible. To be more realistic, some games have a target point on each limb, which is tested in the same fashion.

Let's say that you want to simulate an airplane or vehicle behavior. Do you need to know the exact surface area under the plane to compute the lift? Do you have to dynamically compute the exact area of a tire's contact patches to compute the necessary forces? Even if you have the most precise data available to you, if the computations you perform on the precise data are not exact, you will not get precise results. Furthermore, performing precise computations can prove to be far too expensive to justify.

Many games have used square root and sine tables that store precomputed results for angles at certain intervals. When the sine of an angle needs to be computed, the angle is clamped to a close enough value for which the result has been precomputed. Such techniques approximate the output value. There are also techniques to approximate distance. For example, in some scenarios, it may be sufficient to use the average of delta x and delta y.

Do Not Make Your Data More Detailed Than It Needs to Be

The quality of data on which some computation occurs is directly related to both CPU and memory consumption. The more detailed the data, the more disk space is required and the more RAM is needed to store the data in memory. In addition, higher resolution data means that more processing is required to use the data. This is true for data such as geometry, sound, and textures, or even data that is used to represent the world for the NPCs.

There are tools that can sample textures and generate equivalent textures that have substantially lower color depth without having any detectable impact. In fact, it is possible to have 4-bit textures (only 16 colors) that are as vibrant as 32-bit texture. Good algorithm can look at a source image and select the most important 16 colors that represent the image. If you want to have a rich world that uses only 4-bit textures, you must separate texture to distinguished categories such as sky, trees, and ground.

Even if the data is detailed, the detailed data can be used for some computation, but a lower-resolution copy can be used for another computation. For example, the world used by the NPCs to perform visibility tests can have much lower detail than the representation used for rendering the level. Most games do not use the actual triangles and polygons of the level for collision purposes. Some games use simpler representations such as spheres and boxes. Many games use very low-resolution alternate geometry for collision detection. The alternate representation of the world is created to roughly estimate the actual geometry of the world.

Abstract Data into a Hierarchy

If you must perform computations on a substantial amount of data, you can group small segments together to generate an abstract, lower-resolution representation. If data is represented as a hierarchy, the low-resolution representation can be used to determine which part, if any, of the high-resolution representation should be the focus of the computation.

For example, eight spheres can be used to approximate the limbs of a humanoid character. Each of the eight spheres can point to the actual geometry of the corresponding limb. Another sphere that is large enough to include all the eight spheres can be used to represent an abstract representation of the entire character. This hierarchy, which has three levels, can be used to efficiently compute the point of collision of a bullet. A quick check against the large sphere can determine whether the character has been hit. If the character has been hit, additional checks against the spheres that represent the limbs can determine which limb was hit. If a game needs to know the exact point of collision, the geometry pointed to by the sphere that was hit can be tested to find the exact point of collision. By abstracting the data and generating lower-resolution representations, we avoid having to always perform collision detection against the high-resolution data (that is, the actual triangles of the character).

This concept is applicable to other types of computation as well. For example, if an NPC has to plan its way through an excessively large world, he can use an abstracted or low-resolution version of the level to put together a rough plan and then try to work out the details of his plan using the high-resolution version. This is known as hierarchical path planning. Hierarchical representations are actually much more humanlike than always using fully detailed data.

Be Aware of the Upper Bound of Your Algorithms

Know how much a computation can cost you in the worst-case scenario. If there is a substantial difference between the best-case and worst-case scenarios, it is crucial to know how often the worst-case scenarios can occur. It is not a tragedy for a computation to run faster than necessary, but running too slowly can be a tragedy.

For example, heuristic searches such as A* (A-Star) can run very reasonably. However, in the worst-case scenario, they exhaust the entire search space, making them as bad as brute force algorithms such as Breadth-first and Dijkstra. This means that if worst-case scenarios ever occur, the amount of memory and CPU consumed by the algorithm is extremely high. Therefore, every attempt has to be made either to make sure that searches that result in the exhaustion of the search space never occur, or there is a way to suspect such scenarios and terminate the search.

As another example, consider a rendering system that uses a form of hierarchy such as a quad tree to determine which parts of the scene do not have to be rendered. Just because most of the time you can get good performance does not mean that the game will run well. You have to be aware of how badly the performance can get if the player goes anywhere in the level and looks in any direction. As with the last example, you can try to make sure that extremely bad scenarios can never occur by tweaking the level. Unlike the last example, it is not practical to terminate the rendering of the remaining geometry because the result can be immediately detectible by the player.

Specialized Code Performs Better Than General-Purpose Code

An implementation that has been tailored for a specific task is generally more efficient than its equivalent generic implementation. This advantage comes with higher development and maintenance costs, however. In addition, specialized implementations are usable for fewer problems. This is because specialized code can use problem-specific knowledge to take advantage of every fact and make specific assumptions.

For example, a collision-detection algorithm designed to detect collision between axis-aligned boxes will perform significantly better than a system that needs to handle collision between arbitrary geometry. As another example, a handcrafted linked list can be far more efficient than the generic implementation available in Java collections framework or C++ standard template library. Specific comments are made about the Java collections framework in a dedicated performance tip.

Laziness Can Be Good When It Comes to Computation

When appropriate, you may want to put off expensive computations as long as possible to alleviate sudden computation spikes. Lazy loading, initialization, and computation can help improve the performance of your game by making it appear smoother.

Use Threads with Care

Consider the following question: is it better for a thread to sit and wait or always run as fast as it possibly can? As you might have guessed, it entirely depends on the situation. Some threads should not be blocked so they can constantly perform critical computations. On the other hand, some threads must be blocked often so they do not consume CPU cycles that can be used by other threads with higher-priority tasks.

For example, slight pauses in the thread responsible for rendering can be very undesirable. If the render thread is used to load an opponent model when a new player joins the game, an unwelcome pause will occur. On the other hand, a thread that is supposed to collect network packets or deliver game events should not constantly consume CPU cycles if it doesn't have anything to process. If no events or packets are available, the thread should be blocked until new data is available.

As another example, consider a controller device in streaming mode. If a separate thread is responsible for retrieving the data, the thread may end up wasting a lot of CPU time. If the thread is simply in a loop that reads any available packets and copies them into a structure that can be accessed by the game thread, the thread may end up going back and forth to retrieve the data at a much higher rate than necessary. In this scenario, many CPU cycles are wasted that could have been put to better use by other threads.

As a side note, many console games do not use multiple operating-system-level threads. Instead, they emulate threads at the game level. Tasks are added to a scheduler's list, which then gives each task a chance to run. This approach is sometimes even preferred on PCs because it has low overhead and tasks can be scheduled to start at a specific time in the future. However, if such a scheduler is implemented with a single OS-level thread, the scheduler must have faith in each task and assume that each of them will either complete immediately or return without completing and indicate that it needs to be rescheduled. If any of the scheduled tasks forget to return promptly, the scheduler will not have a clue until the task returns. In fact, if a task never returns, the entire scheduler will halt.

Java-Specific Tips

Better Bytecodes Mean Better Execution Performance

In general, more optimal bytecodes can make your application run faster. This is true for both interpreted bytecodes and bytecodes that have been compiled to native CPU instructions. If you use a VM implementation that is simple and does not have a compiler that can compile the bytecodes to native code, you should use third-party optimizing compilers to get better performance. Sun static compilers do not perform any real optimizations. They perform only basic optimizations defined by the Java language specifications. The optimizations are left for the HotSpot compiler.

Methods that have four or fewer parameters have less overhead because the VM has special instructions for them. For example, `iload_0`, `iload_1`, `iload_2`, and `iload_3` are special opcodes that load an integer from a local variable onto the operand stack. The first local variable of an instance method stores the `this` pointer. The rest are the method parameters and other local variables defined in the method. In addition, the VM has opcodes that refer to constants −1, 0, 1, 2, 3, 4, and 5. For example, the opcode `iconst_1` pushes the integer 1 onto the stack without having to extract the operand from a bytecode.

Because the VM is limited to 256 opcodes, the instructions are not orthogonal. There is not a one-to-one mapping between integer opcodes and byte opcodes. The compiler treats bytes, chars, and shorts as integers and then narrows the result using appropriate cast opcodes. In fact, `int` is the VM's favorite type.

Statically Bound Methods Are Faster than Virtual Methods

When possible use private or static methods because, being statically bound, they are invoked faster. As explained earlier in the chapter, methods that are statically bound can be invoked directly and do not need to be resolved during runtime. Dynamically bound methods are those that are invoked using the `invokevirtual` opcode. It is important to know that using the keyword `final` does not make a method statically bound. In fact, `final` methods are dynamically bound and are still invoked with the `invokevirtual` opcode. You should decide whether a method should be `final` only based on its purpose in the application.

Promote Inlining

Even though it is hard to absolutely control which methods are inlined by HotSpot, some guidelines can increase the likelihood that a method is inlined. Generally, it makes more sense to inline smaller methods because the overhead of calling them can be significant when compared to the actual work they do. In addition, inlining larger methods means that the code can become too bloated. Keep in mind that when a method is inlined, the body of the method is inserted at the call site. If multiple invocations of a single method are inlined, the body of the method is inserted in multiple locations.

Short and simple methods that have no dependencies are ideal candidates for inlining. Note that if a method does not call any other methods and strictly relies on local variables, final members, or static members, it can be copied and pasted by the compiler without any worries. Local variables can be declared and used where the method is inlined. The value of a final variable can simply be copied because they do not change. Finally, static member variables can be resolved without ambiguity because they are statically bound.

In addition, only methods that are statically bound can be inlined. Static and private methods are bound at compile time. Other methods must be devirtualized during runtime before they can be inlined.

Be Careful–Native Methods Are Everywhere

Invoking a native method is more expensive than invoking a Java method. In addition, native methods cannot be inlined, which can lead to additional performance costs. Try to have an idea of which methods are native or call native methods indirectly. It is also good to have an idea of what the underlying native method may be doing. You can always look in the corresponding source files if they are available. Note that JDK does come with most of the Java source. The VM and all its native files are also available for download. In addition, using options such as `-verbose:jni` can help you monitor some JNI activities.

Some native methods use static buffers, and others dynamically allocate memory when they are invoked. If you are calling a native method that dynamically allocates memory, you should make every attempt to reduce the number of times it is invoked. For example, if you write an array greater than 8k to a file, the current implementation of the underlying native function allocates a large enough buffer, copies the data to the buffer, writes the content of the buffer to a file, and then frees the buffer. If you call the method many times, a substantial amount of extra work will be done by the OS, which can cause noticeable performance problems.

Note that some objects use native structures that can be memory intensive and expensive to initialize. You should use such objects with a lot of care. Objects that use native structures tend to have a finalizer to release their native resources when they are collected. Finalizers delay the collection of objects, and there is no guarantee as to how long an object must wait before its finalizer is invoked. Also, keep in mind that it is hard to estimate the amount of native resources used by such objects because the VM does not have the slightest clue about them.

Using native methods, of course, has advantages and is fundamental to Java. However, when a native method is called, the application temporarily gives up many of the guarantees made by Java and the VM. For example, a native library can leak memory or corrupt the memory that is used by the VM and cause it to crash. Chapter 11, "Java Native Interface," discusses how to add native code to your game and covers the implications of using native code in an application.

String Manipulation Is More Expensive than You May Expect

Use strings carefully. Strings are immutable objects, meaning that once they are created they cannot be changed. If you need to manipulate strings, you should use `StringBuffer` objects. In fact, when you use the + or += operators to concatenate strings, the compiler inserts appropriate code to create `StringBuffer` objects so that it can append the strings together. Consider the following methods that concatenate a few strings:

```
String tokens[] = {"s1", "s2", "s3", "s4"};

public String test1(){

    String str = "";
    for (int i=0; i < tokens.length; i++){
        str += tokens[i];
    }

    return str;
}
public String test2(){
```

```
String str = "";
for (int i=0; i < tokens.length; i++){
    str = new StringBuffer().append(str).append(tokens[i])
        .toString();
}

return str;
}
```

If you were to look at the bytecodes generated for the methods, you would see that they are identical. Essentially, the compiler translates:

```
str += tokens[i];
```

to

```
str = new StringBuffer().append(str).append(tokens[i]).toString();
```

As you can see, a simple concatenation has translated to create a new StringBuffer, calling append two times, and finally calling toString. If this wasn't bad enough, note that toString, like most other String methods, creates and returns another String object. The following method accomplishes the same task far more efficiently:

```
public String test3(){

    StringBuffer buffer = new StringBuffer();
    for (int i=0; i < tokens.length; i++){
        buffer.append(tokens[i]);
    }

    return buffer.toString();
}
```

Direct Byte Buffers Are Fundamental to Games

Use direct byte buffers to share data between Java and native code. Direct byte buffers were introduced in JDK 1.4, and games are one of their biggest beneficiaries. Because the memory allocated for a direct byte buffer does not reside in the Java heap, its content can be readily passed to native APIs, such as those of the operating system. Chapter 5, "Java IO and NIO" discussed buffers and direct byte buffers in detail and presented performance comparisons.

The Java Collections Framework Is Good and Bad

The arguments about using generic data structures in games are not new and are not specific to Java. In fact, for years developers have argued this topic, even in C++. The C++ Standard Template Library is essentially the equivalent of Java Collections Framework (JCF). It contains many of the data structures available in the collection's API. It is extremely important that you know the difference between `ArrayList` and `LinkedList` (or the equivalent STL vector and list classes).

You can use the Java Collections Framework in your game, as long as you are careful about a few things. LinkedLists are inefficient for most tasks. Every time you insert an element in a linked list, a new internal object must be allocated to store the element. This internal element is fundamental because it is not practical to require all objects that want to be in a linked list to already have a next reference (or next pointer). Unlike a linked list, an `ArrayList` uses an actual array internally so that it can provide fast random access to its elements. Because of the internal array, there is no need to store next pointers.

Do not use Collection's `Vector`. The `Vector` class was introduced with JDK 1.0, which is before the Java Collections Framework was introduced. The Vector class was changed to be part of the framework, but that was mainly to allow backward compatibility. The main difference between a `Vector` and an `ArrayList` is that the former is synchronized. However, as of JDK 1.2, it has been better to use the following:

```
List list = Collections.synchronizedList(new ArrayList());
```

Even though a Vector is slightly faster than a wrapped `ArrayList`, it is a better practice to use a wrapped `ArrayList` if you need a synchronized list.

Do not use an `ArrayList` when it is more appropriate to use a `LinkedList`. Even though an `ArrayList` is typically more efficient, there are times when you should stick with a linked list. Keep in mind that every time you insert or remove an object from an `ArrayList`, all the elements to the right of the internal array must be shifted to the right or to the left, correspondingly. For a large-enough list, the overhead of shifting (copying) the references can be greater than the disadvantages of the internal allocation and deallocation of `LinkedList` elements.

Because the JCF data structures are written to be as generic as possible, they are not efficient when you want to deal strictly with primitive data types. For example, if you want to have a linked list of ints, you must create a corresponding `java.lang.Integer` object. Even data structures such as hash tables expect an object as the key value of an entry. If a critical module of your game needs to use a hash table, you should typically use a custom-made hash table that uses primitive data types as the key values. Using an `int` instead of an `Integer` object can have substantial advantages in terms of both memory and execution.

More Objects Can Mean Less Available Memory and CPU

Avoid creating unnecessary objects when possible, especially in the hot spots of the application. Even though the GC has been designed to deal with many short-lived objects, it is still a good practice to minimize the number of objects. The more objects created, the more will have to be reclaimed, and the more work the collection and compaction is likely to be. Many times it is possible to reduce object creation by reusing an object. This approach can be problematic when dealing with multiple threads, but it is worth considering.

When using existing APIs, be aware of methods that create new objects, and try to minimize the number of calls to them. When designing an API, to minimize object creation try to receive a reference and populate it with the result. This approach is much better than creating a new object to return some data.

Do Not Leak Objects

Do not forget that objects will not be considered garbage as long as they are reachable. It is easy to inadvertently hold onto objects that are no longer needed. This is especially true during the loading of a game. It does not hurt to explicitly set references to null if they are class members and you are certain that you do not need their corresponding objects. It is generally a good practice to use local references because they help reduce the possibility of such memory leaks in Java.

Minimize the Number of Classes

Avoid making unnecessary classes. More classes mean more memory consumption and longer startup time. For example, if you need a basic vector structure to store three floats, it may be better to use an array of length three as opposed to making a class that has x, y, and z fields. Also, be cautious about using anonymous inner classes. They are common and convenient, especially when implementing Listener classes for GUI components.

```
listener = new Listener() {
    public void actionPerformed(){
    }
};
```

Note that the code segment results in the creation of an extra class file at compile time. It is easy to overlook the number of classes created in this manner.

Take Advantage of Conditional Compilation

The JDK 1.4 compiler (`javac.exe`) allows you to do conditional compilation, which is similar to using C/C++ preprocessors such as `#define_DEBUG`. Defining the

_DEBUG preprocessor allows the code segments that follows a #ifdef _DEBUG state-ment to be included in the compiled representation. Similarly, not defining the preprocessor allows the debugging code to be excluded from the compiled repre-sentation. If you run `javap.exe` on the class file generated from the following code, you will not find any bytecodes that correspond to the code in the conditional check:

```
static final boolean DEBUG = false;

public void test(){
    int a = 10;
    if (DEBUG){
        System.out.println("DEBUG flag is true");
    }
}

0:   bipush  10
2:   istore_1
3:   return
```

Smaller compiled code means fewer bytecodes, which reduces memory con-sumption and load-time bytecode verification, as well as leads to faster execution time. Note that this not only eliminates unnecessary bytecodes from release builds but also prevents the debug strings from being added to the constant pool table.

SUMMARY

To get the best performance for your game, you should understand some of the inner workings of VM. Understanding the structure of the VM, the interpreter, the HotSpot, and the garbage collector are fundamental to writing high-performance Java games. In addition, being able to measure the performance of your game and locate bottlenecks is key to optimizing your code. Take advantage of the perfor-mance tips during the design, implementation, and optimization phase of your game.

7 Local Area Networking for Java Games

by Jeff Kesselman, Game Server Architect,
Game Technologies Group, Sun Microsystems

In This Chapter

- Applets versus Applications
- LAN versus WAN
- The Communication Protocol
- Sockets
- Using the Java Networking APIs
- java.net
- javax.nio
- The Game Networking Process
- Game Networking Protocols
- Conclusion

APPLETS VERSUS APPLICATIONS

Applets are severely limited in the networking they can do to provide security guarantees to the user. This chapter presumes that you are running your Java code as an application. Java applications can be launched on the user's computer like a traditional program or they can be launched from Web pages using Java Webstart.

LAN VERSUS WAN

Networking for games can be broken down into two broad categories: Local Area Network (LAN) games, which are played on computers connected directly to each other, and Wide Area Network (WAN) games, which are generally played over the Internet.

The issues involved with each are fairly different. In general, though, LAN games are much simpler to design and implement than WAN games; therefore, we will focus on LAN games in this chapter. The big ways LAN and WAN games differ are in the latencies they are required to handle and the ways in which computers are connected to them.

Latencies

Networked data is communicated using packets, which are small discrete chunks of data. Latency is the time it takes a packet of data to travel from the originating machine to the machine or machines by which it is being received. If you think of a network as a hose and a packet of data as a cup of water poured into the hose, the latency is the time it takes the water to come out the other end. The longer the hose, the higher the latency (see Figure 7.1).

On the Internet, packet latencies can get quite large and must be dealt with in a way that does not destroy the user experience. Luckily, in a LAN environment the latencies are small enough that they can be safely ignored.

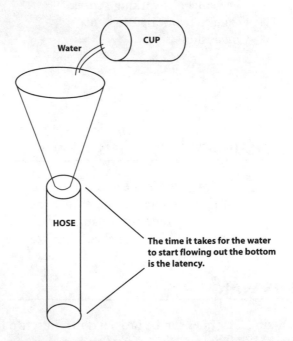

FIGURE 7.1 The latency of water traveling through a hose is determined by the hose length.

Bandwidth

Whereas latency is the time it takes a packet to get from one end of a net connection to another, bandwidth is the number of bytes that can be transferred in a single unit of time. It is typically measured in bytes/second. (The measurement used to be kilobytes; these days it's more likely to be megabytes.)

Looking at the hose analogy, the width of the hose is the bandwidth. Making it wider means it can deliver more water per second, but it still takes a given water molecule the same amount of time to get from the beginning to the end of the hose (see Figure 7.2).

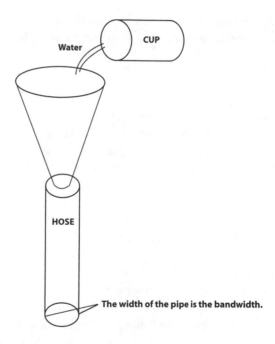

FIGURE 7.2 The bandwidth of water traveling through a hose is determined by the hose's width.

The bandwidth of the player's connection to the Internet is often a critical factor in designing WAN games. Again, on the LAN we generally have so much bandwidth available as to make it a non-issue in your code design.

Connection Types

Computers can connect to the Internet in a variety of ways. Today, these include remote connections such as analog (56-K) modems, DSL modems, cable modems, and more direct connections like T1 and T3 lines. Each of these connection types has its own unique properties. In particular, most of the remote methods add unique challenges in terms of latencies and bandwidth.

Desktop computers connected to a LAN are all connected through either an Ethernet port or a wireless Ethernet connection (80211.b or 80211.g). Both of these connections add trivial latencies and support bandwidths much wider than games require.

THE COMMUNICATION PROTOCOL

Numerous methods are used to move data across an Ethernet connection. These methods are called *protocols*. Two main protocols are used in LAN networking—TCP/IP and UDP.

TCP/IP

The TCP/IP protocol is used for reliable, in-order communications. This means that every packet sent on one side of a TCP/IP connection is guaranteed to arrive at the receiver's end in the same order as it was sent.

For LAN networking, TCP/IP is the simplest and easiest protocol to use. It simplifies many networking problems and allows you to program with the same confidence in the control-flow that you have when you write single-computer games.

The only limitation on TCP/IP is that there can be only one sender and one receiver per TCP/IP connection. Think of it as a virtual wire connecting the sender and receiver across which you can send data. This limitation in most cases is minimal because you can open any number of connections and, thus, string wires to send data down to all those you want to receive the information. It does mean, however, that the data packet must be sent multiple times—once for each connection.

TCP/IP is kind of like the post office. You open a connection to a specific receiver, then the connection guarantees messages sent to that receiver get through, regardless of hail, sleet, or temporary networking problems.

UDP

UDP is a simpler protocol then TCP/IP. It does not guarantee order of delivery or that any given packet actually is delivered at all. This may sound fairly useless. In fact, the uses of UDP are fairly limited in a LAN setting. The biggest benefit of UDP is that it supports multiple receivers for a single packet by using a *multicast channel*.

Everyone who wants to receive packets sent to that channel attach to it. When anyone sends a packet to the channel, the system tries (but may not succeed) to send it to everyone attached to the channel.

UDP multicast is like a bulletin board. Someone posts a message to the board and whomever reads the board can see it. Unfortunately, the readers can't always be relied on to look at all the messages or to read them in the order posted. Nonetheless, UDP multicast is necessary to perform tasks such as the discovery of other players on a network.

JRMS Reliable Multicast

In the previous section about UDP multicast, it was noted that the drawback of UDP is that you aren't guaranteed that the receivers will receive the packets and you do not know the order in which they will be received. Luckily, smart people are out there solving problems like these for us. The Java Reliable Multicast Service (JRMS) API provides an easy way to do multicasting with all the reliability and in-order guarantees of TCP/IP. It is actually a second layer of protocol on top of the ones provided by Ethernet.

The JRMS API is not part of the built-in JDK APIs, but it is an optional package that can be downloaded from *www.experimentalstuff.com/Technologies/JRMS*.

JSDT: The Java Shared Data Toolkit

Another useful API built on top of the basic Ethernet protocol is the Java Shared Data Toolkit (JSDT). This API allows you to create variables in different programs that are linked, so that when you change one in one program, the change is also made to the variable in the other program.

At first glance this might seem an ideal way to do networking, but often it's more convenient to throw packets of data back and forth. The coordination of the shared data requires a fair bit of under-the-hood network packet traffic. It's often more efficient to do simple communications yourself. In addition, the propagation of changes does not happen instantaneously, and it is possible to run into subtle synchronization issues, referred to by multiprocessing programmers as *race conditions*, where two programs are trying to update the same variable to different values.

JSDT provides synchronization mechanisms to deal with these problems, but all these complications can turn what at first seems like an easier solution to networking into a far more complex problem than just sending packets to each other. Nonetheless, JSDT can be ideal for certain kinds of problems.

JSDT is currently in transition. Therefore, at the time this book was written, it was not available for download. The JSDT API has just been re-released as open source by Sun and can be found at *https://jsdt.dev.java.net*.

SOCKETS

Berkeley Unix introduced the idea of a network socket. This terminology has been adopted as the standard way of describing TCP/IP and UDP connections across most other operating systems so that, at this point, it is pretty much a standard in networking. The Java APIs refer to net communications in terms of sockets, so a basic understanding of them is necessary to understand how Java networking works.

TCP/IP Sockets

A socket is an endpoint for network communications—not the most helpful of definitions. If a TCP/IP connection can be thought of as a virtual wire strung between two computers, then a TCP/IP socket is like the socket into which the wire plugs. There are two ways to use a socket: either as a host or as a client. As a host, a socket sits and waits for connections from clients. A host socket has an identifying number called a port, such that the entire range of sockets can be imagined to be a numbered patch panel.

A client, however, does not have a port. It does not need one because it initiates the connection. Think of this process as making a telephone call. The client dials the host's number by specifying the host's address and the host port to which to connect. Once that connection is made, both sides may communicate by "talking" (writing) and "listening" (reading) on their "telephone" (the socket) (see Figure 7.3).

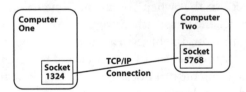

FIGURE 7.3 Sending data via TCP/IP.

UDP Sockets

A UDP socket is more like a wireless connection. Rather than the socket being dedicated to "talking" with a specific port on a specific partner, it can send data and receive data from any other UDP socket on any other machine. UDP is often called a connectionless protocol.

Every packet sent out from a UDP port must be labeled with the machine and port number of the socket that is going to receive it. A computer can receive and send packets to many different partners on the same UDP socket.

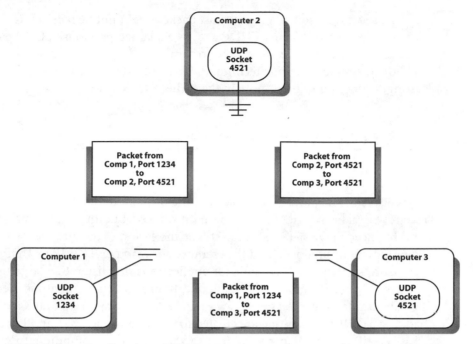

FIGURE 7.4 Sending data via UDP.

Multicast UDP Sockets

Multicast UDP is like a pair of walkie-talkies. Everyone on the same frequency hears every broadcast on that frequency. This setup is accomplished on the network with a special kind of UDP socket called a multicast socket.

Multicast sockets are created as *belonging* to a multicast group. Typically this belonging is referred to as *subscribing to* the group. This group is like the frequency on the walkie-talkie. Every packet sent by a multicast socket can be heard by every other multicast socket subscribed to the same group.

We said *can* be heard not *will* be heard for two important reasons. The first has to do with range. Just as your walkie-talkies have a transmission range, so do multicast sockets. On an Ethernet, range is described in numbers of hops. A hop is the moving of a packet from one router[1] to the next. When a multicast socket is created, it is given a maximum number of hops any packet it sends can travel. This value is called the time to live (TTL). If a subscriber to a multicast group is too many hops away from the sender, he will not receive the message.

---

[1]A router is a special kind of computer used on the Internet. All endpoints for the Internet are tied together through a chain of routers that act sort of like post offices, sorting the messages and handing them off to the next-closest post office to the receiver.

The second reason why a multicast packet might not be received is that multicast is really a special form of UDP and, as explained previously, UDP packets are not guaranteed as to when or if they arrive at all.

For this reason, various techniques have been developed to do reliable multicasting, which is discussed more in the earlier JRMS section.

USING THE JAVA NETWORKING APIS

java.net

The classes in the package java.net are the original networking APIs for Java. In recent years, alternative APIs have been introduced, but for simple, small-scale networking needs java.net classes can still be the easiest to use and they perform fine. Their biggest limitation is that they require a thread per TCP/IP or UDP socket to read from so they aren't suitable for applications that listen to a large number of sockets. (Typically, these are server applications expecting numerous users.)

The fundamental class in java.net is the Socket class. Java draws a distinction between TCP/IP sockets that are created to make connections to another computer and TCP/IP sockets that are created to wait for other computers to connect to them. Sockets that initiate connections to other computers are represented by the Socket class. Sockets that accept connections from other computers are represented by the ServerSocket class.

The ServerSocket class is a special sort of factory class. It returns a separate Socket object for every connection that is made to it. Actual communication back and forth is done using these returned Sockets. Thus, a single ServerSocket can set up separate connections for many different communication partners.

There are also classes for UDP sockets (DatagramSocket) and multicast sockets (MulticastSocket.)

In practice, for LAN games it is generally convenient to do all your game communication with Socket and ServerSocket. MulticastSocket is useful for the discovery process, when you find other players to connect to. DatagramSocket can be safely ignored.

To open a TCP/IP connection in Java, all you need to do is create a Socket and tell it to connect. You can then get an input stream from the Socket and read from it as you would any other data source, with one key difference: socket reads are blocking. Therefore, if you try to read data from the Socket and none has arrived yet, the read call will wait for the data. For this reason Sockets are typically given their own thread to run on so that the wait for data doesn't jam up the whole application.

The SimpleSocketListener sample application does this so waiting for data from one connection doesn't stop it from processing data coming in from another.

```java
package com.worldwizards.shawnbook;
import java.net.ServerSocket;
import java.io.*;
import java.net.Socket;

/** SimpleSocketListener
 * This class is a simple application that opens a TCP/IP socket
 * on port 1138 and prints any data sent there.
 *
 * To try it, run the program and then use telnet to connect to port
1138
 * on the system on which the app is running.
 */


public class SimpleSocketListener {
```

```
ServerSocket myServerSocket;
public SimpleSocketListener() {
  // Create the Server Socket.  This makes an end-point for
  // the telnet sessions to connect to.
  try {
    myServerSocket = new ServerSocket(1138);
  }
  catch (IOException ex) {
    ex.printStackTrace();
  }
}


/**
 * listen
 */
private void listen() {
  while(true) { // loop until program is interrupted
    try {
      // accept() says "I'm ready to handle a connector"
      Socket newConnSocket = myServerSocket.accept();
      Thread socketThread = new Thread(
      new SocketToStdout(newConnSocket));
      socketThread.start();
    }
    catch (IOException ex) {
    }
  }
}

static public void main(String[] args) {
 new SimpleSocketListener().listen();
}
}
```

The SocketToStdout class is a small Runnable that sits in its own thread reading the socket and dumping the received characters to standard out. Runnable is a special interface for writing multithreaded applications. Any class declared as Runnable can be made to run on its own thread. Because java.net Socket read calls are blocking, we want them to have their own thread so they don't block up the rest of the application.

```
package com.worldwizards.shawnbook;
```

```
import java.net.Socket;
import java.io.InputStream;
import java.io.*;


public class SocketToStdout implements Runnable{
  Socket mySocket;
  public SocketToStdout(Socket socket) {
    mySocket = socket;
  }

  /**
   * run
   */
  public void run() {
```

```
Reader rdr;
try {
  InputStream istream = mySocket.getInputStream();
  rdr = new InputStreamReader(istream);
}
catch (IOException ex) {
  ex.printStackTrace();
  return;
}
char[] inchar = new char[1];
while(true){
  // blocks til a character is available
  try {
    rdr.read(inchar);
  }
  catch (IOException ex1) {
    // connection ended.  return
    return;
  }
  System.out.print(inchar[0]);
}
}
}
```

JAVAX.NIO

The one-thread-per-socket approach works well for small numbers of connections and greatly simplifies the code for those cases. Some situations, such as Internet game servers, however, require you to handle hundreds or thousands of connections.

The `java.io` streams are also simple to use but require data to be copied multiple times before it reaches you. This overhead is particularly noticeable in heavy networking applications that need to do multiple layers of custom packet protocols. Each of these layers typically requires the data to be prepended with a protocol-specific header and each of these prepends ends up meaning another copy of the data.

The `javax.nio` package contains classes that address both of these issues. Because `java.nio` isn't really necessary for typical LAN games, it won't be covered in this chapter, but a good reference for learning more about NIO is *http://java.sun. com/j2se/1.4.2/docs/guide/nio*.

THE GAME NETWORKING PROCESS

Software engineers typically learn best from examples, so the rest of this chapter describes a simple example program. Although the actual functionality is simple—just a chat program—this program does everything a game would do to implement LAN networking.

Discovery

Discovery is the process of finding the other chat peers with whom we will connect. The functionality is basically the same as a buddy list. Unlike instant message services that typically have a central machine that keeps the list, LAN discovery must be done *a priori* and in a distributed manner.

UUIDs

To identify the individual programs, each one needs a unique identifier that no other program will have. Such an identifier is called a universally unique identifier (UUID)[2]. The first class needed for LANChat is a UUID class. Java 1.5 is slated to have one built into the JDK APIs, but for now we must make one of our own. It must be able to be compared with other UUIDs, and it must be communicable across the Internet. The easiest way to read and write Java objects is with object serialization, so it should be serializable. An interface that defines what we need follows:

```
package com.worldwizards.shawnbook;

<import java.io.Serializable;
public interface UUID extends Serializable, Comparable{

}
```

There are two kinds of UUID. A truly unique UUID is one that will never conflict with any other UUID. To create a truly unique UUID you need a unique starting seed number. All Ethernet adapters have a unique ID built into them that Ethernet uses called a MAC address. Unfortunately, there is now no way to access the MAC address directly from Java. Therefore, to write a truly unique UUID class, it is necessary to write some native code to fetch the MAC address and a JNI wrapper to allow it to be called from Java. The resulting code would, of course, not be totally portable because the native code would have to be rewritten on every OS on which you wanted to run the program.

---

[2]Another term for a UUID is a globally unique identifier (GUID).

There is, however, a second kind of UUID—a statistically unique ID. A statistically unique ID is not 100 percent guaranteed to be unique, but the chance of a collision is so small as to be virtually impossible. The simplest way to construct a statistically unique UUID is with a combination of a large-bit random number and a time stamp. For two UUIDs to collide, they would have to generate the same random number at the exact same time. This type of UUID can be created completely in Java, so this is the kind used for LANChat.

```java
package com.worldwizards.sbook;

public class StatisticalUUID implements UUID{
  transient static SecureRandom random=null;
  private long randomValue;
  private long timeValue;
  public StatisticalUUID() {
    if (random == null) {
      try {
        random = SecureRandom.getInstance("SHA1PRNG");
```

```java
      }
      catch (NoSuchAlgorithmException ex) {
        ex.printStackTrace();
      }
    }
    randomValue = random.nextLong();
    timeValue = System.currentTimeMillis();
  }

  public int compareTo(Object object) {
    StatisticalUUID other  = (StatisticalUUID)object;
    if (timeValue < other.timeValue) {
      return -1;
    } else if (timeValue:other.timeValue) {
      return 1;
    } else {
      if (randomValue < other.randomValue) {
        return -1;
      } else if (randomValue > other.randomValue) {
        return 1;
      }
    }
    return 0;
  }

  public String toString(){
    return ("UUID("+timeValue+":"+randomValue+")");
  }

  public int hashCode() {
    return ((int)((timeValue::32)&0xFFFFFFFF))^
           ((int)(timeValue&0xFFFFFFFF))^
           ((int)((randomValue)::32)&0xFFFFFFFF)^
           ((int)(randomValue&0xFFFFFFFF));
  }

  public boolean equals(Object obj) {
    StatisticalUUID other = (StatisticalUUID)obj;
    return ((timeValue==other.timeValue)&&
           (randomValue == other.randomValue));
  }
}
```

Discoverer

Now that there is a way of identifying the different runs of the program (sometimes called sessions), the runs can announce their presence on the Internet. An interface that defines the functionality of a `Discoverer` follows.

```
package com.worldwizards.sbook;

import java.net.MulticastSocket;

public interface Discoverer {
  public void addListener(DiscoveryListener listener);
  public UUID[] listSessions();
}
```

To receive discovery events, an interface must be defined as follows:

```
package com.worldwizards.sbook;

public interface DiscoveryListener {
  public void sessionAdded(UUID sessionUUID);
  public void sessionRemoved(UUID sessionUUID);
}
```

The simplest way to coordinate discovery is with multicast sockets. Every game program on the Internet subscribes to a single multicast channel. The hosts broadcast their presence over this channel to all the other players. By repeating that broadcast at regular intervals it becomes possible to tell when a game program leaves the chat by the absence of these updates. The code to implement this follows, starting with the `MulticastDiscovery` class:

(continued)

```java
package com.worldwizards.sbook;

import java.io.*;
import java.net.*;
import java.util.*;
import java.util.Map.*;

public class MulticastDiscovery
    implements Discoverer, DatagramListener,
    Runnable {
  InetAddress discoveryGroup;
  MulticastSocket discoverySocket;
  List listeners = new ArrayList();
  Map timeTracker = new HashMap();
  UUID myUUID;
  private boolean done = false;
  private boolean announcer = false;
// half a second btw them
  private static final long HEARTBEAT_TIME = 500;

  private DatagramPacket hbDatagram;
  private static final int DISCOVERY_PORT = 8976;
  public MulticastDiscovery() {
    try {
      discoveryGroup = InetAddress.getByName("228.9.8.7");
      discoverySocket = new MulticastSocket(DISCOVERY_PORT);
      discoverySocket.joinGroup(discoveryGroup);
// just run on our local sub-net
      discoverySocket.setTimeToLive(1);
    }
```

```java
      catch (Exception ex) {
        ex.printStackTrace();
      }
      myUUID = new StatisticalUUID();
      // create heartbeat datagram
      byte[] hbdata = null;
      try {
        ByteArrayOutputStream baos = new ByteArrayOutputStream();
        ObjectOutputStream oos = new ObjectOutputStream(baos);
        oos.writeObject(myUUID);
        oos.flush();
        hbdata = baos.toByteArray();
        oos.close();
        baos.close();
      }
      catch (Exception e) {
        e.printStackTrace();
      }
      hbDatagram = new DatagramPacket(hbdata, hbdata.length,
                                      discoveryGroup, DISCOVERY_PORT);
      // create and start listen thread  on discovery socket
      DatagramSocketHandler rdr = new DatagramSocketHandler(
          discoverySocket, 1000);
      rdr.addListener(this);
      new Thread(rdr).start();
      // start heartbeating
      new Thread(this).start();
    }


    /**
     * This method starts this discoverer announcing itself to the world.
     */

    public void startAnnouncing() {
      announcer = true;
    }


    /**
     * addListener
     *
     * <param listener DiscoveryListener
     */
    public void addListener(DiscoveryListener listener) {
      listeners.add(listener);
    }
```

```java
/**
 * listSessions
 *
 * <return UUID[]
 */
public UUID[] listSessions() {
  Set ids = timeTracker.keySet();
  UUID[] ar = new UUID[ids.size()];
  return (UUID[]) ids.toArray(ar);
}


/**
 * run
 * This method is a loop that runs on its own thread generating
 * heartbeats.
 */
public void run() {
  while (!done) {
    try {
      if (announcer) {
        discoverySocket.send(hbDatagram);
      }
      checkTimeStamps();
      Thread.sleep(HEARTBEAT_TIME);
    }
    catch (Exception e) {
      e.printStackTrace();
    }
  }
}


/**
 * checkTimeStamps
 */
private void checkTimeStamps() {
  List removedIDs = new ArrayList();
  // find all outdated peers
  synchronized (timeTracker) {
    for (Iterator i = timeTracker.entrySet().iterator();
         i.hasNext(); ) {
      Entry entry = (Entry) i.next();
      long tstamp = ( (Long) entry.getValue()).longValue();
      if ( (System.currentTimeMillis() - tstamp) >
           (HEARTBEAT_TIME * 3)) {
```

```
          // missed the alst 3 heartbeats. we think its gone
          removedIDs.add(entry.getKey());
        }
      }
    }
    // now remove them
    for (Iterator i = removedIDs.iterator(); i.hasNext(); ) {
      UUID id = (UUID) i.next();
      synchronized (timeTracker) {
        timeTracker.remove(id);
      }
      for (Iterator i2 = listeners.iterator(); i2.hasNext(); ) {
        ( (DiscoveryListener) i2.next()).sessionRemoved(id);
      }
    }
  }


  /**
   * datagramReceived
   *
   * <param dgram DatagramPacket
   */
  public void datagramReceived(DatagramPacket dgram) {
    try {
      ByteArrayInputStream bais = new ByteArrayInputStream(dgram.
          getData());
      ObjectInputStream ois = new ObjectInputStream(bais);
      UUID uuidIn = (UUID) ois.readObject();
      ois.close();
      bais.close();
      boolean isNew = (timeTracker.get(uuidIn) == null);
      synchronized (timeTracker) {
        timeTracker.put(uuidIn, new
            Long(System.currentTimeMillis()));
      }
      if (isNew) {
        for (Iterator i = listeners.iterator(); i.hasNext(); ) {
          ( (DiscoveryListener) i.next()).sessionAdded(dgram.
              getAddress(),
              uuidIn);
        }
      }
    }
```

```
      catch (Exception e) {
        e.printStackTrace();
      }
    }


    // test main
    public static void main(String[] args) {
      MulticastDiscovery mcd = new MulticastDiscovery();
      mcd.addListener(new DiscoveryListener() {
        public void sessionAdded(InetAddress address,
                                 UUID sessionUUID) {
          System.out.println("Session joined with ID = " +
                              sessionUUID);
        }

        public void sessionRemoved(UUID sessionUUID) {
          System.out.println("Session left with ID = " + sessionUUID);
        }
      });
      mcd.startAnnouncing();


    }
  }
```

This is a pretty complex piece of code. It is easier to understand if it is broken down by individual methods. It starts with the following declaration:

```
public class MulticastDiscovery implements Discoverer,
DatagramListener,
    Runnable{
```

This code states that this class is going to be implementing three interfaces. We have already discussed `Discoverer`. `DatagramListener` is an interface for clients of another class that is necessary for this discovery—the `DatagramSocketHandler`. The `DatagramSocketHandler` will be responsible for actually reading packets from the UDP multicast socket, much the way `SimpleSocketListener` previously listened for strings coming in through a TCP/IP stream socket. Rather then printing the contents, however, whenever it gets a packet it will call back all its listeners and tell them. `MulticastDiscovery` is declared as `Runnable` as well and will run on its own thread so it can do periodic heartbeats.

The constructor does many things and is best analyzed a few lines at a time.

```
public MulticastDiscovery() {
    try {
        discoveryGroup = InetAddress.getByName("228.9.8.7");
```

Multicast communications are organized into channels called groups. When a program sends a datagram to a group, every other participant in that group receives it. Groups are specified using special Internet addresses within the range 224.0.0.1 to 239.255.255.255.

224.0.0.0 is not included in this range. That address has a special meaning to the Internet and should not be used.

Because all Internet communication is done with sockets, we next need to create a special multicast socket. Multicast sockets are created with only a port number because one multicast socket can belong to many groups.

```
discoverySocket = new MulticastSocket(DISCOVERY_PORT);
```

We must tell it that we want it to belong to the multicast group we just created, as follows:

```
discoverySocket.joinGroup(discoveryGroup);
```

Finally, we need to set a time-to-live (TTL). This setting is really a count of how many subnet boundaries the packet will be allowed to cross. If this were infinite, the multicast packet would travel out over the entire Internet to everyone else's computer,[3] which would create a lot of unnecessary Internet traffic and be an inconvenience to everyone else on the Internet. Because this is a LAN game, we can safely assume we will all be in the same subnet and conservatively set our TTL to 1.

```
discoverySocket.setTimeToLive(1); // just run on our local sub-net
```

Previously, we said UUIDs were a basic necessity for this kind of dynamic discovery. Here we create a UUID that identifies this particular run of the discovery manager and, by association, the program using it:

```
myUUID = new StatisticalUUID();
```

---

[3]This assumes that the entire Internet is multicast capable and willing to accept multicast packets. In fact, this is not true today for a variety of reasons, but you should always be a good citizen of the Internet and write your programs as if it were.

Next, we need to create a Datagram for the heartbeat. This is the data packet we will periodically broadcast to all players to let them know we are still here. Java serialization is a convenient way to transfer objects. It allows us to write code that transmits and receives arbitrary objects with no knowledge of their actual data.[4] The following code builds a Datagram packet that transfers one data object, our UUID:

```
// create heartbeat datagram
   byte[] hbdata = null;
   try {
     ByteArrayOutputStream baos = new ByteArrayOutputStream();
     ObjectOutputStream oos = new ObjectOutputStream(baos);
     oos.writeObject(myUUID);
     oos.flush();
     hbdata = baos.toByteArray();
     oos.close();
     baos.close();
   } catch (Exception e ) {
     e.printStackTrace();
   }
   hbDatagram = new DatagramPacket(hbdata,hbdata.length,
                                   discoveryGroup, DISCOVERY_PORT);
```

It is important that you use the DatagramPacket constructor shown in the previous code because it creates the right kind of packet for transmission through a Multicast socket. If you don't, strange errors can occur.

Next, we must create a DatagramSocketHandler as explained previously to listen for incoming packets and start them running on their own threads.

```
// create and start listen thread  on discovery socket
DatagramSocketHandler rdr = new
DatagramSocketHandler(discoverySocket,1000);
rdr.addListener(this);
new Thread(rdr).start();
```

Finally, we need to start this object also running on its own thread to do heartbeats and heartbeat checks.

---

[4]Serialization is a power tool. Like any power-tool it can hurt you if you don't know how to use it. In particular, naive use of serialization can result in huge data packets. For more information on how to use serialization correctly and economically in other situations, see the author's book Java Platform Performance, *Strategies and Tactics* (*http://java.sun.com/docs/books/performance*).

```
// start heartbeating
  new Thread(this).start();
```

The following short method just sets a flag that tells the code in this object's `run()` method to send heartbeats. If it is not called, the `MulticastDiscovery` object is a passive listener just collecting the discovery announcements of active `MulticastDiscovery` objects. The use for this will become obvious when we actually write the chat host and client code.

```
/*** This method starts this discoverer announcing
itself to the world.*/

  public void startAnnouncing() {
    announcer = true;
  }
```

The next unusual section of code is the `listSessions` method. It is fairly straightforward except for the fact that we are storing the UUIDs in a `Map` class.

```
/**
   * listSessions
   *
   * <return UUID[]
   */
  public UUID[] listSessions() {
    Set ids = timeTracker.keySet();
    UUID[] ar = new UUID[ids.size()];
    return (UUID[])ids.toArray(ar);
  }
```

It might seem counterintuitive that a Set would be more appropriate. The reason a Map is used is because we need to track a tuple consisting of <session UUID, last time it heartbeated>. For tuples, a `Map` is very convenient. If we used a `Set`, we would have had to store some kind of record object that contained the tuple.

As we get updates based on UUID, we would have needed a `Map` anyway, to efficiently find a record when it needed an update to the last heartbeat time. All in all, a `Map` where UUID is the key and the last heartbeat is the value is the simplest solution.

You will note that this method uses two synchronized blocks. They surround places where the `timeTracker` object is scanned or modified. This is because it is the one object that is used to communicate between the `DatagramSocketHandler` thread and the `MulticastDiscovery` thread. We need to make sure they don't get in each others' way.

The next section of code is the Run method. This is the method that is called on its own thread when we start a thread, which is constructed with an object of this class as its Runnable.

```
/**
  * run
  * This method is a loop that runs on its own thread generating
  * heartbeats.
  */
 public void run() {
   while (!done) {
     try {
       if (announcer) {
         discoverySocket.send(hbDatagram);
       }
       checkTimeStamps();
       Thread.sleep(HEARTBEAT_TIME);
     }
     catch (Exception e) {
       e.printStackTrace();
     }
   }
 }
}
```

This logic is simple: it sits in a loop until told to quit or until the program finishes execution. Every time around that loop, if announcer is set to true, it sends the heartbeat packet we constructed previously. Then it checks to see if any session time stamps have expired. Last, it goes to sleep, relinquishing the processor to other threads, and waits until it is time for the next heartbeat. Checking the time stamp for expiration is sufficiently complex (barely) that it deserves its own method, which is next in the file.

```
/**
  * checkTimeStamps
  */
 private void checkTimeStamps() {
   List removedIDs = new ArrayList();
   // find all outdated peers
   synchronized(timeTracker) {
     for (Iterator i = timeTracker.entrySet().iterator(); i.hasNext();
)
       {
```

```
            Entry entry = (Entry) i.next();
            long tstamp = ( (Long) entry.getValue()).longValue();
            if ( (System.currentTimeMillis() - tstamp) > (HEARTBEAT_TIME *
            3)) {
              // missed the alst 3 heartbeats. we think its gone
              removedIDs.add(entry.getKey());
            }
          }
        }
      // now remove them
      for(Iterator i = removedIDs.iterator();i.hasNext();){
        UUID id = (UUID)i.next();
        synchronized(timeTracker){
          timeTracker.remove(id);
        }
        for(Iterator i2 = listeners.iterator();i2.hasNext();){
          ((DiscoveryListener)i2.next()).sessionRemoved(id);
        }
      }
    }
```

This methods contains two loops. First, it loops through all the entries in the timeTracker Map, checking to see if they have expired. Expiration is defined as missing three heartbeats in a row. Heartbeats may be delayed or even dropped entirely, being UDP. Three in a row, however, is a strong indication that the program sending the heartbeats has stopped.

The second loop then reads the list of expired time stamps, removes them from the timeTracker Map, and throws an event to the Listeners telling the listener they have been removed. It is necessary to do this in a separate loop because changing the map while we are traversing it has undefined results.

The next method is the datagramReceived method. This method is called whenever the DatagramSocketHandler receives a datagram. Serialization is again used to unpack the data buffer in the DatagramPacket and retrieve the transmitted UUID.

```
public void datagramReceived(DatagramPacket dgram) {
    try {
    ByteArrayInputStream bais = new
    ByteArrayInputStream(dgram.getData());
    ObjectInputStream ois = new ObjectInputStream(bais);
    UUID uuidIn = (UUID) ois.readObject();
    ois.close();
    bais.close();
```

```
        boolean isNew = (timeTracker.get(uuidIn) == null);
        synchronized (timeTracker) {
          timeTracker.put(uuidIn, new Long(System.currentTimeMillis()));
        }
        if (isNew) {
          for (Iterator i = listeners.iterator(); i.hasNext(); ) {
            ( (DiscoveryListener)
            i.next()).sessionAdded(dgram.getAddress(),
                uuidIn);
          }
        }
      }
      catch (Exception e) {
        e.printStackTrace();
      }
    }
```

The UUID is looked up in the <UUID,timestamp: tuple Map, timeTracker. If no entry for this UUID exists, it is a new session to us. Accordingly, we set a flag so we can do callbacks and let our Listeners know about it. Either way, the new <UUID, current time: tuple is inserted into the Map. If there was an existing one, this method overwrites it; if there was not an existing one, a new entry is made. Either way, it is recorded for checkTimeStamps to use.

This method gets called by the DatagramSocketHandler object. Therefore, it is executed on its thread, not on the MulticastDiscovery object's thread. Accordingly, this is the other place where we need to synchronize access to the timeTracker object.

The last method is just a test we can use to make sure the MulticastDiscovery is working correctly. It uses an anonymous inner class as a Listener to turn the DiscoveryListener callbacks into prints we can see on the command line. Fire up a few of these and see how they report finding themselves and each other. Then kill one and see how the others note its passing.

Creating or Joining a Game

The code so far shows how to know who else is on the Internet with you, but that's about it. Typically, games divide their players by game sessions. One player will be the creator of the session and will set up the game. The others join a game they want to play.

The next sections of code are for creating and joining game sessions.

Creating a Game Session

The goal here is to do two things. First, the code needs to open a server socket to accept joining players. This task can be accomplished using a ServerSocketListener class, which is similar to the SimpleSocketListener already defined at the start of this chapter.

Second, the game must announce that socket to all the other potential players. The MulticastDiscovery class defined previously works perfectly for this task.

Accordingly, the GameSessionCreator class looks like the following sample code:

```java
package com.worldwizards.sbook;

import java.util.*;

public class GameCreator implements ServerSocketListener{
  Discoverer discoverer;
  ServerSocketHandler serverSocketHandler;
  List listeners = new ArrayList();
```

```java
public GameCreator(int gameTCPPort) {
  serverSocketHandler = new ServerSocketHandler(gameTCPPort);
  serverSocketHandler.addListsener(this);
  discoverer = new MulticastDiscovery();
  discoverer.startAnnouncing();
}

public void addListener(GameCommListener l){
  listeners.add(l);
}

// callbacks from serverSocketHandler

public void dataArrived(StreamSocketHandler rdr, byte[] data,
                        int length) {
  for(Iterator i= listeners.iterator();i.hasNext();){
    ((GameCommListener)i.next()).dataArrived(data,length);
  }
}

/**
 * mainSocketClosed
 */
public void mainSocketClosed() {
  String txt = "Server Msg: Error, Server socket as closed!";
  byte[] txtbuff = txt.getBytes();
  for(Iterator i= listeners.iterator();i.hasNext();){
    ((GameCommListener)i.next()).dataArrived(txtbuff,txtbuff.length);
  }
  System.exit(1);
}

/**
 * playerJoined
 */
public void playerJoined() {
  String txt = "Server Msg: Player Connected!";
  byte[] txtbuff = txt.getBytes();
  for(Iterator i= listeners.iterator();i.hasNext();){
    ((GameCommListener)i.next()).dataArrived(txtbuff,txtbuff.length);
  }

}
```

```
/**
 * playerLeft
 */
public void playerLeft() {
  String txt = "Server Msg: Player Disconnected!";
 byte[] txtbuff = txt.getBytes();
 for(Iterator i= listeners.iterator();i.hasNext();){
   ((GameCommListener)i.next()).dataArrived(txtbuff,txtbuff.length);
 }
}

/**
 * sendData
 *
 * <param data byte[]
 * <param i int
 */
public void sendData(byte[] data, int length) {
  serverSocketHandler.send(data,length);
}
}
```

This code is fairly simple and straightforward. It creates a ServerSocket to listen for connecting clients and wraps the returned Socket in a ServerSocketHandler that handles the details of the connection. It then announces its presence on the LAN using a MulticastDiscovery object. It calls setAnnounce() on the MulticastDiscovery object to tell it that we are a host, not a client.

The ServerSocketHandler class is a central component of the chat server and looks like the following sample code:

(continued)

```
 *
 * This software is provided "AS IS," without a warranty of any kind.
 * ALL EXPRESS OR IMPLIED CONDITIONS, REPRESENTATIONS AND WARRANTIES, INCLUDING
 * ANY IMPLIED WARRANT OF MERCHANTABILITY, FITNESS FOR A PARTICULAR PURPOSE OR
 * NON-INFRINGEMEN, ARE HEREBY EXCLUDED.  SUN MICROSYSTEMS, INC. ("SUN") AND
 * ITS LICENSORS SHALL NOT BE LIABLE FOR ANY DAMAGES SUFFERED BY LICENSEE AS
 * A RESULT OF USING, MODIFYING OR DESTRIBUTING THIS SOFTWARE OR ITS
 * DERIVATIVES.   IN NO EVENT WILL SUN OR ITS LICENSORS BE LIABLE FOR ANY LOST
 * REVENUE, PROFIT OR DATA, OR FOR DIRECT, INDIRECT, SPECIAL, CONSEQUENTIAL,
 * INCIDENTAL OR PUNITIVE DAMAGES.  HOWEVER CAUSED AND REGARDLESS OF THE THEORY
 * OF LIABILITY, ARISING OUT OF THE USE OF OUR INABILITY TO USE THIS SOFTWARE,
 * EVEN IF SUN HAS BEEN ADVISED OF THE POSSIBILITY OF SUCH DAMAGES.
 *
 * You acknowledge that this software is not designed or intended for us in
 * the design, construction, operation or maintenance of any nuclear facility
 *
 ******************************************************************************/
```

```java
package com.worldwizards.sbook;

import java.net.*;
import java.util.*;

public class ServerSocketHandler
    implements StreamSocketListener, Runnable {
  ServerSocket myServerSocket;
  List listeners = new ArrayList();
  private List streams = new ArrayList();
  public ServerSocketHandler(int port) {
    // Create the Server Socket.  This makes an end-point for
    // joining games to connect to.
    try {
      myServerSocket = new ServerSocket(port);
    }
    catch (Exception ex) {
      ex.printStackTrace();
    }
    new Thread(this).start();
  }

  /**
   * run
   */
  public void run() {
    while (true) { // loop until program is interrupted
      try {
```

```java
        // accept() says "I'm ready to handle a connector"
        Socket newConnSocket = myServerSocket.accept();
        StreamSocketHandler ssockrdr =
            new StreamSocketHandler(newConnSocket);
        ssockrdr.addListener(this);
        streams.add(ssockrdr);
        Thread socketThread = new Thread(
            ssockrdr);
        socketThread.start();
        doPlayerJoined();
      }
    catch (Exception ex) {
      ex.printStackTrace();
    }
  }
}

public void addListsener(ServerSocketListener l) {
  listeners.add(l);
}

public void doPlayerJoined() {
  for (Iterator i = listeners.iterator(); i.hasNext(); ) {
    ( (ServerSocketListener) i.next()).playerJoined();
  }
}

public void doPlayerLeft() {
  for (Iterator i = listeners.iterator(); i.hasNext(); ) {
    ( (ServerSocketListener) i.next()).playerLeft();
  }
}

/**
 * dataArrived
 *
 * <param rdr StreamSocketHandler
 * <param data byte[]
 */
public void dataArrived(StreamSocketHandler rdr, byte[] data,
                        int length) {
  for (Iterator i = listeners.iterator(); i.hasNext(); ) {
    ( (ServerSocketListener) i.next()).dataArrived(rdr, data,
        length);
```

```
    }
  }

  /**
   * socketClosed
   *
   * <param StreamSocketHandler StreamSocketHandler
   */
  public void socketClosed(StreamSocketHandler StreamSocketHandler) {
    streams.remove(StreamSocketHandler);
    doPlayerLeft();
  }

  /**
   * send
   *
   * <param bs byte[]
   */
  public void send(byte[] bs, int sz) {
    for (Iterator i = streams.iterator(); i.hasNext(); ) {
      ( (StreamSocketHandler) i.next()).send(bs,sz);
    }
  }
}
```

The most interesting part of this code is the loop that handles the ServerSocket itself:

```
/**
 * run
 */
public void run() {
  while (true) { // loop until program is interrupted
    try {
      // accept() says "I'm ready to handle a connector"
      Socket newConnSocket = myServerSocket.accept();
      StreamSocketHandler ssockrdr =
          new StreamSocketHandler(newConnSocket);
      ssockrdr.addListener(this);
      streams.add(ssockrdr);
      Thread socketThread = new Thread(
          ssockrdr);
      socketThread.start();
      doPlayerJoined();
    }
```

```
          catch (Exception ex) {
            ex.printStackTrace();
          }
        }
      }
```

This object sits on its own thread and blocks on the accept() call. Whenever accept() returns, it returns a new Socket connected to a foreign socket that has initiated a connection to the ServerSocket. You can think of accept() as a telephone switchboard. All incoming calls come to it. It then connects those calls to a local telephone and hands the phone back to the program so it can communicate.

The Socket is added to a list of Sockets, so that all data sent to the server by one joiner can be easily echoed to all.

To read the data sent to the Server on that Socket, the code wraps that Socket in a StreamSocketHandler, which is a utility class that functions much like the SimpleSocketListener mentioned previously. Instead of calling a hardwired printing object, however, it calls back registered listeners whenever data arrives.

Finally, it calls back its Listeners, letting them know another joiner has arrived.

Joining a Game Session

The GameJoiner class provides the functionality for client game sessions to discover and connect to the ServerSocket created by the GameCreator. It looks like the following sample code:

(continued)

```
package com.worldwizards.sbook;

import java.io.*;
import java.net.*;
import java.util.*;

public class GameJoiner
    implements DiscoveryListener {
  Discoverer discoverer;
  int port;
  List listeners = new ArrayList();

  public GameJoiner(int hostTCPPort) {
    port = hostTCPPort;
    discoverer = new MulticastDiscovery();
    discoverer.addListener(this);
  }

  public void addListener(GameSessionListener l) {
    listeners.add(l);
  }

  public GameSession joinGame(InetAddress address){
    try {
      Socket tcpSocket = new Socket();
      tcpSocket.connect(new InetSocketAddress(address,port)); // make
      connection to host
```

```
      StreamSocketHandler hdlr = new StreamSocketHandler(tcpSocket);
      new Thread(hdlr).start(); // start listening
      return new GameSession(hdlr);
    }
    catch (IOException ex) {
      ex.printStackTrace();
    }
    return null;
  }


  /**
   * sessionAdded
   *
   * <param address InetAddress
   * <param sessionUUID UUID
   */
  public void sessionAdded(InetAddress address, UUID sessionUUID) {
    for (Iterator i = listeners.iterator(); i.hasNext(); ) {
      ( (GameSessionListener) i.next()).sessionAdded(address,
          sessionUUID);
    }
  }


  /**
   * sessionRemoved
   *
   * <param sessionUUID UUID
   */
  public void sessionRemoved(UUID sessionUUID) {
    for (Iterator i = listeners.iterator(); i.hasNext(); ) {
      ( (GameSessionListener) i.next()).sessionRemoved(sessionUUID);
    }

  }
}
```

The game joiner also begins by creating a `MultiCastDiscovery` object.

```
public GameJoiner(int hostTCPPort) {
   port = hostTCPPort;
   discoverer = new MulticastDiscovery();
   discoverer.addListener(this);
}
```

Because it is interested only in hearing game-session advertisements and not advertising itself as a server, it does *not* call the discoverer's startAnnouncing() method. Therefore, it just sits quietly listening to others' announcements.

A port number is also passed in. This is the port on which the game host will open its ServerSocket. In this simple design, the port is known a priori by the game developer and passed to both GameCreator and GameJoiner. Because only one ServerSocket can listen at a given port at any time, we are limited to one Game-Creator per machine. How to engineer around this limit is discussed briefly in the following section.

Most of GameJoiner methods are just callback routines handling the events sent by MulticastDiscovery. The most interesting part of the class code is what it does when you want to join a game session.

```java
public GameSession joinGame(InetAddress address){
    try {
        Socket tcpSocket = new Socket();
        tcpSocket.connect(new InetSocketAddress(address,port)); // make
        connection to host
        StreamSocketHandler hdlr = new StreamSocketHandler(tcpSocket);
        new Thread(hdlr).start(); // start listening
        return new GameSession(hdlr);
    }
    catch (IOException ex) {
        ex.printStackTrace();
    }
    return null;
}
```

The joinGame() method is called with the Internet address of the game host to which you want to connect. (The Internet address was supplied to the joiner in the sessionAdded() callback, which responds to game announcements from the host.)

The joinGame() routine creates a Socket and connects it to the well-known game session port (see previous) at the supplied Internet address. It then wraps that port in one of our StreamSocketHandler classes, which run the listening thread on that socket and return any arriving data as callbacks.

Finally, it wraps the StreamSocketHandler in a GameSession object. In this example, the GameSession object is a more or less empty wrapper that just converts the StreamSocketListener callbacks received from StreamSocketHandler to GameCommListener events. The same code can be used to respond to game data packets in the Joiner and in the Host and makes the client API layer a bit neater.[5] It could, however,

---

[5]It would be even cleaner if the GameCreator returned a GameSession object as well, but this suffices for illustration purposes.

be extended to include game-specific data filtering or other such game-protocol handling. (See the Conclusion for more information.)

The rest of LANChat is mundane Java plumbing and should be familiar to anyone with moderate Java coding experience. The entire code for LANChat is on the CD-ROM included with this book.

Summary

The point of this chapter has been to demystify the fundamental plumbing needed in Java to hook LAN games together. To make that plumbing clear and easy to follow, many features have been left out that a real game might need, such as dynamic port allocation, attaching data to game sessions for display in the browser, attaching names or IDs to players for identification, and private communication, host migration, and various other extended tasks.

All these can be implemented by protocols on top of the basic networking concepts shown here. Dynamic port numbers and game-descriptive data could be added to the announcement packets. Player information could be sent by the player when it first connects to the ServerSocket and is read by the host from all brand-new connections. Similarly, data about the current game state and players could be sent back down the Socket connection as the first data from the host to the client.

Host migration is the term for handing the "host" designation off to a client in the event that the host suddenly dies. This can be tricky to get right and seriously complicates your logic because each client now has to have direct Socket connections to all other clients and a copy of the current host game state. In general, this sort of failure protection is overkill and few games implement it. Instead they just error out if the host dies and let the players create and join a new session.

The following section of this chapter steps up to the next level of logic and discusses what you might want to be communicating between game sessions and why.

GAME NETWORKING PROTOCOLS

This section discusses in high-level terms the various techniques used to organize the transmission and reception of game data. If you are looking for information on Internet protocols (TCP/IP, UDP), see the previous section.

Game-networking protocols for LAN games can be organized on a two-axis grid where one axis shows how they synchronize with each other and the other axis contains the kind of data they communicate.

Lock-Step versus Open-Loop Asynchronous Synchronization

Lock-Step

Lock-step games arise naturally from the basic single-player game model. In a typical single-player game, controllers are read once a frame, new positions calculated, and game logic handled. A resulting frame is then rendered and flipped to the screen. (See Chapter 2, "Fundamentals of Game Programming.")

A lock-step game works in almost the same way. After it reads the controllers, however, it sends a packet with that data to all the other players in the game. It then waits until all the players have in turn sent it a packet with their controller data before calculating the results. If you think of a real-time game as really a turn-based game where every "move" is one frame in size, then a lock-step game requires that everyone make his move before the game figures the results.

Lock-step games are probably the easiest models to program because they fit so well into what is already in the game. It is also relatively easy to add cheat protection to these games. By sending some data every so often on the state of the game and the controllers, the game sessions can "sanity-check" each other. If one client is saying the world is in a different state than the others, clearly a cheat or a bug is happening.

When creating lock-step multiplayer games, special attention must be paid to random events. Most games contain random elements. It is important that all players use the same random-number generator with the same current seed so the same random events happen at the same time and in the same way in each game session. Usually the host provides the seed on client connection.

The only downside to this approach is that everyone must report his input for the game to continue. This limitation makes lock-step games totally inappropriate for Internet play where latency spikes can stop the game cold in its tracks. It also means that everyone's frame rate is tied to that of the slowest player. In general, however, for LAN-based games, a lock-step game isn't a bad solution.

Open-Loop Asynchronous

Open-loop asynchronous games are very different from lock-step games. These games are based on the idea that small errors you can't see don't matter. They relax the requirement that everyone's gameplay be exactly synchronized and in doing so escape the frame-by-frame problems of lock-step games.

An open-loop asynchronous game is always running around its game loop at the fastest speed it can handle. Periodically, it gets updates about where the other players were and what they were up to at a given time in the past. Based on those updates it adjusts the other players in its game model. Between updates it guesses what the other players will be doing. Such guesses are called dead reckoning, a term invented by the military for military simulations. When an update for a dead-reckoned object comes in, the guesses are adjusted to bring them back in line with what the other player is actually doing.

A variety of techniques are available for making that guess and the subsequent adjustment. Simple adjustments just move the player directly to where he should be, correcting for movement and time elapsed. Such adjustment, although easy to implement, results in the effect game players call "warping," where an object in the world suddenly jumps discontinuously from one place to another. This is a visible and potentially frustrating artifact.

To hide warping, open-loop asynchronous games typically implement some form of interpolation between the old and new positions. The problem is similar to color dithering. When an update comes in, you derive an error term for both position and motion vector. You then add part of that error term in every subsequent frame until you have reduced it to 0.

Another issue with open-loop asynchronous games is the question of world state. In a lock-step game, everyone has a complete and correct picture of an identical world state. In an open-loop asynchronous game, everyone has a correct idea of his own state and an approximate idea of everyone else's. This is generally fine until you hit player-to-player interactions, such as combat. Suppose in my world state I see you in my crosshairs, but in your world state you aren't. I pull the trigger. Are you hit or not?

There is no way to actually reconcile the two views in an open-loop game. However, it is usually possible to pick the best view. In a first-person shooter game, for instance, the person doing the shooting has a reticle and can see exactly where he is aiming, but his target has only a general idea of where the shooter is pointing his gun. The result of this analysis is the conclusion that the shooter should decide if it is a hit or miss and communicate that fact to everyone else. In general, there is always a preferred viewpoint in any situation like this.

Open-loop asynchronous games have a number of great qualities for Internet games. They are reasonably latency-immune, and each player runs at his maximum frame rate. Unfortunately, they have one great weakness—security. In the previous example, the shooter is sending a packet to everyone saying, "I shot Jane!" All it takes is a little hack to the shooter's program so it *always* sends "I shot who-ever" packets rather than "I missed whoever" packets, and you have a player who cannot miss. Various game-specific and partially complete approaches can partially solve this problem, but a complete general solution has not been found. Therefore, it remains a big issue that must be addressed in the design of any open-loop game today.

In practice most Internet games today are modified open-loop games where one of the "players" is a server controlled by the game maker. Generally, this server is considered the one true arbiter of key game decisions. A LAN game could use a similar technique where the host acted as the server, but in practice, LAN games don't suffer from the same cheating problems Internet games do. After all, if Fred-who is in the next cubicle cheats, you can just reach out and slap him.

Controller-State versus Object-State Communication

The first networked games used controller-state communication. This type of communication extends naturally from a simple single-player game model. Once a frame, the game would read the controllers (see Chapter 11, "Java Native Interface") and send a packet to all the other players telling them what was read.

This kind of communication can be rather verbose (one packet per player per frame) and does not provide enough information to guess what the next packet will be. (See the previous discussion of dead reckoning in "Open-Loop Synchronous.") It is well suited to lock-step games but not to open-loop asynchronous games. Nonetheless, hybrids are out there that cross many of these techniques, so it really is a separate (though related) decision from your game-synchronization model.

Object-state communication is different. Rather then sending a raw packet saying, "In this frame, my controllers are doing this," the effect of the user's actions on his in-game representation is calculated first, and then a packet containing his entire state is sent to other players. This packet is time stamped. When it arrives at the other players' computers, the computer calculates the player's current state based on the state sent and the time it took to arrive.

Consider as an example a flight simulator. The object-state packet would describe the plane's location, orientation, and speed, and might even describe the state of its flight control surfaces. The receiving players "cook" that information and make a guess on the plane's current state based on what the plane was doing and the time it was doing it.

If the plane was moved only when state packets arrived, it would not give the illusion of continuous motion but would pop from figured place to figured place. To avoid this type of movement, between the arrival of packets, the guessing continues from frame to frame, and the plane is updated. (The simplest form of guess, and the one usually used, is "I will be doing what I was doing.") Such guessing is called dead reckoning. (See the previous section, "Open-Loop Asynchronous.")

Object-state communication works most naturally with open-loop asynchronous game synchronization, but, as in controller-state communications, hybrids do exist. This approach requires a lot more work to implement well and may be overkill for LAN games, but it is vital to the smooth gameplay of Internet-based games.

CONCLUSION

This chapter has covered the basics of how to make Java games play nicely together on a local area network (LAN) using today's Java. In this next and final section some of the other issues in Java network games are briefly addressed.

Future APIs

JDK 1.5 is right around the corner. It is going to add some key functionality that you had to build yourself in JDK 1.4 or earlier. One key networking addition to JDK 1.5 will be a standard UUID class. This UUID, being part of the environment, will be able to look for MAC addresses and produce the best possible uniqueness. When it is available, it will be preferable to the UUID class presented in this chapter.

In addition, there is ongoing work in Sun's Game Technology Group on a variety of game topics, including networking. Anyone seriously interested in this topic should bookmark the Java Games Community Web pages and visit them reasonably frequently. (You can use either of these URLs: *http://community.java.net/games* or *http://www.javagaming.org.*)

WAN Play

As briefly mentioned earlier, more and more games are dealing with wide area networking (WAN), the most common type being the Internet. The issues and tradeoffs for these kinds of game are very different. Bandwidth can be limited, particularly if you are trying to support analog modem play. Latency can be bad—as high as six-second spikes on analog modems.

If you are designing for broadband users only, these issues become less of a problem but still do exist to some degree. (The Internet itself can cause latency spikes of up to about half a second.)

For LAN games you can get away with lock-step games using controller communication, but a modified lock-step game that isn't tied directly to frame rate is preferable to allow each machine to render at its own pace. For WAN games, you really have no choice but to use some form of open-loop asynchronous synchronization.

Server-Based Games

This chapter addressed only peer-to-peer games. It used a communications architecture where there is one thread per socket that needs to be read. This technique is perfectly fine for games that have up to one or two dozen players. Game servers, however, often need to handle at least hundreds and maybe thousands of sockets at a time. This architecture is not suited to such large-scale problems that you would end up with hundreds or thousands of threads competing for CPU time.

Since JDK 1.4, Java has provided a solution for this with the alternate socket facilities in the `javax.nio` (new IO) packages. Such server coding is beyond the scope of this book, but more information on using NIO can be found at *http://java.sun.com/j2se/1.4.1/docs/guide/nio/*. (This same guide also appears in the guides section of the Sun JDK 1.4 download.)

8 Faster Math

Output looks bizarre.
Oops that was supposed to be
Add not multiply.
—Anonymous Game Developer

In This Chapter

- Introduction—Java Math Performance
- Improving Math Function Usage
- Faster Sine and Square Root
- Vectors and Matrices
- Summary

INTRODUCTION—JAVA MATH PERFORMANCE

Improving mathematical performance in Java has been a topic of interest since Java's creation. When Java was available only as interpreted VMs, many tips and tricks were developed to squeeze the maximum performance out of any Java code because the interpreted mode was so slow compared to native code. In addition, PCs and other computer architectures have special CPU instructions specifically designed for accelerating certain math operations, and Java programmers could not take advantage of them.

At that time, serious math processing was barely on the radar for Java developers. Eventually, Java's JIT compiler was developed and provided such a huge leap in performance that the numeric community took a deeper look at Java. It wasn't long before scientists and developers working on complex and process-intensive mathematics began developing in Java to get all the benefits that other Java developers had enjoyed. Now the latest VMs even take advantage of the specialized instructions previously available only to native-language programmers.

JIT compiling is a huge performance improvement over the interpreted mode, but many math operations are still behind the speed of native languages. This lag happens because of several reasons because part of the Java language design and ever-improved JIT compilers cannot completely remedy it. Also, alternate approximation math methods can be used that can greatly improve performance but that are not necessarily obvious to implement. Their implementation even counters good object-oriented design as well. To make matters worse, what seems to be a global solution may not be globally optimal; what may be a good solution in one small loop may not scale at all, or can be a maintenance nightmare when used throughout. Finding the right balance between usability and performance is often tedious and error prone, but luckily, in the game-programming domain we have the luxury of trading accuracy for speed in many cases. With carefully made trades, we can create great solutions for many core game-math problems.

In this chapter, we will attempt to address several heavily used game-math operations as well as offer a guide in design for future math code. The chapter contains three main sections. The first looks at general math-function usage improvements. The second examines complex functions, such as sine, and functions that typically have iterative solutions, such as square root. This requires that the calling code be a single method or function (x = sqrt(y), for example), but the solution requires the CPU to run many cycles in finding the solution. This class of math operations is a problem in any language, not just Java, and has well-explored solutions. We will implement and test these in Java to see what gains can be made.

The third section focuses on vector and matrix operations. These operations typically use many repetitive operations in high-level code (for example, add and multiply in a matrix multiple) and are required for 3D graphics and games. This code can be tuned specifically for Java, that is, to be as optimized as possible for the Java VM. Because the Java VM is somewhat of a moving target and may have different execution characteristics on different platforms, guaranteed optimal solutions are unlikely, but, in general, well-written solutions can be nearly optimal across a large class of platforms.

IMPROVING MATH FUNCTION USAGE

Most math operations cannot be optimized directly. That is, the user cannot make the add or subtract instructions any faster. They are atomic functions (or nearly atomic), meaning that the add in the Java language maps directly to a processor instruction and, therefore, runs as fast as the processor can execute it. When using most math functions, the first areas that can be optimized are in the math function usage and the algorithms. For those cases, design is the key to performance.

However, some math functions are not atomic. Often, these functions must be iterative to compute a complete and accurate solution and, compared to simple add and multiply functions, are quite costly computationally. The classic examples are sine and cosine (and their trig relatives) and square root. These functions show up in gaming programming often because they are directly related to geometry, and much of game programming deals with geometry. We will take a close look at what can be done to improve performance for these functions. There are many more—for example, log(), which do not show up in game programming as often—but they can be dealt with in a similar fashion.

Minimizing Costly Methods

The first step in minimizing math functions' impact to an application is to examine if the calls to the functions can be reduced. This may not readily yield any gain for well-written code because redundant calls should not be happening anyway. However, this often happens when using APIs that encapsulate these math method calls away from the developer. For example, if application code repeatedly calls a vector object's getMagnitude() method to get the magnitude of a vector for testing and does not store the value in a local variable, the method is probably paying the cost of recalculating the same magnitude value each time getMagnitude() is called by the application code. Because calculating magnitude involves computing a square root—one of the more expensive functions—this repeated accessing is very costly. Most likely, the method documentation will not warn the developer with a note, such as "calling getMagnitude() is costly due to square root," so the developer must simply know this is the case. Careful examination of direct as well as indirect calls to expensive math functions must be considered in any attempt to improve math performance.

Redesign Around Costly Methods

When the application code is making the minimum math calls possible, two more things can be done. One is to examine the technique being used to solve whatever problem needs to be solved. Perhaps knowing that particular math operations are expensive will encourage redesign on a particular routine. Perhaps even foundation data structures will be affected. One example is storing triangle edge and triangle surface normals for computing object collision. Often 2D and 3D collision routines need perpendicular surface vectors that are normalized or unit length for accurate solutions. Normalizing involves computing vector magnitude, which as stated earlier computes a square root. If many normals need to be used in a particular game's collision tests, perhaps computing the normals before runtime and storing them within the collision geometry data structure is a better solution at a greater memory cost.

Deciding when and where to make modifications to basic algorithms and data structures can be challenging, and tradeoffs between speed, efficiency, and memory usage will have to be made.

Rolling Your Own

The last thing that can be done is to "roll your own," or write your own alternative math functions. Writing math functions that are faster than the standard APIs, as well as specialized math functions, are classic gaming crafts. Although the once-large performance gains over standard math implementations are shrinking, this is still an area in which some performance edge can be squeezed out. Simply implementing the alternate math methods in Java is a straightforward process. However, there may be hidden complications to the classic techniques because of how the Java language and VM may affect those techniques and also how the VM handles the standard Java math functions as well.

Troubles with Doubles

At first glance, when attempting to improve on the Java lang.Math methods, one obvious issue sticks out—almost all of the complex functions accept only double-precision (64-bit) numbers, that is, there is no sin(float angle), only sin(double angle). A double is twice as big as a float and takes more processing to compute. One of the easiest changes to be made for mathematical optimization is to use only the lowest-bit resolution data types needed. In fact, on consoles, 16-bit floating-point numbers are typically used versus the 32-bit floating-point numbers on PCs. Java does not have direct 16-bit float support, but it is fine here because it turns out that on PCs it's optimal to be the native data size of 32 bits rather than something smaller. (See Chapter 6, "Performance and the Java Virtual Machine.")

Now, if the application sticks to using 32-bit primitives when its routines call the 64-bit double-based math methods, additional implicit casts from float to double are required in and out of the math function. Because of all of the overhead of casting from 32-bit to 64-bit numbers and back again, as well as the wasted accuracy lost in the conversion, it seems sin(double) would be a great candidate for replacing with a new sin(float).

Here's where the VM starts to complicate things again. The 32-bit float to 64-bit double then double-back to float cast can be avoided by a very smart VM. What's more, sin(double) may actually become sin(float) when an application attempts to pass in a 32-bit float instead of the declared argument of 64-bit double. It seems the latest JIT compilers can be made smart enough to catch that float passed in and the cast to float coming out, and actually switch to calling the float version of a math function instead of the stated double version of the API. This is done purely as an automatic optimization to improve performance when the calling method is working with floats.

This automatic floating of the complex functions is a great improvement for current JVMs over previous versions. However, in some cases, alternative methods can still squeeze out more performance, and in cases where the VM doesn't automatically switch between the double and float math functions automatically, these methods will yield ever-greater speed increases.

Fixed-Point Math

Fixed-point math has a long history of use in games. In the past it was an important technique for performing decimal math operations for PCs and game systems that weren't equipped with floating-point processing units. Today, because PCs have greatly improved floating-point capability and performance, it is a rare case where fixed-point math will give a significant performance increase. Specifically for multiplication and division operations, fixed-point math has a serious performance disadvantage on modern CPUs. Unless you are developing for systems that lack hardware floating-point support, such as smart phones, some PDAs, or other handheld devices, you are unlikely to see a performance benefit using fixed-point math. However, those systems lacking the floating-point support can benefit greatly from fixed-point math

Fixed-point math is a technique in which decimal numbers are encoded into standard integers and processed in that form instead of in the standard floating-point number format. They are called fixed point because the numeral precision on either side of the decimal point is fixed throughout a series of operations. For example, a typical fixed-point representation might use a 32-bit integer where the first 16 bits hold the integer value and the remaining 16 bits hold the decimal value of the number we want to process. To convert a regular integer to this fixed-point number, the value is simply bit-shifted over the number of desired decimal bits, in this case 16, because integers have no decimal component to deal with.

```
fixedPointNumber =  intNumber << 16;
```

Now the int `fixedPointNumber` has the integer value of `intNumber` in its upper 16 bits. One thing that should be obvious is that fixed-point math limits the range of possible integer values because we have just shifted a 32-bit integer into 16 bits. If this is a problem for a given data set, the choice of how many bits to assign to the integer part and the decimal part of the number—in this case, 16 bits each—may need to be reevaluated.

Converting floats is a bit trickier because floats are in IEEE format, so simply shifting them will not work. The correct way to convert these numbers is to multiply the float value by 2 to the power of the bit count we want to shift and cast to an `int`. In this example, that would be 2 to 16th power (1 shifted to the left 16 times, or 65,536, or x1000 in hex).

```
fixedPointNumber = (int) floatNumber * (1<<16);
```

To convert back to an integer from the fixed-point representation, simply shift to the right.

```
int_value = (int) fixedPointNumber >> 8;
```

Unfortunately, this method loses all data in the decimal part of the fixed-point number, which is often data that we want. However, if we want the final number in the form of a floating-point value, the conversion is simply a division by the same number we shift by for the original conversion from floating point to fixed point.

```
floatNumber = (float) fixedPointNumber /(1<<16);
```

This can also be done by multiplying the `fixedPointNumber` and the inverse of (1<<16), which can be precomputed because it doesn't change for a given fixed point, to avoid the slower division operation.

Addition and subtraction of fixed-point numbers work the same as for integers, but multiplication and division do not. The problem is that the fixed-point number is effectively a scaled-up number representation, where the number of shifts holds the amount of the scaling. The CPU does not recognize this fact because we are using regular integers as the native storage. Therefore, when a CPU performs a multiple between these two larger numbers, the result is an even larger number than the result should be in the fixed-point form. For example, if the two fixed-point numbers are meant to be holding the number 1.0, in the same 16-bit shift format used earlier, the actual integer number would be 65536. Multiplying 65536*65536 ($2^{16} * 2^{16}$) yields 2^{32}. After shifting back to get out the regular integer, we get 65536 or 2^{16} again as the final value, but it should still be 1. The value is scaled up because of the multiply operation. To fix this, each result must also be shifted to the right as the multiply operation is performed.

```
fixedPointNumber = (int) (fixedPointNumberA * fixedPointNumberB)
>> 16;
```

Division is handled similarly, but the shift is performed before the division and only to the dividend.

```
fixedPointNumber = (int) (fixedPointNumberA << 16) /
fixedPointNumberB;
```

Because we are basically implementing our own custom math operations and the CPU doesn't really know the representation natively, problems arise, such as integer overflow and precision loss, that must be accounted for and that further complicate a complete fixed-point set of operations.

Sometimes fixed-point representations are good for packing data where precision can be traded for data space, particularly in the cases of animation data, I/O, and networking. 16-bit fixed-point values require half the memory storage that single-precision floating-point values do. Although Java does not directly support 16-bit integers, two can be packed in a single 32-bit integer, doubling the data throughput as compared to floating-point data streams. In fact, fixed-point data packing can be used to pack even more data, as long as numeral precision can be sacrificed or the numeral range of the data is already limited. Using fixed-point representations to pack, stream, and store data is an excellent alternative to standard floats or doubles, even on systems that support floating-point math natively, when conserving memory usage and data bandwidth becomes a priority.

For more on fixed-point representations and operations, see the resources section.

FASTER SINE AND SQUARE ROOT

Sine (with other trig functions) and square root are functions that are ripe for replacement. These functions are relatively costly to execute and often don't need to be exact. In fact, approximations work great in many game uses. Here we are going to create several new versions of existing math functions using two different techniques. For float sine and cosine, we will create a lookup table-based function. For float square root and inverse square root, we will use faster approximation functions. Both techniques trade accuracy for speed, but if applied in appropriate ways, they will give great performance gains with a negligible cost in accuracy.

Sine and Cosine

This text is not a pure mathematics text, and fully defining and explaining sine and cosine (and any other trigonometric functions) is beyond its scope, but here is a limited review.

Sine and cosine come from trigonometry, the branch of mathematics that deals with the relationships between the sides and the angles of triangles and the calculations based on them.

Sine can be defined in different ways, but in this book, we define it in terms of triangles and circles.

The triangle-based definition states that the sine of an angle in a right triangle equals the opposite side length divided by the hypotenuse length.

The circle-based definition states that the sine of an angle can be defined as the y-coordinate of the point on the circle located at that angle from the origin (see Figure 8.1).

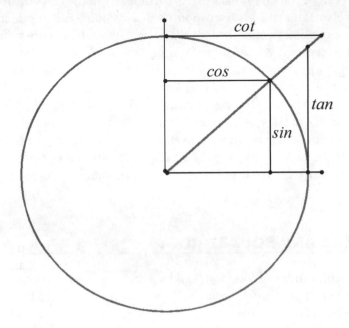

FIGURE 8.1   Trigonometry Functions.

Moreover, sine and cosine are used in all kinds of rotational operations from graphics to collisions to AI decision making.

Sine Lookup Tables

Trigonometry functions are much more difficult to compute than typical polynomials. So much time went into computing them in ancient times that tables were made for their values. Even with tables, using trig functions takes time because any use of a trig function involves at least one multiplication or division. We will create straightforward sine and cosine lookup table functions that trade size for accuracy but have a low constant cost for angle values from 0 to 360 degrees.

The technique of using a sine lookup table is quite simple. Build a table of sine values for all angles needed (usually the full circle of 2 PI radians or 360.0 degrees) at some regular interval. For example, a very small (and inaccurate) table would be as follows:

index	angle	sine
0	0	0
1	45	0.70710678...
2	90	1
3	135	0.70710678...
4	180	0
5	225	−0.70710678...
6	270	−1
7	315	−0.70710678...
8	360	−0

To find `sin(angle)`, simply divide the angle by the table entry interval (here, 45 degrees), use the integer part of the number to get the index, and return that value.

For example:

```
sin(180);
```

Dividing the angle of 180 passed in by this table's interval of 45 yields 4.

The table index 4 returns 0.0, which is, indeed, the sine of 180.

It should be obvious that this table and lookup routine are terribly inaccurate. Not only would 0 be returned for 180 but also for 181, 182, up to 225, depending on whether we round up or not for the index value.

Extra Improvements

Several elements of this table must be improved to bring accuracy to a more usable state.

First, more table entries can be added between the existing values. There will be a direct tradeoff between memory and accuracy, where more memory is required for a larger table with smaller intervals between entries, but the larger table will produce less error, or more accuracy, on average.

Second, the range of table values can be improved. sine and cosine have cycling values. In fact, the values repeat four times in a table going from 0 to 360, with only the signs changing in certain quadrants. We can use this fact to easily shrink the table's range to one-quarter of the original, ultimately allowing for the same accuracy in less space or, alternatively, increase the accuracy in the same size table.

Last, we can interpolate between table values based on the angle passed in. This action will add some more processing to our function and, depending on the need for speed versus accuracy, may be skipped. We have implemented both functions, one with interpolation and one without, for comparison and testing.

To write the lookup table function, the lookup table must first be built. Because we would like to use static math methods, similar to the existing math class, there should be no constructor to call or instance to hold to call our math methods. But before we can call the first look-up, a table building function must be executed.

To do this, we will use what is known as Java's static initializer blocks. We will initialize and fill the lookup table in this block, which will execute once when the class is loaded.

The following code builds a lookup table with 0.01 degree accuracy using 9,000 entries. That may be a bit large (9,000 floats ~36k) for some uses, depending on the target platform. A smaller table would be fine; it would just trade size for accuracy.

```java
// number of table entries per degree
private static final int sinScale = 100;

// float array that will store the sine values
private static final float[] sin = new float[(90*sinScale)+1];

// static initializer block
// fill the sine look-up table
static
{
    // since this table is in degrees but the Math.sin() wants
    // radians must have a convert coefficient in the loop
    // also, this coefficient scales the angle down
    // as per the "entries per degree"
    // A table could be build to accept radians similarly
    double toRadian = Math.PI/(180.0 *sinScale);
    for (int i=0;i<sin.length;i++)
    {
        sin[i] = ((float)Math.sin(((double)i) * toRadian));
    }
}
```

Now that the table is built, we need a new `sin(angle)` method that computes the lookup index and returns the value. Because the table we built is limited to 0–90 degrees, the `sin` method will have to do a little extra work to find the right index and the correct sign for the sine values. Limited function to 0–360 degrees, the mapping looks like the following code:

0–90	index	+sine
90–180	180(*entries per degree) –index	+sine
180–270	index – 180(*entries per degree)	–sine
270–360	360(*entries per degree) –index	–sine

There is one extra "gotcha" that is likely to happen. The angle value must be limited to 0–360 before doing the table lookup processing. Here we use the modulus operator to divide out values greater than 360 and use only the remainder for our final angle lookup. This action is not free but has to be here because the lookup will fail outside of 0–360. Often we know our angles are limited before the `sin()` call. In that case a new lookup function could be made without the check. Later we will look at a technique to limit the range without the modulus for even faster lookups.

```
static final public float sin(float a)
{
    // Limit range if needed.
    if (a > 360)
        a %= 360;

    // compute the index
    int angleIndex = (int)(a*sinScale);
    if ( angleIndex < (180 * sinScale)+1 )
    {
        if ( angleIndex < (90 * sinScale)+1 )
        {
            return sin[angleIndex];
        }
        else
        {
            return sin[(180 * sinScale) - angleIndex];
        }
    }
```

```
        else
        {
            if ( angleIndex < (270 * sinScale)+1 )
            {
                return -sin[angleIndex - (180 * sinScale)];
            }
            else
            {
                return -sin[(360 * sinScale) - angleIndex];
            }
        }
    }
}
```

It may seem that a lot of extra multiples are going on here, but really they aren't. All the (angle*sinScale) values should be computed at compile time because sinScale is final. The compiler knows the values cannot change at runtime and places the constant value in the code instead.

The decompiled code for the method sin(float f) for a particular sinScale value looks like the following lines:

```
public static final float sin(float f)
{
    if(f > 360F)
        f %= 360F;
    int i = (int)(f * 100F);
    if(i < 18001)
        if(i < 9001)
            return sin[i];
        else
            return sin[18000 - i];
    if(i < 27001)
        return -sin[i - 18000];
    else
        return -sin[36000 - i];
}
```

In the end, all the sinScale multiples are gone, replaced with the proper static value. We are left with a small set of operations to get at that sine value.

Array Access Is Not Free

There is a hidden cost in sine lookup table technique in Java over using them in C/C++. Any array access in Java involves a bounds check, as explained in Chapter 6,

"Performance and the Java Virtual Machine." This lookup function is so small and quick that the bounds check is not negligible to its overall execution. However, it happens only once per call and is unavoidable for the VM because we are not accessing in any way that the VM can determine we won't go out of bounds, even though our own angle-limiting code prevents us from doing so. In addition, if the table is quite large, it may not cache well on the host CPU, further increasing the method's runtime cost.

Regardless, this final `sine` method is incredibly cheap. The `cosine` can be computed similarly using the same table. This is possible because the cosine of an angle is equal to sine of that angle plus 90 degrees. With only a few modifications to the `sin(angle)` method, we can also get `cosine(angle)`. Unfortunately, not all complex math functions have order cycles that can be made into a table and work like this. Other functions, such as `Square Root`, don't have this range-limited, repeating behavior and require different techniques.

Faster Square Root

In C/C++ game programming, a now-classic technique was developed for computing a fast square root approximation. From a primitive data perspective, it is a rather complex series of math operations and bit-twiddling steps that clean up into incredibly tight code. Because the technique manipulates the IEEE data encoding of a native floating-point number and Java uses the same native floating-point numbers, the technique can be ported directly to Java and produce the same results. Unfortunately, depending on the JVM version, it's not always faster than the standard Java `Math.sqrt()` method. To see why this is, we must take a closer look at the method.

Implementing a custom square root function is typically done as an iterative approximation function. An iterative approximation function is one in which some part of the solution is processed repeatedly to get the final result where each iteration increases the accuracy of the solution. The nice thing about this kind of solution it that the developer can easily trade speed for accuracy by simply iterating some part of the function more times for better accuracy, fewer for better speed.

To make execution even faster, the function operates directly on the floating-point format. The fast square root function for IEEE-encoded floating-point numbers involves casting the floating-point number to a raw bits integer. This step is done so we can do operations on the exponent part and decimal, or mantissa, of the number separately, and then combine them back for the final floating-point number. This is fairly straightforward to implement in Java, as follows:

```java
//Magic numbers used for computing
//best guess starting square
static final float A = 0.417319242f;
static final float B = 0.590178532f;
static final public double fastSqrt(double fp)
{
    if( fp <= 0 )
       return 0;

    int expo;
    double root;

    // split into hi and lo bits
    long bitValue = Double.doubleToRawLongBits(fp);
    int lo = (int)(bitValue);
    int hi = (int)(bitValue >> 32);

    // pull out exponent and format
    expo = hi >> 20;
    expo -= 0x3fe;

    // clear exponent and set "normalized" bits
    hi &= 0x000fffff;
    hi += 0x3fe00000;

    // assemble back to double bits
    bitValue = ((long)(hi) << 32) + lo;

    // turn bitValue back into decimal float for more processing
    fp = Double.longBitsToDouble(bitValue);

    // find square for decimal using Magic numbers best guess
    root = A + B * fp;

    // repeat for more accuracy, but slower function
    root = 0.5 * (fp/root + root);
    root = 0.5 * (fp/root + root);
    root = 0.5 * (fp/root + root);
    //root = 0.5 * (fp/root + root);
    //root = 0.5 * (fp/root + root);
    fp = root;
```

```
    // find square for expo
    if ( ( expo & 1 ) != 0 )
    {
        fp *= factor;
        ++expo;
    }
    if ( expo < 0 )
        expo = (short)(expo / 2);
    else
        expo = (short)((expo + 1)/2);

    // format back for floating point
    expo += 0x3fe;

    // split back to hi and lo bits
    bitValue = Double.doubleToLongBits(fp);

    lo = (int)(bitValue);
    hi = (int)(bitValue >> 32);

    // put in exponent
    hi &= 0x000fffff;
    hi += expo << 20 ;

    // assemble back to double bits
    bitValue = ((long)(hi) << 32) + lo;

    fp = Double.longBitsToDouble(bitValue);
    return fp;
}
```

This function isn't entirely optimized but instead left in this slightly expanded form for readability. Single-precision floating-point number square roots can be computed similarly.

```
static final public float fastSqrtF(float fp)
{
    if( fp <= 0 )
        return 0;

    int expo;
    float root;
```

```java
// convert float to bit representation
int bitValue = Float.floatToRawIntBits(fp);

// pull out exponent and format
expo = (bitValue >> 23);
// subtract exponent bias
expo -= 126;

// clear exponent in bitValue
bitValue &= 0x7fffff;
// sets expo bits to 127
// which is really 1 with the bais of 126
// effective making the number decimal only
bitValue |= 0x3F800000; // ( 127 << 23 )

// turn bitValue back into decimal float for more processing
fp = Float.intBitsToFloat(bitValue);

// find square for decimal using Magic numbers best guess
root = Af + Bf * fp;

// repeat for more accuracy, but slower function
root = 0.5f * (fp/root + root);
root = 0.5f * (fp/root + root);
root = 0.5f * (fp/root + root);

// find square for expo
if ( ( expo & 1 ) == 0 )
{
    root *= factor;
}
expo++;
expo >>= 1;

// format back for floating point
expo += 126;

// once again turn back to bits for recombining
bitValue = Float.floatToRawIntBits(root);

// clear exponent in bitValue
bitValue &= 0x7fffff;
```

```
        // put in exponent into bitValue
        bitValue += (expo << 23);

        return Float.intBitsToFloat(bitValue);
    }
```

One divided by a square root shows up often in games, particularly because of the operation of vector normalization. In fact, in many cases 1/square root is computed more often that the square root alone. Because of this fact, a fast version of this combination, called inverse square root, has also been developed and used in game code. The Java version of this technique follows, computed similarly to the previous methods.

```
    static final public float fastInverseSqrt(float x)
    {
        float xhalf = 0.5f*x;

        // convert float to bit representation
        int bitValue = Float.floatToRawIntBits(x);

        // find square for decimal using Magic number best guess
        bitValue = 0x5f3759df - (bitValue >> 1);

        // turn bitValue back into decimal float for more processing
        x = Float.intBitsToFloat(bitValue);

        // repeat for more accuracy, but slower function
        x = x*(1.5f - xhalf*x*x);
        //x = x*(1.5f - xhalf*x*x);
        return x;
    }
```

With a working, although approximate square root function, let's do some performance tests against the standard Java Math class methods.

This task is going to be a micro-benchmark, and micro-benchmarks in Java are particularly error prone because the JVM and JIT compiler are going to be doing processing during the execution. To make sure that the JVM and JIT are affecting our benchmark as little as possible, we will do what is known as a warm-up in our test. A warm-up is a place where the test code is run thousands of times so as to trigger the JIT to compile it and also to give the VM time to compile it. In addition, we will use static data so that data-retrieval time is as minimal and consistent as possible.

This performance test creates two arrays of random floats and doubles and performs our different math functions on it, comparing the time results as absolute values and as a performance ratio.

A quick test on JDK 1.4.2 with the default command-line settings produces the following results:

```
C:\j2sdk1.4.2_02\bin\java  MathTestsSquareRoot
Creating random data...
Performing warm-up for square roots test...
Square Root Tests
Base Time Cost = 2336
Double Math.sqrt(double)            Elapsed time 4256 value =
15.915696943287958
Double MathUtils.fastSqrt(double)   Elapsed time 55064 value =
15.915685478989822
Double MathUtils.fasterSqrt(double) Elapsed time 39836 value =
15.91568548271219
Perf Ratios: std Math = 1.0  fast 1 Math = 12.93796992481203
                             fast 2 Math = 9.359962406015038


Base Time Cost = 1303
Float (float)Math.sqrt(float)       Elapsed time 5214 value =
15.915697
Float MathUtils.fastSqrtF(float)    Elapsed time 44256 value =
15.915696
Float MathUtils.fasterSqrtF(float)  Elapsed time 37781 value =
15.9161
Perf Ratios: std Math = 1.0  fast 1 Math = 8.487917146144994
                             fast 2 Math = 7.246068277713848


Inverse Square Root Tests
Double  1/Math.sqrt(double)         Elapsed time 7725 value =
0.06283105311462497
Float  1/(float)Math.sqrt(float)    Elapsed time 8696 value =
0.06283105
Float MathUtils.fastInverseSqrt(float) Elapsed time 15203 value =
0.062725544
Perf Ratios: std Math = 1.0  fast 1 Math = 1.125695792880259
                             fast 2 Math = 1.9680258899676375
```

Any number greater than 1.0 in the Perf (performance) Ratios means that the method is slower than the standard Math equivalent. In every case, the alternate methods were more expensive, and more than 10 times as expensive in some cases. What is happening—these new methods were supposed to be faster!

Just about every operation in the function will execute lightning fast, and the total sum should be quicker than the standard full-precision square root functions. Remember, we are trading accuracy for speed. In Java, however, there is one weakness in this method—the XXXToRawLongBits() and XXXBitsToDouble/Float() methods' calls. This technique requires converting the floating-point number to a bits-only representation. In system languages such as C, this cast operation is unsafe without a copy. In Java, for security reasons, the conversion requires a method call and a copy. This is the only way to perform this C-like cast operation in Java. On a good VM, this method call can be runtime optimized, but the copy will still happen, which slows things down but can't quite account for the difference.

In addition, it turns out that Sun has done quite a bit of work improving the notoriously slow Math methods in Java. The 1.4.2 JVM and JIT compiler are aware of the standard Math API now and are making heavy optimizations to get those methods as close to pure C as possible, so much so that a regular Java method that does even fewer computations is significantly slower than java.Math. This is great news for anyone using Java because it means that by simply upgrading your VM version, you will get some of the best Java math possible.

However, if you cannot upgrade or if you are using some exotic command-line options, even in 1.4.2 these improved functions can help. A rerun of the previous test follows, but with the Xcompile option on 1.4.2. This option forces a JIT at class load time, which seems to prevent the JIT from making the same math optimizations as before.

```
C:\j2sdk1.4.2_02\bin\java -Xcompile MathTestsSquareRoot
Creating random data...
Performing warm-up for square roots test...
Square Root Tests
Base Time Cost = 2072
Double Math.sqrt(double)            Elapsed time 219858 value =
15.915696943287958
Double MathUtils.fastSqrt(double)   Elapsed time 55419 value =
15.915685478989822
Double MathUtils.fasterSqrt(double)  Elapsed time 40011
value = 15.91568548271219
Perf Ratios: std Math = 1.0  fast 1 Math = 0.2520672434025598
                             fast 2 Math = 0.18198564528013536

Base Time Cost = 1135
Float (float)Math.sqrt(float)       Elapsed time 223856 value =
15.915697
Float MathUtils.fastSqrtF(float)    Elapsed time 44282 value =
15.915696
```

```
Float MathUtils.fasterSqrtF(float)    Elapsed time 37629 value =
15.9161
Perf Ratios: std Math = 1.0  fast 1 Math = 0.19781466657136731
                             fast 2 Math = 0.1680946680008577


Inverse Square Root Tests
Double  1/Math.sqrt(double)            Elapsed time 224095 value =
0.06283105311462497
Float  1/(float)Math.sqrt(float)       Elapsed time 221134 value =
0.06283105
Float MathUtils.fastInverseSqrt(float) Elapsed time 14766 value =
0.062725544
Perf Ratios: std Math = 1.0  fast 1 Math = 0.9867868537896874
                             fast 2 Math = 0.06589169771748589
```

As was originally expected, the new approximate square root methods are faster—in the floating point cases, executing in less than ⅕ the time on this test machine and with pretty good accuracy.

Further test combinations are summarized in the graphs in Figure 8.2 and Figure 8.3.

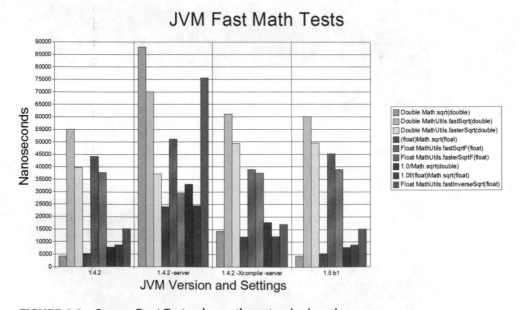

FIGURE 8.2   Square Root Tests, slower than standard math.

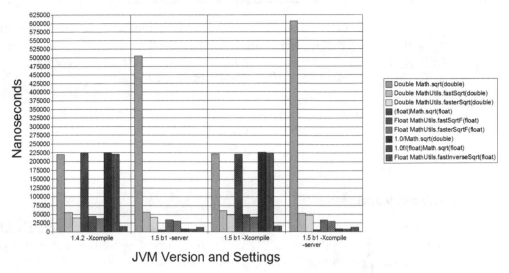

FIGURE 8.3   Square Root Tests, faster than standard math.

Both graphs sum up the time cost of the double square root, float square root, and inverse square root functions as compared to the standard math API across the JVM 1.4.2 and 1.5 beta with default, `-server`, and `-Xcompile` command-line options. The first graph shows the four fastest VMs and settings; the second graph shows the remaining four slowest.

A few interesting things come to light in these tests.

First, in many cases `(float)Math.sqrt(float)` is actually slightly more expensive than double `Math.sqrt(double)`. This result is unfortunate but makes sense because the function is actually processing doubles and has the added overhead of cast to and from floats.

Second, the alternative square root methods are slower than the standard API methods under the default JVM settings but faster than the standard API methods under `-Xcompile` or `-server`, with the exception of combination 1.4.2 `-Xcompile` `-server`. In fact, in the second graph, it is shown that those options make the standard math methods many times more expensive, which is why the alternate methods are cheaper. The alternate methods seem to have less variance than the standard math API across different JVMs and options.

VECTORS AND MATRICES

Vector and matrices APIs have been around for a long time in the Java world. Because the core operations are so basic (add, multiple, sqrt), this is one of the easiest APIs to port across programming languages, and many early vector and matrix APIs were quick ports of existing C/C++ libraries.

They are so generally useful there even exists specific machine architectures built just for computing matrices as fast as possible. The use of vectors and matrices in games is typically 2D and 3D vector manipulation for computing motion and physics, collision detection, and rendering. Vector and matrix math is a foundation of 3D graphics.

Java3D `javax.vecmath`

When Sun released Java3D, it included `javax.vecmath`, a vector and matrix API that is core to Java3D with useful 3D vector operations, as well as classes for general (m x n) matrix computations and other rotation classes, `AxisAngle` and `Quaternion`. Interestingly, it also included the seemingly out of place Java3D `Color` classes. (In `vecmath` there is an inheritance model in which all vectors inherit from Tuple, a generic component vector. Because color is a three-component set, it inherits from Tuple.)

Part of the cost of computing vector and matrix operations is the actual math operations themselves—the adds, the multiplications, and so on. On most JIT-capable VMs, these operations execute as native operations and are as fast as native code. In fact, this is one of the places JIT-compiled Java code can get really close to C++ (and sometimes even better) in terms of performance. Often, however, the performance problem can be the object data access for these operations. Depending on the object structure and the method organization, vector/matrix APIs can be either as fast as C++ or many times slower.

Java3D `vecmath` API is about as good as it gets. It is fairly simple (compared to many other available vector/matrix APIs) and cleanly implemented. It uses instance variables instead of arrays and doesn't generate any object garbage, and the instances are as compact as possible with no extraneous instance data. In our tests on the latest Java VM that support SIMD-enabled JIT compilation, we are seeing appropriate performance gains, meaning the functions are written so cleanly that the SIMD JIT compiler is having great success in matching the instructions. For most purposes, it is a fine vector/matrix API.

vecmath Weaknesses

However, for gaming, `vecmath` has a few weaknesses.

One, it is only distributed as bundled with Java3D, even though you can pull it out of the install and use it separately. No one can download it from Sun as a single API, and it is not bundled with the standard JDK.

Two, where trig and square root functions are needed, it uses the standard Math functions. Therefore, if you want to use the techniques from earlier in this chapter, you'll have to write your own utility class for vecmath and use those functions instead.

For example, rotX creates a rotation matrix using the standard formula from linear algebra, which uses Math.sin() and Math.cos(). If you want to use a lookup table or other sin/cos technique, you must write your own rotX method from scratch. Not a terribly big deal, but once you start, you'll see you will want a new rotY, rotZ, and so on, using the new fast trig functions, too.

Third, there is a float-to-double-to-float conversion in several of the matrix functions where it need not be. Of course, if you never use those methods, you'll never incur the casting cost and heavier data processing, but there is no documentation denoted where this happens, so you are on your own.

Fourth, vecmath was designed and written before ByteBuffers were in the Java platform, and much of the Java Game Technology Group's new APIs use Byte-Buffers for all the reasons covered in Chapter 5, "Java IO and NIO." Because much of game vector/matrix output ends up in ByteBuffers, utility classes for this will need to be written.

Last, it is not open source, so if you did wish to simply modify the routines to make use of faster trig functions, for example, you simply do not have the option.

Even if you choose not to use Java3D vecmath, other available vector/matrix APIs often still suffer from the previously mentioned problems.

It's not a terribly big job to write such a library, because just about all of the algorithms are published in numerous game and mathematical resources. If a project is already using a particular vector/matrix API, it's usually not terribly difficult to port the project to an improved one, either.

One last thing to consider is that these classes are often the core data structures for most games. Having total control over these is a wise design decision, especially for a commercial game.

Faster Vectors and Matrices

There are many ways in Java to create the core vector and matrix classes for a vector math library. The vector classes can use publicly exposed arrays of float, class fields, or even ByteBuffers for the vector components or hide them and provide only accessor methods in an extreme object-oriented design. They could be parent fields in an inheritance hierarchy in a general n-dimensional subclassing design.

Each scheme has its pros and cons, but from the gaming perspective, the reigning issue is performance. In key places in games (and other real-time applications), developers must forgo academic object-oriented design for performance-oriented design. There's never a shortage of discussion and disagreement about where and when performance-oriented design should affect object-oriented design, if at all. In any case, we will develop a performance-oriented vector/matrix API based on the best information we have gathered about doing so in Java. The key thing to remember is to verify that the design and implementation actually improves performance, and not just appears to be improved. That is, all assumptions must be proven correct for the best possible design. The Java VM and JIT compiler must be accounted for as well and embraced as part of the design choices for any Java performance-oriented system. We will see that with the latest VMs, the object-oriented design and performance-oriented design are not as far apart as they once were.

A few easy choices based on current general performance can be made up front. Many of these were also the same considerations for other vector/matrix APIs, such as javax.vecmath, but some are not.

Allow public access to vector and matrix components: Accessors are nice and could also be there, but public access eliminates function overhead (where VMs don't automatically eliminate it) and is often the expected usage for someone who works with vectors. Using getX(), getY(), and getZ() is quite cumbersome and unnatural.

Use only floats: This action will save on memory footprint as well as on processing costs. If, for whatever reason, double accuracy is needed, it can easily be duplicated for doubles, provided source is available. The original Java3D vecmath offered floats and double version of all of its classes.

No inheritance and only final methods: Runtime inheritance has some costs in memory and performance, and in a well-designed set of vector classes, it is not needed. This statement is arguable because vector classes do lend themselves to polymorphism, but because most methods must be reimplemented for each type anyway, we would get no real net gain in terms of method reuse, only method name uniformity, which we can just as well create by design. Therefore, in an effort to be as lightweight as possible, our classes will not have any inheritance (outside of the base Java Object), and thus, each separate 2D, 3D, and n-D class will be completely implemented.

Making the methods final does two things. First, it prevents reimplementation of the methods in a user-derived child class. Sometimes this prevention can be an annoyance, but for vectors it makes sense. There is little need to customize vector operations, and these classes are meant for in-game runtime execution. In any case, the source is open, so the developer can easily refactor the classes if he feels that action is justified.

Second, many JVMs can make special runtime optimizations to methods that are final, although newer JVMs are getting good at doing the same to non-final methods.

Use class fields instead of arrays as components: This rule is particular to Java over a C/C++ version, because in C/C++ most vector/matrix APIs use arrays. However, in Java, as was covered earlier, arrays have a hidden security cost in bounds checking. The way that a vector/matrix API accesses the components is often in semi-unordered fashion, forcing bounds checking on each access on JVMs. So, in most performance tests, even on the latest JVMs, vector component class fields are faster to access than vector component arrays. This situation may change in the future (JVM 1.5 has some new features relating to access arrays in a loop), but today and for the near future, class fields have faster access.

Use a faster math library for the core math operations: Again, the idea here is that the new math functions must really be faster on the target environment. With the latest JVM in the mix, sometimes what looks faster isn't, because the JIT will do interesting optimizations behind the scenes, and the new math method may not actually prove to be faster than the standard, as we saw earlier.

Use any specialized math instructions supported by the CPU: An example of this would be Intel Streaming SIMD Extensions (SSE) and SSE2 instructions for accelerating multimedia applications. SSE is found on Intel Pentium® III processors; SSE2 is Intel's newer instruction set supported on Intel Pentium® 4 processors. SSE and SSE2 are perfect for vector/matrix operations, and specialized C vector/matrix libraries exist that use the SSE instructions to get maximum performance on Intel hardware. It may seem desirable to have a Java vector/matrix API use the SSE instructions, but this would require the vector/matrix API to use the JNI, which introduces complications and costs that make it not worthwhile in terms of performance. (See Chapter 6, "Performance and the Java Virtual Machine.") Fortunately, there is no need to even bother developing an API that accesses these instructions because the latest JVM implementations are beginning to automatically use Pentium SSE/SSE2 features in their JITing and execution, and this will only improve in future versions.

For example, Java version 1.4.2 now uses SSE and SSE2 instruction sets for floating-point computations on platforms that support this. Figure 8.4 shows the performance gain of SSE and SSE2 instruction support as measured by SciMark 2.0, a scientific and numerical computing application that performs floating-point computations.

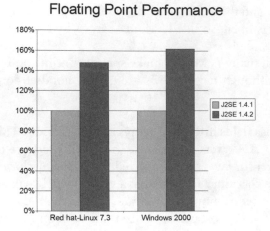

FIGURE 8.4   Floating-point performance improvement.

With this set of guidelines and the previous fast math functions, we create optimal 3D vector and matrix classes, which are nearly compatible with Java3D vecmath Vector3f, Point3f, and Matrix3f/4f.

```java
public class Vector3f
{
    public float x;
    public float y;
    public float z;

    public Vector3f(float xx, float yy, float zz)
    {
        x = xx;
        y = yy;
        z = zz;
    }

    public Vector3f(float vec[])
    {
        x = vec[0];
        y = vec[1];
        z = vec[2];
    }
```

```java
public Vector3f(Vector3f vec)
{
    x = vec.x;
    y = vec.y;
    z = vec.z;
}

public Vector3f()
{
    x = 0.0f;
    y = 0.0f;
    z = 0.0f;
}

public String toString()
{
    return "(" + x + ", " + y + ", " + z + ")";
}

public final void set(float xx, float yy, float zz)
{
    x = xx;
    y = yy;
    z = zz;
}

public final void set(float vec[])
{
    x = vec[0];
    y = vec[1];
    z = vec[2];
}

public final void set(Vector3f vec)
{
    x = vec.x;
    y = vec.y;
    z = vec.z;
}
```

```java
public final void get(float vec[])
{
    vec[0] = x;
    vec[1] = y;
    vec[2] = z;
}

public final void get(Vector3f vec)
{
    vec.x = x;
    vec.y = y;
    vec.z = z;
}

public final void add(Vector3f vec1, Vector3f vec2)
{
    x = vec1.x + vec2.x;
    y = vec1.y + vec2.y;
    z = vec1.z + vec2.z;
}

public final void add(Vector3f vec)
{
    x += vec.x;
    y += vec.y;
    z += vec.z;
}

public final void sub(Vector3f vec1, Vector3f vec2)
{
    x = vec1.x - vec2.x;
    y = vec1.y - vec2.y;
    z = vec1.z - vec2.z;
}

public final void sub(Vector3f vec)
{
    x -= vec.x;
    y -= vec.y;
    z -= vec.z;
}
```

```java
public final void negate(Vector3f vec)
{
    x = -vec.x;
    y = -vec.y;
    z = -vec.z;
}

public final void negate()
{
    x = -x;
    y = -y;
    z = -z;
}

public final void scale(float scalar, Vector3f vec)
{
    x = scalar * vec.x;
    y = scalar * vec.y;
    z = scalar * vec.z;
}

public final void scale(float scalar)
{
    x *= scalar;
    y *= scalar;
    z *= scalar;
}

public final void absolute(Vector3f vec)
{
x = Math.abs(vec.x);
y = Math.abs(vec.y);
z = Math.abs(vec.z);
}

public final void absolute()
{
    x = Math.abs(x);
    y = Math.abs(y);
    z = Math.abs(z);
}
```

```java
public final void interpolate(Vector3f vec1, Vector3f vec2,
float alpha)
{
    x = (1.0f - alpha) * vec1.x + alpha * vec2.x;
    y = (1.0f - alpha) * vec1.y + alpha * vec2.y;
    z = (1.0f - alpha) * vec1.z + alpha * vec2.z;
}

public final void interpolate(Vector3f vec, float alpha)
{
    x = (1.0f - alpha) * x + alpha * vec.x;
    y = (1.0f - alpha) * y + alpha * vec.y;
    z = (1.0f - alpha) * z + alpha * vec.z;
}

public final float lengthSquared()
{
    return x * x + y * y + z * z;
}

public final float length()
{
    return (float)Math.sqrt(x * x + y * y + z * z);
}

public final void cross(Vector3f vec1, Vector3f vec2)
{
    float xx = vec1.y * vec2.z - vec1.z * vec2.y;
    float yy = vec2.x * vec1.z - vec2.z * vec1.x;
          z = vec1.x * vec2.y - vec1.y * vec2.x;
    x = xx;
    y = yy;
}

public final float dot(Vector3f vec)
{
    return x * vec.x + y * vec.y + z * vec.z;
}

public final void normalize(Vector3f vec)
{
    float inverseMag = 1.0f / (float)Math.sqrt(vec.x *
    vec.x + vec.y * vec.y + vec.z * vec.z);
    x = vec.x * inverseMag;
```

```
        y = vec.y * inverseMag;
        z = vec.z * inverseMag;
    }

    public final void normalize()
    {
        float inverseMag = 1.0f / (float)Math.sqrt(x * x + y
        * y + z * z);
        x *= inverseMag;
        y *= inverseMag;
        z *= inverseMag;
    }

    public final float angle(Vector3f vec)
    {
        double d = dot(vec) / (length() * vec.length());
        if(d < -1D)
            d = -1D;
        if(d > 1.0D)
            d = 1.0D;
        return (float)Math.acos(d);
    }

    public final float distanceSquared(Vector3f point)
    {
        float dx = x - point.x;
        float dy = y - point.y;
        float dz = z - point.z;
        return dx * dx + dy * dy + dz * dz;
    }

    public final float distance(Vector3f point)
    {
        float dx = x - point.x;
        float dy = y - point.y;
        float dz = z - point.z;
        return (float)Math.sqrt(dx * dx + dy * dy + dz * dz);
    }
}
```

The complete Matrix classes included on disk are implemented similarly.

SUMMARY

Creating alternate math methods can pay off in certain cases, particularly with lookup tables for functions such as sine and cosine, but may not pay off well for iterative approximation methods for the typical square root implementations. Success in reducing math costs very much depends on higher-level algorithm choice, math function implementation, and the JVM version and settings. In addition, math-focused classes such as vectors and matrices can benefit greatly from careful performance-oriented design.

Java math has come a long way from its interpreted roots, and this sample set shows that trying to improve upon the latest JVM optimizations is getting increasingly difficult, yielding ever-shrinking performance gains over the standard math APIs and only worth the effort in the most specialized of cases—all of which is great news to Java game developers.

9 Game Databases and JDBC

by Will Bracken, Game Server Architect,
Game Technologies Group, Sun Microsystems

In This Chapter

INTRODUCTION

Games are rapidly evolving, growing in complexity and size. Naturally, the amount of game data and the overall persistence requirements are increasing over time. Fortunately, the amount of computing resources and hard disk space continues to grow as well. In fact, the gaming industry is really driving the evolution of computer technology in many ways, more so than many other areas of computing. These days, MMO (massively multiplayer online) games are on the rise, and for this type of system, the game data needs to be managed in an environment where access to the data is fast, efficient, and centralized. At the time of the writing of this book, a prototype engine was being tested to service a million online users in a single virtual environment. There are many challenges to building such a system, and databases play a key role. Actually, a case could be made that plenty of single-player games (such as complex RPGs) could benefit from using a database as well. Think about it. Databases are perfect for the job of managing higher volume and more complex data, as well as reducing development time and providing easier access to data. Databases are an incredibly useful tool, if not the next step in the evolutionary process of game development itself.

Of course, many games out there don't need a database at all. Perhaps small- to medium-size games may never need one. However, some of the off-the-shelf games today can contain gigabytes of data. For a large game like that, the amount or complexity of data can become a bottleneck. When there's that much data running around, it makes no sense to write custom code to store, fetch, and manage the game data—at least, not when robust, fast database technology is already available. One problem with the acceptance of the idea of using a generalized database tool is that most game developers are used to working on making the game lighter and faster, and databases can feel like an anvil. However, it's important to understand the advantages, as well as the disadvantages, of using databases. For example, most of the time game developers instinctively react negatively at the thought of deploying a database with the game because they don't want the runtime overhead that a database engine incurs. Yet it's not always that black and white. Databases can be used for tool development or for speeding up the development process as well, not just at runtime. Furthermore, especially for MMO games or networked games, the database can be deployed onto another machine, separate from the machine that hosts the game. It's important that everyone understands the different applications of the database and keeps an open mind.

This chapter focuses on the design and creation of databases, as well as accessing the database using Java, Java Database Connectivity (JDBC), and SQL. To accomplish this, many concepts will be covered, yet not all of them will be covered in great detail, because there's not enough room in this book for the extensive treatment the topic deserves. The specific concepts and techniques discussed here were chosen based on their viability and general usefulness to the majority of projects and people in the industry. Concepts presented here are meant to be as generic as possible, yet specifics will be covered where performance is concerned. The aim is to provide general and practical knowledge applicable to the most common databases and platforms. Nevertheless, by the end of reading this chapter, you should be able to design, implement, and code against working databases.

RELATIONAL DATABASES

Relational databases are the standard. They are the most widely used type of database and one of the simplest models conceptually. A relational database management system (RDBMS) stores and relates data in tables (that is, rows and columns).

Databases are simply warehouses of data. Each individual table in the database represents an abstract data type or some logical structure. The individual table cells contain the actual data itself. Each row constitutes a record in the database. Records are frequently linked to other records in other tables. Just as a Java object contains references to other objects, the same is true of records and their relationships with each other. Relating data in this way allows for fast and efficient data retrieval.

The RDBMS performs the data-retrieval operations, alleviating the need for the developer to write any code to manage or fetch the data. The use of a database essentially allows the developer to focus on the logical design of the data (and the game code) without having to worry about how the data is accessed and persisted. This level of abstraction comes at a price, though. Relational databases often, but not always, require a significant amount of overhead to run smoothly, and this can be a deterrent. It just depends on the project whether a database is warranted and how well it can fit into the system. Later we'll look at the questions that must be asked to determine whether it makes more sense to use a relational database or some other form of customized data access.

STRUCTURED QUERY LANGUAGE (SQL)

Relational databases are accessed using the Structured Query Language (SQL). SQL is the ANSI standard language for accessing relational databases. Unlike the Java language, which can do just about anything, the SQL language was designed for a single purpose: accessing data from databases. In an RDBMS, the SQL engine performs the real work behind the scenes. The engine accepts queries in the form of SQL code statements. The queries are submitted from a client application to the database server. The SQL queries are received by the database, and a fast path to the requested data is formulated. Finally, requested data is returned to the client. Sometimes, the query or the result can be cached, making future queries even faster. Typically, the queries are submitted from remote machines via network protocols. However, they can be local API calls via DLLs, often called embedded databases. There are a few different methods, which will be covered in more detail later, for communicating between a Java application and the database.

The SQL language itself is very flexible, supporting everything from simple to complex queries. These queries can be formed in a variety of ways. Mastering the SQL language takes time. To truly use the speed, power, and potential the database has to offer, advanced SQL concepts must be learned and utilized. Understanding the SQL language will also greatly improve your understanding of database structure and design. A good comprehension of the language used to access the data will give a better perspective on how the data should be organized. The data should be structured in such a way that the database can search it and traverse through it effectively. Creating efficient and intelligent queries is the key to getting the most out of database performance. Well-written SQL statements running against a well-structured database will significantly speed up database response time, allowing the database to support more concurrent users. This then allows for the fetching of more data more often, because data isn't stored or accessed redundantly or wastefully. A developer's knowledge and skill in the SQL language can have a tremendous impact on the performance of the database, as well as the system overall. SQL syntax differs slightly among databases. However, the differences are usually minor, often in the form of extensions, shortcuts, and convenience features. ANSI-standard SQL will work with most databases.

THE JDBC API

Many databases are available, each having its own unique implementation, feature set, programming interface, and so on. The performance tweaks, features, and functionality available vary and depend on the database and platform chosen. Because of these differences, migration from one database to another can be annoying and difficult. Most databases that follow ANSI SQL standards do support similar data types and can get along at some level, yet they do have their differences.

Luckily for Java developers, database access was standardized a while back. The Java Database Connectivity (JDBC) API defines a simple set of interfaces for accessing any given database, even flat files. At the time of this writing, JDBC was at version 3.0 with the JDBC 4.0 API on the way (JSR 221). The JDBC API is platform independent, as well as database independent. Therefore, no matter which database or operating system, the JDBC code will look and work the same for the majority of operations. Only when using specific proprietary database features or data types will this be a problem.

DATABASE DESIGN ESSENTIALS

This section introduces the basic concepts needed to construct a database. In the spirit of Java and JDBC, the information in this section is meant to be generic, covering fundamental knowledge applicable to all relational databases.

When shopping for a database, there are many factors to consider. For example, how much total disk space is needed? Be sure that the database server chosen can address the amount of data required. How fault tolerant does the database need to be? How well will the database perform under stress? How much data needs to be sent between the client and the database? If large amounts of data are retrieved from the database regularly, things can slow down considerably. How many users will be concurrently accessing the data? Which functionality/features of the database can be leveraged (such as stored procedures, caching, locking strategies, and API)? What about security? What about price? The list goes on and on. A good idea would be to make a spreadsheet, listing in each column the issues mentioned previously. Each row in the spreadsheet would correspond to each database being evaluated. Then, insert a number (say, between 1 and 10) to grade how each database ranks in each column, for each of the criteria. The total points earned for each database would give a general idea for overall performance and reliability. Taking this a step further, a weighting can also be applied to each column. This way, the computed total score for each database would be more influenced by those features most important. Spreadsheets and documents such as this are great for evaluating anything and make a fantastic communication tool between developers and managers. This approach is also well suited for determining if a relational database should be used at all. Simply add another category for each type of custom software being evaluated for data storage and compare it to the databases. Don't forget to add a criterion for development time, if you are thinking of writing your data access software.

Design Patterns

Every project will have unique design challenges. Models, templates, and design patterns should be used whenever and wherever possible. Using a model helps to simplify design and abstracts complex tasks. Using design patterns also gives the code a standardized and consistent look and feel, making it highly readable and attractive for reuse. Custom design is generally required at some point during every project, but should be avoided when a clear solution can be found using a model. Custom design/implementation is likely to introduce bugs into the code as well. It's a good idea to adhere to some set of guidelines when designing anything. Several good sources of design patterns are available both for general and Java-specific software design.

Database Normalization

Database normalization is the process of structuring the database tables in such a way that the data that is stored in those tables is balanced and organized so that searches are executed efficiently and deterministically. The basic idea is to keep related data together in logical groups. In the same way Java objects contain attributes that relate to that object, tables contain data representing a concept or type and are related via pointers, or keys. Data should be distributed across the tables evenly. Why? Each table should represent a related set of data. Avoid storing data redundantly across multiple tables. This practice not only will save disk space but also can reduce search time because there is less data to traverse. However, the most important reason to normalize data is for data integrity. If data is not normalized, any data that is changed has to be changed in several places. A denormalized database can sometimes be faster to query but more complicated to update and maintain. A normalized database will provide solid, reliable performance. Indexes should be used for bigger tables or for often-queried data, minimizing the time spent scanning through potentially large amounts of data. Also, the number of columns in a table shouldn't be very high. If you are designing a database and find yourself putting in lots and lots of columns in your tables, it is often an indicator that your data might need to be reorganized. If a table is not only large but wide as well, it will slow down the search even more if searching for non-key or non-indexed columns. Creating indexes helps the RDBMS to resolve complex and resource-intensive queries because it doesn't need to look at every row in the table.

Data should be logically grouped into tables, which are easy to manage and intuitive to relate. The result of a properly normalized database is one that is well organized and highly deterministic. Database normalization is typically performed through a progressive series of Normal Forms, the details of which aren't covered here, but each form is basically a step or progression in refactoring the database to achieve a higher and higher level of normalization, balance, and stasis. A good rule of thumb to determine whether your data is properly normalized is to make sure that every column in a table is related to "the key, the whole key, and nothing but the key."

KEYS, INDEXES, AND REFERENTIAL INTEGRITY

Primary keys uniquely identify records in the database. These keys can be thought of as the fingerprint of a record. Any number, such as a phone number, can be used as the value for the key, as long as it's unique. These types of keys are called *natural keys*. Natural keys are numbers or values that exist naturally in the world and can be used to uniquely identify somebody or something. Using natural keys can spell trouble, though, because once the primary key has been set, it cannot be updated in the future. Therefore, if a phone number is used to represent the key, and that number changes, nothing short of deleting and reinserting that record can be done. *Synthetic keys* are system-generated numbers, sometimes created by the database itself, which could be a number sequence or globally unique identifier (GUID). Synthetic key values, sometimes called dataless keys, offer an advantage because their value has no meaning to any person or to the application itself. Figure 9.1 shows two database tables, player and item. Each column contains a column named id, which will be used to uniquely identify players and items.

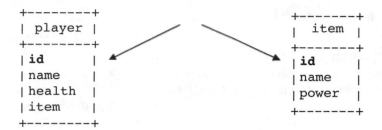

FIGURE 9.1   Player and item database tables.

Foreign keys act as pointers, or references, to the primary keys of records in other tables. Foreign keys maintain the relationships between tables, making the database relational. The tables and their relationships make up the structure of the database system, referred to as the database s*chema*. Figure 9.2 shows the foreign key relationship between the two tables.

Indexes are small, system-generated tables that contain a summary (or subset) of data found in a complete table. Indexing works in a similar manner to the index of a book. When indexes are used, only the relevant data is traversed during a

FIGURE 9.2   Foreign key relationship.

search. Tables can get large and hold many thousands (or millions) of records. The database will check for, and use, any indexes available to it. Indexes are a must for any large database, but the process does slow down data inserts, because the index tables must be written to in addition to the other tables. However, the indexes balance the queries, and overall performance is increased drastically. Without indexes, performance could be potentially dreadful, because searches would involve complete table scans. Primary keys and foreign keys are almost always indexed, but other columns that are frequently used in searches may be indexed as well.

Referential Integrity

Relational databases relate data. *Referential integrity* is the enforcement of these relationships. Java allows an object to hold a reference to another object that is null, right? Well, the database can do the same. If allowed, the database will store records that contain foreign keys into other tables, even if the foreign keys don't reference any valid existing record. For a Java object, using such a reference would result in disaster, and a NullPointerException would be thrown. The database does something similar, and neither is desired. However, if the database does enforce referential integrity, it will not allow keys to point to null data. If referential integrity is enforced, all foreign keys in the record must point to valid records in the database; otherwise, the database will throw an error. This constrains the system, keeping the relational structure intact.

Occasionally, it is necessary to build a database in a generic way, throwing caution and referential integrity to the wind. Generic in this case means that no structure is imposed on the data. Why would someone want this? It's sometimes desirable to build database tables that store data generically, similar to a base class in Java. In this circumstance, a table may store many different kinds of records. Making multipurpose tables can be an attractive solution for larger databases, which can get very ugly very quickly, holding vast amounts of data in numerous tables that have complex relationships. Based on the kind of information written into that table, key relationships may or may not exist. Therefore, to do this, referential integrity must be disabled. Again, with it enabled, key references cannot be null. In spite of this, enforcing referential integrity is always advised, and there should be a really good reason for not using it. Although generic tables can keep the number of tables down, table size, as well as the complexity of the queries, increases.

Online Resources

JDBC Home Page: *http://java.sun.com/products/jdbc*

JDBC Download Page: *http://java.sun.com/products/jdbc/download.html*

JDBC Learning Center: *http://java.sun.com/products/jdbc/learning.html*

JDBC FAQ: *http://java.sun.com/products/jdbc/faq.html*

JDBC Driver Search: *http://servlet.java.sun.com/products/jdbc/drivers*

THE MYSQL DATABASE

Many databases are out there from which to choose. Some of the best ones are even free! MySQL was chosen as a demonstration database in this book because it's fast, popular, stable, and standards compliant. Oh, yeah—it's also free! Seriously,

MySQL is able to handle many concurrent users and store millions of records. It's multithreaded, allowing many concurrent users, as well as able to distribute the database server application across multiple CPUs. Here we'll cover the basics of getting an instance of the MySQL server up and running. This section relates to MySQL-specific tools and features, so if you already have another database vendor in mind, you can skip this section.

Installing MySQL

The first thing to do is to navigate to *www.mysql.com* and download the latest stable version, which at the time of this writing was the MySQL4.0.14b production release. For Windows users, simply download the binary distribution, unzip it, and then double-click the *setup.exe* file and install using the default settings. That's it, done. However, if you're using Unix or another platform, chances are the installation and configuration instructions are more complex and are probably as lengthy as this chapter. If you're using such a platform, you'll have to consult the MySQL installation documentation.

This section assumes you are using a Windows 2000/XP operating system and the installation target directory is *c:\mysql*. No matter which Windows platform you're on, once the installation has completed, add `c:\mysql\bin` to the PATH system environment variable, located in the control panel for the Windows users.

Starting the Server

When the installation is complete and the PATH variable has been set, open a shell or DOS prompt and type the `mysqld` command to start the server:

```
mysql> mysqld
```

If the server started correctly without error, nothing should print to the console, and the prompt will be unavailable, because *mysqld.exe* is now running in that shell.

Connecting a Client

To connect to the server, open another shell (the first shell is hosting the server process) and invoke the `mysql` command:

```
mysql> mysql
```

A password may be required to start the server, depending on the database configuration. If the logon is successful, the following lines will be printed to the console:

```
Welcome to the MySQL monitor.  Commands end with ; or \g.
Your MySQL connection id is 25338 to server version: 4.0.14-log
Type 'help;' or '\h' for help. Type '\c' to clear the buffer.
```

If everything so far has gone well, the client should now be connected to the database server, and the server is now ready to receive commands from the client. To test your connection, try a simply query with the SELECT command:

```
mysql> SELECT version();
+---------------+
| version()     |
+---------------+
| 4.0.14-max-debug |
+---------------+
1 row in set (0.00 sec)
```

If the SELECT was executed successfully and the version information is printed to the console, it's safe to say the database server is up and running, and the client is connected and has access to the data in the database. To get help at any time, type the following command:

```
mysql> help
```

Building a Database

Immediately after installing the MySQL database server, there's not much to look at. However, a couple of databases are already running. To view a list of the currently active databases, use the SHOW command:

```
mysql> SHOW databases;
+----------+
| Database |
+----------+
| mysql    |
| test     |
+----------+
2 rows in set (0.00 sec)
```

The mysql database contains system-level information, and its use is beyond the scope of this chapter. The test database is simply there for practice and learning. A new database can be created using the CREATE command:

```
mysql> CREATE DATABASE gamedb;
Query OK, 1 row affected (0.01 sec)
```

To confirm that the new database was successfully created, use the SHOW command again to list the database instances running on the server:

```
mysql> SHOW databases;
+———+
| Database |
+———+
| gamedb   |
| mysql    |
| test     |
+———+
3 rows in set (0.00 sec)
```

The client (at least from this shell) can be connected to, or operate on, only one database at a time. The process of switching focus from one database context to another involves using the USE command:

```
mysql> USE gamedb;
Database changed
```

At this point, commands will be executed within the context of the gamedb database. The database is, of course, empty, because it was just created. Tables will have to be created and populated with data before things get off the ground. It should be noted that although a shell is being used to send commands to the database, scripts can be written to do the same things, such as creating databases and tables. In fact, it's recommended that the database be created from a script. This way, if a change needs to be made, it can be made to the script itself without having to type individual commands into a shell, one by one. Database scripts can be saved into text files and run any time.

Now that the game database exists, it's time to create a couple of database tables. The following code will create a player and an item table. The player table will contain a foreign key to the item table. The following SQL code will create the two tables.

```
CREATE TABLE player(
    id SMALLINT UNSIGNED NOT NULL,
    name CHAR(60) NOT NULL,
    health SMALLINT NOT NULL,
    item SMALLINT UNSIGNED NOT NULL REFERENCES item(id),
    PRIMARY KEY (id)
);
```

```
CREATE TABLE item (
    id SMALLINT UNSIGNED NOT NULL,
    name CHAR(60) NOT NULL,
    power SMALLINT NOT NULL,
    PRIMARY KEY (id)
);
```

To verify that the tables have been created, use the SHOW command:

```
mysql> SHOW tables;

+----------------+
| Tables_in_gamedb |
+----------------+
| item           |
| player         |
+----------------+
2 rows in set (0.00 sec)
```

The DESCRIBE command can also be used to view details (the keys are shown in bold):

```
mysql> DESCRIBE player;
```

Field	Type	Null	Key	Default	Extra
id	smallint(5) unsigned		PRI	0	
name	char(60)				
health	smallint(6)			0	
item	smallint(5) unsigned			0	

```
4 rows in set (0.00 sec)
```

```
mysql> DESCRIBE item;
```

Field	Type	Null	Key	Default	Extra
id	smallint(5) unsigned		PRI	0	
name	char(60)				
power	smallint(6)			0	

```
3 rows in set (0.00 sec)
```

Before anything useful can be done with the tables, they must be populated with data. Using the SQL INSERT statement, you can easily insert a few records using the following commands.

```
INSERT INTO item values(1,"Dagger",5);
INSERT INTO item values(2,"Sword",12);
INSERT INTO item values(3,"Axe",20);

INSERT INTO player values(1,"Will",75,1);
INSERT INTO player values(2,"Shawn",100,2);
INSERT INTO player values(3,"Chad",87,2);
```

SQL commands will be covered in more detail shortly. For now, these simple commands should be readable enough to get the point across. Now that a few records have been placed in the tables, the SELECT statement can be used to verify/view the data:

```
mysql> SELECT * FROM item;
+----+--------+-------+
| id | name   | power |
+----+--------+-------+
|  1 | Dagger |     5 |
|  2 | Sword  |    12 |
|  3 | Axe    |    20 |
+----+--------+-------+
3 rows in set (0.00 sec)


mysql> SELECT * FROM player;
+----+-------+--------+------+
| id | name  | health | item |
+----+-------+--------+------+
|  1 | Will  |    100 |    1 |
|  2 | Shawn |    100 |    2 |
|  3 | Chad  |    100 |    2 |
+----+-------+--------+------+
3 rows in set (0.00 sec)
```

When the session needs to be ended, the client may be disconnected from the server by issuing the QUIT command:

```
mysql> quit
```

Online Resources

For the complete MySQL Manual online visit: *www.mysql.com/documentation*

For information on technical support from MySQL developers, visit: *www.mysql.com/support*

For information on MySQL books, utilities, consultants, and so on, visit: *www.mysql.com/portal*

GENERAL JDBC USAGE

As mentioned in the beginning of this chapter, JDBC defines a set of interfaces for accessing any given database. The JDBC API facilitates the transfer of data from persistent storage into an application. This section explores loading a database driver, connecting to a database, and accessing the data using JDBC and SQL. To get started with JDBC, all that's needed is the JDK, 1.2 or later.

Quote from *java.sun.com*: "All of the JDBC™ 3.0 API, including both the java.sql and javax.sql packages, is bundled with the Java 2 Platform, Standard Edition, version 1.4 (J2SE). If you have downloaded the J2SE platform, you already have all of the JDBC™ API and do not need to download anything . . .

JDBC Drivers

As mentioned earlier, all databases work in their own unique way. JDBC provides the interfaces that each and every JDBC driver must implement for its corresponding database. JDBC drivers essentially translate function calls into database-specific tasks. Most commercial databases ship with drivers. However, third-party drivers are often available as well and are sometimes better. Driver implementations vary in their speed, efficiency, reliability, and so on. There are also different types of drivers:

Type 1: JDBC-ODBC Bridge, which translates JDBC calls into ODBC calls. Microsoft's Object Database Connectivity (ODBC) is Microsoft's standard interface for accessing relational databases.

Type 2: Converts JDBC calls into native database calls using .dll files or other native binary code.

Type 3: Communicates through middleware/proxy via network protocols. No drivers needed. Broad support for multiple vendors and protocols. Secure.

Type 4: This driver type uses the network protocols of the RDBMS directly and requires no installation of code to the client.

The differences between the driver types are mostly the communications protocols. Despite the differences, the JDBC API is used in the same uniform way, regardless of the driver type. For example, switching from a type 2 driver to a type 4 driver does not require any modification to the code. In fact, switching driver manufacturers, or even databases (with a few exceptions), requires little or no modification of code. One thing to note is that not every database comes with all four types. In fact, some may not ship with any Java drivers, although these days that's pretty rare given Java's incredible popularity and success in so many areas of computing. At any rate, between the database vendor and the third-party driver manufacturers out there, the bases are covered and drivers shouldn't be hard to hunt down.

Connecting to the Database

Drivers are generally packaged in the form of a .jar or .zip archive. Whatever shape or form the driver comes in, it should be incorporated into the project. When using an IDE, the .jar or .zip file can be added to the project classpath, which will hopefully enable the code-complete features of the IDE to work with the driver. If you are not using an IDE, just be sure to add the driver to the build and runtime classpath. When the project configuration is properly set up, the following code will load the driver at runtime, assuming you are using MySQL:

```
Class.forName("com.mysql.jdbc.Driver");
```

If the classpath is not set correctly, the com.mysql.jdbc.Driver class will not be resolved, and the driver will not be loaded. Thus, communication to the database will not be possible. If everything is set up correctly, communication between the client and the database can be established via the java.sql.Connection object. When the driver has been loaded, a connection to the database can be requested from the java.sql.DriverManager class in one of the following ways:

```
Connection conn =
    DriverManager.getConnection(url);

Connection conn =
    DriverManager.getConnection(url, username, password);

Connection conn =
    DriverManager.getConnection(url, propertiesFile);
```

Data Access Using SQL

All database access to standard relational databases is through SQL. Invoking SQL can be done explicitly, such as in the command-line examples mentioned previously or implicitly through a utility or library. A few technologies exist which almost completely abstract developers from the actual SQL used for database access. For example, a certain form of EJB (Enterprise JavaBeans) can be used to hide all of the SQL statements submitted to the database. All the developer must do is request a Java object and supply the primary key. The EJB then uses what is called CMP (Container Managed Persistence) to access the data for you. However, this method is a double-edged sword. Because the SQL is procedurally generated and hidden, there isn't much flexibility or room for tweaking. Most developers prefer to write the SQL, because this option offers the most functionality and flexibility and also allows the SQL to be tuned for specific purposes. SQL is a powerful and rich language, and the full syntax and usage is beyond the scope of this chapter. Many SQL resources are available to describe the full SQL language and its usage, but at its most simple, SQL statements are formed using one of the following keywords:

SELECT: Read data from the database

INSERT: Write data to the database

UPDATE: Update preexisting data in the database

DELETE: Delete data from the database

Examples:

Fetch some player data:

```
SELECT name FROM player WHERE name='Will'
```

Insert a player:

```
INSERT INTO player VALUES (..., ..., ...)
```

Update player information:

```
UPDATE player SET item=3 WHERE id=2
```

Delete a player:

```
DELETE FROM player WHERE name='Will'
```

SQL statements are stored in strings and are executed in the context of a java.sql.Statement object. Statements are created, prepared, and executed via the Connection object. The statement, when executed, may return a Boolean, an int, int[], or a ResultSet, depending on the SQL sent to the database. After a SQL query has been formulated and stored in a string, it may be executed like the following lines:

```
Statement stmt = conn.createStatement();
stmt.execute(query);
```

The way in which the execute() method is used varies, depending on the task at hand. The different method signatures today in the JDK 1.4 follow:

```
boolean execute(String sql)
boolean execute(String sql, int autoGeneratedKeys)
boolean execute(String sql, int[] columnIndexes)
boolean execute(String sql, String[] columnNames)
int[] executeBatch()
ResultSet executeQuery(String sql)
int executeUpdate(String sql)
int executeUpdate(String sql, int autoGeneratedKeys)
int executeUpdate(String sql, int[] columnIndexes)
int executeUpdate(String sql, String[] columnNames)
```

One form of statement called a PreparedStatement can be prepared in advance and executed much more quickly. A PreparedStatement is typically used when the same SQL statement is expected to be executed many times. More information on PreparedStatements is discussed later.

In the case that data is returned to the client, the results may be accessed via the java.sql.ResultSet interface. The data is represented to the client as a table. A cursor, which is like a temporary pointer into the table, is provided and can be positioned anywhere on the table, and getter methods are used to retrieve data from the cells. The code will look something like this:

```
Statement stmt = conn.createStatement();
String sql = "SELECT * FROM player";
ResultSet rs = stmt.executeQuery(sql);
While(rs.next()) {
    rs.getXXX(columnNumber);
}
```

Depending on the data type of the column you're accessing, the getter methods will vary. A few of these methods follow:

```
rs.getInt()
rs.getString()
rs.getBytes()
rs.getDate()
```

If anything goes wrong during execution, a `java.sql.SQLException` will be thrown. The SQLException provides a few useful methods, which help to locate problem areas producing the error condition. A couple of them are worth mentioning.

int getErrorCode(): Each database vendor has its own set of exception codes. The application will typically log the error code received. The error code helps with debugging, because it can be referenced in the database documentation and will hopefully shed some light on an otherwise dark situation.

String getMessage(): This function returns a verbose (hopefully) message indicating what went wrong, or at least how the driver perceived the error condition. This function is inherited from `java.lang.Throwable` and can naturally be used with any Exception.

By default, all of the database inserts/updates are committed as soon as the statements finish execution. However, it is possible to invoke SQL commands in a transactional scope, which is configured using the Connection object:

```
conn.setAutoCommit(false);
```

Sometimes several tables in the database must be updated at once, because they are all executed in the same logical context. Transactions require that either all of the database tables in question are updated successfully, or none at all. The idea is to perform all of the database updates and then commit those changes when they've all been completed, assuming nothing went wrong during the transaction. After all of the appropriate tables have been written to, the data can be finalized simply by calling the commit() function:

```
conn.commit();
```

Your saving grace is that if anything does go wrong, there is always an undo option, typically placed in a catch() block:

```
conn.rollback();
```

The entire code block will look something like the following:

```
Connection conn = DriverManager.getConnection(url);
conn.setAutoCommit(false);
Statement stmt = conn.createStatement();
try {
    stmt.execute(query1);
    stmt.execute(query2);
    stmt.execute(query3);
    conn.commit();
}
catch(SQLException sqlE)
{
    conn.rollback();
}
```

JDBC resources should be released when they are no longer needed. The Connection is automatically closed when it is garbage collected. However, depending on the configuration of the JVM and garbage collection strategy employed, that Connection may hang around a while before it is collected. Thus, avoid tying up database resources by closing the objects manually. It's best to do this in reverse order:

```
results.close();
stmt.close();
conn.close();
```

JDBC PERFORMANCE TECHNIQUES

It's hard to give specific advice on such a vast and complex topic such as databases. Things really depend on the particular project, the requirements, budget, and so on. Before specific techniques are discussed, a few general factors must be considered first, all of which can affect database performance dramatically. The following questions should be considered up front:

Frequency: How many requests per minute/hour will users make? How large is the user group accessing the database? As the number of users increases, so will the number of queries sent to the database. More queries means more compiles on the database server, more disk access, more network traffic, and so on.

Size: How big will the tables get? Large database tables mean slower query execution times, because there is more data to scan. Indexing will help and is highly recommended for tables that are frequently accessed or of significant size.

Complexity: How complex are the relationships between the data? In other words, how difficult will it be for the database to find a path to the data requested? Complexity in the data structure will obviously slow down queries. Indexing can help out here as well.

We should all proactively seek to take advantage of any features (in the database, in Java, in the operating system, or from anywhere) that might help out or speed up development time or runtime performance. Many databases will perform optimizations automatically, without any prompting or extra configuration, but relying solely on the database, the drivers, the garbage collector, and the like to keep your application running clean is not a good idea. Resources should be managed responsibly and efficiently.

Efficient Runtime JDBC Access

Database performance can be excellent, but it is always faster to get data if you know exactly where it is and how it is organized. Where databases really shine is in separating the data storage from the data access, which increases flexibility and ease of development and maintenance. Commercial database technology has been around a long time, and the optimization techniques are good, allowing efficient and high-performance database use without having to know the specifics of the database storage mechanism. You can expect a good commercial-quality database to be fast and support many concurrent users and countless queries. Then again, even the biggest, fastest database will perform dreadfully if it's not accessed properly and efficiently. For example, submitting a large number of queries in a short amount of time could cripple the database. Equally, a small number of queries could do the same given that they force the database to scan through very large amounts of data. Every effort must be made to lift any extra burden off the database. Indexing is one of the most powerful means of reducing the time it takes to search through records. Using well-formed SQL statements, which efficiently access the data, is of utmost importance. Although it is counterproductive to form queries so complex that nobody can read them, submitting a single query for every piece of data is overkill. It's probably best to find a happy medium. Minimize the number of trips to the database to reduce the number of tasks the database is dealing with at any given point in time. For example, it is always better from a performance point of view—although not always from a memory-conservation point of view—to retrieve larger amounts of data less often, rather than submitting a large number of queries for small amounts of data. For example, it's almost always better to do the following:

```
SELECT * FROM TABLE
```

than this:

```
SELECT COL1 FROM TABLE
SELECT COL2 FROM TABLE
SELECT COL3 FROM TABLE
SELECT COL4 FROM TABLE
```

Joins

Joins are operations that merge data from different tables into one context. This operation allows data from various tables to be combined into an efficient, single query and resultant data set. Doing so eliminates the need to query each table independently and allows more of the logic to be performed inside of the RDBMS engine, where it can be optimized for data access, rather than evaluate the values of the data in the Java code. From the application's perspective, complex sets of data can be treated as if they were a single structure. Meanwhile, the SQL (or database access code) acts as a facade, making the interface to the database much simpler. To illustrate this, see Figure 9.3. The figure depicts two sets of data from two tables, one to the left, and one to the right.

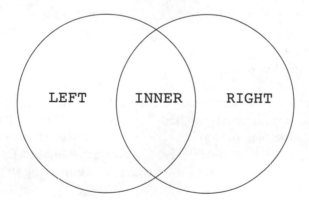

FIGURE 9.3 Two sets of data from two tables.

There are a few different strategies for joining data. Using the previous diagram as a reference, the types of Joins can be summarized as follows:

Inner Joins: Return all the records from the left and right table that match the WHERE clause.

Left Outer Joins: Return all the records from the left, but only those on the right that match the WHERE clause.

Right Outer Joins: Return all the records from the right, but only those on the left that match the WHERE clause.

Full Joins: Return all records from both tables.

The syntax may differ among databases, but should be close to the following format:

```
SELECT column1, column2
FROM table1,table2
WHERE ...
```

Query Plan Caching

The database will always seek the quickest and most efficient path to the data because the RDBMS knows exactly how the data is organized. Caching query plans is one way the database can really save time. When a SQL statement is submitted, the database must:

- Parse the SQL query
- Build a plan/path to the data
- Compile the plan
- Execute the plan
- Return the results

That's a lot of work for the database! Fortunately, most queries are used repeatedly, and they can be cached. There's no need for the database to keep compiling the same plan over and over. To take advantage of caching features, use the `java.sql.PreparedStatement` object. As the name implies, the statement is prepared and remains ready and set for repeated use, eliminating steps 1, 2, and 3 from the previous list.

```
String insertSQL = "INSERT INTO player VALUES(?,?,?)";
PreparedStatement pstmt = conn.prepareStatement(insertSQL);
```

The SQL INSERT has now been parameterized. Player information can now be inserted repeatedly by reusing the `PreparedStatement` pstmt object. The rest of the operation is done as follows:

```
pstmt.setInt(1, 4);
pstmt.setString(2, "Joe");
pstmt.setInt(3, 100);
pstmt.setInt(4, 2);
```

When all of the parameters have been set, the statement can be executed:

```
pstmt.execute();
```

As mentioned earlier, some caching may automatically be performed by the database, with or without your knowledge or intervention. For example, the MySQL Query Cache allows caching of query responses themselves. The database administrator can typically adjust the type (caching algorithm), size (memory usage), and limit (max result size) of the cache. When a client submits a cached query, the value in the cache, rather than the query execution, is returned. When new data is written to the tables, the cached queries are removed from cache. This behavior keeps the important, commonly accessed data in memory, allowing fast access to that data. SQL statements should also be executed in batches whenever possible. Doing so further minimizes trips to the database and excessive use of database resources, as well as disk access. The tradeoff for this improved performance is increased memory usage, so it is important to balance the two for your specific needs.

Stored Procedures

If a significant amount of logic must be applied to the data in the database, stored procedures can be of great help and improve performance of the overall system. Stored procedures are basically functions or logic that get executed on the database server. Therefore, certain tasks can be removed from the game servers and clients and moved to the database servers, freeing up valuable resources on the client and server machines. Unfortunately, not all databases support stored procedures. Stored procedures are similar to methods and functions in Java. They can accept parameters, execute arbitrary logic, and, if the database server supports it, return results. The major difference is that these functions are executed inside the database and not on the JVM.

The language and syntax used for writing stored procedures varies across databases. There is no standard, and depending on the database, stored procedures may be written in one of many languages. Thus, migrating stored procedures to another database may be difficult, depending on how they're written. You should be committed to a database before developing a significant amount of stored procedures, because they are typically not compatible with other databases. Stored procedures may be written using Java, SQLJ, C, and other languages but are most often written using some form of SQL (TSQL, PL/SQL, and so on). SQL and TSQL are preferred because they are much more intuitive languages for operating on data.

MySQL supports stored procedures in version 5.0, which was not available at the time of this writing but is on the way. However, some documentation is already available to illustrate the syntax and use of stored procedures in MySQL:

```
CREATE PROCEDURE
foo([IN] x INT, INOUT y INT, OUT z FLOAT)
...body...

CREATE FUNCTION bar(x INT, y CHAR(8))
RETURNS CHAR(16)
...body with RETURN...

CALL foo(1, 2, var)

SELECT * FROM table WHERE x = bar(y, "foo")

DROP PROCEDURE foo
```

Calling the stored procedure from Java will look something like the following:

```
CallableStatement callStmt = null;

callStmt = conn.prepareCall("{ call function (?, ?) }");
callStmt.setInt(1, intVal);
callStmt.setString(2, stringVal);
callStmt.execute();

callStmt.close();
```

The DAO Pattern

The *data access object* (DAO) design pattern is popular and useful. At a high level, the DAO pattern is a framework or template used to decouple the business logic from persistence logic. DAOs abstract and encapsulate database access, the outcome of which is an object-relational mapping. This mapping (between Java objects and database tables) can be one-to-one, one-to-many, or many-to-many. Each DAO implements a common interface for accessing data, typically implementing read() and write() functions, or something to that effect. This wrapper layer of code allows the database-specific operations to be performed independently of the application logic.

Benefits of using DAO pattern follow:

- Simplifies coding
- Decouples business logic from persistence logic
- Provides transparent access to data
- Has a minimal schedule impact if migration is necessary

The *Java 2 Enterprise Edition* (J2EE) provides something similar to DAOs. Enterprise JavaBeans (EJB) achieves a similar end. In fact, there is tons of functionality in J2EE that could be leveraged by the game-development community. However, the J2EE platform is probably too much baggage for most games. It really depends on the project. EJBs are different in that they are managed in a container environment, which handles the creation and invocation of the beans, as well as the database access, transaction management, failover, clustering, and much more. All the developer must do is define the beans, configure and deploy them, and that's it. This is great! However, the disadvantage of using EJBs is that in their container-managed form, they aren't that extensible and may not perform as optimally as a custom solution. On the other hand, the J2EE is perfect for massive, distributed, online games that must manage vast amounts of resources reliably and securely. The J2EE has been proving itself every day in the enterprise for years in large-scale, mission-critical applications.

The *Java Data Object* (JDO) API is another example of a technology that uses the DAO pattern. Using JDO API is simpler than using EJBs, but it provides the foundation for using an abstract layer between application code and the database itself. Several commercial implementations of the JDO API exist.

DATA CACHING

Using the DAO layer involves instantiating objects and filling them with data to be consumed by the application. When instances of these objects exist, they can be persisted in memory, on a middle tier or somewhere else. In this way, data access not only is efficient but can be centralized, localized, and distributed. The general aim is to make data quickly available to the parts of the application that need it, without hitting the database more often than necessary.

Take, for instance, a multiplayer networked game, which needs to provide a lot of data to a lot of people. Naturally, most of the data being sent to each user is the same for every user, because the data likely describes the environment in which every player is immersed. Given this example, assuming a sizeable number of users exist, it would not then be efficient for every client to send a request to the database for the same data; the database should be accessed only when necessary. When the application needs data, it should check the cache before going to the database. The cache might consist of the DAO instances stored in `java.util.Collection` objects. The DAO objects in cache can then perhaps be updated regularly, as needed, or in response to the database tables being updated. The cached data objects could potentially be managed in a variety of ways and deployed anywhere.

At least one game company, Galactic Village Games, has implemented its own homegrown DAO system, which provides all the advantages mentioned previously. In addition to gaining the performance that caching provides, that company has also been able to deploy to at least five runtime database systems with minimal effort by making good use of the DAO pattern.

SUMMARY

The day has arrived when just about every off-the-shelf PC comes with a video card, sound card, and all the other hardware necessary to play most of today's hottest games. People are abandoning their dial-up connections in favor of the broadband cable and DSL speeds. Many of today's games are quite complex, taking advantage of these evolutionary leaps in computer science and programming. Along with the increased complexity comes a lot of data that must be well managed, and it's just not cost-effective to write file-management software from scratch anymore. We can't deny the increasingly important role databases are playing in game development. In fact, for some games, such as MMOs, databases are already a must-have.

In this chapter, we discussed relational databases and how to access them using JDBC and SQL. Meanwhile, performance considerations are paramount, as they always are in game development. Database design fundamentals were covered thoroughly, as well as database creation, illustrated using the MySQL database.

10 Java as a Scripting Language

In This Chapter

- Introduction
- Overview of a Scripting Language
- Characteristics of a Scripting Language
- Why Use an Existing Scripting Language
- Why C/C++ Cannot Be a Scripting Language
- Why Java Can Be a Scripting Language
- Integrating an Existing Language
- Summary

INTRODUCTION

Productivity of a team as a whole is undoubtedly fundamental to the success a project. It is crucial for a studio to have an efficient development pipeline. This is especially true for highly competitive markets such as gaming. Bottlenecks in the development pipeline can cost a studio a substantial amount of money. In fact, if a game takes too long to develop or is not well polished, the entire project may be canceled. If some tool or technology can save each developer even a few minutes per day, the overall time that could be better utilized can add up to make a substantial difference.

A scripting language allows for a smoother development pipeline, which in turn increases the productivity of the team. Many scripting languages have been used by different applications, including games, and their popularity has been growing over the years. Even though Java is not exactly a scripting language, it is suited and well capable of being used as a powerful scripting language. As far as programming languages are concerned, Java falls between a low-level language such as C/C++ and a high-level scripting language such as Lua or Python. Games use scripting languages for tasks that range anywhere from managing the graphical user interfaces (GUIs) to controlling nonplayer characters (NPCs). In this chapter, we will provide a brief overview of how they work, discuss the characteristics of scripting languages, explain why it is good to use an existing language, discuss the characteristics of Java as a scripting language, and provide an example program that launches the VM and executes a script.

OVERVIEW OF A SCRIPTING LANGUAGE

The common term referred to as *scripting language* is actually more than just a language. It is composed of two separate components: the language that defines the syntax rules for writing the scripts, and an interpreter that can execute the script. Examples of scripting languages are Lua, Python, and MEL™ Script (Maya® Script). They all have their own grammar rules and an interpreter that executes scripts.

The interpreter, which is responsible for carrying out the computations defined in a segment of script, is referred to as the scripting engine or the virtual machine. The interpreter is essentially an emulator. It is responsible for looking at a segment of script and performing what the script is trying to do.

Before a script can be executed by the interpreter, its syntax must be verified to make sure that it follows the rules of the specific language. When the syntax has been verified, the script must be compiled into a series of instructions that can be executed one at a time. Even a simple arithmetic expression has to be broken down. In the following example, code must be broken down so that force/mass is computed, the result is added to velocity, and the final result is stored into velocity.

```
velocity = velocity + force/mass
```

Similarly, a loop must be broken down into several lower-level instructions, such as initializing the loop counter, checking termination condition, and incrementing the loop counter. The interpreter can perform the velocity computation using LOAD, STORE, ADD, and DIV instructions. Likewise, a loop can be carried out using LOAD, STORE, ADD, conditional check, and conditional branch instructions. A form of LOAD and STORE instructions is required to read from and write to variables.

The process of verifying the syntax and translating a script is in many ways similar to what happens when a source of a static language such as C/C++ is compiled. A C/C++ compiler takes the source code and converts it to the assembly instructions of a specific CPU. For example, the Microsoft® Visual C++® 6.0 compiler converts C++ source to Intel 8086 instructions. If the target platform is of a different architecture, the corresponding compiler must be used to generate code that can be executed by the target CPU. For example, the Sony® PS®2 Vector Unit instruction set is entirely different from the Intel 8086 instruction set. In contrast, the compiler of a scripting language always converts the source to the assembly instructions of an abstract or virtual machine. These instructions are typically referred to as bytecodes.

A virtual machine can be modeled after different types of machines. The most generic and simple is a stack-based machine, which does not have special-purpose registers. For example, some Pentium opcodes rely on a specific register for their operands. A stack machine, however, simply uses a stack to store the operands and the output for all operations. The instructions of a stack-based machine pop their operands from the stack and push their results back onto the stack.

An interpreter typically compiles scripts at runtime. When the interpreter comes upon a block that needs to be executed, it compiles the block and executes it. Almost every scripting language also has a support to precompile the scripts. This practice reduces the overhead during runtime and allows for more efficient script execution. In addition, it helps to catch some errors ahead of time.

It is fundamental for a scripting language to provide a mechanism to call native functions (functions implemented in languages such as C/C++ or Assembly) from a script because some tasks must be accomplished in native code. For example, it is not possible to even open a file unless some native code can be executed (directly or indirectly) from the script so that it can talk with the underlying operating system. More important, without the ability to call native functions from a script, it would not be possible to write scripts that manipulate a native application or library such a game engine. A scripting language should also allow a native application to launch its virtual machine. Because both the operating systems and the virtual machines are typically written in native languages, a native application must be launched, which can in turn launch the interpreter.

A scripting engine also has a form of memory manager. The memory manager is responsible for allocating memory and collecting memory that is no longer used. It maintains the heap and compacts data in the heap so that it can have a large contiguous free space ready for future allocation made by a script.

CHARACTERISTICS OF A SCRIPTING LANGUAGE

A scripting language must have several characteristics.

Productive

Scripting languages increase the productivity of the team in various ways. For example, reducing the time it takes to implement something and see the effect of change made to the game is directly related to productivity. In addition, because scripts are easy to write, more developers can add functionality and tweak the game. Scripts also allow for parallel development where multiple scripts can be worked on at the same time without having any dependencies.

One of the most important advantages of scripting languages with respect to productivity is that they allow applications to have a data-driven workflow. Therefore, when the fundamental functionalities for accomplishing different tasks have been developed, you can easily modify and twiddle with the game. Take a real-time strategy (RTS) game, for example. An RTS game that has many different units with different behaviors needs a lot of tweaking and game balancing. If developers can easily modify the game to try out different variations, the development processes will be much smoother.

Some games require a scripting language more than others. Data-driven games can be looked at in two different ways. Some games may strictly need different sets of data. For example, a racing game can benefit from a data-driven design by describing a car as a list of numbers. Some cars may have different gear ratios, steering radius, power, and so on. Many racing games have one central physics model, and the variation is achieved through different settings for the physics model. In this scenario, a scripting language is not necessary. A simple text file can be used to store the different parameters. If you need to store tables or lists of information, Microsoft® Excel files can be useful. If you want a structured text format, you can also use XML files. The popularity of XML files has been growing over the past few years. In fact, many in-house tools made by game studios use XML files as their intermediate and even primary file format.

On the other hand, some games need variation through both data and functionality. For example, the puzzles of a game may require both different data set as well as some new functionality. Unlike the previous example, in which the behavior of different cars could simply be defined by a list of simple data, every puzzle may require its own special code or functionality. The same holds true for a game where the world needs to be populated by triggers that activate unique functionality, such as moving a platform, turning on a light, or controlling the camera. In these scenarios, you need a way to provide different data and define new ways to manipulate the data. In other words, you actually have to write some code as opposed to some simple data.

Easy to Learn

Scripting languages typically are and should be easy to learn. By being so, novice programmers such as artists and level designers can learn the language and experiment with the game without having to go to the programmers. As a result, the programmers can spend more time on tools and technologies rather than writing the game logic. In addition, level designers can be even more creative and get a better feel for what is possible with the technologies provided by the game engine.

The simpler the language, the less time is needed to learn enough to accomplish different tasks. If a language contains a lot of difficult-to-understand concepts, it can be overwhelming for developers. For example, the more features the language has, the more complicated it tends to be. Another reason why scripting languages are easy to learn is that they are more forgiving when the developer makes a mistake.

Development support such as documentation, tutorials, existing libraries, and debugging tools can significantly reduce the learning curve. They allow novice developers to get started, learn proper practices, and accomplish tasks in a shorter amount of time. Inadequate documentation is a serious problem. Regardless of how easy a language is, if a developer cannot easily find out how to use the language constructs, the learning process will still take a long time.

Existing libraries are also an important factor in making a language easy to learn as well as increasing productivity. A language that is simple but does not have enough libraries can still be challenging to use. In fact, not having a sufficient amount of libraries can cause novice developers to replicate a lot of functionality in their code, which can increase bugs, bloat the code, and lead to unnecessary inefficiencies. If a programmer is responsible for writing the libraries, that person should also be responsible for providing adequate documentation and code sample to demonstrate how the libraries should be used.

If a game needs to be extensible by the user community, using a scripting language that is easy to learn becomes even more important. Modifying an existing game to make different games has been proven essential to the longevity of several games. If the language is difficult or requires a lot of preparation and setting up, far fewer users will be able to modify the game. For example, *Quake III* required a more substantial amount of expertise and commitment to modify than *Unreal Tournament* or even *WarCraft III*. The number of custom games implemented with *WarCraft III* is substantially higher than those that use *Quake III*, even though the latter has been around for quite some time and has been used for making numerous commercial games.

Flexible, Powerful, and Extensible

A scripting language should be powerful enough so that the necessary tasks can be accomplished in the scripts. The simplicity and power of a language tend to work against each other. The more powerful a language, the more sophisticated it tends to be. For example, scripting languages that have objects are more powerful but also have a higher learning curve.

The flexibility of a scripting language is also important. Many games use scripting languages for a wide variety of tasks. The game code, menus, and cut scenes are just a few examples of tasks that have been accomplished in scripts.

If a language is too limited, it is critical to have a way to extend the language because certain features may not be necessary until you actually realize they are needed. The language must be extensible, especially if the scope is extremely limited. Languages that are powerful enough and have already been used for the tasks you need to perform do not need to be as extensible.

Stable and Efficient

The stability of an interpreter or the virtual machine is vital. The last thing any game needs is a scripting language that fails internally for reasons beyond the control of the developers. An interpreter or virtual machine has various components that can be rather complicated. An unstable interpreter will cause problems that can undo any benefits that scripting language provides.

The efficiency of the interpreter can be important but can also be irrelevant if the number of scripts used in a game is trivial. This is in part because all performance-critical tasks are typically handled in native code. If the scripting language is efficient, more code can be handled on the script side. If scripts are used only for tasks such as the menus, efficiency may not be as big of a concern as it would be if the entire game logic or opponent AI were written in scripts. Generally, the more scripts and the longer the scripts, the more efficient the interpreter must be. Note that memory management must also be efficient enough not to cause noticeable problems. Memory management is easy to do but hard to do efficiently.

Safe and Secure

The safety and security of a scripting language is a characteristic that should not be overlooked. A script should not be able to crash the entire game. It is hard to describe the enormous bottleneck that an unsafe scripting language can cause. Consider trying to tweak the game, and mistakes in a script crash the entire game. Let's say the game is being tested and halfway through a level, the game crashes. As you can imagine, for a novice programmer, debugging the scripts can become as difficult as debugging a C/C++ project. If the game crashes, it needs to be rerun many times just to get a feel for what may be causing the problem. Keep in mind that unlike debugging a small stand-alone project, just to test whether a bug has been fixed you may have to play through part of a level, which can be very time consuming.

What can crash the entire game? Any direct memory access from scripts is dangerous. Even if direct memory access does not exist, arrays should be indexed within the valid bounds. Any improper array access should be caught and disallowed, because if some array overflows, it can corrupt data used by other scripts or components of the game. As a result, another component whose data has been corrupted may crash first. These types of problems are unwelcome and should not be possible in a script. Even if an illegal operation is performed, the interpreter should handle it gracefully.

The interpreter should not execute invalid code. For languages that allow precompiling of the scripts, the compiled representation may have to be checked to make sure it does not contain invalid compiled code. For example, a branch statement may be trying to jump to an invalid line. This step is especially important if scripts or modules can be downloaded in compiled form.

A secure scripting language is one that does not allow for cheating, does not allow any illegal operation to occur from the script, and even prevents information stored in a script from being accessed from native code. Not all games need to be concerned with security, but those that do need to guarantee secure scripts have a tremendous task before them. For a language to be as secure as possible, it has to be designed with security in mind.

Runtime Code Execution

A system that allows code to be executed during runtime can be used to configure and tweak an application while it is running. In fact, this ability is the most important characteristic that makes scripting languages vital to most applications. Runtime code execution is useful for debugging and allowing for a comprehensive in-game console. If a game or application has a console that allows the user to execute code, values that are used by the game can be tweaked to get immediate feedback about minor changes without having to restart the game. This characteristic is especially important for configuring and manipulating programs that run for a long period or are costly to restart. For example, a game server must be manipulated without shutting down a game in progress. Because testing a game can be very time consuming—because it takes some time to launch the game and reach the point in the level where things need to be tweaked—being able to run code at runtime can be a handy feature.

WHY USE AN EXISTING SCRIPTING LANGUAGE

After you determine whether you need a scripting language, you must decide whether to use an existing one or roll your own. This decision has to be made thoughtfully because it can have serious implications either way.

Creating and maintaining a scripting language from scratch is a significant undertaking. Having good scripting support for a game means that both the language and the interpreter must be designed, implemented, and maintained well. Many games use in-house scripting languages that are very poor, many times because the task was underestimated. Other reasons include lack of careful design or the assumption that the language would be used only to solve the specific problem that was originally in mind.

Even though scripting language is adopted in games to solve single specific tasks, such as menus, by the time a game is done scripts tend to be used for far more things than originally intended. Even if a scripting language stays true to its specific mission, by the time the next game comes around, it is just too inconvenient to give up a system in which the team has invested so much time and is so familiar. Of course, a new project can require tasks that are entirely different from those of the original game for which the scripting language was designed.

For example, BGScript, which is the scripting language created for *Baldur's Gate,* was intended only for scripting the combats. Yet, it was eventually used in multiple games and used for tasks that were beyond the sight and intention of its original designers. By the time the language and the interpreter were changed to meet the radical new requirements, it was nearly unusable. It become so convoluted and hard to use that after the substantial amount of time and money spent for its development and maintenance, it had to be put aside. In fact, two of the developers at BioWare wrote an article titled "How Not to Implement a Basic Scripting Language," which discusses all the problems they had.

As another example, Ensemble Studios had used a custom scripting language for *Age of Empires II*. Even though the language was well designed and thought out, it suffered from inherit limitations that were not a problem or concern for *AOE II*. The limitations were enough to render the system inherently inappropriate for *Age of Mythology*. The language allowed a developer to define rules by mapping a set of conditions to a set of actions. The engine behind the script would trigger a rule when its conditions were met. When a rule was triggered, its corresponding actions were executed. This rule-based system was simply not powerful enough to represent and manipulate data that was more sophisticated. A rule-based system is in a sense similar to a function that has a list of if-then checks. What if there is a need to loop through a list of objects? What if there is a need to define and use custom data structures to represent alternate views of the world to give the NPCs a more humanlike view? Such tasks could not be implemented directly in the scripts.

You should be cautious about designing a new language, even if it is a simple one. If a language is very simple, it is likely that it will need a lot of growth before it can handle more sophisticated tasks. Over the years, a substantial amount of effort has been put into designing the languages we use today. Even if you were to create a custom scripting language, you should use the syntax and rules of an existing one. When possible, you should make every effort to avoid creating a new language. By adopting an existing scripting language, you can save a lot of time and money by using a language that has matured and been used by many developers.

Keep in mind that if you have a large number of scripts written and you need to make a change that breaks the backward compatibility of the language, you either must make double standards to hack the change or modify all the old scripts. As you can guess, neither solution is pleasant or safe. As a mater of fact, you can use a subset of an existing language. This is what *Quake III* does. They use a subset of C as their scripting language. *Unreal* uses a Java-like language and *WarCraft III* uses a language similar to Basic.

If you don't go with an existing scripting language, after you design a language or go with the syntax of an existing language, you must write a parser and a compiler. Writing a parser is not necessarily a difficult task. Actually, it sounds easy enough to make anyone think that it can be written without any problem. Writing a parser, however, is very time consuming, and the code tends to be very long. A full-blown scripting language has so many dependencies that it will be rather easy to create bugs and even harder to maintain. Even if you write your own scripting language, do not write the parser. Writing your own parser is the easiest way to waste a lot of time. Instead, use Lex and Yacc or their equivalent tools to alleviate some of the burden.

Making your own language means that you also have to design and implement your own interpreter. An interpreter is composed of components that can verify and translate the source to the language of the virtual machine, and execute the compiled representation, and a memory manager, which can allocate, free, and compact the memory used by the scripting engine. How much time does it take to design, implement, and test these components? They are definitely not trivial tasks. The interpreter is actually more important than the specific scripting language. One way to measure the amount of work involved is to look at an existing interpreter and try to see how much time went into it to make it work well. These tasks are so involved that they can take a single person a year of solid research, design, and development before the interpreter can be used. Many companies that use an in-house scripting language have a dedicated developer to design, implement, and maintain the system. If this is not the case, it is because they cannot afford to do so, they do not realize how big of a task it is, or someone else is maintaining the language for them, perhaps an independent group or a third-party company.

Plenty of open-source systems are available that can be used to avoid implementing such a system from scratch. Of course, if a studio can afford to tackle the problem by having dedicated developers, it will work out just fine. For example, even though *Quake III* uses C files as its scripting language, the C files are compiled to bytecodes that are interpreted by the Quake Virtual Machine (QVM).

It is also important to know that compilers exist that can convert existing languages to the bytecodes of an existing virtual machine. This is exactly what Jython (or JPython) does. Jython is a compiler that compiles Python code to Java bytecode. Many different compilers are available that can convert other languages to Java bytecodes. Similarly, Microsoft .NET VM is just a C# VM. Languages such as Visual Basic®, Managed C++, and J# are simply compilers that convert different languages to C# bytecodes

It is also important to note that if you want to use an existing language to run on a platform for which a VM does not exist, you must compile the interpreter for the specific platform. Interpreters written in ANSI C can easily be compiled for various platforms. For example, Lua can be compiled to run on PCs as well as on PS2.

WHY C/C++ CANNOT BE A SCRIPTING LANGUAGE

C/C++ are unproductive, unsafe, and have an extremely high learning curve. Of course, for someone who has been using C/C++ for several years, these statements may seem untrue. Because C/C++ do not have a runtime engine, all the code must be compiled and linked ahead of time to a specific CPU's instructions. In other words, it is not possible to execute arbitrary code during runtime.

A new developer can easily be baffled by the fact that there are many ways to do the same thing. To understand C++, a developer must understand C and C++ as well as the difference between the two. For example, in a cpp file you can allocate memory using the `new` keyword, the `malloc` function, or the `calloc` function. Similarly, to read a file you can use the `fread` or the C++ file input stream. Strings may be C-style character arrays, C++ strings, or MFC strings, and each has its own representation and ways of manipulation.

In addition, seemingly similar ways of doing things can give very different results or may even be entirely wrong. For example, an array can be conveniently initialized at declaration time as long as it is not a class member. The equals operator can be, and often is, overloaded to compare data other than the expected data.

C/C++ compilers generate errors that are excessively convoluted for a novice programmer. This is in part because of the complexity of the language and the fact that the compiler has to deal with a lot of legacy. For example, leaving out a semicolon results in rather interesting error messages. Leaving out a semicolon after declaring a class in a header file results in error messages that point the developer to the wrong files.

Dealing with header files is an unnecessary headache that a new developer should not have to deal with. Consider the fact that declaring global variables in a header file is perfectly fine until more than one source file includes the same header. Doing so results in the creation of multiple symbols with the same name, and an error is generated only when it comes time to link the object files. Circular inclusions can also be problematic and rely on the use of macros. In some situations, even if macros are used, you will need to add forward declarations to trick the compiler.

Pointers are one of the hardest topics to learn for new developers, and they are also unsafe. A pointer can be cast to any type and then used. Because of the complete access to the memory, a mistake in one module can cause a completely separate and unrelated module to fail because the first module can mistakenly corrupt the data used by the other module.

Besides the fact that C/C++ requires longer implementation time and debugging time, compiling a large C/C++ project can take a substantial amount of time. Simple projects may only need a minute, but an entire game or its tools can take anywhere from tens of minutes to a few hours. The time spent on simply compiling and linking the code is a bottleneck in the development pipeline.

WHY JAVA CAN BE A SCRIPTING LANGUAGE

Java is in many ways similar to a scripting language. The Java language defines the constructs and syntax rules, and the JVM can execute Java bytecodes. JNI allows Java to invoke native methods and native functions to execute Java code.

Productivity

As with typical scripting languages, Java offers a fast edit-test cycle, which is important. Unlike C/C++, Java has a substantially faster compile time, mostly because compiles are incremental and no linking is performed at compile time.

Ease of Learning

The simplicity and power of a language tend to work against each other. Java has the power of a complete object-oriented language but tries to do without unnecessary things. For example, multiple inheritance is possible but limited so that it does not get out of hand. Some may argue that an object-oriented language is overkill for a scripting language. If you are sure that you do not need an object-oriented language, then you should look into other scripting languages. However, keep in mind that objects are an intuitive way of grouping data and functionality. Many languages that did not originally support objects now support them.

Keep in mind that familiar languages are easier to learn. Developers who are familiar with an existing scripting language such as Macromedia® Flash® script (ActionScript) or Maya script (MELScript) can learn Java's syntax without any difficulty. This is in part because many languages including Java have C-like syntax.

Strongly Typed versus Loosely Typed Languages

To make a language easier, some languages use runtime or loosely typed variables. In other words, they do not map a variable to a specific type. Each variable is instead a reference to a structure that contains a field indicating its current type. By doing so, the type of the variable can be changed when necessary. For example, if an integer is passed to a function that takes a string as its parameter, the integer value can be converted to the equivalent string that contains the number.

Some languages do not require a variable to be declared before the language is first used. Instead, when the language comes across a name that has not been seen before, it assumes that the variable is new and therefore registers it. Can you imagine the bugs that can show up if the name of a variable is misspelled?

There is no question that such features make writing scripts more convenient and, as a result, reduce the learning curve. However, they are open invitations for bugs. It is important to know that the mistakes made in such languages do not show up until the interpreter actually tries to execute them. Such features make it more convenient not only to write scripts but also to overlook mistakes and write bugs. This is not to say that such languages are fundamentally flawed. If there is the need to write a few short and isolated scripts, using such languages can be extremely helpful, in part because a small and isolated script can be tested quickly. On the other hand, as the length of a program grows, the amount of effort required to test and debug it tends to grow exponentially.

Another important point is if you have to rely on the interpreter to find mistakes, you must test every single control path to make sure the script is sound. Can you imagine testing every possible control path, just to find out if you have misspelled the name of a variable?

If your team writes scripts that are bug prone, they will spend a lot of time trying to find the bugs. Do not forget that debugging skills are not easy to learn and can take a while to hone. Having to spend more time to learn a language that makes it harder to write bugs is generally an investment worth making.

Continuation Support

A potential disadvantage of using Java as a scripting language is the fact that there is no support for *continuations,* which are supported by some scripting languages such as Python, Scheme, and Lua. Continuations can make scripts much easier to read and write. Coroutines, generators, and microthreads are different approaches to continuations. A language (or VM) that supports continuation is one that allows a function to call another function without requiring the second function to return execution to the caller. In other words, control can be forwarded to any frame in the call stack, not only to the top frame, and a function's frame can be saved and restored at a later time so that it continues where it left off. This is in some sense like using the devious goto statement, but before leaving a function, the state of the function is stored and the state of the other function can be restored before entering it. As messy as this sounds, it can make implementation of many systems significantly simpler. Take, for example, the task of traversing a tree recursively. If there were only one thread in the game, it would not be possible to perform a task recursively unless it guarantees not to take a significant amount of time. The recursion would have to be unrolled and emulated to allow the thread to leave in the middle of recursing to allow the game to perform other things. With the use of continuations, you could simply yield to the game even if you were 20 plies deep, and pick up right at the 20th ply later. A more game-related example would be the implementation of a state machine. A state machine written in a language that supports continuations does not need a variable to keep track of the current state. Instead, the program counter keeps track of the current state, which makes the code much easier to read and write.

You might have realized that some of the previously mentioned tasks can be emulated by the use of threads. It is correct to say that continuations can be adequately emulated using threads in Java. One of the disadvantages of this approach would be sizable overhead of threads if there were many NPCs. Because microthreads use assembly code to store the execution state, there can be thousands micro-threads with an extremely small amount of overhead.

Tools and Documentation

Java has many development tools that can make life easier. Features such as syntax highlighting and pop-up helpers can be useful, especially for new developers. Project files can also be beneficial for grouping script files and providing easy navigation between them when working on larger projects. Besides the basic development tools, debugging and profiling tools are also important. Even though it is easier to write high-level scripts, debugging and profiling them is not as easy. In fact, using a basic scripting language can become worrisome if a project requires numerous intricate scripts. Many scripting languages try to provide profiling and debugging support, but it is safe to say that achieving the completeness of tools available for a language such as Java is not trivial.

Many Java books are available, as well as many online tutorials that can help your team learn Java. Many in the user community already know Java or can easily learn it because of the tremendous amount of books and tutorials, and will, therefore, be able to modify the game. In addition, most colleges and universities now teach Java. Some have even adopted it as their main programming language.

Efficiency

Even though Sun Microsystems has defined the language, many different vendors besides Sun have implemented JVMs. If you read the Java language specifications, you will not find many details about how the VM should do things. This lack of information is so the implementers of a VM do not have to face unnecessary restrictions and make decisions that are more appropriate for their target platform. In this book we focus on Sun VMs. The Sun VM has gone through a significant amount of change since its first version. Sun has focused on improving memory management and performance in different releases.

Performance

As far as performance goes, Java is not what it used to be. The 1.0 VM acted as a typical and basic interpreter. It simply interpreted each bytecode. In the following releases, Sun added JIT compilers that converted Java bytecodes to native instruction corresponding to the CPU of the host machine. Therefore, after the VM ran for a little while, the VM would not have much interpreting left to do. This, of course, resulted in a tremendous amount of speed increase. One of the disadvantages of the JIT VM, however, was that it eagerly loaded class files and tried to compile them, which resulted in substantial consumption of memory. In the later releases, the HotSpot VMs were introduced. Instead of compiling every possible bytecode to native CPU instructions, they tried to convert only the most important parts of the code to native instructions. The HotSpot VMs rely on the 10-90 rule, which states that only 10 percent of the code runs 90 percent of the time. In fact, when the hot spot of the code is found, the VM tries to do many other optimizations before it converts the code to native instructions. For example when possible it converts virtual methods to final, eliminates null checks and bounds checks, and inlines methods. In addition, because HotSpot is aware of the host CPU on which it is running, it can generate native instructions specific to the design of the CPU, including hardware-specific optimizations such as taking advantage of special registers and instructions. Keep in mind that a C/C++ program compiled to take advantage of hardware-specific features cannot run on a machine that does not have the features. It is, therefore, common for developers to compile their code for an older machine.

Having mentioned this, have no doubt in your mind that Java is one of the absolute fastest scripting languages you can get your hands on. Any documentation that you find that states languages such as Python, Perl, or Lua run faster than Java are almost certainly comparisons performed with older versions of the VM. It is also important to note that it is likely for Java to run more slowly than other interpreted languages if it is run in interpreted mode. When run in interpreted mode, the performance is almost like that of the 1.0 VM, which was anything but fast.

You may wonder, if running in interpreted mode can be slow, why would anyone run in the interpreted mode. Even though Java bytecode is platform independent, as with other scripting languages, the VMs are highly platform dependent. If you want to run Java on a platform for which a VM is not available, you must compile the VM for the specific platform, or write your own VM. Then, if you have some extra resources to spare, you can write compilers to convert bytecode to the corresponding native code during runtime.

Memory

The smarter a VM, the more memory it is likely to use to perform certain optimizations. For example, hot spot detection consumes some resources. In addition, when the code must be compiled, the VM has to keep track of the bytecodes as well as the native assembly code. The memory footprint of Sun's VMs are definitely not as small as the footprint of the interpreter of languages such as Lua. Lua's binaries are the absolute minimum amount of code that does only the basic tasks.

The VM does a superb job at memory management. Sun's VM has been used by many developers and has had many years to mature. The VM comes with multiple garbage collection algorithms to deal with programs that have different behavior. The garbage collector is also highly tunable. You can use parameters that give you total control over the size of the heap and how often collections occur. Chapter 6, "Performance and the Java Virtual Machine," provides detailed information about the memory management and the runtime optimizations.

Safety and Security

Java is inherently safe. There is no direct memory access. Every array access is checked to make sure that an illegal index is not used to access memory outside of the array. The language was also designed with exception support. In addition, before a class file is executed, the VM verifies its bytecodes to make sure it does not contain any inappropriate instructions. By doing so, some bad bytecodes cannot crash the VM and simply result in exceptions that can be caught and dealt with gracefully. The check is extensive, and the details are explained in Chapter 6, "Performance and the Java Virtual Machine." In addition, features such as runtime type checking are designed to make the language safe.

Making a language safe and secure takes a tremendous amount of effort. By using Java, you have a team of developers keeping you as safe as possible. Some studios have had to spend a substantial amount of effort to make sure that their scripting engine is secure.

Runtime Code Execution

A potential disadvantage of Java is that you cannot execute Java source code during runtime as easily as you can in a language such as Lua. This is because the source must be compiled to bytecodes before it is handed off to the VM. A scripting language such as Lua can readily execute source code. If you want to execute Java source code during runtime, you have to compile it using an appropriate compiler. It is possible to compile Java source code to bytecodes during runtime and then execute it. `Javac.exe` is simply a wrapper for `com.sun.tools.javac.Main`, which is part of `tools.jar` that comes with JDK.

INTEGRATING AN EXISTING LANGUAGE

When it comes to using a scripting language, the decision has to be made as to which parts of the game should be written in the script language and how much of the game data should be maintained on the script side. One extreme of the spectrum is to implement all the functionality and manage all significant data on the native side. The other is to keep as much functionality and data on the script side. The former is most common because too much data and code on the script side can have substantial performance implications. This is not the case if the scripting language is Java, for reasons explained in the previous sections. In fact, *Vampire: The Masquerade* used Java to implement more than just basic scripts. The Nod SDK came with about 500 Java source files. The scripts communicated with objects on the native side as well as objects that were fully maintained on the script side. *Chrome* is an example of a more recent game that uses Java strictly as its scripting language.

As with the other extreme, choosing to maintain all significant data on the native side is as practical for Java as it would be for any other language. Scripts can manipulate the game objects using native accessors. It is typical for this approach to simply store an object identifier on the script side. When a native function is invoked, the identifier is used to indicate which object the function should manipulate.

The first step to using a scripting language is to be able to launch its VM. Chapter 11, "Java Native Interface" has a section titled, "The Invocation Interface," which shows how to launch the VM from C/C++ code. The next step is to expose native methods so that they can be accessed from the script side.

ON THE CD
The source for a demo that shows how to use Java as a scripting language has been provided on the CD-ROM in code/Chapter 11/Scripting Example. ScriptBase acts as the base class for other script files. The base class allows a script file to have convenient access to the common methods, constants, and variables. A sample script file extends the ScriptBase class and creates several units, as follows:

```java
class Script1 extends ScriptBase{
    void run(){
        print("Script1.run()");
        Unit peons[] = new Unit[10];

        for(int i=0; i<peons.length; i++){
            peons[i] = createUnit(UNIT_TYPE_PEON);
        }

        for(int i=0; i<peons.length; i++){
            destroyUnit(peons[i]);
        }
    }
}
```

The demo shows how to launch the VM, register the native functions for creating and destroying units, load the compiled version of the script file, and execute it.

SUMMARY

Scripting languages allow games to have a more data-driven workflow. Even though many games start with a simple and basic scripting language used for a specific task, their scope is significantly broadened during the development of the game or across projects. After spending a significant amount of time and money to create and maintain a custom language, the language can end up being poorly designed or implemented. Instead of creating a custom language, it is better to take advantage of existing languages that have had many years to mature and are maintained and used by many other developers. If you need a scripting language, Java is one of your options.

An implementation of the VM does not exist for different game consoles, so using Java on a console means that you would have to implement a VM yourself. Alternatively, you can compile an open implementation of the VM for the target console. If your target platform is a PC, as it stands today, Java (language and virtual machine) can be used as a perfect scripting language. The strengths of Java can be advantageous for a game that requires a reasonable amount of reliable scripts.

11 Java Native Interface

INTRODUCTION

The ability to communicate with native code such as Assembly, C, or C++ is fundamental for the operation and extensibility of nonnative languages such as Java. Applications that need to utilize OS or hardware capabilities need to do so in the appropriate language. Java code is compiled to bytecode, which is understood by the VM and not necessarily by the OS or the hardware. By allowing a program to execute some native code, the VM can avoid having to know about all the features of the underlying OS and hardware. This design allows for creation of packages that in turn use native code to utilize OS and hardware features. For example, when we create a new file in Java we use a package that in turn uses some native code to communicate with the OS. Because Java comes with extensive libraries, you can write

315

entire applications without having to write any native code or even call native functions directly. Yet, there are times when you need to perform tasks not supported by the standard packages. In addition, a package may support certain operations but you might need to do them differently for reasons such as performance purposes. In addition, you might want to access existing native libraries such as OpenGL, DirectX, OpenAL, or even ones that you have created yourself.

Java Native Interface (JNI) allows you to mix native and Java code. If you want to make a professional Java game, it is vital to have at least one person on your team who is familiar with JNI. As it stands currently, you are likely to have to deal with native code directly. Even if you do not, it will be beneficial to be aware of your options during the development of your project. To understand this chapter, you should be familiar with C or C++. This chapter will teach you how to communicate with native code and vice versa. We will review the functionalities, provide examples, discuss the implications of using native code, and suggest usage patterns. For those already familiar with JNI, we recommend that you read sections that discuss direct byte buffers, which were introduced in JDK 1.4 as part of the `java.nio` package. Direct buffers have made it possible to share data between Java and native code in a direct and efficient manner. Games are one of the biggest beneficiaries of direct byte buffers.

WHERE IS JNI USED?

JNI is the official interface of Sun Microsystems that can be used to communicate between native and Java code. As mentioned earlier, many Java packages use native libraries. The idea is that once you have access to native code, you can do just about anything. If you search the JDK directory, you will find several binaries (such as .lib, .dll, or .so files) that are used by the Java libraries. For example, you may find *awt.dll, jsound.dll, zip.dll, j3d.dll,* or *win32com.dll*. These libraries correspond to abstract windowing toolkit (AWT), Java sound, Zip utilities, and comm port API, respectively. They contain native functions that are called from the Java side by their corresponding packages. If you view the function table of these libraries with tools such as Microsoft Dependency Viewer, you can get an idea of when their corresponding libraries rely on native code. Additionally, if you launch the VM with `-verbose:jni`, you can see some JNI activities. The following is only a segment of the output when running an empty `Main` method of an empty class:

```
Dynamic-linking/Registering native method:
java.lang.StrictMath.pow
java.lang.Float.intBitsToFloat
java.lang.Object.registerNatives
```

```
java.lang.System.registerNatives
java.lang.Object.has
java.lang.Object.clone
java.lang.System.currentTimeMillis
java.lang.System.arraycopy
java.lang.Thread.yield
java.lang.Thread.sleep
java.lang.ClassLoader.retrieveDirectives
java.lang.Class.getName
java.lang.Class.getSuperclass
java.lang.Class.isArray
sun.misc.Unsafe.getObject
java.lang.Compiler.compileClass
java.io.FileSystem.getFileSystem
java.io.FileInputStream.open
java.io.FileInputStream.readBytes
java.lang.String.intern
java.util.zip.ZipFile.open
java.util.zip.ZipFile.getEntry
```

COMMUNICATING BETWEEN JAVA AND C/C++

When deciding on how to approach the problem, Sun engineers considered existing solutions, such as their Native Method Interface shipped with JDK 1.0, Netscape Java Runtime Interface, Microsoft Raw Native Interface, and even Microsoft COM interface. JNI was designed with several goals in mind, of which binary compatibility was one of the most important ones. That is, programmers should not have to recompile their native libraries when using different versions of virtual machines. To ensure binary compatibility, certain restrictions are imposed. Because the Java language specifications do not define a specific internal representation of Java objects that has to be used by a VM, JNI grants the developer no knowledge of a VM's internal representation of objects. This approach is substantially different from the Native Method Interface. Even though the old approach was more efficient, it meant that changes to the VM could result in binary incompatibilities. In addition, direct access to Java objects imposed serious restrictions on the garbage collector and its performance. It is true to say that JNI costs us some efficiency. The resulting code is also less readable, but this is all for good reason. Even though none of the existing solutions to the problem met all the goals, the result is in some ways similar to Netscape Raw Native Interface and Microsoft COM.

The communication between Java and native code can be bidirectional, that is, you can access native code from the Java side and access Java code and objects from the native side. More specifically, from the Java side you can call native functions and even access memory outside the Java heap. The latter capability is a new feature introduced in JDK 1.4. We will go over examples that demonstrate both functionalities. When Java code invokes a native function, you can do anything that you can do in C/C++. For example, you can allocate memory, manipulate files, or talk to the video card through OpenGL. However, if you want to talk back to the Java side from the native side, you must choose from a set of functionality provided by the JNI. The interface lets you do many different things. For example, from the native side you can instantiate a Java object, access its member variables, or pass it to a Java method. Even though you cannot directly manipulate objects in the Java heap, you can do so through the JNI interface pointer. Before getting into details of JNI, let's first look at a basic sample.

Sample Native Library

From the Java side you can call native functions and access memory in the C heap outside the Java heap. From a Java developer's perspective, calling a native function is no different from calling a Java method. The idea is that a dummy Java method is declared so that other Java code can call it as if it were a typical method. When you declare a dummy method, it must be preceded by the keyword `native` and must not have a body. The keyword `native` flags the method so that the VM knows it has to do some special work when the method is called. When a native method is invoked by some Java code, the VM does some extra work and then calls a C/C++ function that has been mapped to the dummy method. Before a dummy can be called, its corresponding native function has to be loaded and linked. The following example declares `MyNativeMethod` as a `native` or dummy method and loads the native library that contains the native function that should be called when the dummy method is called.

```
class Sample{

    Sample(){
        System.loadLibrary("MyNativeLibrary");
    }

    // dummy method
    private static native void MyNativeMethod();

    public static void main(String args[]) {
        Sample sample = new Sample();
        sample.MyNativeFunction();
    }
}
```

Notice that when the argument is passed to loadLibrary, it does not specify a platform-dependent extension such as a *dynamic link library* (DLL) or Unix *shared object* (SO). Also, note that the library is loaded from the constructor of the class. What do you think would happen if we invoke the static native method before making an instance of the class? Because the native library is not loaded until the constructor is called, there would be an UnsatisfiedLinkError exception because the VM would not be able to link the method to a corresponding native function. It is generally a better practice to place the load call in a static block, which would cause the library to get loaded when the class is loaded. Note that there are times when you may not want to load a library until you really need it.

```
class Sample{

    static{
        System.loadLibrary("MyNativeLibrary");
    }

    private static native void MyNativeMethod();

        public static void main(String args[]) {
        Sample sample = new Sample();
        sample.MyNativeFunction();
    }

}
```

Preparing the native function and library is a little more work. First, we must write a function prototype that matches the arguments and the return type of the dummy method. Furthermore, we must inform the VM which dummy method should be mapped to the native function. The mapping between a dummy method and a native function can be done from some C code, as we will see later. Fortunately, if the native function follows a specific naming convention, the VM will automatically map the dummy Java method to the corresponding native function. The naming convention is to name a function so that its name shows exactly to which Java package, class, and method the native function corresponds.

JDK ships with a tool that autogenerates a header file, which contains the prototypes of the native (or dummy) methods in a given Java class. The tool is Javah.exe. Running it on the Sample class shown earlier generates a header file named Sample.h that has the prototype for the MyNativeMethod method.

```
/* DO NOT EDIT THIS FILE - it is machine generated */
#include <jni.h:
```

```
#ifdef __cplusplus
extern "C" {
#endif
/*
 * Class:     Sample
 * Method:    MyNativeFunction
 * Signature: ()V
 */
NIEXPORT void JNICALL
Java_Sample_MyNativeMethod(JNIEnv *,jclass);

#ifdef __cplusplus
}
#endif
```

Let's go through some of the details of Sample.h. The included jni.h contains the necessary JNI declarations. jni.h includes the only additional external header file, jni_md.h, which declares some machine-dependent definitions. The machine-generated comment above the function prototype shows the class name that was inputted to Javah.exe as well as the method name. In addition, it comments that the method signature is "()V", which means that the method takes no parameters and returns void. We will discuss method signatures later. JNIEXPORT is a simple macro that indicates that this function should get added to the function table of the library. The two parameters of the function are the JNIEnv (JNI environment) pointer and a reference to the class to which this function is linked. We will later talk about how to use the environment pointer to communicate with the Java side. We can now make a C or C++ file that looks like the following:

```
#include "Sample.h"
#include <stdio.h>

JNIEXPORT void JNICALL
Java_Sample_MyNativeMethod(JNIEnv *env, jclass clazz){
    printf("Java_Sample_MyNativeMethod was called\n");
}
```

We next must compile the file to a dynamically linkable library. The library will have one entry in its function table. If we then launch Sample.class, Java_Sample_MyNativeMethod will be written to the console window. Even though a class file that has a few native methods can do many useful tasks, there is often the need to talk back to the Java side from a native function. Therefore, JNI functions must be called. Before looking at the available functions, let's look at how Java types map to native types.

Mapping of Java Types to C/C++ Types

To interface two languages, a mapping of different types must be established. If you want to pass some data from language A to language B, you have to make sure that the data is preserved properly. Table 11.1 shows the mapping of Java primitive types to their C/C++ equivalents. Note that some C/C++ types such as short, int, and long are compiler dependent, and the table uses int16, int32, and int64 correspondingly.

TABLE 11.1   Java versus Native Primitive Types

Java	C/C++	JNI	Bytes
boolean	unsigned char	jboolean	1
byte	signed char	jbyte	1
char	unsigned short	jchar	2
double	double	jdouble	8
float	float	jfloat	4
int	int32	jint	4
long	int64	jlong	8
short	int16	jshort	2

For nonprimitive types, the solution is not as simple. Passing objects by value is not a viable option and can result in many issues. Take, for example, the scenario in which you need to pass a structure that has a reference to another. What should be done then? Even if it were possible and the data were copied byte by byte, how would the other language know which bytes correspond to which members of the structure? A practical solution is to pass an object by reference and use accessor functions to manipulate the object.

The JNI Interface Pointer

JNIEnv is the JNI environment that is basically a table of function pointers. It is passed to every native function as its first parameter. If a native function chooses to communicate to the Java side, it has to use this interface. JNIEnv contains more than 230 function pointers, and as newer versions of JDK become available, more functions may be added to the end of the table. The structure looks like the following:

```
Struct {
    void *functionName1(JNIEnv *env)
    jint *functionName2(JNIEnv *env, ... )
    jobject *functionName3(JNIEnv *env, ... )
    ...
}
```

In C, `env` is a pointer to another pointer that points to the function table. The reason for an extra level of indirection is that the JNIEnv not only points to a function table but also stores additional data local to the thread that is managed internally. You can simply dereference the double pointer and call one of its functions. The syntax is a bit more convenient when using a C++ compiler as opposed to a C compiler.

```
// When using C compiler you call the functions as:
(*env)->FunctionName(env, ...)

// But when using C++ compiler you write:
env->FunctionName(...)
```

The functions in the table can be broken down to different categories. Some deal with Java references, which are used to point to Java objects. Class functions are those that deal with instances of `Java.lang.Class`. Object functions are those that can be used for typical Java objects. Field and method functions are those that allow you to access the fields of an object or invoke its methods. Array functions deal with arrays, and string functions deal with instances of `java.lang.String`. Exception functions allow you to deal with Java exceptions from the native side. Direct Byte-Buffer functions allow you to make arbitrary regions of the system memory accessible from the Java side. The last category covers other miscellaneous functions.

Reference Functions

In Java, objects are referred to by references, not direct pointers. Even though newer VMs use direct pointers internally, the pointers are nondirect from the developer's view. A reference contains a direct pointer to an object in the Java heap. The following Java segment shows three references, two of which are of type `ClassA`, but the `reference3` is of type `java.lang.Object`:

```
Object ReferenceTest(){
    ClassA reference1 = new ClassA();
    ClassA reference2 = reference1;
    Object reference3 = reference1;
    return reference1;
}
```

Note that when this method returns, reference1, reference2, and reference3 are destroyed, and if the code that invoked this method does not save a reference to the object that was created in this method, the object will be considered a candidate for garbage collection.

When manipulating Java objects from native code, we cannot use direct pointers. That is, you cannot simply use the memory address to manipulate a Java object. Instead, you must have some sort of Java reference to the object. This is in part because the garbage collector may move objects when performing housekeeping. As expected, when objects are moved, the pointer contained within a reference is updated accordingly. In Java, references are typed, and you cannot use a reference of type ClassA to set a reference of an arbitrary type. For example, the following code results in an incompatible types error:

```
class ClassA{
    int x, y, z;
}

class ClassB{
    String name;
}

Object ReferenceTest(){
    ClassA referenceA = new ClassA();
    ClassB referenceB = referenceA;
    return referenceB;
}
```

When dealing with Java objects on the native side, however, all references are of type java.lang.Object, so you do not have as much compile-time type checking as you do in Java. When using a C compiler, all references to Java objects are simply of type jobject, which is the equivalent for java.lang.Object. However, some extra dummy types are defined when a C++ compiler is used so that some compile-time type checking can be performed for common types. Figure 11.1 shows the types defined when using a C++ compiler.

Because the garbage collector collects objects that do not have a reachable reference to them, an important issue has to be dealt with when manipulating Java objects from the native side. What if there is only one reference to an object from the native side? Should the object get collected? JNI provides special reference objects that must be used to manipulate Java objects from the native side. They have different scopes that allow us to have limited control over when an object is garbage-collected. References can have either local or global scope. JNI also provides a special type of global reference called weak global reference.

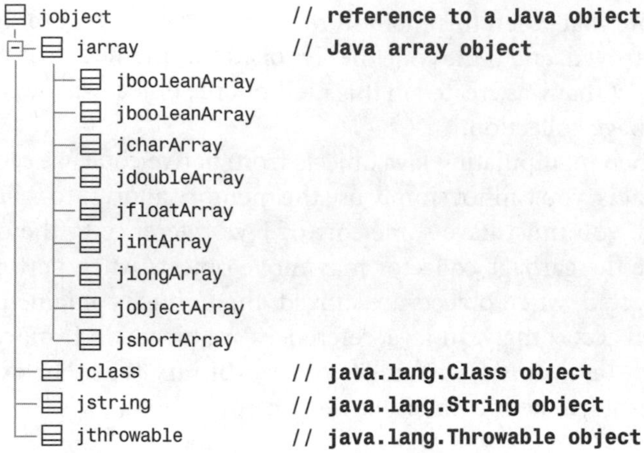

```
⊟ jobject              // reference to a Java object
⊟ jarray               // Java array object
    ⊟ jbooleanArray
    ⊟ jbooleanArray
    ⊟ jcharArray
    ⊟ jdoubleArray
    ⊟ jfloatArray
    ⊟ jintArray
    ⊟ jlongArray
    ⊟ jobjectArray
    ⊟ jshortArray
⊟ jclass               // java.lang.Class object
⊟ jstring              // java.lang.String object
⊟ jthrowable           // java.lang.Throwable object
```

FIGURE 11.1 JNI reference types.

Local references are used most commonly. Local references live only during the execution of a native function, just as typical Java references are destroyed when they go out of scope. In other words, when a native function returns, any local references created during its invocation are automatically released. This is convenient and more than often frees you from having to explicitly destroy (or release) a reference object that points to an object in the Java heap. For example, if an object is created and passed to a native method, a local reference is created to point to the object being passed in. This action ensures that the object does not get collected, even if there are no references to the object on the Java side. The local reference in this example is automatically created and, as mentioned, automatically released when the function returns. If the local reference was the only reference to the passed-in object, the object will then be ready for garbage collection. When a function is called by JNI, some local references have been created already. Consider the following:

```
JNIEXPORT void JNICALL
Java_Sample_MyNativeFunction(JNIEnv *env, jclass clazz){
    jobject reference2 = env->NewLocalRef(clazz);
}
```

The local reference clazz, which is of type jclass, has already been created when the following function is called. In the function, another local reference of type jobject is created to refer to the object referred to by the clazz reference. Both references will automatically be deleted when this function returns.

Even though this behavior is appropriate for most cases, there are times when a reference should persist, even when the native function returns. For example, what if you want to store a reference in native code for use across calls? Alternatively, what if the object is created from the native side and only relevant to the native code?

Unlike local references, global references are not released when a native function returns. The only way to release them is to explicitly call the `DeleteGlobalRef` function. To create a global reference you must do so explicitly using the `NewGlobal-Ref` function. Unless explicitly released, global references can result in objects not getting collected during the lifetime of the VM. If you use a global reference you must make sure to call a corresponding delete at the appropriate time. Weak global references relax this idea a bit.

If you want to have a global reference but want the reference not to prevent the garbage collector from reclaiming the object, you can use a weak global reference. This type of reference is similar to the `java.lang.ref.WeakReference` object. This brings up another question: what if you go to use a weak reference but its corresponding object has been reclaimed? If you check to make sure that the weak global reference has not been reclaimed, is there any guarantee that it will be there immediately after you check it? The trick is that you cannot use a weak reference directly. First you must use it to create, say, a local reference. If you want to use a weak global reference, you should not simply check the weak reference to see if it has been collected and then use it. The object may happen to get collected immediately after you check its validity.

Frames are used to manage the scope of local references. When a native function is called, a new frame is created and then destroyed when the function returns. If you want to manage local references yourself, you can explicitly push and pop frames. Explicit management is useful when you have native functions that create many local references that are needed only in a specific block. In such cases, instead of waiting for the function to return, you can cause the references to be freed when you complete a block. `PushLocalFrame` and `PopLocalFrame` do exactly what their names imply.

Class Functions

In Java, instances of `java.lang.Class` are used to represent classes and interfaces in a running Java application. The `java.lang.Class` class has no public constructor and is instantiated by a class loader when class files are loaded. It is extremely important to understand the difference between an instance of `java.lang.Class` that a class loader creates from, say, `ClassA.class` file and an object of type `ClassA` that is created when executing:

```
ClassA ref = new ClassA
```

Only one instance of java.lang.Class is created to represent ClassA during the life of the VM. On the other hand, many objects of type ClassA can be created using the new operator. When using JNI with a C compiler (as opposed to C++), you should be careful not to confuse them with typical Java objects because you will not have compile-time type checking. When using a C compiler, an instance of java.lang.Class is referred to by jobject. If using a C++ compiler, they are referred to be jclass.

To load a class file through JNI you can call the FindClass function. FindClass takes a descriptor that identifies the class you want to load. The descriptor is simply a string that represents the class name and its package.

```
jclass classMyClass = env->FindClass("MyClass");
```

Because arrays are special objects, to describe an array object the type of the array is preceded by "[". Table 11.2 shows the descriptors for different types, and Table 11.3 shows how to describe primitive types.

TABLE 11.2   Example Class Descriptors

java.lang.Object	"java/lang/Object"
Array of java.lang.Object	"[java/lang/Object"
Array of bytes	"[B"
2D array of Integers	"[[I"

TABLE 11.3   Primitive Identifiers

boolean	Z
byte	B
char	C
double	D
float	F
int	I
long	J
short	S

You can also load a class by passing its raw bytes to DefineClass. The Get-SuperClass function returns a java.lang.class reference to the super class of a class, and IsAssignableFrom determines if an object can be safely cast from one type to another. Two of the rarely needed but interesting calls are RegisterNatives and UnregisterNatives. They can be used to manually link a Java native method to a native function. This is the alternative to calling System.loadLibrary() and allowing the VM to link the functions to native methods based on the names of the functions. The following segment registers the functions function1 and function2 with the class referred to by clazz so that they correspond to methods createUnit and destroyUnit:

```
JNINativeMethod methods[2] = {0};

methods[0].name = "createUnit";
methods[0].signature = "(I)LUnit;";
methods[0].fnPtr = function1;

methods[1].name = "destroyUnit";
methods[1].signature = "(LUnit;)V";
methods[1].fnPtr = function2;

g_env->RegisterNatives(clazz, methods, nMethods);
```

These calls are especially useful when you want to link a method to a function in a static library. They are also the only option for linking native methods when a platform does not support dynamically linkable libraries. In addition, they are useful when you want to embed the VM in a C/C++ game. By using these functions, the function that a native method has been linked to can be dynamically changed.

Object Functions

If you look through jni.h you will see that jobject is defined as _jobject pointer. jobject is really a pointer that points to a reference. Comparing two jobjects using the == operator can return false, even if they both refer to the same object. Doing so results in the references, as opposed to the objects referred to by the references, being compared. To compare two Java objects referred to from the native side, you should use the IsSameObject function. You can also use IsSameObject to test whether the object referred to by a weak global reference has been garbage collected. To do so, you can pass in NULL or 0 as one of its parameters.

```
jobject reference1 = env->NewLocalRef(myObject);
jobject reference2 = env->NewLocalRef(myObject);
jobject reference3 = reference1;
```

```
// this will evaluate to **false**
if (reference1 == reference2){...}

// this will evaluate to true
if (env->IsSameObject(reference1, reference2)){...}

// obviously this evaluates to true
if (reference1 == reference3){...}
if (env->IsSameObject(reference1, reference3)){...}

// this will evaluate to true if the object referred
// to by myWeakGlobalReferece is not live
if (env->IsSameObject(myWeakGlobalReferece, NULL)){...}
```

There are two different ways to create objects from native code. The `NewObject` function creates an object in much the same way that the `new` operator does in Java. It can be used to allocate an object and call a constructor. If you want to create array objects, you should use `New<type>Array` instead. Unlike `NewObject`, `AllocObject` allocates memory for an object but does not call any of its constructors. If necessary, you can call the constructor explicitly later. Other functions such as `GetObjectClass` and `IsInstanceOf` are very intuitive. `GetObjectClass` returns a `jclass` (instance of `java.lang.Class`) and `IsInstanceOf`, a `jboolean` that can be either `JNI_TRUE` or `JNI_FALSE`.

Field Functions

To access the fields of an object, we must first obtain a *field identifier* or `jfieldID`. The `GetFieldID` and `GetStaticFieldID` functions take a reference to a class, the field's name, and a field descriptor and returns the field ID. The descriptor is simply the signature of the field, as previously presented in Table 11.3. References are described by L + class descriptor + ;. As with class descriptors, array fields are preceded with "[". Table 11.4 provides several examples.

TABLE 11.4   Example Field Descriptors

float	"F"
int[]	"[I"
Integer	"Ljava/lang/Integer;"
Object array	"[Ljava/lang/Object;"

Once you have a field ID, it is a good idea to cache it so you do not have to look it up every time you need to use it. After resolving the field IDs, you can use the set/get functions to access the fields of an object. Note that there are separate accessor functions for static fields. The functions are of the following form where <type> can be "Object," "Boolean," "Byte," "Char," "Short," "Int," "Long," "Float," or "Double."

```
GetFieldID
GetStaticFieldID
Get<type>Field
Set<type>Field
SetStatic<type>Field
GetStatic<type>Field
```

The following line looks up the ID of the field named health, which is of type integer and is a member of a java.lang.Class instance referred to by clazz.

```
jfieldID field = env->GetFieldID(clazz, "health", "I");
```

There are also two functions that allow you to convert field IDs into instances of java.lang.reflect.Field and vice versa. These functions are useful if you want to take advantage of reflection from the native side. The functions are From-ReflectedField and ToReflectedField.

Method Functions

Calling functions through JNI is similar to accessing fields. To call methods we first must obtain a *method identifier* (jmethodID), and then invoke the method using one of the following:

```
Call<type>Method
CallStatic<type>Method
CallNonvirtual<type>Method
```

A method ID can be retrieved by using GetMethodID or GetStaticMethodID. These functions take a class reference, method name, and the method descriptor as parameter. A method descriptor or signature is composed of the return type and the parameter types of the method. You can also look up the ID of the constructor as if it were a typical method that returns void. When doing so, you have to use <init> as the method name.

```
jmethodID method1 = env->GetMethodID(clazz, "run", "()V");
jmethodID method2 = env->GetMethodID(clazz, "<init>", "()V");
```

The previous segment retrieves the ID of the run method and the default constructor of the class referred to by `clazz`. Table 11.5 contains several examples of method descriptors.

TABLE 11.5 Example Method Descriptors

void method(int a)	"(I)V"
boolean method(int a, byte b)	"(IB)Z"
char method(String s, int a)	"(Ljava/lang/String;I)C"
Object[] method()	"()[Ljava/lang/Object;"

Unlike C++, Java methods are `virtual` by default. That is, if class B extends class A and class B overwrites the `foo` method, if we call the `foo` method on an instance of class B that has been cast to A, the `foo` method in class B will be called. If you want to call the foo method in A through JNI, you should use the `CallNonvirtual <type>Method` family of functions.

Array Functions

Java arrays are unlike arrays in C. Java arrays are special objects. You can use the `New<primitiveType>Array` functions to create an array and `GetArrayLength` to get its length. Three sets of functions can be used to retrieve elements of primitive arrays, and it is crucial to understand their differences.

```
Get<primitiveType>ArrayRegion
Get<primitiveType>ArrayElements
GetPrimitiveArrayCritical
```

`Get<primitiveType>ArrayRegion` simply copies a region of the array into a provided buffer. On the other hand, `Get<primitiveType>ArrayElements` attempts to retrieve a direct pointer to the first element of the array, and if the attempt fails, it will return a pointer to a copy of the array. The attempt will fail if the array cannot be *pinned* or if the VM implementation does not store arrays as would typically be expected. For example, a VM implementation may not represent arrays as contiguous memory. A VM implementation may represent, for example, boolean arrays as a collection of bits. Because pinning an object so that the garbage collector does not move it may not be supported due to implementation complications, the VM may return a copy. In addition, even if pinning is supported by a VM, it may just happen that the call will result in too much fragmentation of the heap. The isCopy parameter informs you whether the returned pointer is a pointer to a copy of the array. Either way, you must call Release<primitiveType>ArrayElements when you no longer need the elements.

Unlike Get<type>ArrayElements, GetPrimitiveArrayCritical makes every effort to return a pointer to the body of the array. If possible, it will even temporarily disable the garbage collector. Every call to GetPrimitiveArrayCritical needs to be paired with ReleasePrimitiveArrayCritical. Be careful not to perform blocking operations or even call arbitrary JNI functions because such operations can result in a deadlock. In addition, disabling and enabling the garbage collector has some overhead that may undo the benefit of obtaining a direct pointer. Retrieving a direct pointer may sometimes be preferred because some CPU cycles do not have to be wasted to copy the content of the array. The larger an array, the more beneficial obtaining a direct pointer can be. In addition to CPU consumption, creating a copy can also become a concern if an array is extremely large. As with Get<type>ArrayElements, if the VM uses special internal representation for arrays, even GetPrimitiveArrayCritical can result in a creation of a copy. Setting the data in a primitive array is always done by value because the data must end up in the Java heap and not remain in the C heap or stack.

Accessing arrays of objects are done using GetObjectArrayElement and SetObjectArrayElement. You can obtain a reference to the objects referred to by the array elements only one at a time.

String Functions

JNI provides a set of functions specific for string manipulation. This may seem odd because java.lang.String objects are like any other Java objects, and it should not be necessary to have functions specific to a type. Strings have been treated differently because they are common to many applications. It is much more convenient and faster to call these functions instead of the equivalent calls that treat strings like typical objects. In Java, strings are Unicode strings, but in C they are ASCII, so you have to be more careful when dealing with strings. JNI provides functions that deal with UTF-8 and not specifically ASCII. Even though UTF-8 strings can contain multibyte characters, a UTF-8 string that uses only single-byte characters is identical to an ASCII string. An ASCII string and its equivalent UTF-8 string have the same length, and, unlike Unicode strings, they are both null-terminated. The NewStringUTF takes a pointer to a char buffer and returns an instance of java.lang.String, which is always represented as Unicode. On the other hand, NewString takes a pointer to a jchar (Unicode character) buffer and, like NewStringUTF, returns a jstring (reference to an instance of java.lang.String). Because Unicode strings are not null-terminated, you must pass the length of the buffer when calling New-String. Given a jstring, both GetStringLength and GetStringUTFLength can return the same length. In fact, the only time they return different values is when a jstring contains characters that are non-ASCII (or multibyte when converted to UTF-8). GetStringRegion and GetStringUTFRegion work like Get<primitiveType>Array-Region. They copy the data into a preallocated buffer.

```
Java_Sample_MyNativeFunction(JNIEnv *env, jclass clazz,
    jstring string){

    jsize stringLength = env->GetStringLength(string);
    char *buffer = (char *)calloc(stringLength+1, 1);
    env->GetStringUTFRegion(string, 0, stringLength, buffer);
    printf("buffer: %s", buffer);
    free(buffer);
}
```

GetStringChars and GetStringUTFChars work similar to Get<primitiveType>ArrayElements. Finally, GetStringCritical is similar to GetPrimitiveArrayCritical. The isCopy parameter of these functions lets you know if the call results in the creation of a copy. Regardless, be sure to call the corresponding Release functions.

In Java, instances of the java.lang.String class are constant. In other words, once created, they cannot be changed (unlike java.lang.StringBuffer). By being immutable, the VM can share string objects. This means that you should not be surprised to find out that they return constant pointers and that there are no Set-StringChars functions.

Exception Functions

The Java programming language specifies that an exception will be thrown when semantic constraints are violated, in which case it causes a nonlocal transfer of control from the point where the exception occurred to a point that can be specified by the programmer. An exception is said to be thrown from the point where it occurred and is said to be caught at the point to which control is transferred. When using native code, you can throw and catch Java exceptions, but unlike in Java, the transfer of control must be done explicitly. For example, if a method invoked by some native code throws an exception that is not caught on the Java side, control is transferred back to the native code. The native code should explicitly check for any pending exceptions and then transfer control appropriately so that the exception can be dealt with gracefully. When an exception is detected in native code, you can choose to return from the native code and let the caller of the native function handle the exception. Alternatively, you can choose to deal with the exception in native code and continue with the execution of the native code. The following sample shows how to check for an exception and handle it in native code:

```java
class Sample{

    Sample(){
        System.loadLibrary("MyNativeLibrary");
    }

    private native void myNativeFunction();

    public void myMethod() throws NullPointerException{
        throw new NullPointerException("Sample.myMethod...");
    }

    public static void main(String args[]) {
        Sample sample = new Sample();
        sample.myNativeFunction();
    }
}


#include "Sample.h"
#include <stdio.h:

JNIEXPORT void JNICALL
Java_Sample_myNativeFunction(JNIEnv *env, jobject obj){

    jclass clazz = env->GetObjectClass(obj);
    jmethodID mid = env->GetMethodID(clazz, "myMethod", "()V");

    env->CallVoidMethod(obj, mid);

    if (env->ExceptionCheck()){
        printf("An Exception has occurred\n");
        env->ExceptionDescribe();
        printf("clearing Exception\n");
        env->ExceptionClear();
    }
}
```

The sample code demonstrates a native function that calls the `myMethod` method, which throws an exception. The native code checks for any pending exceptions, and after printing out some message, it clears the exception.

To check for pending exceptions you can use `ExceptionCheck` or `Exception-Occurred`. The former is more efficient and useful when you simply want to know if an exception has been thrown. `ExceptionOccurred` returns a reference to the exception. Once you handle an exception in native code you should clear it by calling `ExceptionClear`. Because native code has to check for exception to transfer control, failing to clear a handled exception can result in unexpected behavior. This holds true for JNI functions themselves, meaning you should not call arbitrary JNI functions when there is a pending exception.

Native code can also throw an exception by calling `Throw` or `ThrowNew`. You can declare a native method with the `throws` keyword so that catching of the exceptions thrown from the native code is enforced at compile time. JNI function may throw exceptions themselves. Some JNI function returns success or failure that can be used as a more efficient way of error checking.

Direct Buffer Functions

Direct buffers were introduced in JDK 1.4 as part of `java.nio`. They provide the means to make data visible to both native and Java code by directly exposing the data to both sides. Before going any further, it is important to know the difference between the Java heap and the system memory. As shown in Figure 11.2, we will define the Java heap as the memory maintained by the garbage collector, and the system memory as all the memory of the host machine minus the Java heap.

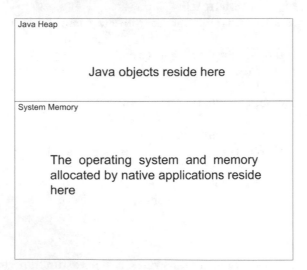

FIGURE 11.2   Java heap and system memory.

Because the garbage collector moves the data in the Java heap when performing housekeeping, direct access to the data cannot be possible unless either the VM supports pinning of objects or the garbage collector can be disabled temporarily. As discussed earlier, JNI functions such as `GetStringChars` and `GetPrimitiveArray-Critical` attempt to pin objects or disable the garbage collector to avoid having to copy the data. However, even if a VM implementation supports these techniques, they can impose serious overhead and limitation.

If native code cannot manipulate data in the Java heap, the data must be copied from the Java heap to system memory, manipulated, and then copied back. Copying data back and forth can result in substantial performance loss for sizeable amounts of data. Passing primitive types or even accessing object data through JNI means that data is copied. Direct buffers, on the other hand, allow both Java and native code to access a buffer of data without causing the data to get copied, relying on the VM implementation to support object pinning, or disabling the garbage collector. A direct buffer is essentially a Java object that contains a pointer to an array (or buffer) that is not maintained by the garbage collector and is typically in the system memory. This means that both native and Java code can access the content of the buffer. In addition, an implementation of the Java platform may support the creation of direct-byte buffers from native code. This means that the native code can allocate a chunk of memory and assign it as the buffer of a `java.nio.Byte-Buffer` object. Figure 11.3 shows this concept.

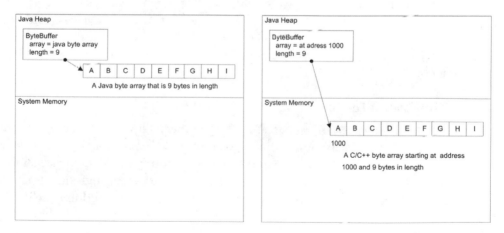

FIGURE 11.3   Java ByteBuffer object that contains a pointer to a native buffer.

Let's consider a scenario where we need to load an image, modify it dynamically, and then draw it in a window. From the native side, we can load the image into the system memory and then use a direct ByteBuffer to wrap the loaded image.

Once we have a direct buffer reference that points to the image data as its buffer, we can pass it to the Java side so that the image can be manipulated from the Java side. Because the image resides in the system memory, if the direct ByteBuffer is passed to a native draw function, the address of the image can be obtained from the Byte-Buffer and used to draw the image. Without the use of a direct buffer, we would run into a few problems. First, we would have to decide where to store the loaded image. If stored on the Java side, after modifying the image, it would have to be copied to system memory before being passed to a draw function. Again, this is because the garbage collector can move an object when performing housekeeping. If the image is stored in system memory, it would not be possible to directly modify the image data from the Java side unless a direct ByteBuffer object wraps the content of the image. In fact, this is the reason why it is necessary to use an instance of `java.awt.bufferedImage` to access the data of an AWT image. A buffered image is essentially an object that is used to indirectly manipulate the image data stored by default in the system memory. If direct buffers were available when AWT was designed, the solution would probably be different. The following segment shows how to create a direct buffer that wraps an arbitrary region of the system memory:

```
jobject jDirectByteBuffer =
env->NewDirectByteBuffer(startAddress, length);
```

Note that from the Java side you cannot set a direct ByteBuffer's buffer address. If this were not the case, Java would lose its inherently safe nature. It is, however, possible to write a quick native method that takes the `startAddress` and `length` as parameters and returns a newly created buffer.

Other buffer-related JNI functions are `GetDirectBufferAddress` and `GetDirect-BufferCapacity`.

Miscellaneous Functions

The two handlers, `JNI_OnLoad` and `JNI_OnUnload`, allow you to perform some initialization and finalization in the native library. When a library is loaded by the `System.loadLibrary` method, the `JNI_OnLoad` function is called. You can allocate any memory that should live during the life of the library through this function. The function is also a good place to compute and cache method and field IDs. The value returned by the function allows the loader to determine if the library is compatible with the version of JDK. For example, if you have a native library that uses newer functions in the JNI function table, the library should not be used in an older VM. It is important to note that the `JNI_OnUnload` handler is not called until the class loader of the class that caused the library to load is garbage-collected.

Therefore, it would be a good idea not to wait for the `JNI_OnUnLoad` handler to free a large amount of system resources.

The Invocation Interface

JNI also includes an invocation interface that can be used to launch the VM from a native program. By using the functions provided by this interface, you could create and destroy a VM. In fact, this is how `Java.exe` launches the VM. The invocation interface is used to launch the VM from C/C++ code, which is also known as embedding the VM. If you want to use Java as a scripting language for a C/C++ game, you must use this interface. Note that Java is not exactly a scripting language. For more information please read Chapter 10, "Java as a Scripting Language."

The `AttachCurrentThread` function can be used to let the VM know that you want to allow the current native thread to communicate with the VM. This step is important because the VM must give each thread a pointer to a different JNI environment instance.

As the following segment shows, launching a VM is pretty straightforward. The only requirements are that the project links to `jvm.lib` and the directory of `jvm.dll` be visible. Note that you cannot copy the `jvm.dll` to your directory because it uses its relative location to find other files.

```
JavaVM* g_jvm = 0;
JNIEnv* g_env = 0;

int StartVM(){
    JavaVMInitArgs jvmArgs;
    jvmArgs.version = JNI_VERSION_1_4;
    jvmArgs.ignoreUnrecognized = JNI_TRUE;

    result = JNI_CreateJavaVM(&g_jvm, (void**)&g_env, &jvmArgs );

    if (result){
        printf("Error:  JNI_CreateJavaVM failed");
        return -1;
    }
}
```

The following code segment destroys the VM, but note that because the *jvm.dll* uses internal global variables, after destroying the VM, a VM cannot be created in the same process again. This was not the original intention, and in the past, destroying the VM would return an error. Even though the destroy function no longer returns an error, the VM cannot be restarted.

```
void StopVM(){
    if (g_env){
        if (g_env->ExceptionOccurred()) {
            g_env->ExceptionDescribe();
        }
    }

    if (g_jvm) {
        jint result = g_jvm->DestroyJavaVM();
        if(result){
            printf("Error: g_jvm->DestroyJavaVM() FAILED\n");
        }
    }
}
```

If you want to find out if a VM exists, you can call the following:

```
JavaVM* createdVms[1] = {0};
jsize numberOfVMs;
JNI_GetCreatedJavaVMs(createdVms, 1, &numberOfVMs);

if (numberOfVMs > 0) {
    g_jvm = createdVms[0];
    g_jvm->GetEnv((void**)&g_env, JNI_VERSION_1_4);
}
```

USING NATIVE CODE IN YOUR GAME

There are many scenarios in which you may need to use native code in your game. Many times, rather simple native libraries can help you work around some issues and accomplish tasks that might not be possible otherwise. If you want to use an existing native API, you can write one-to-one bindings. That is, you can create a native method for each of the API functions so that they can be called from the Java side. The disadvantage is if the API for which you are writing the bindings is platform specific, you will have some work and redesigning to do when and if you wish to port your game to other platforms. For example, writing one-to-one bindings for DirectX may not be a good idea. Of course, if you are developing a game only for the Windows platform, you will be just fine. APIs such as JOGL and JOAL are good examples of one-to-one bindings. Because the APIs are themselves available across platforms, writing direct bindings is a good idea. Many times, a better way to extend the functionality of your Java game is to design a platform-independent layer and use any platform-dependent API underneath that layer. It is important to note that using native libraries has some implications that we will discuss in a later section.

When writing native libraries, even your native code should be separated into platform-dependent and platform-independent files. You can have header files that contain machine-dependent declarations and other headers that conform to your API. You can also abstract APIs to allow for communication between native and Java code at a higher level. For example, Java3D does not have bindings for OpenGL or Direct3D calls and defines its own API that internally uses OpenGL and Direct3D. You can even write a generic interface to call arbitrary functions in arbitrary native libraries. Such an interface would need to take a library name, function name, and parameter list. You can even return the memory address of an object in the system memory to the Java side as an integer and pass it to other native functions. This approach is obviously not very safe. The code samples that follow show examples of direct bindings.

High-Resolution Timer

This example demonstrates a simple binding for retrieving the CPU counter's frequency as well as its current tick count. By using the frequency, we can convert the value of the counter from ticks to time. The resolution of this timer depends on the speed of the CPU itself. The performance counter is the value of a register that is incremented by the CPU every cycle. The more cycles the CPU can have in a second, the higher the resolution of the timer, which even on slower CPUs is much higher than milliseconds. Unfortunately, the resolution of System.currentTimeMillis() is platform dependent and can have resolution as low as 50 milliseconds on an older Windows platform. Such poor resolution means that measuring small time slices is impossible. For example, if you are doing animation or time-based physics, low time resolution does not allow for smooth and accurate calculations. The Query-PerformanceCounter class shown in the next code segment allows for retrieval of the counter and the frequency of the counter.

ON THE CD
      The following code can be found on the book's companion CD-ROM (Chapter 11/High Resolution—Timer folder):

```
public class QueryPerformanceCounter
{
    private QueryPerformanceCounter(){} // cannot be instantiated

    public static boolean loadNativeLibrary(){
        try{
            System.loadLibrary("QueryPerformanceCounter");
```

```
            }catch(UnsatisfiedLinkError e){
                e.printStackTrace();
                return false;
            }
            return true;
        }

        public static native long nativeQueryPerformanceFrequency();
        public static native long nativeQueryPerformanceCounter();
    }
```

The `QueryPerformanceCounter` loads the library through a static method and returns whether the load was successful. For example, if the .dll is not found, the standard timers can be used instead. The class provides bindings for the `Query-PerformanceFrequency` and `QueryPerformanceCounter` functions, which are part of WinAPI. The corresponding native functions defined in `QueryPerformance-Counter.dll` are simple, as can be seen here. The `HighResolutionTimer` class uses the frequency and the current tick count to compute the time. The `QueryPerformanceCounter` method is similar to the `sun.misc.Perf.getPerf().highResCounter()` method. A call to `getElapsedTimeInSeconds` returns the time since the reset method was last called.

```
#include "windows.h"
#include "QueryPerformanceCounter.h"

LARGE_INTEGER    largeInt;

JNIEXPORT jlong JNICALL
Java_QueryPerformanceCounter_nativeQueryPerformanceFrequency
    (JNIEnv *, jclass){
    QueryPerformanceFrequency(&largeInt);
    return largeInt.QuadPart;
}

JNIEXPORT jlong JNICALL
Java_QueryPerformanceCounter_nativeQueryPerformanceCounter
    (JNIEnv *, jclass){
    QueryPerformanceCounter(&largeInt);
    return largeInt.QuadPart;
}
```

LISTING 11.1   High-resolution timer class.

```
public class HighResolutionTimer
{
    ...
    public HighResolutionTimer(){

    boolean success =
            QueryPerformanceCounter.loadNativeLibrary();

            if (success){
            frequency = QueryPerformanceCounter.
                nativeQueryPerformanceFrequency();
        }

        if (success && frequency != 0){
            highResSupported = true;
            System.out.println(" frequency: " + frequency);
            frequencyInverse = 1.0/frequency;
            reset();
            return;
        }

        System.out.println("====: WARNING: PerformanceCounter not
            supported. System time will be used instead");
        reset();
    }

    public void reset(){
        if (highResSupported){
            counterStart = QueryPerformanceCounter.
                nativeQueryPerformanceCounter();
        }else{
            timeStart = System.currentTimeMillis();
        }
    }

    public double getElapsedTimeInSeconds(){
        if (highResSupported){
            counterEnd = QueryPerformanceCounter.
                nativeQueryPerformanceCounter();
            elapsedTime = (counterEnd - counterStart)*
                frequencyInverse;
```

```
            }else{ ... }
            return elapsedTime;
        }
    }
```

Joystick

This example demonstrates simple bindings for joystick calls available in the Windows multimedia library. One way to do this would be to simply write native functions that retrieve data, such as X-Axis, one at a time. Here we take a different approach to demonstrate direct buffers. A direct buffer is used to wrap an instance of the JOYINFOEX structure that is passed to the GetJoyPos function. The function writes the joystick data to an instance of JOYINFOEX, and its data is read directly from the Java side. Because the call is part of wmm.lib, the joystick can be calibrated from the control panel, and there is no need to have Direct Input installed. The definition of the JOYINFOEX structure and the bindings for the win32 joystick API are provided in Listing 11.2. Note that the direct buffer that wraps an instance of this structure can be indexed with precomputed indices. The buffer is read as an array of integers because every DWORD corresponds to a 32-bit value.

```
typedef struct joyinfoex_tag {
    DWORD dwSize;                  // size of the struct
    DWORD dwFlags;                 // flags that specify which
                                   //     data should be read,.....
    DWORD dwXpos;                  // axis 1
    DWORD dwYpos;                  // axis 2
    DWORD dwZpos;                  // axis 3
    DWORD dwRpos;                  // axis 4
    DWORD dwUpos;                  // axis 5
    DWORD dwVpos;                  // axis 6
    DWORD dwButtons;              // masked button states
    DWORD dwButtonNumber;        // number of buttons held down
    DWORD dwPOV;                  // point of view (8 digital)
    DWORD dwReserved1;
    DWORD dwReserved2;
} JOYINFOEX;
```

ON THE CD

The following code can be found on the book's companion CD-ROM in Code/Chapter 11/JoystickWin32Ex:

LISTING 11.2   Bindings for win32 joystick API.

```
public class JoystickWin32Ex {
    ...
    public static final int
        FIELD_INDEX_dwSize        = 0,
        FIELD_INDEX_dwFlags       = 4,
        FIELD_INDEX_dwXpos        = 8,
        FIELD_INDEX_dwYpos        = 12,
        ...
        JOY_BUTTON1      = 0x0001,
        JOY_AXISX        = FIELD_INDEX_dwXpos,
        JOY_RETURNX      = 0x00000001,
        ...

    private static ByteBuffer   joyInfoStructs[];

    private static void initialize(){
        joyInfoStructs = new ByteBuffer[2];

        for(int i=0; i<2; i++){
            joyInfoStructs[i] =
                (ByteBuffer)nativeWrapJoyInfoStruct(i);

            joyInfoStructs[i].order(ByteOrder.nativeOrder());

            joyInfoStructs[i].putInt(FIELD_INDEX_dwSize,
                joyInfoStructs[i].capacity());
            joyInfoStructs[i].putInt(FIELD_INDEX_dwFlags,
                JOY_RETURNALL);
        }
    }

    // joyAxis parameter can be JOY_AXISX, ...
    public static
        float getAxis(int joyId, int joyAxis){
        return normalizeAxisValue(
            joyInfoStructs[joyId].getInt(joyAxis));
    }

    // joyAxis parameter can be JOY_BUTTON1, ...
    public static
        boolean getButton(int joyId, int joyButton){
        return ((joyInfoStructs[joyId].getInt(
            FIELD_INDEX_dwButtons) & joyButton) != 0)?true:false;
    }
```

```
public static void dumpJoyInfoExStruct(int joyId){
    System.out.println("---- JOYINFOEX Struct ----");
    System.out.println("dwSize:        " +
        joyInfoStructs[joyId].
        getInt(FIELD_INDEX_dwSize));
    System.out.println("dwFlags:       " +
        Integer.toBinaryString(joyInfoStructs[joyId].
        getInt(FIELD_INDEX_dwFlags)));
    System.out.println("dwXpos:        " +
        normalizeAxisValue(joyInfoStructs[joyId].
        getInt(FIELD_INDEX_dwXpos)));
        ...
}
...

// returns a ByteBuffers mapped to a JOYINFOEX instance
private static native
    Object nativeWrapJoyInfoStruct(int joyId);

private static native int
    nativePoll(boolean pollBoth);
}
```

LISTING 11.3 The native code for the bindings.

```
JOYINFOEX joyInfoExs[2];

JNIEXPORT jobject JNICALL
Java_JoystickWin32Ex_nativeWrapJoyInfoStruct(JNIEnv *env, jclass,
    jint joyId){
        ...
    memset(&joyInfoExs[joyId], O, sizeof(JOYINFOEX));
    jobject jDirectByteBuffer =
        env->NewDirectByteBuffer(&joyInfoExs[joyId],
        sizeof(JOYINFOEX));
    return jDirectByteBuffer;
}

JNIEXPORT jint JNICALL Java_JoystickWin32Ex_nativePoll(JNIEnv
    *env, jclass, jboolean pollBoth){
    ...
    return joyGetPosEx(JOYSTICKID1, &joyInfoExs[0]);
}
```

Embedding the VM and Using Java as a Scripting Language

ON THE CD
The code for this example can be found on the book's companion CD-ROM in Code/Chapter 11/Scripting Example.

The source for a demo that shows how to use Java as a scripting language has been provided on the CD-ROM. ScriptBase acts as the base class for script files. A sample script file extends the ScriptBase class and creates several units as follows:

```
class Script1 extends ScriptBase{
    void run(){
        print("Script1.run()");
        Unit peons[] = new Unit[10];

        for(int i=0; i<peons.length; i++){
            peons[i] = createUnit(UNIT_TYPE_PEON);
        }

        for(int i=0; i<peons.length; i++){
            destroyUnit(peons[i]);
        }
    }
}
```

The demo shows how to launch the VM, register native functions for creating and destroying units with the ScriptBase class, load a script file, and execute it.

Direct Memory and IO Access from Java (UnsafeNativeUtil)

This example demonstrates how to have the same level of control over memory and file IO as you have in C/C++. The main purpose of this example is to show that if you must have as much control as you do in C/C++, you can. Please note that in general, it is not a good practice for a Java program to perform the tasks outlined here, and you should avoid them. In fact, justifying the need to perform some of these operations from Java can be quite a challenge. Having said that, we highly recommend that you look through this example.

The UnsafeNativeUtil class provides bindings for ANSI C functions such as malloc, free, memcpy, memset, fopen, fclose, fread, fwrite, feof, fseek, and ftell. The utility class uses longs to pass around memory addresses, which is typically represented as unsigned longs in the native side. Instead of using a long to represent a file pointer, the library defines the FilePointer class:

```
class FilePointer{
    private long pointer;
    private FilePointer(){};
}
```

Because the class has a single private constructor, objects of type FilePointer cannot be created on the Java side. In addition, the pointer member cannot be accessed, which makes the type an opaque structure to a Java program. Instances of the class can be made only from native code. In fact, the native fopen method is the only function that can create a file pointer object and return it to a Java program. UnsafeNativeUtil is a simple class that contains several native methods, which are listed here.

ON THE CD

The code for this example can be found on the book's companion CD-ROM in Code/Chapter 11/ UnsafeNativeUtil:

```
//---- memory bindings ----
long malloc(int size);
void free(long pointer);
byte read(long pointer);
void write(long pointer, byte value);
void memcpy(long dest, long src, int count);
void memset(long dest, int value, int count);

//---- ByteBuffer ----
ByteBuffer    wrapbuf(long pointer, long size);
long          getbuf(ByteBuffer byteBuffer);

//---- file bindings ----
FilePointer fopen(String filename, String mode);
int fclose(FilePointer stream);
int fread(long buffer, int size, int count, FilePointer stream);
int fwrite(long buffer, int size, int count, FilePointer stream);
int feof(FilePointer stream);
int fseek(FilePointer stream, int offset, int origin);
int ftell(FilePointer stream);
```

For details about all but read, write, wrapbuf, and getbuf, refer to the corresponding C function documentation. The read method reads the value of a byte at the provided memory address, and the write method writes the provided byte to the specified memory address. They can be used to access any byte of the system memory. The wrapbuf method uses the JNI NewDirectByteBuffer to create a Byte-Buffer that wraps the memory region passed to the method. The getbuf method uses the JNI `GetDirectBufferAddress` to return the address of a direct ByteBuffer's buffer.

The following Java segments are from a class provided on the CD-ROM that demonstrates how to use the `UnsafeNativeUtil` to duplicate a 24-bit bitmap file and modify its content directly as well as through direct ByteBuffers. This segment shows how to duplicate a file. As you might expect, this segment of Java code looks a lot like a segment of C code.

```
FilePointer fileInput = UnsafeNativeUtil.fopen("In.bmp", "rb");
FilePointer fileOutput = UnsafeNativeUtil.fopen("Out.bmp", "wb");

// compute file size
int bufferSize = 0;
UnsafeNativeUtil.fseek(fileInput, 0, UnsafeNativeUtil.SEEK_END);
bufferSize = UnsafeNativeUtil.ftell(fileInput);
UnsafeNativeUtil.fseek(fileInput, 0, UnsafeNativeUtil.SEEK_SET);

// allocate memory and set its content to 0
long buffer = UnsafeNativeUtil.malloc(bufferSize);
UnsafeNativeUtil.memset(buffer, (byte)0, bufferSize);

// read from input file into buffer, then write buffer to out file
UnsafeNativeUtil.fread(buffer, 1, bufferSize, fileInput);
UnsafeNativeUtil.fwrite(buffer, 1, bufferSize, fileOutput);

UnsafeNativeUtil.fclose(fileInput);
UnsafeNativeUtil.fclose(fileOutput);
```

The following segment uses the `wrapbuf` method to create a ByteBuffer that wraps the memory region starting at `buffer` and ending at `buffer + bufferSize`. It then traverses the middle third of the buffer and modifies its bytes. Bytes that represent 255 (a component of the white color) are converted to 192 (gray component), and any black bytes (value of 0) are converted to white. Note that the segment uses both the `put` and `get` methods of the ByteBuffer as well as direct memory access through `read`/`write`.

```
ByteBuffer bBuffer = UnsafeNativeUtil.wrapbuf(buffer, bufferSize)

for(int i=bBuffer.capacity()/3; i<bBuffer.capacity()*2/3; i++){

    if (bBuffer.get(i) == (byte)255){
        bBuffer.put(i, (byte)192);
```

```
        }else if (UnsafeNativeUtil.read(buffer+i) == (byte)0){
            UnsafeNativeUtil.write(buffer+i, (byte)255);
        }
    }
```

The last section of this example allocates a direct ByteBuffer by calling allocateDirect, and then uses memcpy and memset to copy and set a section of the image back to white, and write out another file. It finally calls free to release the buffer. Note that failing to call free on the memory allocated through malloc will result in memory leaks. The memory allocated through malloc is not managed by the garbage collector. In fact, the garbage collector does not even know about the memory allocated here.

```
ByteBuffer byteBuffer2 = ByteBuffer.allocateDirect(bufferSize);
long byteBuffer2Buffer = UnsafeNativeUtil.getbuf(byteBuffer2);
UnsafeNativeUtil.memcpy(byteBuffer2Buffer, buffer,
    byteBuffer2.capacity());
UnsafeNativeUtil.memset(byteBuffer2Buffer + bufferSize/3,
    (byte)255, bufferSize/3);

// write the buffer to a file
FilePointer fileOutput3 =
    UnsafeNativeUtil.fopen("Output3.bmp", "wb");
UnsafeNativeUtil.fwrite(byteBuffer2Buffer, 1,
    byteBuffer2.capacity(), fileOutput3);
UnsafeNativeUtil.fclose(fileOutput3);

// free memory that was allocated using malloc
UnsafeNativeUtil.free(buffer);
```

PERFORMANCE

One of the most important aspects of interfacing with native code is to make sure that you are passing data efficiently. Passing primitive types to native functions is a perfect solution for a few and fixed number of parameters. Primitive arrays can be viable when passing more than a few or a variable number of parameters. They are also useful when you need to return multiple values. Passing the data as Java objects does have some disadvantages, primarily due to the overhead of accessing the objects from native code. Reading from and writing to a Java object from the native side means that JNI functions have to be used as accessors to set and retrieve data by value. Direct buffers are by far the best approach for passing or sharing a large amount of data between the two worlds. They are especially important when dealing with large chunks of data and can pay off even for a small amount of data.

Mixing native code and calling native functions from the Java side can have reasonable effects on the performance of your game. Table 11.6 shows the timing comparison of native and nonnative methods running with different VM settings. To time the overhead of calling a native function, a test was set up where the Main method called an update method and its equivalent nativeUpdate(). The bodies of the methods simply incremented a counter. Each method was called 100,000,000 times after the VM had the chance to warm up. The settings include the default VM settings that allow the HotSpot to compile the Java code to native CPU instructions, as well as inline qualified methods. The column labeled **No Inlining** indicates that the VM was also not allowed to perform any inlining by specifying the command-line option -XX:MaxInlineSize=0. Last, the tests were also performed in fully interpreted mode (-Xint), which is similar to the classic Java VMs. The numbers in the table have been normalized using the timing of the update method when running in interpreted mode.

TABLE 11.6   Timing of Native and Nonnative Methods

		Default	No Inlining	Interpreted
JDK 1.4.1	update()	4%	39%	100%
	nativeUpdate()	110%	109%	108%
JDK 1.4.2	update()	4%	42%	103%
	nativeUpdate()	98%	76%	112%

There are a couple of points to note. Intuitively, the default setting resulted in a far better performance than the interpreted mode. This is because the VM was able to inline the method call and then compile the byte code to native CPU instructions. As expected, without inlining, the JIT compiler resulted in reasonable performance increase. On the other hand, the timings of nativeUpdate() are roughly the same, regardless of the VM settings. This is because a native function is not inlined and the resulting bytecode remains unoptimized. The data presented in the table indicates that the pure overhead of calling native functions is only about 10 percent.

Calling Java methods and accessing object fields from native code does have some overhead as well. The overhead is due mostly to using JNI functions as assessors, which results in an extra level of indirection. Note that these overheads are relatively trivial. The most important point to realize is that the more expensive the task performed by a function, the less noticeable the overhead will be. For example, if you call a render function that takes up the most significant chunk of time in your game, the overhead will be imperceptible. The overhead may even be too small to measure for some applications.

IMPLICATIONS OF USING JNI

Even though adding native code to your Java games can have many benefits, you should be aware of its implications. There are scenarios when porting a section of your Java code to C code can result in some performance increases, but you should keep in mind that C/C++ compilers output code that is optimized for a specific target CPU. On the other hand, HotSpot VMs compile bytecode to machine code for any hardware on which the bytecode is running. In addition, HotSpot VMs perform optimizations during runtime. One of the optimizations is inlining bytecode.

If you use native functions, the HotSpot will not be able to inline them and perform additional optimizations. Please refer to Chapter 6, "Performance and the Java Virtual Machine," for more information on the optimizations performed by the VM. You should also keep in mind that some overhead is involved when using JNI. As discussed earlier, some JNI functions may even disable the garbage collector temporarily. When using native code, it is harder to keep track of how much memory is used by an application. Intuitively, the VM does not know about any memory that it is allocated by other native functions.

Another significant implication of using native code is the portability issues. If you want your application to remain cross platform, you must provide your native libraries for every platform of interest. This means that at the very least you must recompile the native source files for each platform. This task can be much more complicated if you are using OS functions or other libraries that are not available across platforms. For example, the joystick example we provided earlier is useful only on Windows. In fact, because it is a binding for part of the OS API, you will not be able to port the code without modifying the Java code that uses the bindings. One of Java's most important characteristics is its safety. By mixing native code with your Java code, you are in a way reducing the reliability of your application.

SUMMARY

Using native code has both advantages and disadvantages. If the use of native code can be avoided, you should make every attempt to do so. Sometimes it is your only option and, unfortunately, as it stands right now, if you want to make a professional Java game, you will likely have to write some native code for your game. As more libraries such as JOGL and JOAL become available, the need to write native code will be reduced.

12 3D Graphics Foundations

In This Chapter

- Introduction
- 3D Graphics in Computer Animation and Real Time
- 3D Hardware Acceleration
- A Brief History of 3D Game Graphics
- 3D Graphics Condensed Soup
- Summary

INTRODUCTION

Just about any computer game these days uses some form of 3D graphics. Most major titles now are completely real-time 3D-graphics based. The gameplay takes place as a real-time 3D rendered experience, and these same games usually require 3D hardware acceleration to execute.

In the coming chapters we will examine what developers need to understand and to do to make real-time hardware accelerated 3D graphics work for a game. This can be a complex and daunting task. Fortunately, there is OpenGL, a well-developed standard 3D graphics API, to help with this task as well as higher-level APIs such as Java3D and other techniques to help us assemble a rich 3D game engine—the basis for any 3D game.

3D GRAPHICS IN COMPUTER ANIMATION AND REAL TIME

3D graphics is heavily used in many industries, including aerospace, medical visualization, simulation and training, science and research, and entertainment. In entertainment, two fields stand out in their 3D graphics use—movies and computer games. Movie and game 3D graphics are divided into two disciplines for their creation, where computer animation is used for movies and real-time 3D is used for games, although games sometimes also play movies.

Any type of 3D computer graphics typically uses a mathematical model, for example, groups of triangles or points, to represent a 3D object on screen. The final on-screen display is simply a 2D image computed from various parameters, such as position relative to the viewer, lighting effects, and surface color. The process of making this 2D image from the 3D information is called rendering.

The rendering happens similarly in computer animation and real-time 3D, and both techniques must render for the user to have something to view. However, there are some important differences. Movies are rendered in advance of viewing, almost always on a different computer than the user is using, and the rendering takes as much time as the rendering software needs to finish the images. When the movie is complete, it is obtained by the user, who watches the movie playback on his computer.

Real-time 3D (RT3D) uses special software and hardware to render and display the graphics on the user's computer while the user is viewing them. That is, the software and hardware renders a frame, immediately displays it to the screen, and then repeats this process until the experience is done or the user halts it. The final displayable image is often called a frame, like a frame in a movie reel.

Because the software and hardware is rendering while the display is happening, the amount of time available for this rendering must be very small (a fraction of a second) in comparison to pre-rendered movies. In big-production movies using 3D computer animation, complex single frames have been known to take 48 hours to render! The time to render can vary, but a RT3D application's render must typically be finished and displayed within 1/30th of a second. How fast the software and hardware can do this is measured by frame rate. The frame rate is how many full screens or frames a given application refreshes or redraws per second. The goal in real-time graphics is to have a frame rate high enough that the viewing experience is smooth and seamless and yet allows interactivity. What makes real time real time is that it is interactive. Therefore, when 3D graphics are rendering and displaying fast enough to interact with, then it can be called real time.

This begs the question—how fast is fast enough to interact with? Unfortunately, there is no universal answer, but for games, we can have an idea. Fast enough is entirely dependent on the type of gameplay you are trying to create. A top-down or isometric-view type game may need only 15 frames per second (fps) to satisfy the player. However, a cutting-edge first-person shooter or race game will require 60 fps or greater. Still other games may simply be short segments of movie playback and do not require truly interactive 3D graphics at all.

One last thing to remember about movies is that although prerendered movies can have a fast enough frame rate—for example, 30 fps for video—they are still not considered interactive because the playback will always be the same. By rendering in real time, the renderer can change what will be shown in the next frame, based on user input and game logic, making the experience potentially different every time.

Software versus Hardware

There are two main ways to render 3D graphics, software rendering and hardware-accelerated rendering. It is possible to combine the two, but most RT3D games stick to hardware-accelerated rendering in an effort to maintain interactive frame rates.

Software rendering is what the movie industry typically uses to render frames. Software rendering means that the rendering code runs on a general purpose CPU using specialized graphics algorithms. Software rendering for computer animation is notoriously slow because the scene complexity and frame resolutions are so high, but they can be sped up if limited to quicker algorithms and simpler scenes. Software rendering is often an attractive alternative for 3D games because it doesn't require special 3D hardware. However, the graphics quality must be highly limited in this case, particularly the screen resolution, to maintain interactive frame rates. Software rendering is popular on handheld devices because handheld displays have a low resolution, and most handheld devices have no 3D hardware acceleration.

Today, most PC games require 3D hardware acceleration if the game is to be RT3D.

3D HARDWARE ACCELERATION

Because rendering 3D graphics requires too much computation for a lone CPU to handle in real time, specialized RT3D graphics hardware has been developed. These 3D video graphics cards were developed for PCs, and similar specialized 3D graphics processors were added to game consoles, such as the PS2 or Nintendo® GameCube®. Consumer handheld devices and phones do not have specialized 3D hardware today but will in the near future.

To better understand what this hardware does for the task of 3D rendering, the origins and evolution of this hardware will be examined.

A BRIEF HISTORY OF 3D GAME GRAPHICS

The Games

In the beginning, there was 320 × 240, then 640 × 480 . . .

FIGURES 12.1 AND 12.2   Screenshot of early 3D games.

And it was good!

The game companies began to create games when no real-time 3D hardware was available for PCs other than expensive computer-aided design and virtual reality (VR) systems. Although these early games appeared to use 3D graphics, the characters were 2D images and the environments were not true 3D. Because there was no RT3D graphics hardware, the developers created custom software renderers that used techniques such as raycasting. The graphics were quite simple and low quality by today's standard but still 3D-like and dazzling in their time.

The Hardware—Heavy Metal

In response to game players' desire (and money) for improvements on existing and next-generation games, consumer-level graphics accelerator cards such as the Voodoo by 3dfx were produced. The Voodoo, as well as others, was a good start but depended a great deal on the CPU for frame rate. They used proprietary APIs to access the card's full features, but it helped speed rendering up nonetheless. Unfortunately, at the time many 3D games and 3D cards were often incompatible, but it was still solid progress from the nonaccelerated hardware days.

After many years of 3D hardware production and competition, the 3D graphics video cards have become incredibly powerful components of a modern game system.

Even before PC games started using 3D graphics hardware, the U.S. military was using 3D graphics hardware for vehicle simulators. Evans and Sutherland were among the first to create RT3D for the military. Host computers were hooked up to separate boxes of graphics hardware called Image Generators (IGs). IGs were large machines costing millions of dollars, but they did the job at a time when nothing else could, and they are still used today for certain simulation applications.

The hardware used in RT3D started as federally sponsored university research. Ivan Sutherland, one of the founders of Evans and Sutherland, pursued a federally funded program of research in 3D graphics hardware at the University of Utah. Sutherland was also advisor to Jim Clark, who received his Ph.D. from the University of Utah and founded Silicon Graphics, Inc., in 1982. Joining the faculty at Stanford, Clark received support from the DARPA VLSI Program for his geometry engine project, with a goal to harness modern custom integrated-circuit technology to create cost-effective high-performance graphics systems. It was this geometry engine that formed the basis of Silicon Graphics' technology.

Combining Graphics Hardware and Software with OpenGL

Silicon Graphics was the first company to merge IG-level graphics with computer workstations. To use that hardware they also created the very popular OpenGL RT3D rendering library. Although OpenGL was originally created for visualization on SGI's high-end Unix workstations, as PCs became more powerful it eventually made its way onto consumer-grade systems. Once OpenGL was running well on PCs, game developers began using it for their 3D game engines.

Due to the enormous success of these games and the excellence of OpenGL-based graphics, OpenGL found a new life in the game industry. In addition, OpenGL was portable, that is, it worked (for the most part) across different graphics cards and hardware platforms, so it was ideal for developers who wanted cross-platform games.

OpenGL is now the foundation for many 3D game engines as well as a version of Java3D and JOGL, the Sun Game Technology Group Java OpenGL wrappers, which we will examine and use in later chapters.

OpenGL is the essential 3D library that lets you harness the power of hardware acceleration to thrust games into the realm of professional-quality rendering, texture mapping, and special effects. Almost all of the leading games (such as *Quake III, Half-Life, MDK2, Baldur's Gate, Decent 3,* and *Madden NFL 2001*) require OpenGL for hardware acceleration.

Empowered and Bound by Hardware

With APIs such as OpenGL opening the door for game developers to control sophisticated graphics hardware, it wasn't long before specialized graphics hardware became one of the major driving forces behind RT3D advancements. There are many things it can do, and even more it cannot. Often movie-frame renderers need far greater control and complexity than the specialized hardware can provide, and this is one of the many reasons movie rendering does not typically use 3D hardware for its rendering.

However, for 3D games, interactivity is a higher priority than absolute image quality. Therefore, the hardware is usually required to get the performance needed. Because the rendering is usually done entirely by this RT3D hardware, it is also limited by what the hardware can't do. Those limitations are key issues to take into account when developing a full-blown 3D game engine.

The primary graphics primitives for 3D graphics hardware are triangles, lines, and pixels. There are many reasons why these are the only accelerated drawing primitives, including computing lighting, depth testing, and transformations. Some of these reasons will be examined later in this chapter; however, others are beyond the scope of this text. See the resources for more information.

The 3D hardware accelerates these specific primitives, so rendering performance can be measured by how fast these primitives can be processed and rendered.

Vendors use two major metrics to measure 3D hardware performance: the triangle process rate, or how many triangles the graphics card can process per second, and the pixel fill rate, or how many pixels the graphics card can draw on screen per second, usually measured in millions of pixels per second (megapixels/sec) Figure 12.3 shows renders of varying triangle and fill rate amounts.

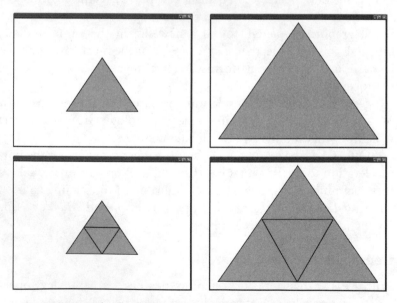

FIGURE 12.3 The pixel fill rate and triangle process rate.

Although the final game performance is affected by many things, such as processing game objects, sound, and other game code, the hardware's triangle process rate and pixel fill rate often have a direct effect on the game's final frame rates.

3D GRAPHICS CONDENSED SOUP

Although the rendering hardware is built to primarily draw 3D triangles, how you set them up and manipulate them has evolved into a rich system of algorithms using 3D mathematics and other techniques. This section is meant to be a broad overview of these 3D concepts. This material is considered the foundation for many of the techniques in later chapters but is in no way all-inclusive of the world of 3D graphics. See the resources for more information.

Coordinate Systems

Everything in 3D graphics takes place in mathematical or virtual space.

A coordinate is a series of numbers that describes a location in that space.

The space used in most 3D graphics is called the 3D Cartesian coordinate system, after René Descartes (1596–1650). It uses a series of intersecting line segments to describe a location relative to the origin. The origin is the point in space where all coordinates in a coordinate system are 0. The intersection lines are orthogonal or perpendicular to each other.

By convention, the intersecting lines are named the x-, y-, and z-axis, and the standard order is to use a right-handed orientation (see Figure 12.4).

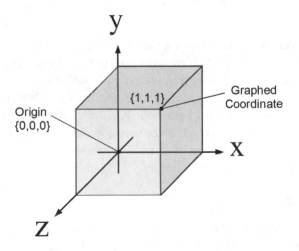

FIGURE 12.4 Coordinate triad and origin.

Cartesian coordinates are written as an ordered set, often called x, y, z, corresponding to the coordinate axis. These coordinates can then be graphed or rendered, for example, (5.0, 4.0, –1.5).

3D Objects

A 3D model is composed of relational information and geometric information. This information is usually stored in the form of polygons or triangles and vertices.

Polygons

A polygon is a multisided, closed surface composed of vertices connected by closed, chained lines (see Figure 12.5).

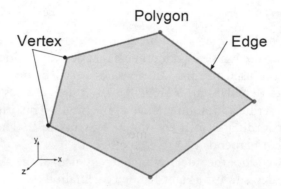

FIGURE 12.5   Polygon.

A vertex is where the coordinates of a polygon are actually stored. For mathematics this may be all a vertex needs, but for 3D graphics a vertex still has much more data associated with it, for example, color.

A triangle is simply the most basic form of a polygon with exactly three vertices.

A triangle is useful because it is always planar and convex, which can be important for lighting as well as for collision detection, as we will see in later chapters.

3D objects don't have to be made of only triangles, but they are often triangulated, or converted into triangles.

Winding Order

Another important thing to note about polygons and triangles is the winding order. Winding order determines what is the front and what is the back of a polygon. OpenGLs default winding order is counterclockwise, that is, when looking at a polygon, the front will be facing the viewer when the vertex order is counterclockwise. The winding order can be changed when rendering, but typically it is left as counterclockwise. Counterclockwise winding order will be assumed from now on unless otherwise specified (see Figure 12.6).

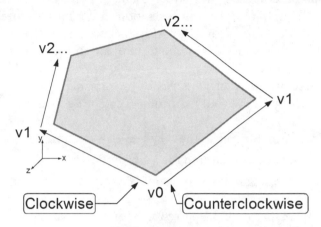

FIGURE 12.6 Polygon winding order.

3D objects are rendered from meshes of triangles. Often a geometric object can be thought of as a set of coordinates or points that have a common origin and a set of triangles made with those coordinates. Because they share a common origin they can also be thought of as translation vectors from that common origin.

Current 3D hardware and OpenGL can process this geometric data for rendering if it is properly formatted.

A note on 3D object or content creation: creating 3D objects in code can be very challenging and sometimes disappointing. Some objects, such as terrain, lend themselves to programmatic generation. Others, such as fantasy characters, do not. In addition, just as artists don't tend to make great programmers, programmers don't tend to make great artists. In any case, sophisticated software applications have been created over the years specifically for assisting in 3D content creation. Maya from Alias and 3d studio max® from discreet® are two of the most popular commercial packages, each costing thousands of dollars. Shareware and freeware 3D-modeling software is also available, such as Milkshape and Blender. Any professional-level 3D game development will be using some form of 3D content-creation software with skilled artists creating the bulk of the content. The programmers' job at a minimum will be to give that content life, by first loading the content into the game engine, and second, giving it motion appropriate for the games. Building content loaders and animating the content will be examined in later chapters.

Transformations

To create a change or "motion" in a 3D object or a coordinate system, we use a transformation. A simple definition of a transformation is any operation that uniformly changes the coordinates of a piece of geometry. By uniformly, we mean that the same operation is done to each coordinate and, thus, the overall shape is preserved.

In 3D graphics, the transformations are typically stored as 3D matrices, but often, due to wrappers and tool APIs, the matrices are not processed directly by the code but are abstracted by some form of a transformation class. Java3D does this, as do many other 3D APIs and tools.

There are three major types of transformations in a 3D graphics system as shown in Figure 12.7, but many others can be applied:

Translate: Moving in the x-, y-, and z-direction

Rotate: Rotating around the x-, y-, and z-axes

Scale: Scaling in the x-, y-, and z-direction

A 3D matrix multiplied to a vector or coordinate applies that matrix to the vector or transforms that vector by the matrix. For example, if the matrix represents a 45-degree y-axis rotation, multiplying it times the vector will return the transformed vector rotated 45 degrees around the y-axis.

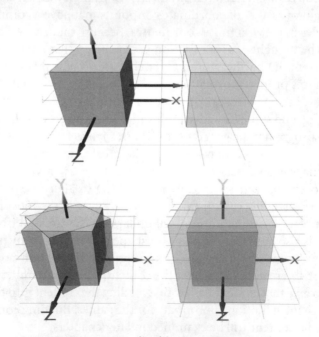

FIGURE 12.7 Example object transformations.

Transformation matrices can be associated with 3D objects, and then the renderer can apply the transformation to the 3D object for rendering when processing the graphics pipeline.

Derived from linear algebra, performing the matrix multiple on a single vertex involves 16 multiply and 12 add operations. That is quite a few operations in a single mathematical operation, but when this is multiplied by the thousands of vertices that may need to be transformed in a single frame, it really starts to add up. Luckily, this is yet another one of the operations that the 3D hardware has been designed to handle.

Transformation Stacks and Hierarchies

Associating a 3D object with a single transform matrix for transforming its vertices works well for simple objects. However, more complex objects such as characters and vehicles that are made up of more than one object often need transform hierarchies, such as in Figure 12.8

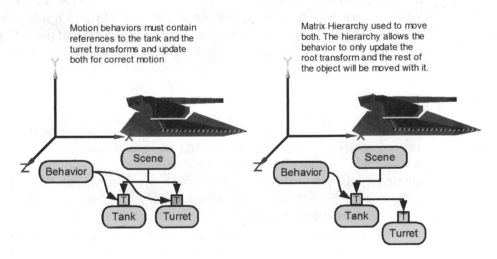

FIGURE 12.8   Transformation hierarchies.

This situation leads to much more complex scene representations and rendering pipelines, but often this hierarchical representation actually makes managing the scene simpler. Hierarchical and graph-based scene representations are often called scene graphs and will be discussed further in Chapter 15, "3D Render Using JOGL."

Camera and Projection

The final render of our 3D object is a 2D image, but so far we have been learning about 3D data. To get from the 3D virtual space to the 2D screen display involves two more important concepts. One is the camera, and the other is projection.

The idea of a camera is that the developer can place a camera virtually in the 3D space and have the system render from that point of view. However, a camera is really an illusion in which the world's objects are really inversely transformed by a camera transform. In OpenGL, there is not a real camera but a ModelView matrix that is used to create the effect of a camera in the world. To make the controls easier to use, setting up a camera object is one of the first things a 3D game engine provides on top of OpenGL. Manipulating the camera is a critical part of 3D games, and each game has its own needs for what the camera should do. Often this is one of the most difficult parts of a final game to get right. Anyone who has played 3D games knows camera motion can make or break a game.

A projection is performed on the 3D polygons to make 2D polygons. This process is done using a projection matrix that the rendering system creates based on the state of the camera and other factors, such as the field of view. In general, projections transform points in a coordinate system of dimension n into points in a coordinate system of dimension less than n. The good news is that the 3D hardware handles this fairly automatically, so rarely nothing more than the initial setup is needed.

Lights and Shading

Lighting is one of the most important elements of the visual appeal of a 3D game and is currently one of the hottest topics in real-time 3D graphics. Simulating real light accurately is a difficult problem. Although real light is made up of photons, the fundamental particles of light, trillions of photons interact in any simple lit surface. Light also has special behavior characteristics such as refraction, reflection, and obstruction that can further complicate the render. Because accurately simulating light is far too computationally complex, lighting models have been developed to create the illusion of illuminating the surfaces of 3D models. These models are approximations of the real effect of light but are often good enough to fool the human eye.

Ray Tracing

One model, ray tracing, is often used in computer animation. Ray tracing uses the computer to create a realistic graphic image by calculating the paths taken by rays of light hitting objects from various angles, creating shading, reflections, and shadows, which give the image a convincing look. Figure 12.9 shows an image produced by ray tracing.

FIGURE 12.9 Ray tracing producing accurate shading, reflections, and shadows.

Unfortunately, ray tracing is computationally intensive, too much for real-time rendering currently. Therefore, other models have been developed for real time that are faster but less accurate.

Real-Time Lighting and Shading

Real-time lighting can be split into two categories: static and dynamic.

Static shading is when the shading effect is meant to be permanently colored into the 3D object itself and does not change at runtime. This technique is often used on world models and typically relies on the 3D content-creation software to create the effect.

Dynamic shading is computed during the rendering of each frame and is used on moving 3D objects and lights. Dynamic shading uses 3D vector math and incorporates ambient illumination as well as diffuse and specular reflection of directional lighting.

The basic shading function for static or dynamic is a modulation of the polygon surface color based on its angle to a light direction. These parameters are expressed as vectors and vector operations. After a short vector refresher, the shading function will be examined in greater detail.

Brief Vector Review

Vector: A quantity that has magnitude and direction is known as a vector. For example, force, displacement, velocity, and acceleration are vectors. A vector can be represented by a directed line segment in space. Usually vectors are denoted by a letter with an arrow over it, such as $\vec{A}$, $\vec{a}$, $\vec{x}$. In the component form it is represented by a series of numbers, just like a coordinate, x, y, z. See Figure 12.10.

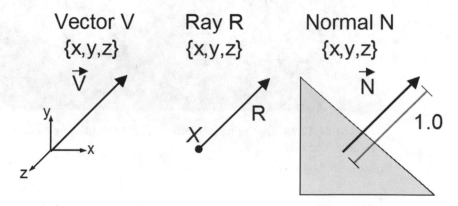

FIGURE 12.10 Vector types.

Unit Vector: A vector with a magnitude or length of 1.0. A unit vector is said to be normalized and can be created by the normalization vector operation, which is found by dividing each of the vector components by the original vector's magnitude.

Ray: A translated half-line. We call x the root, and we say that the ray is rooted at x. Another way to think of this is to imagine a ray as a vector with an infinite length. Because we often mean to use a ray as a representation of direction, a unit vector in the same direction as the ray is substituted in computer algorithms.

Normal: A vector that represents the orientation of a plane or surface. The normal of a surface is perpendicular to that surface. Often a normal is also normalized.

The Scalar Multiply: The following equation computes a vector **A** by **S**:

$$Ax' = Ax * s, \; Ay' = Ay*s, \; Az' = Az *s.$$

The Dot Product: The following equate computes the two vectors **A** and **B**:

$$(Ax*Bx)+(Ay*By)+(Az*Bz).$$

Shading Function

Computing the shading function for real-time 3D graphics is a feature built in to 3D hardware and would not need to be reimplemented by a game developer, but it is still useful to understand the process because it directly affects how 3D models are made.

First, the dot product of the direction to the light in the form of a unit vector and the surface normal is computed. The resulting scalar value will be between −1.0 and 1.0.

Next, the value is clamped to the range 0.0 to 1.0 and now represents the intensity of the light for that surface. The surface color is multiplied or scaled with that intensity. Because the intensity is between 0.0 and 1.0, the color will become darker accordingly. See Figure 12.11

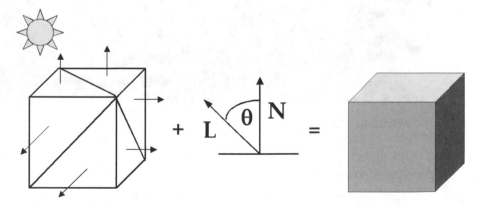

FIGURE 12.11 Simple shading function.

Finally, the given triangle is then rendered with the resulting color for each surface.

The shading function is one of the simplest vector operations done in 3D graphics, but because it is done so many times in a typical scene, the hardware needed to be built to accelerate its computation.

Types of Shading

There are two main types of hardware accelerated shading. Both compute shading using the shading function, with the difference being what normals they use and how the shading is applied to the surface.

Lambert or Flat Shading

The simplest shading is called Lambert or flat shading. The shading function is calculated and applied for each polygon surface of a given object. Each polygon is uniformly colored based on its single-surface normal and the direction to the light.

Flat shading is simple and quick but gives a faceted appearance. See Figure 12.12.

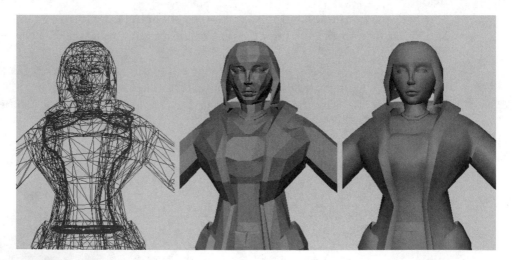

FIGURE 12.12 Shading types comparison.

Gouraud or Smooth Shading

Gouraud developed the technique to smoothly interpolate the illumination across polygons to create shading that is smooth and continuous, even for triangle-based objects that are not actually smooth and continuous.

A vertex normal must be added to each vertex in a 3D object. This new normal at the vertices can be calculated by averaging the adjoining face normals. The vertex intensity is then calculated with that new normal and the shading function. The intensity is interpolated across the polygon based on the vertices just like vertex color.

OpenGL and modern 3D hardware support both shading models. Either may be chosen, but smooth shading is usually more pleasing and can be more realistic. Smooth shading is usually used unless flat shading is needed to represent a 3D object more accurately. Remember, smooth shading will not work correctly unless the appropriate vertex normals for the 3D object are specified. It is a common mistake to have incorrect normals for a code-produced model. Quality 3D modeling software will usually create the proper normals for shading.

Types of Lights

There are three types of hardware-supported lights (the effects are shown in Figure 12.13), with many names:

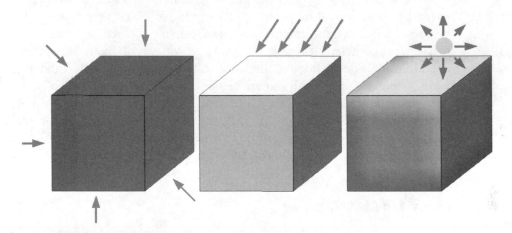

FIGURE 12.13   Light types comparison.

Ambient, Non-, or Omni-Directional

Ambient light comes from many directions, as a result of multiple reflections and emission from many sources. The resulting surface illumination is uniform.

Directional or Global

Directional light comes from a source that is located an infinite distance away. Thus, directional light consists of parallel rays coming from the same direction. The intensity of directional light doesn't diminish with distance, so identically oriented objects of the same type will be illuminated in exactly the same way.

Positional, Point, or Local

Position lights originate from some specific location. The light rays that emanate from the source are not parallel, and they typically can diminish in intensity with distance from the source. Identically oriented objects of the same type will be illuminated differently, depending on their position relative to the light source.

The Shadow Problem

When first working with real-time 3D graphics, one disappointing realization happens. Because the lighting and shading models are local, shadows are not automatically rendered as with ray tracing.

Hardware-based real-time lights have no complete shadowing or light-occluding features built in. The 3D objects are lit regardless of other objects blocking the light, because each triangle's shading is computed independently of any other triangles in the scene. Taking into account all of a scene's geometry for each shaded triangle would be prohibitively expensive on current graphics hardware, besides the fact that the graphics hardware doesn't necessarily have access to all of the scene's geometry. However, shadow effects do exist in many 3D games, but they are additional effects added to the scene and not completely supported in 3D hardware. There are several ways to create the effects of shadows, which is usually the combination of a 3D hardware feature and a clever 3D engine. Shadow effects are currently a developing topic in real-time 3D graphics, but classic techniques include simple textured polygons, projected geometry, and more advanced techniques, such as using a hardware feature like the stencil buffer and the depth buffer.

Transparency and Alpha Blending

Alpha blending is the technique for creating transparent objects. It works by blending an object as it is rasterizing with whatever has been rendered to the frame already. That way the foreground object appears see-through and the background object appears behind the foreground object (see Figure 12.14). Proper handle transparency is an important, but an often difficult to get correct, part of 3D engines. Transparency will be examined in more detail in Chapter 15, "3D Render Using JOGL."

Textures and Texturing

A texture or texture map is an image (such as a bitmap or a GIF) used to add complex patterns to the surfaces of objects in a 3D scene without adding any geometry. Textures enable developers to add much greater realism to their models. Applying a texture to the surface of 3D models can better create the look of walls, sky, skin, facial features, and so on (see Figure 12.15).

FIGURE 12.14 Opaque and transparent objects.

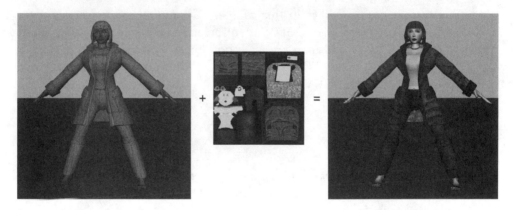

FIGURE 12.15 Girl geometry with texture.

Another way to consider how textures can improve a 3D object is in the way that textures can lower a model's polygon count. Often a model's shape can be simplified to contain fewer polygons when an appropriate texture is applied to that model. The model will still look as good (probably better) than the original, untextured higher-polygon model.

Because the texture adds so much more detail to the surfaces without costing more polygons, texturing is heavily used in 3D games, to the point where nearly every triangle that makes up a typical game scene has one or more textures rendered on it.

Texture Mapping

Texture mapping is the process of applying a texture to the surface of 3D models. Because real-time 3D models are made of vertices, the texture will be mapped to that part of the model. Therefore, to map a texture to the vertices of the 3D object, each one must have extra data added that contains the mapping at that vertex.

In a 3D object, each vertex already has a set of coordinates that represents the vertex's location in 3D Cartesian coordinate space. To support texture mapping, each vertex can also have texture coordinates. Texture coordinates are 2D image coordinates in texture space stored in the associated vertex that correspond to the part of the texture meant to be rendered at that vertex in the final 3D render. These coordinates are often called U-Vs, and sometimes S-Ts.

Additionally, the term texture mapping can mean the ability of a particular piece of graphics hardware to support accelerated rendering of texture objects. We would say that XYZ's latest graphics card has texture mapping.

How Is a Texture Applied?

One way to apply a texture is to program or compute a 3D object's U-Vs. However, as was discussed earlier in this chapter, 3D modeling software is the preferred process for most objects. 3D content-creation software allows artists to apply a texture to a face and then set corresponding U-V coordinates in each vertex on the face using many different tools. Figure 12.16 shows an example of mapping between vertices and UV coordinates.

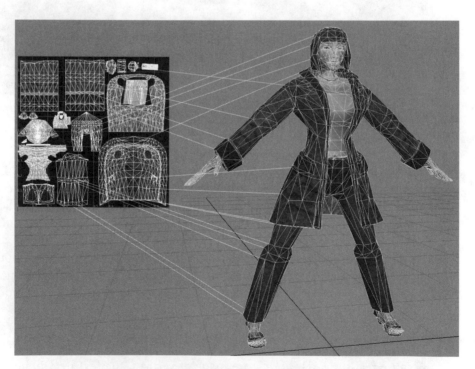

FIGURE 12.16 Texture map and 3D object showing corresponding image U-Vs and object vertices.

Textures can also have alpha, just like untextured geometry. However, the alpha textures contain the transparency information per texel. This arrangement increases the detail possible for certain types of models that can use this effect, such as fences, grading, trees, and plants, as shown in Figure 12.17.

FIGURE 12.17   Textured plant with regular and alpha texture maps (outlined).

Texture Artifacts and Filters

As mentioned earlier, images are made up of pixels, whereas textures are made of texels. The names are just shortened forms for their full names —a texel is a texture element, and a pixel is a picture element.

They are essentially the same thing in computer memory. Both represent one unit of an image, and both have red, green, and blue components. However, in the final render they aren't always the same size on screen, which creates some render problems. We can see why this happens by further examining the process of rendering textures.

The simplest method of texture map rendering is known as point sampling. For each final pixel on screen from a polygon, a simple and fast lookup is performed for the corresponding single texel in the texture image, based on the polygon's vertices U-V coordinates, treating them as a point falling in texture space. Whichever texel the U-V point falls in will be the returned color.

Unfortunately, this simple method can lead to problems when the screen pixels and the final rendered texture texels don't match up closely. When zooming in or out on a texture, the number of pixels on screen representing each texel of a texture changes, depending on how the final object is scaled in screen space. However, the number of texels in the texture does not change. Because of this, a simple lookup does not yield the best results when the texels don't match closely to the pixels on screen and unwanted texturing artifacts can appear in the final render.

Texturing artifacts—or any kind of graphics artifacts, for that matter—are simply rendering errors that distort or otherwise affect the final image in an unwanted way. For texturing, there are two main types of artifacts: pixelization and texel swimming.

Pixelization or blockiness happens when the texture on screen is rendered with more pixels in the final display area than texels in the original texture. Texel swimming and Moiré patterns happen in the opposite case, that is, when the texture is rendered in fewer pixels in the final display than texels in the original texture. Pixelization is fairly obvious in a single frame, as shown in Figure 12.18, but texel swimming, shown in Figure 12.19, is largely a dynamic effect, because the change from frame to frame creates a distracting moving pattern in the textured triangle.

Again, hardware solutions in the form of texture filters come to the rescue and help reduce these artifacts. Texture filters are added processing done to the texture data at the time of rendering to alter the final render, usually in the effort to improve it but sometimes for special effects as well.

FIGURE 12.18 Texel pixelization.

FIGURE 12.19   Texel swimming.

For these two texture artifacts, there are two texture filter techniques.

The first texture filter is called magmapping, and it is used to remove pixelization. Magmapping blends pixels together by interpolating between texel colors when one texel maps to many pixels as seen in Figure 12.20. The effect is usually an improvement, but sometimes, if the texture is too low resolution or if the camera view can move too close to the texture triangle, the blurring effect of magmapping is just as undesirable. In these cases, higher-resolution textures, more frequent texture repeating, or camera-motion limits will need to be made in addition.

FIGURE 12.20   Magmapping texture filtering.

The texel swimming effects can be reduced completely with the texture filter technique called MIPmapping. The MIP in MIPmapping comes from the Latin Multum In Parvo, meaning a multitude in a small space. MIPmapping attempts to reduce texture swimming by switching between preblended, lower-resolution textures, in which many texels map to one pixel.

The problem is that to accurately render each pixel when many texels map to one pixel, the renderer must combine the contribution from all the texels that fit in the pixel. Using only one texel lookup is what produces the texel swimming effect. However, accurately finding all the texels that fall in a single pixel's space for each and every final image pixel is too much work to do on current graphics hardware.

MIPmapping reduces the task of correcting texel swimming by pre-generating and storing multiple versions of the original texture image, each with lower and lower resolution (thus effectively larger texels for the same U-V set). When a pixel is to be textured, the version of the texture image or layer with the right-size texels relative to the final onscreen pixel size is selected. Figure 12.21 shows a render with and without MIPmapping.

FIGURE 12.21   MIPmapping texture technique removes texel swimming.

To improve this process even further, several texels can be averaged together, similar to magmapping. The three most frequently accelerated options follow:

Linear MIPmapping: Averages the texels from the nearest two texture layers; one from the larger, and one from the smaller

Bilinear MIPmapping: Averages the four texels on the nearest texture layer

Trilinear MIPmapping: Averages all eight texels from the nearest two texture layers each; four from the larger, and four from the smaller

The averaging that's done usually uses the same interpolation used in magmapping.

MIPmapping can greatly improve the final image by preventing texel swimming, but it comes at a cost of one-third more texture memory usage. Figure 12.22 shows how this can be visualized.

New texturing techniques for image correction are always available, for example Anisotropic MIPmapping and even new pixel shaders, which further improve upon these basic texture filters techniques.

FIGURE 12.22   MIPmapping requires one-third more texture memory.

Texture Formats

Because game textures are using hardware acceleration and not software rendering, the texel color formats and texture size are limited to those specifically supported by the hardware. The texel color formats have a fairly large range and using them doesn't affect texture creation adversely. However, texture size requirements are quite limiting and must be followed for the best results. Specifically, texture made for real-time hardware must be sized to a power of 2—1, 2, 4, 8, 16, 32, 64, 128, 256, 512, 1024, and sometimes larger counts. Note this is not multiples of 2. (That would allow many more options than are possible with the power of 2 sizes.) For the most part, this is an industrywide standard, and violations can cause all sorts of problems to occur, from MIPmapping problems to rendering slowdown to even crashes. There does exist some specialized extension on the latest graphics cards for non-power-of-2 sizes, but that is still fairly rare.

Conserving Texture Memory

Because graphics memory is limited and textures tend to use large amounts of memory, techniques for conserving texture memory can be important for getting the most out of 3D hardware. Briefly, a few of the most popular and useful techniques follow:

Reusing textures: The most obvious and used technique because it is the easiest to implement. Unfortunately, it can lead to monotonous-looking models, so it must be used wisely.

Shrinking textures: A simple process of reducing a texture to the next smaller power of 2 size. The tradeoff is less-detailed textures.

Lowering color bit depth: You can often get back lots of memory with almost no visual cost. Use 8-bit or 16-bit instead of full 24-bit color images, where appropriate.

Crop textures closely: This process can help you avoid wasting texels. When making a texture and applying it to a model, care must be taken to be sure that as much of the texture is used as possible, with as few unseen texels as possible.

Collaging: The technique of combining many different textures onto a single image (see Figure 12.23). This texturing technique is used mostly in characters and vehicles but can be applied to just about any kind of object.

Proper texture application: Further extends reuse. Applying nature textures such as rock patterns, slightly tilted (see Figure 12.24), as opposed to horizontally aligned textures tricks the eye somewhat and hides the fact that the texture is repeating more often than it appears.

Texture compression: Textures are stored in a compressed format in memory to conserve memory. This is now directly supported in 3D hardware. Texture compression allows games to have greater effective texture memory by making more efficient use of the available texture storage. In addition, texture compression maximizes AGP transfer performance because each texture can be smaller in size, minimizing the bandwidth impact, which can make games run faster as well as allow more textures to be used in a scene.

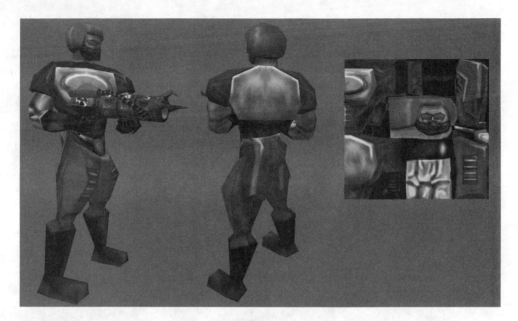

FIGURE 12.23   Example of texture collaging.

FIGURE 12.24   Aligned versus tilted texture.

Textures Everywhere!

Texturing is another area of great activity in real-time 3D graphics, and many amazing effects can be created by manipulating textures. Some involve animating object's U-Vs to create motion, simulated reflection effects, and shadows, as well as other shading effects such as cel-shading, bump mapping, and many, many others, with new ones being developed all the time (see Figure 12.25).

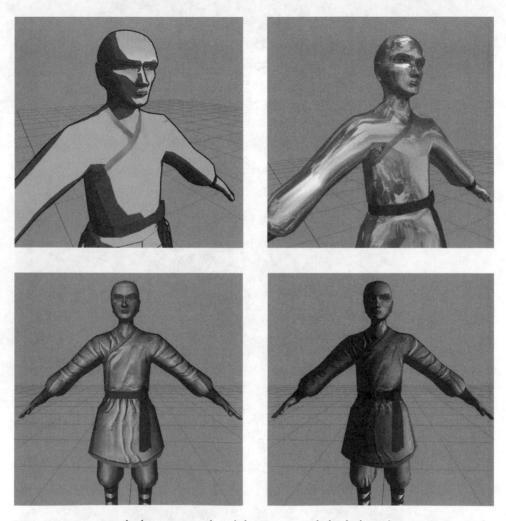

FIGURE 12.25 Monk character rendered three ways: cel-shaded, environment mapped, and bump mapped.

SUMMARY

Programming real-time 3D graphics can be a massive and even overwhelming undertaking at worst and challenging at best. But, as you probably can imagine, the rewards are well worth the effort! Fantastic, immersive 3D worlds and characters await the dedicated and persistent 3D game developer.

13 Java Bindings to OpenGL (JOGL)

In This Chapter

- Introduction
- OpenGL Overview
- JOGL-Specific Features
- JOGL and OpenGL Differences
- Using JOGL
- Summary

INTRODUCTION

OpenGL is the industry standard 3D library that lets game developers capture the power of hardware acceleration. Many of the leading games require OpenGL for hardware acceleration. OpenGL enables today's top games to manipulate massive amounts of data in real time using hardware-accelerated geometry, real-time lighting, clipping, transformations, and rasterization. OpenGL has all kinds of special features for a dazzling array of effects, such as real-time fog, anti-aliasing, volume shadows, bump mapping, motion blur, transparency, reflections, 3D textures, volume rendering, and more.

OpenGL is designed to support the future of graphics in software and hardware through its extension mechanism. It can expose brand new features that didn't even exist when it was originally designed.

The OpenGL API is highly stable. Workstations and supercomputers have been running OpenGL-based applications for more than a decade. OpenGL is also the most popular 3D solution for professional and consumer use.

Finally, OpenGL is cross-platform. The software runtime library ships with all Windows, Macintosh, Linux, and Unix systems.

Using OpenGL with Java has been possible for several years now by using one of several publicly available Java bindings to OpenGL. Unfortunately, not all of these bindings were of top quality or complete enough for many applications; some violated the Java security model. Fortunately, developers at Sun sought to remedy the situation as a community-driven project under the management of Java Games Technology Group. They seeded it with their implementation of Java bindings for OpenGL, simply called JOGL, which is the result of picking the best elements of previous designs and utilizing the latest Java platform features to create the best possible real-time 3D graphics system for the Java developer.

In the first section of this chapter, we will explore OpenGL a bit more deeply. Then we will further examine JOGL, the Java bindings to OpenGL. Because OpenGL is a C library, Java does not by default have instant access to it. In addition, because Java is object-oriented and OpenGL is functional-based C, simple one-to-one JNI wrappers to OpenGL are not a robust and secure solution. Thus, Sun's Game Technology Group developed JOGL to solve this problem for game developers.

You don't have to have C OpenGL programming experience to develop with JOGL, and you can learn all about OpenGL by programming with JOGL. In fact, almost any OpenGL book, tutorial, sample C program, or other source can easily be ported to JOGL; in fact, many already have. Many excellent OpenGL resources exist, and this chapter is not meant to replace a solid OpenGL development book. However, because JOGL is meant to be as similar to OpenGL as possible yet still hold true to Java standards, there are some key differences between JOGL and OpenGL, and this chapter seeks to address those key differences.

Finally, we will look at an example and develop a basic 3D object renderer using JOGL.

OPENGL OVERVIEW

If you are familiar with OpenGL and have programmed with in the past, this section may serve as a brief review. The more experienced OpenGL programmer may choose to skip this section and continue on to the JOGL section.

As stated in the previous chapter, OpenGL is a widely used industry-standard real-time 3D graphics API. OpenGL is currently up to version 1.4.

OpenGL is no small system. It is large, complex, and often perplexing because errors (actual programming errors or just incorrect visual effects) can be hard to identify due to OpenGL's state-based rendering. This section in no way covers everything a developer can create using OpenGL. Dozens of books are dedicated to that subject. At the same time, though, it is possible to use OpenGL (or JOGL) through a render-engine layer that simplifies the task of controlling, manipulating, and rendering a 3D scene, which is typical for 3D games as well. A solid understanding of OpenGL will benefit any developer using a 3D engine, whether or not they are called on to write actual OpenGL code.

High-Level or Low-Level API?

Depending on which group of developers you ask, OpenGL may be considered a low-level or high-level API. Because it allows the developer to work with geometric primitives such as triangles instead of pixels, it can be considered high-level. However, in the world of 3D game development, it is usually considered low-level because it is hardware supported, and you cannot program any lower while still using the hardware to its fullest capabilities. This is due to how video drivers use OpenGL as their main access layer. In theory, a developer could write his own device driver and use that to access the hardware, but it would have to be reverse-engineered because the specific hardware communication is almost always proprietary.

OpenGL provides access only to graphics-rendering operations. There are no facilities for obtaining user input from such devices as keyboards and mice, because it is expected that any system (in particular, a Windows system) under which OpenGL runs, must already provide such facilities.

One of OpenGL's major strengths from the perceptive of a Java developer is that OpenGL is by far the most cross-platform 3D hardware-accelerated API available. Combining OpenGL with Java gives game developers an excellent cross-platform 3D game-technology foundation.

OpenGL Render Features

OpenGL has numerous features, many of which are not used in typical OpenGL-based games (such as anti-aliased lines) because most games simply don't need them. It also has even more features that are not used regularly in games for other reasons, such as performance costs. A short subset of hardware-accelerated OpenGL features that do end up in games follows, many of which will be used in our example render engine:

- Polygon/triangle, line, and pixel rendering
- Smooth (Gourand) and Flat (Lambert) shading (with diffuse, ambient, and specular lighting effects)
- Z buffering and double buffering
- Stencil buffer
- Colored directional and point light sources
- Texture mapping
- Texture filtering (MIPmapping and magmapping)
- Texture environment controls, such as automatic texture coordinate generation
- Backface culling
- Matrix transformations
- Perspective and parallel projections
- Vertex programmability (on the latest hardware)
- Fragments shaders, coming soon as a standard feature, currently supported through extensions

In addition, through the OpenGL extension mechanism, the latest hardware-accelerated features are readily accessible, even if the features are not part of the OpenGL standard yet. This is an excellent benefit for building and testing ahead of the curve for 3D game engines.

Immediate Mode Rendering

The basic model for OpenGL command interpretation is immediate mode, in which a command is executed as soon as the hardware receives it; vertex processing, for example, may begin even before specification of the primitive of which it is a part has been completed. Immediate mode execution is best suited to applications in which primitives and modes are constantly altered.

An example of immediate mode commands follow:

```
void display(void)
{
// draw diamond with radius of 10
glBegin( GL_QUADS );
    glVertex3f( 10.0, 0.0, 0.0 );
    glVertex3f( 0.0, 10.0, 0.0 );
    glVertex3f( -10.0, 0.0, 0.0 );
    glVertex3f( 0.0, -10.0, 0.0 );
glEnd();

// flush GL buffers
glFlush();
}
```

In immediate mode, a set of `glBegin()` and `glEnd()` calls establishing the primitive type contain the appropriate calls for that primitive to be rendered. This is sometimes called a *batch*.

Whereas immediate mode provides flexibility, it can be inefficient for large and unchanging parameters because each execution of the batch is respecifying the render object's parameters redundantly. In the past, to accommodate such situations, OpenGL provided a feature known as *display lists*. A display list encapsulated a sequence of OpenGL commands and stored them on the hardware. The display list was given a numeric ID by the application when it was specified, and the application needed only to reference the display list ID to cause the hardware to effectively execute the list. Another similar option is vertex arrays and vertex buffer objects; we will examine those in a later section.

State Control

OpenGL is a state machine, meaning OpenGL's render pipeline is defined by certain states at any given time, and those states control how the final image is rendered. Geometric primitives are also specified in a standard way. The current render state determines their shape, material properties, and orientation.

For example, setting the current drawing color could be executed by simply calling `glColor3f (float red, float green, float blue)` with the color represented as floats.

Calling `glColor3f (1.0, 0.0, 0.0)` would set the current color to bright red. Once set all geometric primitives rendered are affected by that red state until the states are changed.

Many states can be changed at any time, even per vertex. For example, the current color can potentially be set to a different color for each vertex in a batch, as shown in the following code:

```
glBegin( GL_QUADS );
    // set this vertex's color
    glColor3f( 1.0, 0.0, 0.0 );
    // set this vertex's coordinate
    glVertex3f( x1, y1, z1 );

    // same as above, but for each new vertex
    glColor3f( 0.0, 1.0, 0.0 );
    glVertex3f( x2, y2, z2 );
    glColor3f( 0.0, 0.0,1.0 );
    glVertex3f( x3, y3, z3 );
    glColor3f( 1.0, 1.0, 1.0 );
    glVertex3f( x4, y4, z4 );
glEnd();
```

Light and lighting effects are also states in OpenGL. Like many other states, they must first be enabled to be used. In addition, other render states must be properly set in coordination with the lighting states to get the desired lighting effects. For example, object material states and vertex normals are needed for correct lighting, which can also be changed per vertex.

```
glEnable(GL_LIGHTING);
glEnable(GL_LIGHT0);
glLightfv(GL_LIGHT0, GL_DIFFUSE, color);
```

Triangle style is another controllable state in OpenGL. For example, you can control whether to draw the front or back of polygons (known as face culling) as well as whether they should be completely filled in or only in outline.

```
glPolygonStyle(GL_FRONT, GL_FILL);
glFrontFace(GL_CCW); (How is front defined)
glCullFace(GL_BACK);
glEnable(GL_CULL_FACE);
```

Additional useful miscellaneous functions include setting the background color and clearing the screen and Z-buffer.

```
// Clears Color buffer and resets Z-buffer
glClear(GL_COLOR_BUFFER_BIT | GL_DEPTH_BUFFER_BIT);
// Sets the clear color often thought of as the background color
glClearColor(....);
```

Transform Control

3D matrix transformations are key to manipulating 3D graphics. Therefore, OpenGL supports matrix transformations in the form of a render state. The current matrix state is applied to each vertex (and existing normals) during the geometry specification. On the modern graphics cards these transformations are accelerated by the graphics hardware.

There are several commands in OpenGL for matrix state manipulation, including load and multiple for complete, user-supplied matrices, and utility commands such as glLoadIdentity(), glRotate3f(d, x, y, z), glTranslate(tx, ty, tz), and glScale3f(sx, sy, sz). Also, OpenGL currently specifies three matrix modes—GL_MODELVIEW, GL_PROJECTION, and GL_TEXTURE—with the current mode set with the glMatrixMode command. OpenGL also implements for each of the matrix modes a matrix stack, which the user can then utilize with glPushMatrix and glPopMatrix.

The stack depth is limited, depending on the mode—at least 32 for `GL_MODELVIEW` and at least 2 for `GL_PROJECTION` and `GL_TEXTURE`.

The `glPushMatrix` function duplicates the current matrix and then pushes that matrix into the stack. The glPopMatrix function pops the top matrix off of the stack and replaces the current matrix with that matrix. Each stack contains the identity matrix at initialization.

A typical routine setting up a basic camera matrix state (given the camera matrices) might look like the following code sample:

```
// set up camera view
glMatrixMode(GL_PROJECTION);
glLoadMatrixd(camera.eyeFrustumMatrix);

glMatrixMode(GL_MODELVIEW);
glLoadMatrixd(camera.eyeViewMatrix);
```

The camera or view matrix is usually thought of as the product of the Projection matrix and the ModelView matrix, where the ModelView matrix represents the global camera/model transformation and the Projection matrix contains the view from which the related Projection matrix is to be applied.

Additional Resources

For more on OpenGL from its history to the future, current game-related activity, as well as great tutorials, check out the following Web sites:

www.opengl.org: The official OpenGL Architecture Review Board Web site. Get all the latest news in the OpenGL world here.

www.sgi.com/software/opengl/: SGI's Web site on OpenGL.

nehe.gamedev.net/: NeHe Productions has a great Web site for pure OpenGL tutorials with a gaming slant.

www.mesa3d.org: Mesa 3D is an open-source software implementation of the OpenGL specification. It is great for testing as well as running on systems without hardware acceleration.

JOGL-SPECIFIC FEATURES

JOGL is the shortened name for the Java bindings to OpenGL developed and maintained by Sun Microsystems' Java Game Technology Group and distributed on the

Web at their main Java game development site, *www.javagaming.org*. Whereas JOGL serves to provide clean, object-oriented access to standard OpenGL features, it also adds additional features beyond standard OpenGL. The JOGL team took the best ideas from several other previous Java OpenGL wrapper projects, such as GL4Java, while keeping it fast, clean, and easy to use.

JOGL is intended to be a community-development process. Developers and users can get involved through existing forums and mailing lists at *www.javagaming.org* and the *java.net* Web site on game development. Everyone is encouraged to post, and the participants on those sites are eager to hear about impressions and suggestions for its development.

JOGL is integrated with Java's Abstract Window Toolkit and Swing widget sets. JOGL provides access to the latest OpenGL 1.4 with vendor extensions. JOGL also provides popular features introduced by previous Java bindings, including a composable pipeline model that can provide simpler debugging for JOGL applications than the analogous C OpenGL program. The GL class provides a minimal and easy-to-use API designed to handle many of the issues associated with multi-threaded OpenGL applications. JOGL uses the most recent Java Platform features and, therefore, supports only J2SE 1.4 and later. Several complex and leading-edge OpenGL demonstrations have been successfully ported from C/C++ to JOGL. Finally, the JOGL binding is written almost completely in the Java programming language. The native code is autogenerated during the build process by a tool called GlueGen, which is also publicly available.

Integration with AWT

Java's Abstract Window Toolkit, or AWT, is the set of standard Java APIs for GUI building and is part of the larger group of APIs called the Java Foundation Classes (JFC), included with the standard Java distributions. The vast majority of Java applications that use a graphic interface use the display classes from the JFC. Because JOGL is also a display technology, it was built to be integrated with AWT and compatible with AWT components.

The main display class in JOGL is an interface called GLDrawable. JOGL provides two implementations of this interface, GLCanvas and GLJPanel.

GLCanvas is a heavyweight AWT component, and GLJPanel is a lightweight Swing component, both of which provide OpenGL rendering support. The class inheritance structure for GLCanvas and GLJPanel follows, showing their relationship to AWT:

```
net.java.games.jogl
Class GLCanvas
```

```
java.lang.Object
  |
  +—java.awt.Component
       |
       +—java.awt.Canvas
            |
            +—net.java.games.jogl.GLCanvas


net.java.games.jogl
Class GLJPanel


java.lang.Object
  |
  +—java.awt.Component
       |
       +—java.awt.Container
            |
            +—javax.swing.JComponent
                 |
                 +—javax.swing.JPanel
                      |
                      +—net.java.games.jogl.GLJPanel
```

Because `GLCanvas` and `GLJPanel` inherit from AWT and Swing components, respectively, they can be added to standard AWT and Swing applications and used directly there. This ability makes for nice integration options with existing as well as new AWT/Swing applications, gaming or otherwise.

Neither `GLCanvas` nor `GLJPanel` can be instantiated directly; the class `GLDrawableFactory` is used to create them. The `GLDrawableFactory` creates the canvas or panel based on default or user-defined `GLCapabilities`, which configure things such as the display area's color depth, Z-depth, and other frame bufferer settings. See the API docs for more information.

Supports OpenGL 1.4

JOGL is completely up-to-date and supports the latest OpenGL 1.4 release. This is important for JOGL to be considered a leading-edge technology, and it will need to follow closely future OpenGL releases. OpenGL is a fairly large (and growing) API, and although designed to be as simple as possible, it is still fairly complex by most standards. Keeping the Java wrappers current would be a tedious task if it were done by hand as it was done in the past with other Java OpenGL bindings. One way this process is improved with JOGL is the use of a new tool, GlueGen.

GlueGen

GlueGen is an automatic tool for creating JNI wrappers from regular C code to become part of Java APIs.

JOGL is completely automatically generated from the OpenGL C header files. When a new GL version or function is released, GlueGen can reprocess the C source, and the new JOGL will instantly have access to the new functions.

GlueGen parses C header files using a full GNU C grammar and builds a memory mapping of all typedefs, enums, structs, pointers, function pointers, and other C structures. It then builds a parallel mapping of Java methods and structures to the C equivalents and writes all the Java code and JNI code necessary to link the two. In fact, it's powerful enough to allow you to call C functions that use C structs as parameters or return values and builds Java-side accessor classes that wrap NIO buffers. This gives you fast, completely safe access to native data.

It cleanly handles all the platform-dependent complexities involved with determining whether or not a GL function is supported at runtime. This process takes into account the GL versions of the server and client and the extensions that are exposed on the client and server. At this writing, GlueGen is also used to build Java bindings for NVidia's Cg language for JOGL. This is currently experimental, but it shows the power of GlueGen and the forward thinking of the JOGL team.

Vendor Extensions Exposed

All public OpenGL 1.4 vendor extensions are exposed directly in the GL interface. This does not mean that they are all implemented on any given system and will most likely need to be queried with the `isExtensionAvailable()` and `isFunction-Available()` GL methods, similar to regular C OpenGL. On many platforms, most functionality is still only OpenGL 1.1, so, in theory, any routines first exposed in OpenGL 1.2, 1.3, and 1.4 as well as vendor extensions should all be queried. Still, should an application call an unavailable or unsupported OpenGL function on the existing hardware, JOGL will gracefully throw a runtime `GLException`.

Designed for NIO

JOGL uses NIO's ByteBuffers for many data access and manipulation operations. Rendering APIs such as OpenGL access much data and need it as fast as possible. Copying large arrays of floats between Java and the underlining system memory is prohibitively slow for a cutting-edge rendering system. Therefore, JOGL uses direct `ByteBuffers` for data wrappers where the Java and JNI OpenGL-side need to share data. More on this in the next section.

Composable Pipelines and DebugGL

JOGL has what is called composable pipelines. Composable pipelines are alternate render objects that can provide debugging and error-checking options in OpenGL. The DebugGL object can be swapped for the standard GL object at will, and DebugGL will do automatic error-checking "under the hood" to catch GL error conditions in application commands. This tool is valuable for debugging, as will be shown in the easy use of this in the main example.

Open Source

Finally, although not really an API feature, the designers choose to author the JOGL implementation as open source. As with any open-source project, one of the greatest benefits is that the developer always has the option to dig into the binding and make changes if needed. This flexibility is extremely helpful when a particular feature is not yet available in the current release build, or the implementation is buggy, or the interface disagrees with another possible design. During the course of writing this book, we built our own custom build of JOGL to allow access to features that were planned for future JOGL releases but not yet implemented in the public releases. This was of great help, allowing us to make progress on our projects independently of the current public release. When the following public release supported those features that we had added in our custom builds, we easily switched back to the standard public release.

JOGL AND OPENGL DIFFERENCES

There are key differences between using JOGL and OpenGL, due partly from the fact that JOGL maps a function-based C API to object-oriented Java, and partly from the fact that Java is secure, (here we mean in terms of illegal memory access) and OpenGL is not. These differences instantly make the JOGL interface slightly different everywhere, and very different in a few critical places. In addition, not every single API difference is documented here (depending on how you look at it, there are hundreds!), and inevitably there will be new differences in future JOGL versions. This book is meant to help you understand the major differences and learn to use them in Java.

OpenGL's Static Constants and Functions

The C version of OpenGL makes heavy use of static constants throughout the OpenGL API, particularly for function parameters. It is an accepted way to create some level of type-safety for the C language interface it uses. However, in Java there is no such thing as true, stand-alone (classless) static variables or constants. All Java constructs are either a field or method of a class. Java objects may have static class variables but not any global classless static variables such as those used in C and OpenGL.

OpenGL also uses static functions. This is the nature of pure C code. Similar to the static constants, Java has no true classless methods that can be mapped directly to the OpenGL C functions.

This is a typical problem when mapping a functional C API to a object-oriented language such as Java. Fortunately, the solution is simple and effective in most cases. A single Java class is created that has all the C APIs static variables and functions, which are mapped to identically or similarly named static (or instance) variables and methods. The developer then either accesses the variables/functions through the classes' static variables/functions directly, or, depending on the design, a runtime instance is created and used as the accessing object.

JOGL uses this second method of a runtime class instantiation for various reasons. That is, a special GL object is created, and most JOGL operations are done using that single instance. To an experienced OpenGL programmer this process may appear strange at first, and to anyone using existing OpenGL resources, any sample C-based OpenGL code will not port unmodified but must be converted to this class instance-accessing method.

Fortunately, for a Java programmer the conversion is quite simple and straightforward. An example code segment follows, first in C, then in Java with JOGL:

```
// Original C OpenGL source
glBegin( GL_QUADS );
    glColor3f( 1.0, 0.0, 0.0 );
    glVertex3f( 10.0, 0.0, 0.0 );
    glColor3f( 0.0, 1.0, 0.0 );
    glVertex3f( 0.0, 10.0, 0.0 );
    glColor3f( 0.0, 0.0,1.0 );
    glVertex3f( -10.0, 0.0, 0.0 );
    glColor3f( 1.0, 1.0, 1.0 );
    glVertex3f( 0.0, -10.0, 0.0 );
glEnd();

// Ported to JOGL
// using local gl instance reference
// and GL class reference
// and explicit f for floats
```

```
gl.glBegin( GL.GL_QUADS );
    gl.glColor3f( 1.0f, 0.0f, 0.0f );
    gl.glVertex3f( 10.0f, 0.0f, 0.0f );
    gl.glColor3f( 0.0f, 1.0f, 0.0f );
    gl.glVertex3f( 0.0f, 10.0f, 0.0f );
    gl.glColor3f( 0.0f, 0.0f,1.0f );
    gl.glVertex3f( -10.0f, 0.0f, 0.0f );
    gl.glColor3f( 1.0f, 1.0f, 1.0f );
    gl.glVertex3f( 0.0f, -10.0f, 0.0f );
gl.glEnd();
```

OpenGL's Use of C Pointers to Arrays

Several functions in OpenGL make use of pointers to arrays in C. This is done as a mechanism to return a series of OpenGL *names,* or handles, for what it calls server-side data objects. For example, multiple texture names can be generated at once in the C API by calling:

```
void glGenTextures(GLsizei n,
                   GLuint *textures)
```

whcre *n* specifies the number of texture names to be generated and **textures* specifies a pointer to an array in which the generated texture names are stored. The GLuint *textures is a C pointer to GLuint that should be at the beginning of an array of GLuint type that is the length of *n*. Because arrays are a formal type in Java, JOGL simply uses Java array objects instead.

```
public void glGenTextures(int n,
                          int[] textures)
```

After calling this method, the Java int[] array argument "textures" will contain the texture names OpenGL has generated (just like it would for GLuint *texture in C) and can be accessed in the usual Java way.

This method shows another difference as well. In C, OpenGL has all sorts of additional primitive data types usage beyond standard C types to help type-safe OpenGL.

JOGL has mapped the OpenGL types to native Java types in the JNI layer where applicable, so standard Java types are supported directly. See Table 13.1.

TABLE 13.1 OpenGL Types Mapped to Native Java Types

OpenGL Data Type	Internal Representation	Defined as C Type	C Literal Suffix	Java Type
Glbyte	8-bit integer	Signed char	b	byte
Glubyte	8-bit unsigned integer	Unsigned char	ub	byte
Glboolean	8-bit unsigned integer	Unsigned char		boolean
Glshort	16-bit integer	Short	s	short
GLushort	16-bit unsigned integer	Unsigned short	us	short
GLint, Glsizei	32-bit integer	Long	l	int
GLuint, GLenum, GLbitfield	32-bit unsigned integer	Unsigned long	ui	int
GLfloat, Glclampf	32-bit floating point	Float	f	float
GLdouble, GLclampd	64-bit floating point	Double	d	double

The C literal suffix is used in the function names in OpenGL, and the same suffixes are used in JOGL for compatibility and listed here for reference. The way the functions are named generally follows as shown in Figure 13.1.

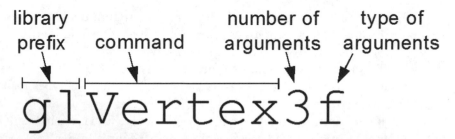

library prefix · command · number of arguments · type of arguments

glVertex3f

FIGURE 13.1 The first two letters are the library prefix, which is a common design in C APIs. *gl* means that the function is part of the gl library, *vertex* is the command, *3* gives the number of arguments for this function, *f* denotes that the arguments are of type *float*.

Creating JOGL Textures

To reveal a more profound JOGL difference, we will further examine setting up textures in JOGL.

Java has existing standard images classes, including image loaders, and it would be nice to be able to use those to create the textures for OpenGL. It's not automatic, but it's not terribly difficult, either. It also exposes another significant difference in JOGL—its use of `ByteBuffer` objects.

ByteBuffers

JOGL needs fast and efficient ways to process and reference chucks of "raw" memory that would contain texture data or geometry data to which the OpenGL layer can have direct access, just as it does in C. The Java solution is to use NIO's `ByteBuffers` wherever JOGL needs that kind of direct access. So, many functions that expect C pointers in OpenGL alternatively access `ByteBuffers` in the Java bindings and under-the-covers on the JNI-side OpenGL, which can have direct access to this data without any wasteful copying.

Let's look at how this affects the texture functions by following the process of creating a texture from a standard Java BufferImage.

Getting a texture into an OpenGL environment is at least a three-step process on any system. Because of all the existing standard Java image APIs, it's probably one of the easiest environments.

> **Step 1—Load a image from the file system:** Image loading is a well-supported functionality in Java, so this is probably the most familiar step for the typical Java developer. Several supported mechanisms are available for loading images, and this can always be done though direct file access as well, if needed.
>
> **Step 2—Format the image data appropriately:** The JOGL texture methods accept texture data as `ByteBuffers` where the buffer data must be encoded to a format that the OpenGL standard accepts. Unfortunately, this is almost never going to be the same format as the data format returned from a loaded image, unless the image loader was specifically designed for JOGL, which none of the existing standard image loaders are. Therefore, some data conversion will be required to get from the loaded image data to the OpenGL required data format.
>
> **Step 3—Create OpenGL texture binding for the new texture and set the texture data and parameters:** After the `ByteBuffer` is packed with the image data correctly formatted, we can get a texture bind ID from OpenGL and pass the texture `ByteBuffer` along with any OpenGL texture parameters that we want to set with it.

Of the methods to load images in Java that the example uses, is `ImageIO.read()`, which returns `BufferedImages`. `BufferedImages` are the preferred type because they support a pathway to get the image data to a `byte[]` array with which we can load up a `ByteBuffer` for OpenGL. One problem that we wouldn't catch until actually viewing in OpenGL is that the image would be upside down in most cases. This happens in many systems; it is not a Java-specific issue.

What happens is that the convention for assigning texture coordinates is with positive U (X in the image) to the right and positive V (Y in the image) up. But most image formats consider the positive y-direction as down, as it is in screen space. It is simple to flip the image with the `AffineTransformOp` class right after loading but before the OpenGL formatting, if needed. Given the correct string file-name for an image file, here's how it can be done:

```
static public  BufferedImage loadImage(String resourceName)
throws IOException
{
    BufferedImage bufferedImage = null;

    try
    {
        bufferedImage = ImageIO.read(new File(resourceName));
    }
    catch (Exception e)
    {
        // file not found or bad format maybe
    // do something good
    }
    if (bufferedImage != null)
    {
        // Flip Image
        //
        AffineTransform tx = AffineTransform.getScaleInstance(1, -
    1);
        tx.translate(0, -bufferedImage.getHeight(null));
        AffineTransformOp op = new AffineTransformOp(tx,
    AffineTransformOp.TYPE_NEAREST_NEIGHBOR);
        bufferedImage = op.filter(bufferedImage, null);
    }
    return bufferedImage;
}
```

At this point we have a `BufferedImage` in memory. Now it must be formatted for OpenGL.

This process could be a bit messy in practice, because BufferedImages can themselves be many different data formats. The trick is to use the Java image APIs and let them handle the conversion for you. Using ComponentColorModel and the Raster class, we can set up a utility routine that can convert any BufferedImage to an OpenGL-acceptable data format. First, we will make two reusable ComponentColorModels, one for regular RGB color images and another for RGBA (color-transparent) images. Then we will use the ComponentColorModels to build a Raster from which we can get bytes.

One last detail is that textures need to be sized to powers of 2 due to most graphics hardware requirements. It is simple to check the image's width and height, and upsize the image height and/or width to the next power of 2. This action is typically considered wasteful in terms of graphics memory because the image will be larger but not anymore detailed. However, it will allow loading of non-power-of-2-size images without failing out, which is especially useful when testing.

ByteBuffer AllocateDirect and Native Order

There are two additional important points about using ByteBuffers in OpenGL. The ByteBuffers need to be created with ByteBuffer.allocateDirect() so that the ByteBuffers are C accessible without copying, and the byte order must be set to native order with byteBuffer.order(ByteOrder.nativeOrder()) to work correctly. Failing to do this is a common error when first starting out with JOGL.

Putting this all together, we have a versatile image conversion routine.

```
glAlphaColorModel = new
ComponentColorModel(ColorSpace.getInstance(ColorSpace.CS_sRGB),
    new int[]{8, 8, 8, 8}, true, false,
ComponentColorModel.TRANSLUCENT, DataBuffer.TYPE_BYTE);

glColorModel = new
ComponentColorModel(ColorSpace.getInstance(ColorSpace.CS_sRGB),
    new int[]{8, 8, 8, 0}, false, false, ComponentColorModel.OPAQUE,
DataBuffer.TYPE_BYTE);

public static ByteBuffer convertImageData(BufferedImage bufferedImage)
throws TextureFormatException
{
    ByteBuffer imageBuffer = null;
    try
    {
        WritableRaster raster;
        BufferedImage texImage;
```

```
        int texWidth = 2;
        int texHeight = 2;

        while (texWidth #### bufferedImage.getWidth())
        {
            texWidth *= 2;
        }
        while (texHeight #### bufferedImage.getHeight())
        {
            texHeight *= 2;
        }

        if (bufferedImage.getColorModel().hasAlpha())
        {
            raster =
Raster.createInterleavedRaster(DataBuffer.TYPE_BYTE, texWidth,
texHeight, 4, null);
            texImage = new BufferedImage(glAlphaColorModel, raster,
false, new Hashtable());
        }
        else
        {
            raster =
Raster.createInterleavedRaster(DataBuffer.TYPE_BYTE, texWidth,
texHeight, 3, null);
            texImage = new BufferedImage(glColorModel, ####dis:raster,
false, new Hashtable());
        }

        texImage.getGraphics().drawImage(bufferedImage, 0, 0, null);

        byte[] data = ((DataBufferByte)
texImage.getRaster().getDataBuffer()).getData();

        imageBuffer = ByteBuffer.allocateDirect(data.length);
        imageBuffer.order(ByteOrder.nativeOrder());
        imageBuffer.put(data, 0, data.length);
    }
    catch (Exception e)
    {
        throw new TextureFormatException("Unable to convert data
for texture " + e);
    }
    return imageBuffer;
}
```

At last we have the `ByteBuffer` correctly formatted for OpenGL. All that is left is to get a bind ID and hand over the data to OpenGL. Everything we've done until now could have been done offline—that is, before OpenGL is configured, initialized, and rendered—and is recommended when possible. Loading and converting images in the middle of an OpenGL render cycle will inevitably decrease runtime performance.

To get a bind ID as well as to pass over the texture data to OpenGL, we will need a valid GL reference. Also, it must be done within the thread that is assigned to the OpenGL context. Often that means the texture binding will be done in the `init()` method of `GLEventListener`, but if it happens later on during execution, it will most likely be inside the `display()` method. In any case we must have a live and current GL object. The JOGL bind ID calls are straight, standard OpenGL texture commands with the exception of the `int[]` handle for the bind and `ByteBuffer` syntax. Putting it all together would look something like the following code:

```
static public int createTexture(String name,
                                String resourceName,
                                int target,
                                int dstPixelFormat,
                                int minFilter,
                                int magFilter,
                                boolean wrap,
                                boolean mipmapped) throws
IOException, TextureFormatException
{
    // create the texture ID for this texture
    //
    int[] tmp = new int[1];
    gl.glGenTextures(1, tmp);
    int textureID = tmp[0];

    // bind this texture
    //
    gl.glBindTexture(GL.GL_TEXTURE_2D, textureID);

    // load the buffered image for this resource - save a copy so
    we can draw into it later
    //
    BufferedImage bufferedImage = loadImage(resourceName);

    int srcPixelFormat;
```

```java
if (bufferedImage.getColorModel().hasAlpha())
{
    srcPixelFormat = GL.GL_RGBA;
}
else
{
    srcPixelFormat = GL.GL_RGB;
}


// convert that image into a byte buffer of texture data
//
ByteBuffer textureBuffer = convertImageData(bufferedImage);



// set up the texture wrapping mode depending on whether
// this texture is specified for wrapping or not
//
int wrapMode = wrap ? GL.GL_REPEAT : GL.GL_CLAMP;

if (target == GL.GL_TEXTURE_2D)
{
    gl.glTexParameteri(target, GL.GL_TEXTURE_WRAP_S,
    wrapMode);
    gl.glTexParameteri(target, GL.GL_TEXTURE_WRAP_T,
    wrapMode);
    gl.glTexParameteri(target, GL.GL_TEXTURE_MIN_FILTER,
    minFilter);
    gl.glTexParameteri(target, GL.GL_TEXTURE_MAG_FILTER,
    magFilter);
}

// create either a series of mipmaps or a single texture image
// based on what's loaded
//
if (mipmapped)
{
    glu.gluBuild2DMipmaps(target,
            dstPixelFormat,
            bufferedImage.getWidth(),
            bufferedImage.getHeight(),
            srcPixelFormat,
            GL.GL_UNSIGNED_BYTE,
            textureBuffer);
```

```
        }
        else
        {
            gl.glTexImage2D(target,
                    0,
                    dstPixelFormat,
                    bufferedImage.getWidth(),
                    bufferedImage.getHeight(),
                    0,
                    srcPixelFormat,
                    GL.GL_UNSIGNED_BYTE,
                    textureBuffer);
        }

        return textureID;
    }
```

After this, the OpenGL textures and IDs are properly set up and ready to use.

Vertex Arrays and ByteBuffers

ByteBuffers are also the mechanism used to set up vertex arrays in JOGL. Whereas OpenGL takes C float-array pointers for vertex arrays using the following function:

```
void glVertexPointer(GLint size,
                     GLenum type,
                     GLsizei stride,
                     const GLvoid *pointer)
```

Similar to texture ByteBuffers, the JOGL method is:

```
public void glVertexPointer(int size,
                            int type,
                            int stride,
                            Buffer ptr)
```

The easiest way to use vertex arrays is to make a regular Java float[] array containing the appropriate vertex, color, normal, or texture coordinate data and pass the array into a ByteBuffer in the array put() call. A simple triangle vertex array for a unit square follows:

```
float[] verts = new float[]
{
    -1.0f,  1.0f, 0.0f,
    -1.0f, -1.0f, 0.0f,
     1.0f, -1.0f, 0.0f,

    -1.0f,  1.0f, 0.0f,
     1.0f, -1.0f, 0.0f,
     1.0f,  1.0f, 0.0f;
};
FloatBuffer vertexArray =
ByteBuffer.allocateDirect(verts.length*4).order
(ByteOrder.nativeOrder()).asFloatBuffer();
vertexArray.put( verts );
```

Getting it to render is nearly identical to standard OpenGL:

```
gl.glVertexPointer(3, GL.GL_FLOAT, 0, vertexArray);
gl.glEnableClientState(GL.GL_VERTEX_ARRAY);
gl.glDrawArrays(GL.GL_TRIANGLES, 0, vertexArray.capacity());
```

Multithreading

Multithreading is another issue that creates some difficulties for developers first working with JOGL. Usually this step occurs in basic GUI test applications that aren't designed around the single-threaded nature of OpenGL. Most errors happen when the user sets up some GUI components such as a button, wants to catch that button's press-action event, and then wants the event action to do some direct OpenGL state setting.

For example, the developer might wish to have a GUI button enable or disable texturing in the OpenGL renderer. The developer makes the GL instance object available to the anonymous event Listener object, either by a static reference or through an accessor method, and then proceeds to call that GL object's glEnable/Disable() on whatever state they want to affect. Unfortunately, this is not going to work because the GUI event thread now performing the GL call is *not* the assigned rendering thread. This is a violation of the threaded access to OpenGL and at best will result in no change or possibly a runtime exception, and at worst an application or system crash.

Two popular solutions are available for this problem. One is to have the desired modifiable states in OpenGL declared as Java class variables that are used to modify the OpenGL render states using the assigned render thread when display() is called.

The second is to set up a messaging system, where messages or requests for OpenGL changes are made and queued up until the next `display()` is called when the rendering thread reads though the messages performing the requested OpenGL operations. This is a typical design pattern in Swing and other GUI apps.

Either design is acceptable, but no matter which way multithreading is managed, it is likely that this issue will need to be addressed in all but the simplest of JOGL applications.

USING JOGL

JOGL is very easy to set up and use. JOGL does not currently have an install system because it is simply two files: the *jogl.jar* containing all the JOGL Java binary, and an additional native code file that is machine specific and links to that architecture's OpenGL implementation. On Windows, that file is simply *jogl.dll*. These two files can be put in the JVM directories for the system to use anywhere the Java classpath would find them, or the classpath could be appended to a new location for them, whichever the developer chooses.

In beginning a new class to make use of JOGL, we add the main JOGL import:

```
import net.java.games.jogl.*;
```

Any application that intends to display a JOGL render will need to make a AWT or Swing frame. In addition, the example will catch a key press for stepping through the different render states, so it will also need AWT events imported. Therefore, we also import:

```
import java.awt.*;
import java.awt.event.*;
```

Last, we are going to use vertex arrays and vertex buffer objects, and for that we will need two more imports, Java's NIO and a JOGL utility class that makes the special offset `ByteBuffer` used by vertex buffer objects.

```
import java.nio.*;
import net.java.games.jogl.util.*;
```

To keep this as simple as possible, we are going to make one class called `Sample`, which will implement the `GLEventListener` interface, expecting it to respond to the `display()` events generated by the main `GLCanvas`. The interface `GLEventListener` declares events that client code can use to manage OpenGL rendering onto a

`GLDrawable`. When any of these methods is called, the drawable has made its associated OpenGL context current, so it is valid to make OpenGL calls within them.

Let's take a look at main():

```
public static void main(String[] args) {
    Frame frame = new Frame("Spinning Cube Four JOGL Ways!");
    GLCanvas canvas =
        GLDrawableFactory.getFactory().createGLCanvas(new
        GLCapabilities());
    canvas.addGLEventListener(new Sample());

    System.err.println("CANVAS GL IS: " +
    canvas.getGL().getClass().getName());
    System.err.println("CANVAS GLU IS: " +
    canvas.getGLU().getClass().getName());

    frame.add(canvas);
    frame.setSize(500,500); // hard coded width/height
    animator = new Animator(canvas);
    frame.addWindowListener(new WindowAdapter() {
        public void windowClosing(WindowEvent e) {
            animator.stop();
            System.exit(0);
            }
        });
    frame.show();
    animator.start();
    canvas.requestFocus();
    }
```

The `GLDrawableFactory.getFactory().createGLCanvas()` is the simplest of the series of `create()` methods for `GLCanvases` or `GLJPanels`. We use the "new `GLCapabilities()`" for the display settings, which simply means to use the defaults.

Next, we add this Sample class to the canvas's `GLEventListener` list so `Sample` can receive the callbacks:

```
void    display(GLDrawable drawable)
            Called by the drawable to initiate OpenGL rendering by
            the client.
void    displayChanged(GLDrawable drawable, boolean modeChanged,
void    boolean deviceChanged)
            Called by the drawable when the display mode or the
            display device associated with the GLDrawable has
            changed.
```

```
void      init(GLDrawable drawable)
          Called by the drawable immediately after the OpenGL
          context is initialized for the first time.
void      reshape(GLDrawable drawable, int x, int y, int width, int
          height)
          Called by the drawable during the first repaint after the
          component has been resized.
```

The rest of the code is the typical frame initialization, window-setting size, adding an anonymous WindowListener for quitting, and finally showing the frame.

One other interesting piece is the Animator class. Animator is a JOGL utility class that sets up a looping thread that continually triggers a repaint on the canvas. An Animator can be attached to a GLDrawable to drive its display() method in a loop. For efficiency, it sets up the rendering thread for the drawable to be its own internal thread, so it cannot be combined with manual repaints of the surface.

It is a simple class with the full interface being the only the constructor—the start() and stop() methods:

```
Animator(GLDrawable drawable)
          Creates a new Animator for a particular drawable.
void      start()
          Starts this animator.
void      stop()
          Stops this animator, blocking until the animation
          thread has finished.
```

More full-featured applications may wish to create their own Animator-type class with more functionality, but this one will do fine for this example.

When the Animator start method is called, it creates an internal Thread instance and sets the GLDrawables rendering thread reference to it. It then goes into a loop that will repeatedly call display() on its GLDrawable, which is, in this case, our Sample class.

When GLDrawable.setRenderingThread() is called, JOGL will carry out a series of initializations triggering the canvas to call GLEventListener.init() on our Sample class. Here we will do a bit of setup of our own and see some typical OpenGL calls pass in the Sample object as the KeyListener to the GLDrawable. In addition, doing so will build up our geometry to be used later in display() and check for availability of vertex buffer objects in this OpenGL implementation. This gives an example of how to use gl.isExtensionAvailable() to check which ARB and vendor-specific extensions are supported on the current system. Extension functions can also be checked using the method isFunctionAvailable(java.lang.String).

This example tries to use vertex buffer objects, but if they are not supported on the current system, it will skip both building the vertex buffer objects and rendering them in `display()`:

```
/** Called by the drawable immediately after the OpenGL context
* is initialized for the first time. Can be used to perform
* one-time OpenGL initialization such as setup of lights and display
lists.
* <param gLDrawable The GLDrawable object.
*/
public void init(GLDrawable gLDrawable) {
    final GL gl = gLDrawable.getGL();
    gl.glShadeModel(GL.GL_SMOOTH); // Enable Smooth Shading
    gl.glClearColor(0.0f, 0.0f, 0.0f, 0.5f); // Black Background
    gl.glClearDepth(1.0f); // Depth Buffer Setup
    gl.glEnable(GL.GL_DEPTH_TEST); // Enables Depth Testing
    gl.glDepthFunc(GL.GL_LEQUAL); // The Type Of Depth Testing
    gl.glHint(GL.GL_PERSPECTIVE_CORRECTION_HINT, GL.GL_NICEST);
    // Really Nice Perspective Calculations
    gLDrawable.addKeyListener(this);
    // Use Debug pipeline
    // comment out to use standard pipeline
    gLDrawable.setGL(new DebugGL(gLDrawable.getGL()));

    supportedVBO =
    gl.isExtensionAvailable("GL_ARB_vertex_buffer_object");
    if ( supportedVBO )
        System.out.println("Vertex Buffer Objects Supported");
    else
    {
        System.out.println("Vertex Buffer Objects NOT Supported - part
of this example will not execute");

    }
    buildCubeDisplayList(gl);
    buildCubeVertexArrays(gl);
}
```

The last two methods are called to build a display list and vertex arrays and also bind OpenGL buffers for vertex buffer objects, if they are supported.

This simple display method is where the rendering actually gets done every frame. In this example, we do the typical operations of clearing the buffers, translating and rotating the objects for viewing, and finally drawing the cube. This example has the four main render methods set up—batched vertex calls, a display list of those calls, an indexed vertex array of the same shape, and a vertex buffer object of those same vertex arrays. All are set up in other later methods for cleanness, except for the display list render, which is simply one glCallList() command anyway.

```
public void display(GLDrawable gLDrawable) {
    GL gl = gLDrawable.getGL();
    gl.glClear(GL.GL_COLOR_BUFFER_BIT | GL.GL_DEPTH_BUFFER_BIT);

    gl.glLoadIdentity();
    gl.glTranslatef(0.0f, 0.0f, -6.0f);

    gl.glRotatef(rotX, 1.0f, 0.0f, 0.0f);
    gl.glRotatef(rotY, 0.0f, 1.0f, 0.0f);

    rotX += 1.0f * scale;
    rotY += 0.5f * scale;
    //for(int i = 0;i<10; i++) // uncomment to slow down
    {
    switch( renderType )
    {
        case rtVertex:
            drawCubeVertex(gl);
        break;
        case rtDisplayList:
            gl.glCallList(gear1);
        break;
        case rtVertexArray:
            drawCubeVertexArrays(gl);
        break;
        case rtVertexBufferObject:
            if ( supportedVBO )
            drawCubeVertexBufferObjects(gl);
        break;
    }
    }
}
```

The rest of this Sample is the actual render methods, the object build methods, and the KeyListener methods, of which keyPressed() catches the spacebar for toggling through the different render modes and Escape for exiting.

And there you have it—Java bindings for OpenGL rendering an amazing spinning colored cube.

SUMMARY

OpenGL is the industry standard for real-time 3D graphics, and many developers have used it as the core rendering system for the industry's leading games. JOGL, the Java bindings to OpenGL, brings all the power, efficiency, and cutting-edge features of OpenGL to Java while extending the OpenGL feature set to blend well in the Java runtime environment. At the same time, it stays true to Java standards and conventions. JOGL takes Java to the highest level of professional real-time 3D graphics, finally "rendering" the Java platform a top choice for 3D games.

14 Overlays and Menus Using JOGL

In This Chapter

- Introduction
- Setting Up a 2D Coordinate System
- Text Rendering
- HUD and GUI
- Summary

INTRODUCTION

There are many reasons to render 3D geometry that appears 2D. For example, rendering text on the screen can be done by rendering polygons with textures of the corresponding letters. Similarly, textured polygons can be used to display the menus and the heads-up display (HUD) of your game. In fact, most games use this technique instead of pasting an image on top of the 3D context. In this chapter, you will learn how to set up the coordinate system so that you can use typical 2D coordinates to draw the geometry on screen. The section on text rendering shows different ways of drawing text on the screen, which is a good way to see the different approaches to getting 2D-looking content on the screen. Also, note that text rendering is necessary for just about every game. After learning the basics, you will learn how to create GUI APIs that can be used to create the menu and HUD for your game. This chapter comes with a working demo that shows animated and interactive in-game menus that run in a 3D context. The examples section explains the demo and shows how the in-game menu, console, and HUD work.

SETTING UP A 2D COORDINATE SYSTEM

Typical perspective frustums are set up such that the lower-left corner is coordinate (-1, -1) and the upper-right corner is (1, 1), which would make the center of the screen (0, 0). If you want to render primitives such as quads as if they were 2D, it will be convenient to define a coordinate system where the upper-left corner is (0, 0) and the lower-right, say, (640, 480).

The glOrtho and glFrustum methods can be used to set up the frustum and the coordinate system in which the objects are rendered. The difference between them is perspective and the sense of depth. When using a perspective projection, objects that are farther from the camera appear smaller and move more slowly. The glOrtho method can be used to produce a parallel projection in much the same way that the glFrustum method can be used to produce a perspective projection. The following line sets up a parallel projection matrix. The upper-left corner is (0, 0) and the lower-right corner is (640, 480).

```
//          left, right, bottom, top, zNear, zFar
gl.glOrtho(   0,   640,   480,    0,   -1,    1 );
```

Note that the zNear and zFar have been set to -1 and 1 correspondingly. When drawing, you can simply set the z-coordinate to 0 or use glVertex2i instead of glVertex3i. It is a good practice to avoid using perspective projection if you want to render polygons right in front of the camera. But if you want to use a perspective projection instead, you must render the geometry right passed the near clip and use the new and far clip appropriately. An example of a quad drawn using the orthographic projection matrix we set up earlier follows:

```
gl.glBegin(GL.GL_QUADS);
g gl.glVertex2i(100, 200); // South West
g gl.glVertex2i(200, 200); // South East
g gl.glVertex2i(200, 100); // North East
g gl.glVertex2i(100, 100); // North West
g gl.glEnd();
```

Unlike console games, PC games must be able to run in different screen resolutions, so menu systems may have to compensate for the possible changes. By using a virtual 640 × 480 coordinate system, you can choose to change the coordinate of the projection matrix, or leave it as is. If the width and height parameters that are passed to glOrtho change, the size of the components will shrink and allow more components to fit. On the other hand, by not changing them, the components take the same amount of space, regardless of the screen resolution.

TEXT RENDERING

Text rendering is necessary for just about every game. Text rendering is used for tasks ranging from in-game console windows used to execute commands and send text messages, displaying mission descriptions, and GUI component labels. There are different techniques for drawing text in a 3D window. One approach is to use images; another is to use textured polygons.

Bitmap Fonts

The glBitmap method can be used to set the value of each pixel to the current color. Unlike the well-known bitmap file format, an OpenGL bitmap is literally a bitmap, where each bit corresponds to a pixel and indicates only whether a pixel is on or off. The following code segment draws a 32 × 8 pixel square with a cutout center. Pixels that correspond to the "on" bits are set to the current color, and pixels that correspond to "off" bits are left alone.

```
byte[] bitmap = {
    (byte)0xFF, (byte)0xFF, (byte)0xFF, (byte)0xFF,
    (byte)0xFF, (byte)0xFF, (byte)0xFF, (byte)0xFF,
    (byte)0xFF, (byte)0x00, (byte)0x00, (byte)0xFF,
    (byte)0xFF, (byte)0x00, (byte)0x00, (byte)0xFF,
    (byte)0xFF, (byte)0x00, (byte)0x00, (byte)0xFF,
    (byte)0xFF, (byte)0x00, (byte)0x00, (byte)0xFF,
    (byte)0xFF, (byte)0xFF, (byte)0xFF, (byte)0xFF,
    (byte)0xFF, (byte)0xFF, (byte)0xFF, (byte)0xFF,
};
gl.glRasterPos2i( 300, 300 );
gl.glBitmap(4*8, 8, 0, 0, 0, 0, bitmap);
```

The first two parameters of glBitmap are the width and the height of the bitmap, and the last parameter is a reference to the bitmap data. Note that bitmaps are drawn to the current raster position. You must set the raster position accordingly, before using glBitmap.

To draw text, you can use a separate bitmap for each character. You can make each bitmap yourself, or use actual Java (or Windows) fonts to draw every character on a 2D context and then read the pixels to create the bitmaps. This can be done by using a rather simple and small external tool to create the bitmaps and saving them to a stream.

Alternatively, you can use the `glutBitmapCharacter` method, which has been exposed through the `net.java.games.jogl.util.GLUT` class. Even though it has only a few fonts with only a few different fixed sizes, it is just fine for getting something up quick. This method uses `glBitmap` to draw the characters, as explained earlier. The following segment uses `glutBitmapString`, which calls `glutBitmapCharacter` for every character. The text is drawn at the current raster position.

```
GLUT glut = new GLUT();
glut.glutBitmapString(gl, GLUT.BITMAP_TIMES_ROMAN_24,
                      "Text using GLUT");
```

The problem with using `glBitmap` is that the text cannot be rotated, zoomed, or made transparent. The text does not look very nice because the edges are too crisp. In addition, each character can only have one color. You can use `glDrawPixel` to draw pixels as opposed to bits. When drawing, you can also enable blending so that the image blends with the screen contents.

Using Textures

Another technique is to use a textured geometry. The texture can be made in an art package and highly customized. For example, the *you won* message at the end of a fighting game can be made as a single texture. Just about every game uses this technique for some of its text. The main disadvantage of this technique is that it consumes a lot of texture memory. It also works only for static text or text that is not generated during runtime from the game data or user input.

To reduce texture memory consumption, instead of making a texture for every string, we can make a single texture that contains the entire alphabet. To draw the text, we can use quads that use the texture and have appropriate texture coordinates. The following method renders a string at the provided coordinates. The ID of the texture that contains the characters is passed in as an integer. The texture is assumed to be a square texture with 16 columns and 16 rows. The first character in the texture is assumed to be the space (or empty) character, which has the ASCII value of 32. In addition, the coordinate system is assumed to be set up as described in the previous section.

```java
public void renderText(GL gl, int x, int y, String string,
                       int fontTexture){
  gl.glPushAttrib(GL.GL_CURRENT_BIT |
                  GL.GL_COLOR_BUFFER_BIT);

  gl.glColor4f(1.0f, 1.0f, 1.0f, 1.0f);
  gl.glBlendFunc(GL.GL_SRC_ALPHA, GL.GL_ONE);
  gl.glEnable(GL.GL_BLEND);

  gl.glBindTexture(GL.GL_TEXTURE_2D, fontTexture);

  for(int i=0; i<string.length(); i++){

    float cxIndex = ((string.charAt(i)-32)%16)/16.0f;
    float cyIndex = ((string.charAt(i)-32)/16)/16.0f;

    gl.glBegin(GL.GL_QUADS);
    gl.glTexCoord2f(cxIndex,1-cyIndex-0.0625f);
    gl.glVertex3f(x, y+16,  0.0f);               // SW
    gl.glTexCoord2f(cxIndex+0.0625f,1-cyIndex-0.0625f);
    gl.glVertex3f(x+16, y+16,  0.0f);            // SE
    gl.glTexCoord2f(cxIndex+0.0625f,1-cyIndex);
    gl.glVertex3f(x+16, y,  0.0f);               // NE
    gl.glTexCoord2f(cxIndex,1-cyIndex);
    gl.glVertex3f(x, y,  0.0f);                  // NW
    gl.glEnd();

    x += 16;
  }
  gl.glPopAttrib();
}
```

If the texture is 256×256, there will be a one-to-one mapping of texture pixels to screen pixels. Lower-resolution texture will result in the same size text with a lower quality. The texture can be generated from existing system fonts at some specific point size. If each character is 16×16 pixels, you can fit 256 characters in a 256×256 texture. Because you typically do not need a full character set for any given font, you can store multiple fonts in one texture. If you need to use variable-width fonts, you will have to keep track of the width of each character. You can create a Font class that stores the texture, character widths, and such information.

HUD AND GUI

The complexities of HUDs vary largely from game to game. Games of certain genres, such as RTS, are guaranteed to have rather involved HUDs. For example, a game such as *WarCraft III* has an interactive HUD, which understands mouse and keyboard input. There are buttons on the left side of the screen that can be used to select the heroes. There is also an interactive overhead map and even a viewport that shows a close-up of the currently selected unit or building. In addition, there is a text field that acts as the in-game console and is used for passing messages to the players. The HUD is practically a fully functional window that has different components such as buttons, text fields, and progress bars. Even though FPS games tend to have very little, if any, interactive HUDs, the in-game console is still an interactive GUI component.

Besides HUDs that are rendered in a 3D context, many games render their menus in a 3D context as well. The main menu of *WarCraft III* and *Quake III* are in a 3D context. In this section, we will build a GUI system that can be used to create interactive HUD and menus. The code that comes with this chapter demonstrates the infamous spinning cube game, with main menu, options menu, HUD, and in-game console.

By creating your GUIs as demonstrated here, you will be able to have nice menus that can even be transparent and rendered right onto the 3D context. In addition, the menus and dialog boxes will be local to your game. That is, pressing Alt + Tab will not cause the focus to be stolen from the game and given to a top-level container. In addition, clicking the wrong window will not cause another window to be inadvertently hidden from the user. The approach presented here is also extremely light and will not require much startup time or resources.

ON THE CD
The code for this chapter can be found on the book's companion CD-ROM in Code/Chapter 14/HGUI.

Components

The GUI system that we implement here has to model some of the functionalities of AWT and Swing. We define a component as an object, such as a button or a text field. All the components we define here inherit from the HComponent base class. Some of the more important members of this class are shown in Figure 14.1.

The members x, y, w, and h are used to define the position and the boundary of the component. They are also used to render the component and serve as a bounding box used to find out if the mouse is on the component. The coordinates of this box are integer values that assume a coordinate where the origin is the upper-left corner of the screen. Note that even though the boundary is a rectangle, it does not

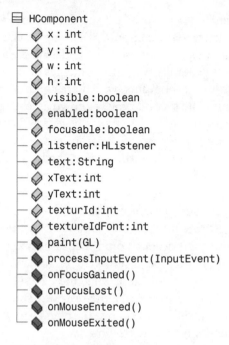

FIGURE 14.1 The more important members of the HComponent class.

mean that a component cannot be round. The boundary can simply be an estimated bounding region.

The member visible is used to indicate whether a component should be rendered. This can be useful when, for example, a simple image or text has to flash or pop up as the result of the user's interaction. As another example, when a button is triggered, additional components may need to become visible on the same screen. The member enabled is used to indicate whether the component should receive input. A component that is not enabled should typically be rendered so that it appears grayed out, indicating that the component is there but not active. The member focusable is used to indicate whether the component can gain focus. A focused component is the component to which the keyboard input is sent. Note that at most, one component can have the keyboard focus at any given time.

The member listener is a reference to a listener whose actionPerformed method is called to handle the events generated by this component. As with a typical listener, it is notified when input to the component translates into actions. For example, a button can be assigned a listener so that when it is clicked, the listener can start the game. For the sake of simplicity, a component can have a single listener reference as opposed to a multiple list of them.

The member text stores a string that is rendered at coordinates (xText, yText), which are relative to the component's position. The member textureIdFont is the texture that contains the font used for rendering the text member of this component.

There are generally two different types of events in a GUI system. The first type is known as low-level events, which are composed of events such as keyboard and mouse events. The second type is known as semantic (or high-level) events. High-level events are those that are typically generated by a component and have a higher level of meaning. For example, a "triggered" event can be generated by a button and passed to its listeners to indicate that the button was clicked by the mouse or the Enter key was pressed when the component had focus.

A component can receive low-level events through its processInputEvent method. Every component can choose to call its super class's processInputEvent method to get the functionality supported by the super class.

The paint method of a component is called to allow the component to render itself. The paint method receives the GL object, which is used to invoke OpenGL methods. A component can change the OpenGL state and do just about anything it wants, as long as it restores the previous state when it is done. For example, a component may decide to change the blend function or even change the projection matrix to render a complex geometry.

Figure 14.2 shows a hierarchy of components implemented in the example that comes with this chapter.

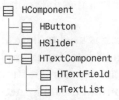

FIGURE 14.2 The component types defined and used here.

An instance of the HComponent can be used as a simple component that displays an image or some text. It does not generate any high-level events and ignores low-level events. As mentioned previously, HComponent is the base class for other components.

HButton is used as a button or check box. It contains a member called toggle-Botton that can specify whether the button is a typical one or one that can be toggled. A toggle button can be used as a check box component. An HButton can generate CLICKED, CHECKED, or UNCHECKED events. When the button is pressed, the default paint method of this component renders a smaller textured quad with a different texture. By doing so, there is a sense that the button is pushed away from the camera.

The HSlider component is a simple slider. It is an example of a component that cares about the MOUSE_DRAGGED in addition to the MOUSE_PRESSED event. A floating-point value is used to store the current value of the slider. It is also used to compute the position at which the slider knob is rendered. The value can be changed by clicking or dragging the mouse, or by using the page up and page down keys. This component generates VALUE_CHANGED events.

HTextComponent is the base class of components that need to do text editing. The processInputEvent of this component can distinguish typeable characters and concatenate them. It also defines the behavior for keys that are important for text editing, such as backspace, Home, End, or Event Copy and Paste.

HTextField component extends HTextComponent and catches the Enter key so that it can generate an ENTER event. If you want to be able to validate the text being entered, you can generate TEXT_CHANGED events to make sure the text is valid. After this component separates the input events in which it is interested, it sends the events to its super class, which can do the text editing.

HTextList is a component that keeps track of a list of strings and renders the most recent strings. You can easily catch behaviors, such as page up/page down. You can also set up an HSlider to scroll the strings that are rendered.

Containers

Now that we know the components we will be dealing with, let's see how we can put them together to build a menu. To put a menu together, we need to have some sort of containers that group the components together. A container is an object that manages a list of components. Dialog boxes, windows, and panels are examples of containers. The more important members of the container class are shown in Figure 14.3.

A container has many members and methods that are similar to those of a component. For example, a container needs to have a position, processInputEvent method, and a paint method. In fact, AWT's java.awt.Container class extends the java.awt.Component class. By doing so, a container can have other container objects in its list. For example, an AWT Panel can have other components as well as another Panel in its list. Swing takes this one step further. A JComponent actually extends the AWT container class. This means that every Swing component is a container. For example, the JScrollPane component is a container that has JScrollBars and a JViewPort component.

Unlike AWT and Swing, the container class we use here does not inherit from the component class or vice versa. We want to keep our hierarchy flat, instead of

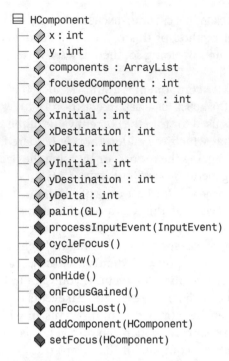

FIGURE 14.3 The more important members of the `HContainer` class.

having a tree of components and containers. Having a list instead of a tree greatly simplifies the problem. Even though this may seem overly simplified, it is sufficient for the HUD and GUI of most games.

The order of components in a container's list dictates their draw order. The list is drawn from head to tail. That way, if some components overlap, the one that was added last will be drawn last. This means that the last component will appear on top of the others.

The `processInputEvent` method of the container has to forward the events to the appropriate components. To pass the keyboard events, the container must keep track of the component in focus. The focused component is the component to which the key events are sent. Intuitively, the focused component can be changed by clicking another component. Alternatively, a key such as the Tab key can be used to cycle the focus by simply walking the component list. As a side note, if a mechanism is set up to navigate through the menus by using only the keyboard, a controller's input can be translated to equivalent keyboard events. For example, a button of the controller can be translated to the Tab key and another to the Escape key.

Mouse events are a little different. MOUSE_MOVED events should be forwarded to the component that has the mouse on it. Similarly, MOUSE_PRESSED events should be sent to the component over which the mouse was pressed. On the other hand, MOUSE_DRAGGED and MOUSE_RELEASED events should be forwarded to the component that received the corresponding MOUSE_PRESSED event. In other words, if you click a component and drag the mouse so that it is no longer on the component, the drag events should still be sent to the same component. Moreover, when the mouse button is eventually released, the component should still be notified about the MOUSE_RELEASED event, regardless of whether the mouse is directly over the component. Another relevant concern arises when the mouse is on overlapping components. In such cases, the topmost component should receive the input.

The processInputEvent of the container can also trap some keys and define a default action for them. For example, by default, the Escape key requests to close the container.

Most GUI components used in games have some sort of rollover effect to emphasize the component that is directly under the mouse. To implement rollovers, a container can draw a highlight texture on the component or allow the component to draw the rollover effect itself. By testing the position of the mouse against the bounds of the components, the component that is directly under the mouse can be determined. It is also useful to notify a component when this state changes. The onMouseEntered and onMouseExited methods of a component are used to notify it. Because our components are not managed by AWT or Swing, we must emulate these events ourselves.

In addition to rollovers, it is also useful to highlight the component that currently has the keyboard focus. Note that just because the mouse is over a text field does not mean that the keyboard input should be sent to that component.

Container Management

There are times when you may need to have multiple containers showing at the same time. Take, for example, the scenario where you are at the main menu and you want to quit the game. It may be appropriate to display another container that displays a message asking whether you really want to quit the game. The ability to show multiple containers at the same time is particularly important if you want to use the menu system to display a HUD. This is because while the HUD container is showing, you may want to show a console container or some sort of dialog box.

As its name implies, the HContainerManager class is responsible for managing the containers. It is actually a simple class. Figure 14.4 shows the more important members of this class.

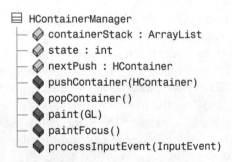

FIGURE 14.4 The more important members of the `HContainerManager` class.

The most important member is the stack, which is an `ArrayList`. When the `pushContainer` method is called, the container is passed in as the parameter is pushed using the `ArrayLists`'s add method. The `popContainer` method pops the topmost container from the stack.

When a container is pushed on the stack, its `onShow` method is invoked. Similarly, when a container is popped, its `onHide` method is called. In addition, the `onFocusGained` and `onFocusLost` methods are invoked when a container becomes the topmost component or loses its spot as the topmost component. Note that a container may gain or lose focus if it is either pushed or popped from the stack or another component is pushed or popped immediately in front of a container. In other words, the `onShow` and `onFocusGained` methods are not necessarily called the same number of times. When a container's `onFocusGained` or `onFocusLost` method is called, any component that has the mouse over it or has the keyboard focus should also be notified. This is useful, for example, when a component is rendering its own highlighting effect.

The `paint` method of the container manager calls the paint method of all the containers in its stack. The `paint` method is performed from the bottom of the stack to the top. In other words, the topmost container is painted last. In addition, the `paint` method of this class is responsible for setting up the frustum so that the components can draw themselves in a convenient 2D coordinate system. Such settings that are global across the GUI components can be set up in this method. This method is also responsible for storing the render states and states such as enabling textures and disabling lighting. After this `paint` method calls the `paint` method of all the containers in the stack, it should restore the render state. Note that the `paint` method of the container manager should be called after the game has been rendered. By restoring the render state, the game will not be affected as a side effect of rendering the GUI.

The `paintFocus` method draws a highlight texture on top of the component that is under the mouse, as well as a texture to emphasize the component that has the keyboard focus.

The `processInputEvent` method simply directs the events to the topmost container.

Unlike menus and GUIs used for most applications, game menus are typically animated. For example, the menus may slide in from the side, or the in-game-console may slide down from the top. Animation support can be easily added to the container manager. If every container has a position, and the position of the components are relative to their container's position, by simply moving the container, all of its components will move accordingly.

To handle the animation, every container stores its initial position, destination position, and a delta vector. The delta vector is simply a pair of x- and y-values that specify the velocity of the container when it is being animated. In addition, the container manager needs to know the state of the animation for purposes such as ignoring user input while a container is being animated. The container manager can act as a simple state machine with the following states:

```
static final int  STATE_IDLE        = 0,
                  STATE_PUSH_ENTER   = 1,
                  STATE_PUSH         = 2,
                  STATE_PUSH_EXIT    = 3,
                  STATE_POP_ENTER    = 4,
                  STATE_POP          = 5,
                  STATE_POP_EXIT     = 6;

int state = STATE_IDLE;
```

Even though there are a total of seven states, there are only three general states. The states are IDLE, PUSH, and POP. The IDLE state does not do much. The PUSH state indicates that the topmost container should be animated from its initial position to its destination position. The POP state indicates that the topmost container should be animated from its destination position to its initial position.

Before the state of the container manager is set to push or pop, the corresponding ENTER state is set so that some initializations can be performed before the animation starts. Likewise, the corresponding EXIT state is set to indicate that the animation has completed.

When a container is pushed, the state is set to STATE_PUSH_ENTER. This state is responsible for notifying the topmost container that it is losing focus, calling the onShow method of the container being pushed and adding the container to the stack. This state is also used to decide when to set the current position of the container to its initial position. Typically, the initial position of a container is set such that it is not on the screen. After the aforementioned changes are made, the state is set to STATE_PUSH, which simply adds the delta values to the x- and y-position of the container. It also checks to see if the destination position has been reached so that it can set the state to STATE_PUSH_EXIT. This state is used to notify the new topmost container that it has gained focus. The POP states perform the same tasks in reverse order, with some minor differences.

If you want to hide the components when the container is being animated, you can set the visibility flag of the components to false in the onShow method, and set them to true in the onFocusGained method.

When the container manager is not in the IDLE state, the processInputEvents method simply ignores the input events. Depending on the requirements of your menu system, you may have to set up the container manager so that it queues up push and pop requests. That is, when multiple calls to the push and pop methods of the container manager are made, the container manager can store the request and process them one at a time.

Demo

The following code can be found on the book's companion CD-ROM in Code/ Chapter 14/HGUI.

The demo discussed in this section uses a spinning cube as the placeholder for any 3D content you may want to have in the background while the menus are displayed. Using geometry to render the menus or display graphics in the background is a common practice. For example, both *WarCraft III* and *Quake III* use this approach. *WarCraft III* renders a world with weather effects, flying crows, and such in the background. Most games, especially console games, have menus more like *Quake III*. The menus are basically geometry right in front of the camera, as we have been doing here. For example, *Quake III* uses polygons to render the fire effect on the main menu. Some games may have a selection screen where a spinning model such as a vehicle or character is rendered. Either way, the spinning cube represents some 3D geometry that may be displayed during the menus or on a specific screen.

To create a menu, we can extend the container class. This allows us to create the components relevant to the specific menu in the constructor, catch any interesting keys by overwriting processInputEvent, perform any resetting by overwriting methods such as onShow, and, most important, define the actions that should be performed when the user interacts with the components.

The MainMenuContainer has a few member variables that are instances of different components. An instance of HComponent is used to draw a background for the container, which is just a textured quad. Instances of HButton are used for the Start, Options, and Quit buttons. The components are created in the constructor of the container. Each component is set up and added to the container using the addComponent method. The add method ends up adding the component to the component list of the container, which, as mentioned already, is used for tasks such as rendering the components. By making the MainMenuContainer implement HListener, the container can serve as a listener for its components. When the components are created, their listener is set to the instance of the MainMenuContainer. When the actionPerformed method of the container is called, we can distinguish which component generated the event and carry out the appropriate action.

When the application is launched, the main menu is animated such that it slides down from the top. This action is accomplished by setting the initial position of the container to some negative number. As the container manager calls the paint method of the container, it also updates the position of the container using the deltaX and deltaY values of the container.

If you move the mouse over the components of the menu, you will see that a texture is used as the rollover texture to emphasize the component that is immediately underneath the mouse. There is also another texture used to indicate the component that has the keyboard focus. You can press the Ctrl key to cycle the keyboard focus or click a component to potentially trigger a change in keyboard focus. You can click a button to trigger it, or press the Enter key while the component has the keyboard focus.

When the Start button is triggered by the user, the main menu is popped from the container manager's container stack, and the HudContainer is pushed on. Again, the main menu animates upward until it disappears. When the main menu is completely out of sight, the background color is changed as an indication that the game has started. This action is done by calling glClearColor through the overwritten onHide method of the MainMenuContainer.

You have to be careful about invoking GL calls through the GUI methods. It is important to note that you cannot invoke the glClearColor method (or other GL methods) from the processInputEvent or the actionPerformed methods. This is because these methods are indirectly called through the mouse and keyboard listeners on the GLCanvas, which are called by the AWT event thread. Keep in mind that GL calls should not be made by arbitrary threads. Instead, we must notify the render thread that we want to change the clear color so that it can change it for us. The notification can be accomplished by simply flipping a boolean value. Even though unlike actionPerformed and processInputEvent the onHide method is called by the render thread (through the paint method of container manager), it is still a good practice to request the GL operation.

The HUD container is similar to the main menu container. Because the initial position of the container is the same as its destination position, it appears without any animation. Note that clicking the components of the HUD does not cause them to gain the keyboard focus. None of the components of the HUD is focusable—even pressing the Ctrl key does not cause them to gain the keyboard focus.

The Escape key is trapped by the HUD container's `processInputEvent` method, which in turn pushes the main menu without popping the HUD. Note that at this point there are two containers in the stack of container manager.

The Options button on the main menu causes the main menu to be popped and the options container to be pushed on the stack. The components of the Options menu simply affect the behavior of the cube that is spinning in the background. The Options container emulates a container with multiple tabs. The tabs are triggered by triggering the toggle buttons on the left of the menu. One of the buttons on the first tab resets the rotation of the cube. The other button, which is also a toggle button, scales down the rotation velocity when it is toggled to be on and undoes the effect when the button generates an UNCHECKED event. Clicking the second tab causes the component of the first tab to be hidden and the components of the second tab to become visible. The second tab has a slider bar that controls the rotation velocity of the cube about its x-axis. See the `OptionsMenu-Container` class for additional details.

Triggering the Quit button from the main menu causes the program to exit. If the game has not been started by triggering the Start button, the application terminates immediately. However, if the main menu has been brought up after that game has started, a dialog box opens to confirm that you really want to exit. In that situation, three containers will be in the container stack.

Unlike the main menu, Options menu, and the HUD container, the Quit dialog box was not implemented by extending the container class. Instead, the background and *yes* and *no* buttons are instantiated and added to an instance of the `HContainer` class. Similarly, the listeners are created separately as anonymous inner classes. They are then added to the *yes* and *no* buttons. This is to show you that you do not always have to make a custom container class just to show a simple container. It is important to keep in mind that the startup time and memory footprint of the game will be increased by using anonymous inner classes. However, they are convenient, because they allow you to place the action code next to where the component is created. As long as you do not abuse them, you will be okay.

As mentioned previously, pressing the C key while the HUD is showing brings up the in-game console. The console is a container that has a text field and a text list. The text list component is set up so that it is not focusable. Moreover, the text field is set up to be in focus when the container is shown. When the Enter key is pressed, the corresponding listener receives an event, reads the text from the text field, and adds it to the text list. The text list always renders as many of the most recent entries as possible.

SUMMARY

In this chapter, we have looked at how to create simple and light API that can be used for making in-game menus and HUD. We have also looked at creating rendering text, which is a necessary ingredient for every game. The demo presented here is a starting point to show you how you can create and animate your GUIs. It is also worth mentioning that a few attempts have been made by the Java gaming community to integrate existing APIs such as Swing with JOGL. As of this writing, none of the attempts can be considered entirely successful. If you need extensive functionalities, such as the ones found in Swing, you may want to follow up on the attempts made to find out about any new progress. However, integrating Swing is not a trivial task, and the complications involved may prove this approach to be impractical.

15 3D Render Engine Using JOGL

In This Chapter

- Introduction
- A Simple Retained-Mode Render Engine
- Scene Graph: Object-Oriented Scenes
- Scene Graph Components
- Scene Graph Visibility Culling
- Final Thoughts on Scene Graphs
- Real-Time 3D Character Animation Primer
- Summary

INTRODUCTION

With the release of JOGL, just about any C/C++ OpenGL-based render engine can now be ported to Java. But not everyone has the C/C++ engine handy or one with the up-to-date features they want. In this chapter we will begin by building a simple retained-mode JOGL renderer, then further examine the 3D engine process using scene graphs, a generic and popular system for 3D rendering.

A SIMPLE RETAINED-MODE RENDER ENGINE

Using OpenGL directly in small or specialized applications (such as the menus Chapter 14, "Overlays and Menus Using JOGL") is relatively easy. Often the geometry data and OpenGL render calls are all contained in the same methods and possibly only a few display lists are created and used. But programming OpenGL in this direct-access inlined fashion becomes messy when trying to scale up the application in size or functionaltiy. Most full-blown 3D games are much bigger than these easy-to-manage applications, so a better way of organizing and manipulating the scene must be developed.

A major improvement is to create a OpenGL application that uses a technique known as retained-mode rendering.

OpenGL is considered an *immediate mode* API, meaning that the developer uses commands to tell the OpenGL renderer how to proceed, and then OpenGL does it immediately. (This is somewhat of a misnomer because, in fact, the commands may not execute immediately. OpenGL may queue up the commands. However, the effect is the same as immediate execution in terms of graphical output.) This is a functional approach to graphics, and just like most computing systems, functional control is what is really at the core.

What we want to do is use a more object-oriented approach in which we create 3D objects that exist independently of the specific OpenGL code. That way we can manipulate them independently as well. If we can make an OpenGL renderer that understands these objects, then functionality and scalability are much easier to grow. These independent 3D objects are called *retained* because we retain the data that describes them separately from the render code. Using this data as the basis for render engine is known as *retained-mode* rendering. Operating in retained mode is also a stepping-stone to full-blown geometry hierarchies and scene graphs, which we will examine later in the chapter.

Geometry Containers

The first significant object type we need to build for a retained-mode renderer is a geometry container. In a simple retained-mode renderer, geometry containers and the OpenGL code that can render them is all that we need.

Many different formats and types of geometric data are available that OpenGL supports, and this is one of the things that makes OpenGL so versatile. Some of these types don't really lend themselves well to a geometry container, and other legacy types may not be as useful now, compared to the latest types. To show a simple working example of retained mode, we will stick to only one category of geometric types, the vertex array, and the two ways OpenGL can render it—what we will call immediate and cached (similar to how we use it in the JOGL chapter sample). The difference here is that we will formalize the related geometric data into one object that we will call a VertexArraySet. Also, we will put all related render-state parameters, such as material and associated textures, into another object called an Appearance and a container for both called a RenderShape. Theses three elements form the core of our retained mode data (see Figure 15.1).

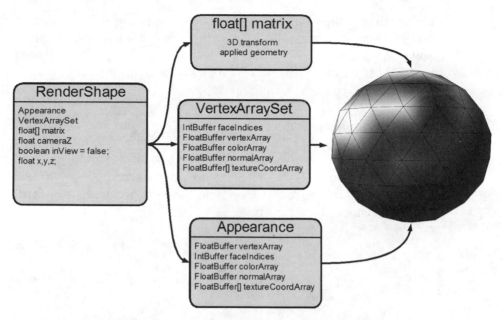

FIGURE 15.1   Retained mode structures. `RenderShape` contains references to a `float[]` matrix, a `VertexArraySet` object, and an `Appearance` object.

It is important to understand why all this related data gets divided up this way. All the data could simply be in one class because it all describes one 3D object and will all be combined to render a single 3D object. So why split it up like this?

The major reason is reuse. By reuse, we mean sharing the `VertexArraySets` and `Appearances` across many different `RenderShapes` in a scene. In practice, for even the simplest scenes, it often turns out that `Appearance` data alone can (and should) be shared across many of the `RenderShapes` in that scene. The big gains from sharing data in a retained-mode renderer are both in memory savings and improved rendering performance. The less new data to move around and the less new states that must be changed in the render pipeline, the better the render performance. By reusing as much data as possible and setting up the rendering operations to take advantage of the reuse accordingly, we can increase the possible performance for a given scene. Designing the renderer in this way is a careful balance of object-oriented and performance-oriented design.

The renderer will also need scene container or be passed a scene container that has all the 3D objects desired to render in a particular frame. The renderer will also need a few other pieces of global information, such as the view transformation or camera position and the direction and lighting configuration. In the procedural reality of OpenGL, lighting is actually a per-object local effect, but it can be treated as a global effect in the retained-mode system if it is meant to be the same for all objects or groups of objects. This is a very limiting lighting model, but it will serve as a solid beginning. The way lighting should be handled is different from game to game and can be one of the more complex areas of 3D engine design. The model here is intended to be the simplest possible but still allow basic control for dynamically lit objects.

To add this new global rendering information to our system we will create several new classes with the relationships shown in Figure 15.2. A new Scene class will have a reference to a Camera class containing basic view parameters, a Light class containing light position or direction, and a container for RenderShapes. The renderer will have a reference to a Scene object and other OpenGL required classes to display the render on the screen.

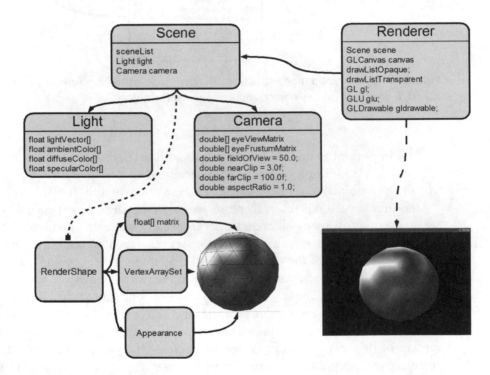

FIGURE 15.2 Simple render engine structure.

Now that we have a rough overview, let's go into more detail with some of the issues of rendering the RenderShapes. With this design and current OpenGL 1.4 capabilities the vertex arrays in VertexArraySet can be set up to use VerterBuffer-

`Objects` or Display Lists for the fastest performance. But if `VerterBufferObjects` or Display Lists were created automatically by the renderer for every `VertexArraySet`, we would have a problem with dynamic geometry data.

Static and Dynamic Geometry

Some geometry in a scene is static. That is, the geometry will never change from when it is first created. Usually these are elements such as buildings, terrain, trees, and everything we consider world geometry. 3D objects that move around, such as cars or characters, are usually considered dynamic. However, from the perspective of OpenGL vertex arrays, dynamic geometric data is data that actually changes the *values* in the vertex arrays, not just the transformation of the vertex array. We can easily move objects around by applying transforms in the render pipeline, without ever actually changing the vertex arrays' values, because the render-time transformation is done only at render time and never affects the original vertex array data. Therefore, static rendered objects could include moving vehicles and objects and some types of characters, all of which can be put into `VertexBufferObjects` and referenced only with the VBO IDs for rendering. We define these objects that can use VBOs for their internal representation as uniformly transformed because this type of transformation is performed by OpenGL without affecting the vertex array data.

If all vertex arrays were created as VBOs, OpenGL would not correctly render certain 3D objects such as skin, animated characters, particle systems, and other deformable surfaces that are changed by altering the vertex array data. These kinds of geometries must be transferred to OpenGL every time they change, which is usually once every frame. These objects are called nonuniformly deformable because whatever transformations or custom effects are made to the vertex array data are not the same for each vertex, and they need to use regular vertex arrays for their internal representation (see Figure 15.3).

Static geometry-based objects and characters are made up of several separate vertex arrays grouped together. To create the look of bending joints, separate objects overlap slightly at the joints where local transformations control the final global position and orientation, creating the look of a continuous geometry. These separate transformations don't actually deform the individual geometries; they only uniformly transform them, similar to how a real toy action figure is constructed.

Dynamic vertex arrays must be used (along with a more complex transformation system) to create the effect of a continuous deformable mesh, more like real skin, cloth, water, or particle systems.

OpenGL doesn't formally make the distinction between static and dynamic. It is all about which data representation is used and how a given rendering system uses it to render.

<table>
<tr><td>

"Static" VertexArraySet
- Uses Display Lists or VertexBufferObjects
- Transferred once at load or creation and uses transforms to move
- Examples include:
  - Disjoint Characters
  - Vehicles
  - World Geometry

</td><td>

"Dynamic" VertexArraySet
- Uses regular VertexArrays, which are transferred every frame
- Can be deformed any way the user wishes to create motion
- Examples include:
  - Skinned Characters
  - Particle Systems

</td></tr>
</table>

FIGURE 15.3   Example static and dynamic VertexArraySets.

Rendering

With all the vertex data and render state data neatly contained in a RenderShape and global camera and light in our Scene, we can begin to implement the Renderer.

Render Pipeline

The renderer has to perform a series of operations in each frame, based on all the retained-mode data. This series is called the render pipeline. There are almost as many variations of render pipelines as there are game engines, but a few key operations are fairly constant. For our engine, our steps will look as follows:

1. Clear frame buffer and Z-buffer.
2. Set the `Modelview` and `Projection` transforms from the `Camera` object's data.
3. Set the `Light` states from the `Light` object's data.
4. For each `RenderShape` in the `Scene` list:
   a. Apply the `RenderShapes` matrix. With OpenGL, we use `glPushMatrix()` followed by `glMultMatrixf(shape.myMatrix)` to achieve this.
   b. Set the appropriate states for the current `RenderShape Appearance`.
   c. Set the current vertex array `ByteBuffers` references or Bind IDs for the RenderShapes's `VertexArraySets`.
   d. Execute the appropriate OpenGL draw function.
   e. Reset the matrix state. Similar to step 4a, in OpenGL we use `glPopMatrix()`.
5. One frame is complete! Return from `display()` where JOGL will perform a buffer swap to display the final render on screen. For continuous rendering, as in a game, repeat this procedure from step 1. This is a brief overview of the process, and it should be noted that this describes only the 3D render engine stage of a game engine, not a complete game engine. User input, sounds, and object updates all need to happen before this render stage is executed.

Render Order

Unfortunately, depending on what the 3D objects are in the scene and how complex the final scene is, this basic pipeline may not be enough to get a *view-dependent* correct render. By view dependent we mean render results that depend on how the view or camera is positioned and oriented. It turns out that simply rendering objects in whatever order they exist in the scene list will probaby not work for most scenes. One reason is that transparent objects will probably not end up rendering correctly. Creating the effect of object transparency is not automatic in modern 3D hardware, but instead requires significant effort to be correctly implemented in a 3D engine. There are a few more things that can done to get a correct scene render, as well as possibly improving render performance.

Opaque and Transparent Graphics

For transparent objects to look right in the final frame, they must be rendered with the proper OpenGL blending function *after* all other opaque objects have been rendered to actually look transparent. In addition, within that transparent object render pass the transparent objects must also be rendered *farthest to nearest* from the camera's perspective, a technique known as Depth or Z-sorting. To be absolutely correct, the 3D objects must be rendered far to near on a face-by-face basis, and for any intersecting geometry those faces would have to be split and sorted. Whew! That could be a lot of work to set up.

Depth-Sorted Transparency

Totally correct scene transparency is often incredibly expensive to compute, especially for dynamic transparent geometry such as particle systems, so real-time 3D engines do the best they can by usually supporting only depth-sorted transparent objects (not individual triangles) and rendering them after all the opaque objects.

To properly support depth-sorted transparency, our renderer will need to have two distinct lists of RenderShapes to draw each frame—the opaque list and the transparent list. That is simple enough to add, but it means that the renderer should probably no longer maintain a reference to the Scene object for accessing the scene list and that some additional process must step through the Scene RenderShapes list and sort it into the opaque and transparent object lists, or *bins*, in the renderer. Sorting is probably an overglorified word for what needs to be done at this point, but we call it sorting because as the engine becomes more complex, this step will transform into a more complex sort. If our container classes are java.utils.ArrayLists, the next code shows this can be quite simple:

```
static public void generateRenderBins(
    ArrayList drawListOpaque,
    ArrayList drawListTransparent,
    ArrayList list)
{
    for (int i = 0; i < list.size(); i++)
    {
        Object obj = list.get(i);
        if (obj instanceof RenderShape)
        {
            RenderShape renderShape = ((RenderShape)obj);
            if (renderShape.appearance.hasAlpha)
                drawListTransparent.add(renderShape);
            else
                drawListOpaque.add(renderShape);
        }
    }
}
```

This functionality could be set in the Renderer class or in the Scene class, or even some new class. The reason we may want to place it in so many locations is that it depends on how the Scene class holds the RenderShapes. It can be a simple ArrayList, such as in this example, or it can be a much more complex structure, more related to the actual game design. In fact, by making the renderer process only an opaque draw list and then a separate transparent draw list, we can make the renderer as dumb (meaning simple) as possible and yet be useful for many different Scene container implementations. Also, this simple renderer will not perform the sort operation on the transparent list, but only just step through what is there and render it in list order. If the list of transparent objects needs sorting, it should be sorted before it is given to the renderer for rendering. That may seem problematic, but it actually makes the renderer more generally useful because some games or portions of games will not need any transparency sorting or may need greater control over how the sorting is done than the renderer's default implementation.

For example, it may be that in one particular game, the camera does not move freely but rather is constrained in some way. In that case, the transparency may only need to be sorted infrequently at game-specified times. Having the sorting happen automatically by the renderer would mean that the renderer's method would need to be overridden by the game application code anyway or controlled in a some other game-specific way. Why not just have the game handle that directly because it knows best when and how to do it?

This doesn't mean we will skip the sorting in our example engine. We will make our engine do a general Z-depth sort on all transparent objects, but the sorting will happened outside of the Renderer class and without its knowledge.

Correctly rendering transparent objects is at least a three-step process, two of the steps being splitting the objects into two opaque and tranparent object lists and ordering the transparent list from far to near. The remaining step is finding the right depth values with which to sort the transparent objects. This is not as simple as it may seem at first because the proper depth value is relative to the camera position, not some inherit object value that can be retrieved. The depth value changes depending on how the camera transform changes, even if the object never moves, because the sort-depth value is relative to the camera's location and orientation, that is, we need the *camera space* Z-depth of the object to use in the sort.

If the camera position is maintained as a 3D matrix, a quick transform of the object's position will do. Depending on how a renderer's camera data is stored, this may need to be an inverted camera matrix to tranform the object position correctly. Also, some objects may not have an associated matrix, or the matrix they have may not represent the position that we want to use for Z-sorting, especailly if the objects were modeled as translated from the origin without a translation matrix. Therefore, an additional position may need to be stored for the object that represents its intended center point:

```
static public void computeDrawListTransparentZDepth(
    Scene scene,
    ArrayList drawListTransparent)
{
```

```
        for (int i = 0; i < drawListTransparent.size(); i++)
        {
            float x,y,z;
            RenderShape renderShape =
(RenderShape)drawListTransparent.get(i);

            // Check if object has a matrix or not
            // so we can get the position to use
            // for Z-sorting
            if (renderShape.myMatrix != null)
            {
                // Get object position from matrix
                x = mat[12];
                y = mat[13];
                z = mat[14];
            }
            else
            {
                // Get object position as stored
                x = renderShape.x;
                y = renderShape.y;
                z = renderShape.z;
            }

            // transform the object position in Camera space
            // but only need to keep the resulting Z coordinate
            // for later sorting
            renderShape.cameraZ =
                VecMatUtils.transformZ(

    scene.getCamera().eyeViewMatrix,
                x,
                y,
                z);
        }
    }
```

The steps go as follows:

1. Create a list of tranparent-only objects. In our case, we generate it from the total list of objects in the Scene list.
2. Compute the Z-depth for each object from the camera's current frame of reference.
3. Sort the list from farthest to nearest based on each object's camera Z-depth values.

Incidentally, any popular sort (quicksort, merge sort, and so on) will work here, but a sort that leverages already-sorted lists, such as an insertion sort, is nice because most games have high-frame coherency, that is, from frame to frame the scene doesn't change too much. This frame-to-frame coherency leads to all kinds of interesting optimizations that can be done, but they complicate the renderer design and are certainly not guaranteed to always be beneficial. We will look at some of these ideas later in this chapter.

Geometry and Matrix Hierarchies

At this point we have a pretty good 3D object renderer. It can handle multiple objects, with different kinds of render states, including textures, lighting, and Z-depth-sorted transparency. Moving objects is a snap with matrix transforms, and even dynamic geometry is optimized. However, manipulating groups of objects together can be quite cumbersome because everything is in list form.

A classic example of the problem of moving groups of objects together is a simple vehicle. Probably the simplest case is a tank with turret. Our example will be a fictional hover tank.

The problem is obvious once we start trying to make the tank drivable. The tank and turret are two different shapes and, therefore, would be two different RenderShapes in our renderer. When the driving motion code executes and updates the tank transform to make it move in a particular direction, it leaves behind the turret object floating in midair. The reason this happens is that the turret does not know it should move with the tank, because it exists as a separate object.

One possible solution to this problem is to modify the tank-driving-motion code to know about the tank body and the turret and to update the turret's transform to move forward when it does the same for the tank body. For a simple tank and turret example, this is not that bad of a solution. But what if the design calls for more articulated parts, such as another weapon or maybe a hatch on the tank body? The tank motion code would need to be written to know about all the separate parts of a tank to move all those objects as well. This can get to be tedious and error prone as object groupings become more and more complex.

What we need is a *geometry hierarchy*. A geometry hierarchy replaces the list-based scene structure with a tree structure of groups of objects. What makes it fix our moving-object problem is that the tree will also contain local transformation matrices between grouped objects and the final transformation state of any leaf RenderShape will be the matrix concatenation of all the tree transformations from the root to the RenderShape.

Instead of representing the whole tank as a *list* of independent RenderShapes, it can be a simple *hierarchy* of transformed objects, where the final global object transformation is inherited from all the transforms above it in the hierarchy (see Figure 15.4).

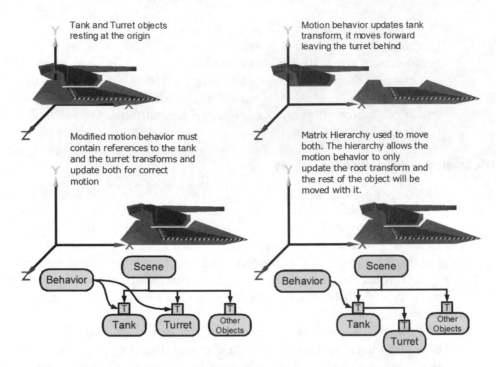

FIGURE 15.4 Transformation hierarchy.

Matrix hierarchies are not an automatic creation, just as correct transparency isn't automatic. That is, simply creating the hierarchy data structures does not also create the correct final render; it will take more work than that. The transform state of the render pipeline needs to be modified to follow the matrix hierarchy for each final object that must be rendered.

One possible implementation of dealing with the hierarchy is to make the render engine itself contain a reference to the hierarchical structure, and many 3D engines work this way. Unfortunately, this complicates the render engine again by forcing it to know how to process tree structures but, more important, ultimately it limits the render engine's general usefulness by forcing it to be based on a specific tree implementation or interface.

To avoid this, we will keep the hierarchical structure abstracted from the final render engine's data. The render engine will operate as it always has, simply rendering out a list of singly transformed objects. However, we will build a new structure for containing the objects in a transform hierarchy that is held by the Scene object. When the Scene executes its usual process of generating the opaque and transparent render bins for the renderer, it will also perform the extra step of flat-

tening the transform hierarchy, also known as converting from local to global coordinates. It will compute the final per-object transform, based on the hierarchies'
transformations and the objects' hierarchical relationships.

To do this, the Scene class will perform a recursive depth-first traversal of the
entire hierarchy, multiplying each matrix to its child as it descends the hierarchy
until it reaches an actual RenderShape. It will then set the RenderShape myMatrix to
the current accumulation. This accumulated transform is called the global transform and is what the renderer will use for that particular object. It is possible to do
this directly in OpenGL using its push and pop matrix calls, but then the final
transform would not be computed by the engine and would not be readily available
for use as the object transform for depth-sorting transparencies or other collision
processing. In addition, most OpenGL matrix-stack implementations are limited to
a max size of 32, and in a complex scene this may fall short of the scene hierarchy
depth.

To set up this transform hierarchy we must make a few new classes. We will use
a Java object as our base, Group to act as the branching node that holds other nodes
using a java.util.ArrayList, and TransformGroup to be a special type of group that
contains the local matrix at that point in the hierarchy.

```java
public class Group
{
    ArrayList children = new ArrayList();
    /**
     * <return
     */
    public ArrayList getChildren()
    {
        return children;
    }
}


public class TransformGroup extends Group
{
    Matrix4f matrix = new Matrix4f();

    /**
     * <return
     */
    public Matrix4f getMatrix()
    {
        return matrix;
    }
```

```
/**
 * <param matrix4f
 */
public void setMatrix(Matrix4f matrix4f)
{
    matrix = matrix4f;
}
}
```

Because our Group class is using ArrayLists to act as its container mechanism, we can add any Java object to it, including other Groups, TransformGroups, and the actual RenderShapes the renderer will render. The modified generateRenderBins(), which is now recursive and incorporates the flattening operation, looks like this:

```
static public void generateRenderBins(
    ArrayList drawListOpaque,
    ArrayList drawListTransparent,
    Object node,
    Matrix4f matIn)
{
    // Object is RenderShape, place into
    // appropriate bin and assign
    // current matrix accumulation
    if (node instanceof RenderShape)
    {
        RenderShape renderShape = ((RenderShape)node);
        renderShape.myMatrix = matIn.toFloatArray();

        if (renderShape.appearance.hasAlpha)
            drawListTransparent.add(renderShape);
        else
            drawListOpaque.add(renderShape);
    }
    // Object is TransformGroup
    // Acculumation current matrix transform
    // and then recursively call children
    if (node instanceof TransformGroup)
    {
        TransformGroup transformGroup = (TransformGroup)node;
        // New matrix for keeping the global current global
        // accumulation
        Matrix4f matG = new Matrix4f();
        matG.mult( matIn, transformGroup.mat );
```

```
        Group group = (Group)node;
        for (int i = 0; i < group.getChildren().size(); i++)
        {
        // recursion call
            generateRenderBins(
                drawListOpaque,
                drawListTransparent,
                group.getChildren().get(i),
                matG);
        }
    }
    // Object is Group
    // Recursively call children
    else if (node instanceof Group)
    {
        Group group = (Group)node;
        for (int i = 0; i < group.getChildren().size(); i++)
        {
        // recursion call
            generateRenderBins(
                drawListOpaque,
                drawListTransparent,
                group.getChildren().get(i),
                matIn);
        }
    }
}
```

When this is called, it passes the root of the hierarchy and a Matrix4f, which is an identity matrix. Several optimizations are done in production systems, for example changing the TransformGroup class to contain two matrices—one that is the local and one that is global—so during this traversal the need to keep creating new Matrix4f matrices for the current global matrix is eliminated. Also, the initial passed-in identity matrix is a bit wasteful but is needed to keep the recursion as simple as possible. Allowing for a NULL matrix to be used is also a good improvement.

Putting this all together in a custom Animator class, the final render cycle might look like this:

```
while (!renderStop)
{
    generateRenderBins(renderer.drawListOpaque,renderer.drawListTransp
arent,renderer.getScene().getSceneList());
```

```
        computeDrawListTransparentZDepth(renderer.getScene(),
    renderer.drawListTransparent);
        renderer.sortDrawListTransparentByDepth();
        renderer.render();
}
```

What we have created here is a versatile and useful system for general object rendering. It doesn't hide the details, but it also isn't overly complex. It's still not quite complete for many types of applications. For example, if we try to render really large and complex scenes, a city environment perhaps, we will get a very poor performance because we would be processing every object in the scene, even though the majority of the scene would not actually be in view of the camera. It turns out this particular problem has a high variance in terms of optimal solutions, depending on the type of scene itself. We will look at several approaches of dealing with this, but first we will take a slight detour and reexamine this rendering engine from a more top-down perspective. Geometry and matrix hierarchies are a great way to handle groups of objects cleanly and efficiently. However, in 3D graphics there exists an immediate successor to the simple geometry hierarchies, called the scene graph, which adds even more functionality, albeit by adding more complexity as well.

SCENE GRAPH: OBJECT-ORIENTED SCENES

A scene graph is a directed acyclic graph (DAG) that contains all of the data needed to render a 3D scene. Scene graphs are typically *n*-ary tree data structures, in which any node can contain any number of children. Scene graphs are also an object-oriented way to handle objects for a practical and organized 3D engine. These objects can be graphical objects, such as shapes and meshes, or nongraphical entities, such as lights, cameras, and sound objects, all organized in a scene hierarchy. Another thing that is special about scene graphs is that any particular node will inherit and concatenate the transformations and render states of its parents, just as our previous geometry hierarchy did.

Java is one of the easiest languages in which to write scene graphs because it is object oriented, and scene graphs are inherently object oriented, including the use of base classes, garbage collection, runtime type identification, and multithreading. Much of the design and implementation effort for C/C++ scene graphs is spent dealing with these issues that are already part of the Java platform.

Why Use a Scene Graph?

A well-implemented scene graph will take advantage of various techniques to achieve better performance with the graphics hardware without forcing the developer to be familiar with the complex algorithms it employs to achieve this. In addition, scene graphs abstract the rendering operations from a process-oriented problem to a data-oriented problem. This is the crux of what is considered retained-mode graphics, but scene graphs take this idea even further by adding additional scene-based behavior support, such as switching geometry, LOD geometry, and even updating the use of scene-based behaviors.

These techniques are generally designed to minimize the number of operations done on the host CPU and graphics commands sent to the graphics hardware API. In Java, this design has additional performance benefits because this means there should be fewer overall JNI calls and their associated overhead, as well.

Some of the techniques are hardware specific, such as OpenGL display lists, vertex arrays, and vertex buffer objects, just like our RenderShape used. Other techniques include many different types of *view culling* and render *state sorting*. View culling is used to determine which geometry lies either partially or wholly within the camera view. By eliminating the geometry that lies wholly outside the viewport, the number of geometry commands that are sent down the graphics pipeline is reduced. State sorting is also important because, if done properly, it can minimize costly render-state changes by optimally ordering the commands that it sends to the graphics hardware.

SCENE GRAPH COMPONENTS

Many different scene graphs have been developed down through the years, and their collective structures can vary quite a bit. However, there is a fair amount of common structures between them in general, and their basic structure can be distilled into a minimal set of unique classes that together make up the nebulous thing we call a scene graph and renderer.

The node types in a scene graph can be split into roughly two categories, Group nodes and Leaf nodes. Interior Group nodes structure the graph into logical groups and Leaf nodes carry the displayable geometry. The few classes that we created for our geometry hierarchy are a good place to start.

Group Nodes

As with our Group class, this is the core container class in the graph and contains a list of child nodes. They can be used for organizing the scene as well as a host of other operations. There can be many different derived types in any given scene graph API. For example:

- Transform groups store the transformation for child nodes (same as the earlier `TransformGroup`).
- Switch groups incorporate a mask or selection to hide or block traversals from particular child graphs. Switches can be used to dynamically change the look of a group of objects in a scene, switching between different sets. One example of this would be to switch from a regular-looking tank group to a damaged-looking tank group when a game tank is damaged. Additional variants of switches include the LOD group, where the group switches between child groups, based on distance to the camera, which changes the displayed geometry to a precreated lower-detail version. Sometimes this LOD action is handled through a behavior instead of an explicit graph-node type.
- Shared groups are a way to reuse or instance part of a scene graph. This allows for more efficient memory use when creating a more complex scene with numerous objects. In practice, though, it is quite difficult to implement and use correctly, and the idea of instancing is implemented in lesser ways.

Leaf Nodes

Leaf nodes hang at the bottom of the graph and have no children, but they may have other node-specific data and come in many different types.

3D Objects are the most important leaf node type in a scene graph because they specify the geometry objects that are to be rendered. This is analogous to our earlier `RenderShape` but can also include things such as raster images. A common interface style has proven to be useful and is used with little variation by most current scene graphs. It is based on splitting the data into separate arrays and is close to the OpenGL `VertexArray` interface, the same as our `VertexArraySet` class.

Rendering States

Rendering states are parameters of the rendering pipeline that relate to the appearance of an object. These parameters include color, texturing, and materials state as well as others, such as lighting and fog.

Materials are used to define the surface properties of the geometry. The attributes of the materials are mostly direct mappings from the OpenGL material states, that is, emissive, ambient, diffuse, and specular color and shininess.

Render state maintenance and control is one of the areas of greatest variance across different scene graphs.

Bounding Volumes

All nodes in a scene graph have some common attributes, one of them being the bounding volumes. The bounding volume of a node is a simple volume, usually an axis-aligned box or a sphere, that encloses the contents of all the nodes below the current one in the hierarchy. It is used by the scene graph to check the node for visibility and possibly for lighting scope and collision detection. If the bounding volume of the node is outside the visible area, all other nodes below in the hierarchy are also outside of the visible area, thus halting any further processing by the renderer and preventing the objects from being wastefully passed on to OpenGL. For large scenes, this can have a significant impact on rendering speed. See the following Visibility Culling section for more information.

Multithreading

Multithreading is an aspect that is growing in importance, given the current trend in processor designs to support multithreaded applications in the processor core. A number of scene graphs provide simple multithreading support, which allows simultaneous reading or rendering of the scene graph. For many applications, this is fine, but for more demanding applications that use asynchronous simulation threads needing consistent data, strong threading support will need to be built into the scene graph. For games, however, most renderers treat the application update and rendering as a single thread system, even if the game is multithreaded.

The previous nodes define just about everything needed to render rich 3D scenes without actually referencing specific OpenGL functions. Only the lowest-level rendering process actually has OpenGL calls in it, thus successfully abstracting the graphics commands from the developer-level scene graph objects.

SCENE GRAPH VISIBILITY CULLING

There are many useful operations that a scene graph system provides. Most critical operations involve graph traversals. Just like flattening a transform hierarchy for rendering, scene graphs are traversed to compute global object transforms. Some are also traversed to accumulate the render states when they are not leaf-node based. Sometimes they are traversed for a search to find all nodes of a particular type, and other times for specific individual nodes for game logic processing (that is, find all "door" nodes in a particular area).

One of the most important traversal operations is *view culling*. View culling is the process of removing from the render pipeline geometry that is not visible in the current view. Visibility-culling algorithms reduce the number of polygons sent down the rendering pipeline based on the simple principle that if something is not seen, it does not have to be drawn.

There are many popular algorithms for visibility culling in scene graphs. They can generally fall into the categories of backface culling, view frustum culling, occlusion culling, and portal culling.

Backface Culling

Backface culling is the simplest culling technique. It removes individual triangles in any given frame that are facing away from the viewer.

The idea is to treat polygons and triangles as essentially one-sided. If the polygon is turned so that the front surface is facing the viewer, then it is called frontfacing. Any polygons that are turned away are called backfacing. A frontfacing polygon needs to be rendered, but a backfacing polygon can be skipped. This step can be expected to cull roughly half of all the polygons in a given view (see Figure 15.5).

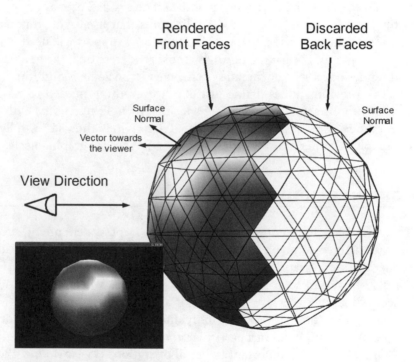

FIGURE 15.5   Backface culling applied to objects.

The basic test is that if the surface is normal and the vector formed to the viewer from the polygon is greater than 90 degrees (dot < 0.0), then the polygon must be backfacing and can be discarded (see Figure 15.6).

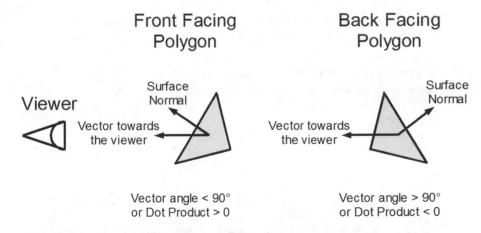

FIGURE 15.6 Backface culling single triangles.

There have been many optimizations developed for computing this test. Some attempt to speed surface-normal calculation; others transform the camera view vector into an object's local space to minimize vertex transformation. Still others use quick screen space algorithms to determine face direction. With graphics hardware ultimately handling the face render, there is little need to directly implement backface culling because it is a feature of modern 3D graphics hardware. Also, it is supported directly in OpenGL, so we can simply enable it through OpenGL in our render engine by adding the state to the Appearance class as an object attribute and update the renderer to use it.

In OpenGL glEnable(GL_CULL_FACE) is used to enable backface culling. As with all states enabled and disabled using glEnable and glDisable, it is disabled by default. In addition, OpenGL is not limited to backface culling. The glCullFace command can be used to specify the type of face culling desired, when face culling is enabled.

View Frustum Culling

View frustum culling is culling that uses the current view frustum to determine what is unseen. Perhaps the most implemented form of culling, it is based on the idea that only the scene objects that are in the current view volume need be drawn. To fully understand view frustum culling, we must first define what a view frustum is.

View Frustum

The *view frustum* is the shape of the viewing volume of space that includes everything currently visible from the viewpoint. It is defined by six clipping planes in the shape of a pyramid with the top chopped off. The six planes are typically named Near, Far, Top, Bottom, Left, and Right (see Figure 15.7). The Near and Far clipping planes could theoretically be defined as the viewpoint and infinity, but in practice they are not. Usually the Near plane is defined to be at a close forward distance, such as 0.1, and the Far plane at some greater distance relevant to scene size, such as 1000.0.

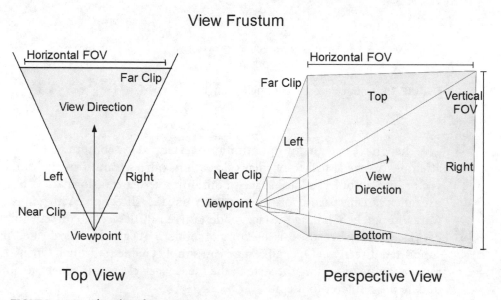

FIGURE 15.7 The view frustum.

If a polygon is entirely outside the view frustum, it cannot be visible and can be discarded. If it is completely inside, it should be sent down the rendering pipeline. If it is partially inside, it may be clipped to the planes so that its outside parts are removed.

Testing each individual polygon as is done with backface culling is almost never done these days because of 3D objects' complexity. Triangle count can be quite high because of the graphics hardware capabilities. Because the less-capable host CPU is doing the view frustum test, it would get bogged down testing so many triangles. Just as with 2D testing, pixel-to-pixel collision detection is usually preceded with a rectangle- or box-collision detection test to reduce overall tests. In 3D, per-triangle collision detection is first done with bounding volume tests.

Bounding Volumes

A bounding volume is a simplified approximation of the volume of a 3D object, used in, for example, view frustum culling. Although it is commonly a box, it can be almost any shape, such as a sphere, cylinder, or convex polyhedron (see Figure 15.8). Different shapes may be selected, depending on the nature of how the 3D object will be manipulated.

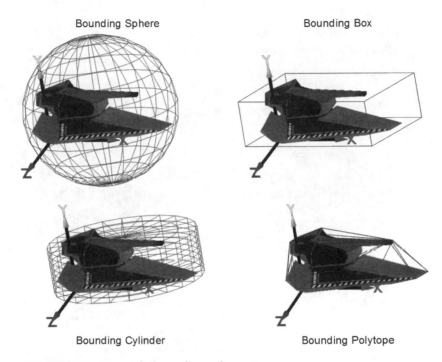

FIGURE 15.8 Example bounding volume types.

Often movable 3D objects will use a sphere because it requires minimal operations to update the sphere with the objects' motion, whereas static 3D worlds fill space with boxes that fit tightly together.

In a simple version of view frustum culling, each 3D object's bounding volume in the scene is tested against the six planes. Although this is a huge improvement over testing each individual polygon, the running cost of the algorithm scales linearly with scene object count. For a few hundred 3D objects, this may be okay, but for larger, more complex scenes, we can do much better than this by using a bounding volume hierarchy.

Bounding Volume Hierarchies

Bounding volume hierarchies are hierarchal data structures where each group node's bounds surrounds all of its children's bounds. Just as matrix hierarchies are a natural evolution for singly transformed 3D objects, bounding volume hierarchies help 3D object bounding volume tests scale to much larger 3D object groups.

There are two major types of bounding volume hierarchies—hierarchies that fit the underlining 3D objects as closely as possible, and spatial partitioning hierarchies that completely fill space so that every location within the hierarchies falls into at least one bounding volume.

Bounding volumes can start off simple but can quickly become complex, depending on the objects or scene, as shown in Figure 15.9 and Figure 15.10.

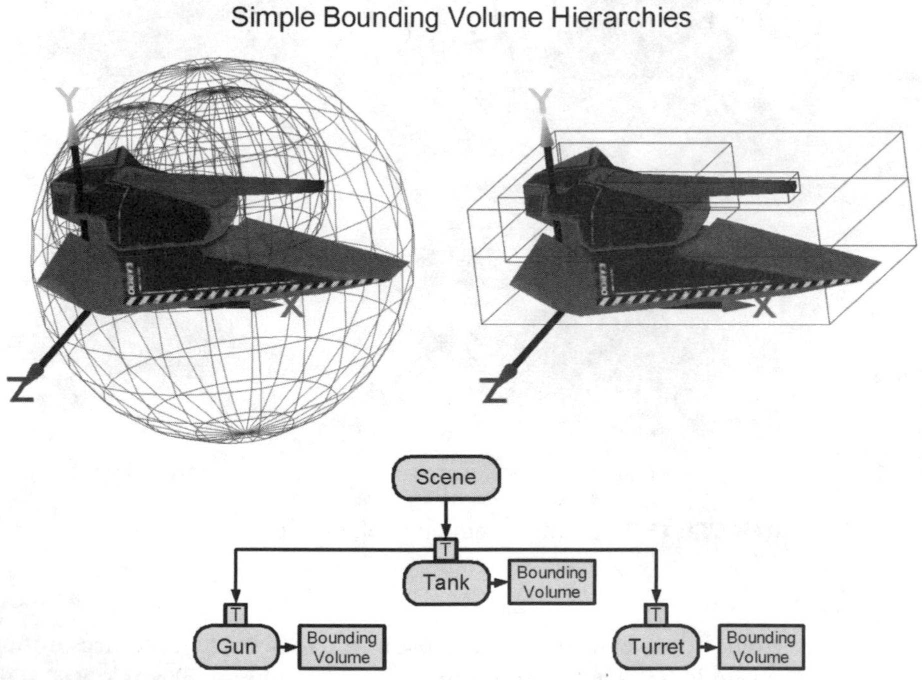

Simple Bounding Volume Hierarchies

FIGURE 15.9 Simple bounding volume hierarchies.

For view frustum culling, the bounding volume hierarchy is traversed top-down. If a node's bounds are completely in the view frustum, that entire subgraph can be marked for rendering or added to the render bins. If a node's bounds are

Complex Bounding Volume Hierarchies

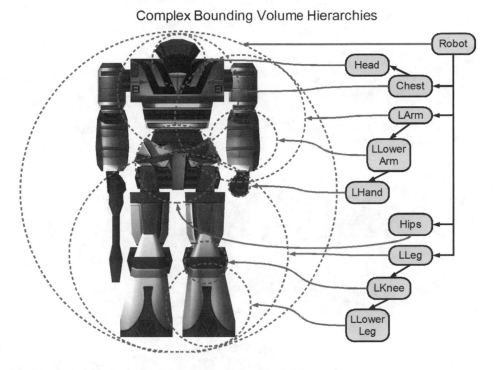

FIGURE 15.10   Complex bounding volume hierarchies.

completely out of the view frustum, the node and its remaining child graph can be skipped. If the bounds cross the frustum planes, then recursion continues on all of the children until done.

Spatial Partitioning Hierarchies

Spatial partitioning hierarchies typically subdivide 3D space into smaller sections using different dividing techniques, such as boxes or planes, and their resulting hierarchical organizational structures.

Two popular related techniques are the Quadtree and the Octree. Both use axis-aligned bounding boxes that are progressively subdivided into smaller boxes until some criteria is satisfied to stop the subdivision process (see Figure 15.11). This criteria is usually box size or number of objects contained in the box. Densely occupied areas will have many small bounds, whereas larger empty areas will be bounded with just one large box.

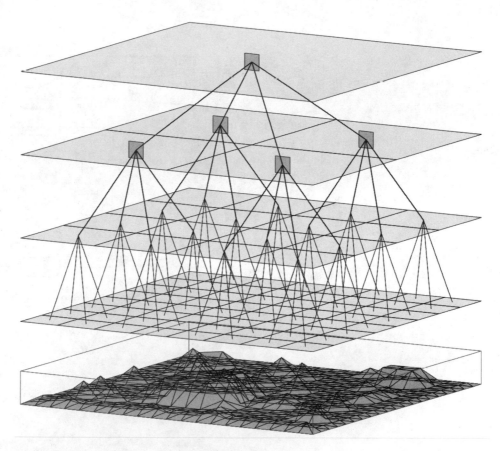

FIGURE 15.11   Quad tree spatial partitioning structure.

Occlusion Culling

Occlusion culling is a type of view culling where geometry that is occluded is not rendered, that is, geometry that is inside the view frustum but not visible in the final image because it is blocked from view by other geometry. This type of culling can offer an excellent performance gain for certain scenes with large numbers of 3D objects and large-size objects that block the view. An example case is a city scene, where large buildings block the view of many other large buildings.

Occlusion culling for static-world geometry can be precomputed somewhat, but for dynamic objects it is costly to determine totally correct occlusion culling. Finding occluded objects is akin to shadow algorithms and is typically more expensive to compute than the gain from removing the occluded objects. Other techniques such as cells and portals offer a good gaming alternative.

Cells and Portals

Full treatment of cells and portals are beyond the scope of this book but are mentioned because they are in growing use among 3D game renderers. The basic idea is to partition the world into chunks or cells, usually based on the geometry of the world. Portals connect the cells to each other, very much like nodes are connected by links in a graph structure. In the 3D world, the portals are typical doorways, windows, or other objects that the view can see through to other cells. The render pass begins in whatever cell the view is currently, and only needs to process this cell and any cells reachable through this cell's portals. With a well-organized cell-and-portal system, the renderer will be able quickly to cull large portions of the surrounding world.

FINAL THOUGHTS ON SCENE GRAPHS

Scene graphs are meant to be fairly automatic. After the graph is created and any other render parameters are set, the graph and renderer should update and render on its own. But that doesn't mean it will do anything interesting! User-defined behaviors and game logic are just as important as ever to make this automatic rendering system into a game. Hooking into and controlling the graph is the main way game logic makes a scene graph into an actual game.

Updates and Interaction

Because scene graphs can get fairly large in terms of nodes in the graph, traversing and searching in the graph for every game update frame is prohibitively expensive. What most games do is build their scene graphs at startup and also build a secondary layer to the graphs that enables easier and direct manipulation of scene graph nodes from outside of the graphs themselves. Often this secondary layer is more of what the game developer thinks of as the game engine. It is the data structures that are relevant to the actual game design, with objects that make sense in the game. For example, in a race game, the game design may wish to have a car class that contains all the data and methods a player's car needs in the game, including a reference to the car's 3D model.

Creating this game-oriented access layer can be done in many ways, and sometimes is even embedded in derived-scene graph nodes. Only the specific game's needs can determine the best design for this, and often this mapping of game-level objects to the scene graph representation can be quite challenging.

Content Loaders

The value of content loaders for a scene graph and even simpler geometry hierarchy renderers cannot be underestimated. A scene graph's ability to import specific content formats has been known to be the deciding factor for choosing one graph over another. This is one of the more tedious parts of building a custom scene graph system because marrying a scene graph's tree structures with file IO can be error prone. In addition to getting data loaded and mapped to scene graph nodes correctly, often the loader must do additional processing to optimize the scene graph it outputs because the data format it is loading is rarely in a runtime-optimized organization.

The subject of content loaders also leads to content creation, that is, creating the content that will be loaded into a scene graph. Content creation is the realm of the 3D artist and beyond this text but incredibly important nonetheless. Without the initial content, loaders have no meaning. Because of this, developers and artists have to work hand-in-hand to complete the 3D content production pipeline for quality 3D games.

Scene Graphs and Games

As was stated earlier, scene graphs are high-level graphics tools that hide the procedural realities of the low-level graphics API such as OpenGL. Because full-featured scene graphs such as those used in the simulation industry and VR are usually concerned with data management and not graphical special effects, sometimes they are not suitable for certain games. The problem is that this high-level layer often makes it difficult (or impossible) to create low-level graphics special effects that are possible and desired in games. What is desirable is a well-defined retained-mode renderer that has several of the useful features of scene graphs, such as a geometry hierarchy with inherit transforms, bounds support, and view culling, but that doesn't hide the underlying rendering process or exclude direct access. The following example attempts to satisfy this, although it is incomplete in terms of supporting the numerous possible geometric and rendering state data possible in OpenGL. Instead, it focuses on the immediately useful and practical, while being ready for extension through a number of programming options.

Scene graphs are often intended to heavily abstract away the complex and particular details of the underlying rendering software and hardware. Depending on the actual game requirements, a scene management system that is meant to give more object-oriented organization to rendering and not obstructing its fundamental functional nature, is optimal. It is a difficult balance to create a rendering system that is a higher level than OpenGL and generally enabling, but that isn't overly restrictive at the same time. One way to stay on course is to always choose the most straightforward technique or method when committing to a solution for a significant issue. When using or developing scene graphs, remember the mantra: Keep It Simple, Stupid (K.I.S.S)!

REAL-TIME 3D CHARACTER ANIMATION PRIMER

Character animation is a huge topic, with entire volumes dedicated to it. However, as a 3D game developer, it is important to understand the most general concepts and terms and their effect on renderer design. Straightforward coverage of character animation techniques relevant to 3D games is discussed in this section. It is intended to describe the current state of real-time 3D animation techniques as well as identify essential components for a useful and usable animation system.

The techniques are separated into three main layers, where each new layer builds on the previous one. The three layers will be referred to as core techniques, mid-level techniques, and high-level components.

Core Techniques

All geometric animation requires altering render vertex data in some way in each frame to create motion. There are several techniques for performing these alterations, and the final render object will need to be supported as a dynamic geometry type.

Camera animation does not use these vertex-based techniques, but it does use the techniques explained in the mid-level section.

Vertex Transformation

Vertex transformation is a vertex animation technique that dynamically alters vertex data in a polygon set in which all the vertices in a given set are uniformly transformed by applying a parent matrix. This action gives the effect of translating, rotating, and scaling the entire geometry object. The general shape of the object defined by the vertex set is unchanged. Usually, the original vertex data is left unchanged because the transformation is stored in a matrix separate from the vertex data and used only to produce the render geometry for a given frame or for accurate collision tests. This type of animation can be done using static vertex array data, as explained in the previous Static and Dynamic Geometry section.

Vertex Deformation

Vertex deformation is a vertex animation technique that dynamically alters vertex data in a polygon set in which particular vertices are transformed or otherwise altered independently of other vertices in the polygon set. This action gives the effect of deforming the sets geometry. The general shape of the object defined by the polygon set can be completely changed to a new shape. As with *vertex transformation*, usually the original vertex data is left unchanged because the transformation is stored in a matrix separately from the vertex data and used only to produce the render geometry for a given frame or for accurate collision tests. However, sometimes the deformation is meant as a permanent change to the vertex data, for example, in the case of dynamic vehicle or terrain damage. This type of animation would use what was previously called dynamic vertex arrays in the Static and Dynamic Geometry section.

Vertex Blending

Vertex blending generates a new model geometry by doing N-linear *interpolation* between blend shapes, based on given blend-shape weights. This type of animation would also need to use dynamic vertex arrays as the renderer retained-mode structure. *Blend shapes* are what we call the individual geometries used in vertex blending.

These three techniques can be encapsulated in various scene-object-based architectures.

Transformation: Simple insertion of a matrix transformation object upon the target polygon set.

Deformer: Object used to control a set or subset of vertices in a polygon set, possibly independent of the other vertices in the polygon set.

Sculpt deformer: Deformer that uses geometry to influence the shape of other geometry.

Morph object: Object that stores the blend shapes for vertex blending and performs the blending based on its current weights. For more see, "Morphing under Freeform Animation."

It is important to note that all or part of these techniques often end up being implemented directly in hardware, because graphics hardware has evolved to support the operations needed for these techniques.

Mid-Level Real-Time Animation Techniques

The core techniques are expanded on to build more sophisticated animation techniques. These higher-level animation techniques can be separated into two categories—hierarchical based and everything else. Here, everything else will be referred to as Freeform animation.

Hierarchical Animation

Hierarchical animation is any animation technique that uses a hierarchical data structure to animate the visual geometry.

Articulated animation: The simplest type of hierarchical character animation, where the character model is made up of groups of individual disjointed geometries that are animated using the vertex transformations technique based on keyframe data or procedural kinematics, usually in a hierarchical structure.

Skinned, *Skin and bones animation* (**or simply Skinning**): Similar to articulated animation, except that the final animated surface is made up of a continuous polygonal mesh that deforms to the underlining animated hierarchical structure. Skinning uses the vertex deformation technique. Because the "skin" geometry is deformed by some underlying structure, local transformations need to be computed to correctly deform the mesh, and *vertex weights* are often used to improve deformation across joints.

Vertex Weights: The amount of contribution an assigned bone, joint, transform, or other deformer applies to the given vertex. Multiple deformers can influence a vertex by assigning the associate deformers and determining how much each deformer influences the vertex by using a weight. Weights usually range from 0.0 to 1.0, where the total of all weights for a given vertex usually must equal 1.0.

Facial animation: Animation that uses skinning as its basis but has the added requirement of playback blending, usually multiple weights, and audio synchronization.

Rigid-body dynamics: A type of physics simulation where the individual objects act as rigid bodies, that is, they have physical-based motion and collision, but do not deform during motion and collision. This type of animation can be achieved using *articulated animation* and kinematics.

Templates: Reusable animation hierarchies, often parameter controlled, used to minimize memory for hierarchical character animation.

Freeform Animation

Freeform animation is any animation technique that makes changes to the vertex data in polygon sets to animate the visual geometry that does not follow a strict structure. Examples include the surface of water, special effects, deformation due to collision, morphing, and so on. There are potentially an unlimited number of animation possibilities that fall under Freeform animation, but all require dynamic vertex data sets as their core retained data structure.

Cloth animation: Animation that deforms nearly every, if not all, vertices in a polygon set and often performs some physics and collision detection to affect that deformation.

Morphing: Almost the same as vertex blending but often formalized as a higher-level object, as presented here. Morphing generates a new model geometry by doing *N*-linear interpolation between blend shapes, based on given blend shape weights.

Soft-body dynamics: A type of physical simulation where the individual objects act as soft bodies, that is, they have physical-based motion and collision but deform during motion and collision. This type of animation can be simulated using skinned animation but usually is implemented as freeform animation and dynamics simulation.

Animated textures: Textures that change from frame to frame. The textures are usually preloaded static texture images that repeat, for example, fire or flame textures for a torch object.

Dynamic textures: Animated textures that use dynamic texture images. These can be compressed movie formats rendered on a polygon, such as .mpg or .avi. The movie files can be loaded into main memory or come from a streaming source. They can also be dynamically generated as in the case of a changing fractal cloud texture or a mirror effect that uses an actual view rendered to a textured surface.

Support Objects

Also worth noting is the role of other support objects for mid-level animation. Bounding volumes are nonrendered geometry used to represent other geometry for spatial testing, as described earlier, but here can be used for point containment for joint, bones, or other deformer assignments.

Interpolators: Objects that perform the process of determining from two or more values what the in-between values should be.

It is important to note that the implementations of these techniques can vary somewhat, but for the most part the techniques are well known and alternate implementations should not affect a well-designed interface.

High-Level Animation Components

Finally, at the highest level of real-time 3D animation, the animation data needs to be managed in an efficient and flexible manner as well as support integration with other motion systems, such as physics or direct game logic control.

These techniques include but are not limited to:

Keyframe data management, control, playback, blending, and loading: This is often what is thought of as the Animation engine, but as we can see, this is only the top layer of a large process.

Animation data loaders: Needed for popular animation packages and of primary importance to developers. These loaders load the animation data generated by animation packages into the *keyframe data management* system.

Physics and dynamics systems: Can use the underlying animation support for managing and maintaining the objects the physics simulators want to manipulate. Physics systems often need access to higher-level information as well, such as an object hierarchy that it is meant to control and have the animation system deform to the manipulated hierarchy.

It is important to note that the high-level animation components vary greatly in their implementations and capabilities from system to system and from game to game.

SUMMARY

Creating a developer-friendly, robust, full-featured 3D render engine can be a large and difficult task but not without its rewards. Balancing the need for automation and direct control can be particularly difficult. Even for a well-defined domain such as 3D games, design and implementation may be at odds, and for wide domains, may not be resolvable. Fortunately, there is plenty of help in the form of Java and JOGL and well-developed structures and techniques for specific capabilities can be assembled into a usable, working render engine that can satisfy the most demanding game design.

16 | 3D Collision Detection and Response

In This Chapter

- Introduction
- Static Object-to-Object Collision-Detection Techniques
- Foundation Object Collision Tests
- Linear Feature Collisions
- Plane Collisions
- Summary

INTRODUCTION

Simply put, *collision detection* is the process of determining if two objects have collided by testing their bounds or a spatial overlap. The word *objects* can be used to mean many different things, such as statistical data or even ideas, but in 3D games we usually mean geometric objects. Collision detection is inherently a boolean operation, that is, for any given objects there exists either a collision or there does not—their collision is either true or false. Often, determining this is enough to handle the collision and then continue with other collision testing or game logic. However, simply determining collision detection may not provide enough information to handle the collision in a particular way, for example, when affecting object motion. In this case, we may need to compute object *intersections* as well. An intersection is the point or set of points at the location where one line, surface, or solid crosses another during a collision.

The process of collision detection can generate what we call *collision events*. An event is simply a point in time and space. Collision events would typically also have references to the two colliding objects and any other useful information based on how the collision should be handled.

The process of handling the collision is called *collision response* or reaction. What should happen or how the objects or surfaces involved in the collision event react is based on game design. Collision response can be as simple as removing the colliding objects, say, in the case of a weapon projectile hitting a target, or as complex as simulating the physical reaction that would result when two real objects collide.

In addition, for resolving contacts, a description of the contact area is often required. This is often called the *penetration depth* of the collision. The penetration depth of a pair of intersecting objects is the shortest vector over which one object needs to be translated to bring the pair in touching contact so that they are no longer interpenetrating. This is often the first step in creating a physical-looking collision response.

Collision detection has been studied and developed in many different disciplines far beyond games, including robotics, computer graphics, computer-aided design, and computational geometry. There are as many approaches and algorithms for collision detection as there are systems computing it. More specifically, there is no standard way to do general 3D collision detection. Some systems precompute collision detection in advance of the motion they are analyzing, such as in some factory robotic systems. Other systems can afford only inaccurate collision detection, possibly for object selection or high-level decision making, which can be implemented with approximation techniques.

Collisions in Games

Depending on the actual gameplay desired, 3D games can sometimes require the most demanding real-time collision detection systems. The constraints are confining and demanding. The collision detection must execute as quickly as possible and as accurately as possible given the game geometry, on consumer-level processing hardware and in relatively low-memory systems. Implementing collision-detection techniques within these constraints makes game-collision detection a challenging topic in game development.

Good collision detection and reaction is fundamental to a positive gaming experience. Collision detection is central to 3D games that simulate interactions of the physical world. Even in games that are not performing physical simulations, collision detection is important for all kinds of other gaming operations. For example, as was expressed in Chapter 15, "3D Render Using JOGL," view frustum culling for render engines is at its core a collision-detection problem. One of the best ways game AI can assess the game world situation for decision making is by using data gathered from collision detections. Finally, player game control is often based on interaction through collision detection.

Collision detection can be done in many ways. There isn't a single generic algorithm that works for all collision types. Depending on the objects being represented by the game, completely different-collision detection techniques may be used for different classes of objects. In addition, what the objects are doing at the stage where collision will be computed can affect which collision detection algorithm to use. For example, fast-moving objects often need collision detection algorithms that are significantly modified from their static and slower moving objects' counterparts. Often they will use different geometry than the actual object being represented.

Usually game data is organized to make collision testing as efficient as possible. Only the bare minimum should be computed to prevent wasting any runtime cycles. There is no point in computing the intersection volume of a sphere and a cylinder if simply finding that an overlap exists will do. In addition, there are often different techniques for computing collision detection versus computing intersections of a set of objects, and it pays to know what needs to be computed in advance of the tests.

Basic Collision-Detection Processing

Collision detection requires special data structures and management, and objects often need to be processed together in groups to achieve maximum performance for general scenes. Also, at what point in the game execution collision detection is processed can have direct impact on the accuracy and response perceived by the player. Typically, it is the last thing done before the scene is set for the render frame. Using collision detection for game objects could be processed as described in the following stages as shown in Figure 16.1.

For each game object:

1. Compute the object's new movement based on user input, AI control, game events or physics.
2. For collidable objects, check if the new movement violates any other game geometry via collision detection.
   a. If no collision occurs, then the motion is allowed. Do nothing.
   b. If collision occurs, determine the desired reaction, such as generating a game event (power up, explosion, and so on), correcting the movement based on collision information, or compute reaction motion.
3. Render scene.
4. Rinse and repeat.

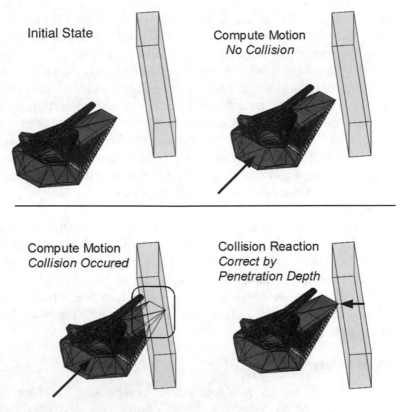

Initial State

Compute Motion
No Collision

Compute Motion
Collision Occured

Collision Reaction
*Correct by
Penetration Depth*

FIGURE 16.1 The Collision detection process.

Even with this general sequence, it's possible that some game collision testing won't quite fit in so well. For example, user input in the form of mouse clicks or other picking mechanisms, as well as instantaneous weapons such as a laser beam or even bullets, may need to have collision detection computed in the action routines. Because these types of actions are not implemented as objects moving through the world, they require immediate collision tests and collision events processing outside of step 2, where the general object-to-object collision detection is processed.

In a ideal game engine, collision detection would be precise, efficient, and very fast. These requirements mean that the collision-detection process will need to have fast access to the scene geometry. Unfortunately, modern games contain too much 3D data for per-frame brute-force methods to finish quickly enough. More elegant methods have been developed, because checking each polygon of an object against every other polygon in the scene takes too long. Even determining whether an object's geometry only penetrates the world's geometry would be too computationally expensive with this method.

A note about 2D collisions: when applicable, use 2D collision tests for 3D worlds. There are many cases where a cheaper 2D test can be used in place of a more expensive 3D algorithm. For example, finding the local ground triangle on which a character is located may be possible to do in 2D if the ground on which the character is standing holds its basic shape when projected flat. Many terrain collision systems use only a character's x- and z-coordinates to quickly find the triangle they would be standing on from a table and then compute the y-coordinate (height) at the point on the triangle. This method is much cheaper than performing general 3D triangle tests, which would yield the same results.

Bounding Volumes

The most popular way of improving collision-detection performance is to approximate each object or a part of the object with a *bounding volume*, and then process the bounding volumes of collision (see Figure 16.2). This method is widely used for approximate collisions but also in place of accurate and exact collisions instead because it's much more computationally efficient than computing exact collisions.

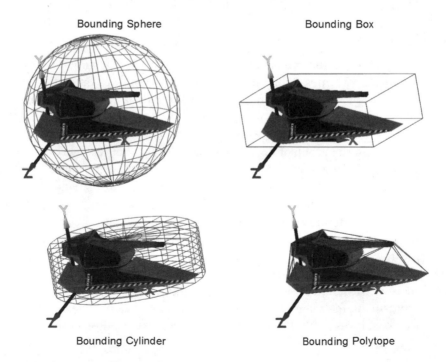

FIGURE 16.2 Example bounding volume types.

Whereas simpler bounding volume collision calculations are much quicker than processing the more complex visual scene geometry, the collision results are imprecise and may often require further refinement, depending on the need for accuracy. Using bounding volumes collision detection as a first step before processing the bounded geometry for the final, more accurate tests offers a good balance between final execution speed and collision accuracy.

In addition, it is possible to process individual object bounding volume pairs one at a time, followed by exact collision detection on passing candidates or while queuing the candidates for later bulk exact collision-detection processing. Unfortunately, this is terribly inefficient for the large scenes of today's games.

Efficient and Accurate Collision Detection for Complex Scenes

As scene complexity increases, even scene geometry wrapped in bound volumes will become too expensive to test because in a general collision system, each collidable bounding object needs to be compared to every other one, making the final bounds-to-bounds test equal to the square of the number of collidable objects. For example, in a scene with 100 possible collidable bounding volumes, there would be 99 * 99 = 9801 collision tests! (99 because for any object it must test against the remaining 99, but not itself.) That is a lot of tests for 100 objects, and a typical game these days could contain more than a 1,000 collidable world objects or surfaces.

Bounding Volume Hierarchies

One technique for greatly reducing the n^2 object pair testing is to use a hierarchy of bounding volumes. A hierarchy of bounding volumes or spatial partition groups greatly improves performance, albeit with a tradeoff in memory use. Let's look at an example.

We could represent a whole group of objects as one large sphere completely containing the group of objects and then check whether the large sphere intersects with any other objects' bounds in the scene. If collision is detected, to increase the precision we can subdivide the big sphere into a set of smaller spheres and check each one of those for collision as well. (See Figures 16.3 and 16.4.) We can then continue to subdivide and check until we are satisfied with the approximation. This is the basic idea of a bounding volume hierarchy. If the hierarchies' subdivisions and group bounds are properly built in advance of the collision testing, the bounding collision tests can be performed quickly and efficiently at runtime.

Collision object hierarchies and bounding volume collision detection really go hand-in-hand to complete an optimal collision system. The overall collision detection cost is decreased because the hierarchy makes finding potential collisions faster than large linear searches that would be used on a scene list. Also, in an elegant way,

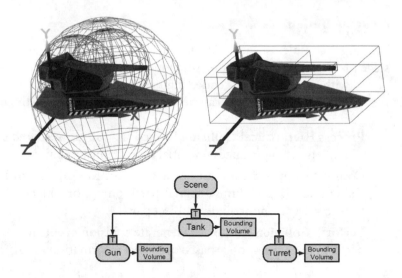

FIGURE 16.3 Simple bounding volume hierarchy.

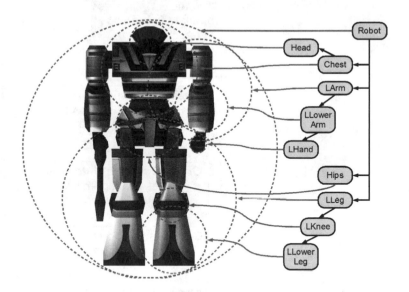

FIGURE 16.4 Complex bounding volume hierarchy.

they allow us to trade accuracy for speed, depending on how we build and use the hierarchy.

Collision Engine Design

For large, complex scenes, collision detection can be implemented as a several-stage process and can be further developed into an engine of sorts that can be integrated with game logic and render engines as illustrated in Figure 16.5. Specifically, real-time collision detection can be split into at least three distinct steps:

Process Hierarchical Collision Detection: Called *sweep and prune* or *collision culling*, this step produces potential object collision pairs.

Compute Approximate and Exact Object-to-Object Collision Detection: Using bounding volumes, spatial partitioning, or object geometry collision tests to reject all noncolliding object pairs.

Perform Collision Response: Generate collision events for the game logic, or perform proper response based on object information or engine design.

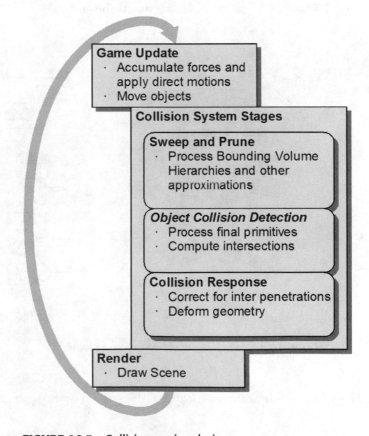

FIGURE 16.5 Collision engine design.

To be able to get this engine up and running, we need classes for building collision hierarchies and spatial partitioning structures, collidable objects, techniques for representing different types of bounding volumes, and the algorithms for determining their collisions, as well as equivalent classes for processing exact collisions with scene object geometry or its proxies.

Object to Object versus Object to World

In addition to using bound hierarchies to speed up things, we can also divide our collision tests into two major categories, object-to-object collisions and object-to-world collisions. This is an artificial division because in reality there is no difference between these two types of collisions. However, in games, often the objects and resulting collision information needed for gameplay is very different. Typical object-to-object collisions require only a true-or-false-type detection for triggering game events, such as a weapon hit or picking up a powerup. Object-to-world collisions often require additional information about the collision, usually in the form of intersection, particularly for computing the desired collision response for player motions, such as navigation. There is no reason why collision detection techniques for either type can't be used in either situation, but as we will see, it is advantageous to view these techniques from this perspective.

Static Objects versus Dynamic Objects

Another reason we denote collision tests as object-to-object or object-to-world is because quite often the game "world" is a static set of geometry, in which case these world objects' bounds are unchanging. This means the world objects' bounds will not need to be dynamically updated during the game, which can lead to many optimizations.

Any moving object can then be said to be dynamic, which means that the object's bounds must also be moved along with the object. Because the bounds of moving objects will be changing by definition, dynamic objects in collision hierarchies require additional runtime hierarchical processing. Parent nodes in the hierarchy are meant to contain all of their children's bounds, so any object below them in the hierarchy that is dynamically changing its bounds must bubble up the changes, that is, it must somehow notify its parent(s) that its bounds have changed and, therefore, they too must modify their bounds accordingly. This process can get complex and expensive at runtime, depending on many factors, such as the depth of the hierarchy, amount and frequency of the movement, and the cost of modifying or recalculating bounding volumes. Therefore, dynamic objects are often managed in their own structure, separate from the main scene bounding volume hierarchy.

Static versus Dynamic Collisions

In addition, moving objects may require a slightly different set of collision-detection algorithms than nonmoving world geometry. Updating a moving object and then testing its updated bounds for collisions against the rest of the scene is the typical process, as described earlier. However, *static collision detection* tests, which examine only the current object's bounds with other objects' current bounds, may fail, depending on the object's velocity as relates to its size and other possible collision objects.

The reason is that because of the discrete nature of a 3D game (or any computer-based simulation), when the collision system executes it processes only a snapshot of the game's collidable objects' current states. It is possible that between the last game state and the current game state, fast-moving objects will pass right through each other and basic static collision tests will not detect the collision that would have happened between the last frame and the current. This situation is illustrated in Figure 16.6. In the first frame, the static collision test luckily detects the bounding sphere collision as it collides with the box. In the second frame, the displacement between frames is great enough that the static frame-to-frame collision detection fails to catch the bounding sphere passing through the box. To properly prevent this collision failure, either the object must not be allowed to move more than its width in one frame, multiple static collision detection tests must be run, or a more sophisticated dynamic collision test accounting for the volume the object traveled between the frames must be used.

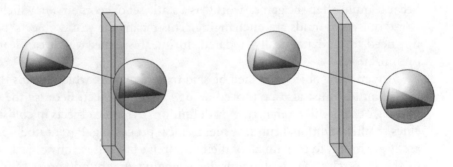

FIGURE 16.6 Static collision success and failure.

STATIC OBJECT-TO-OBJECT COLLISION-DETECTION TECHNIQUES

As stated earlier in this chapter, there is no universal or single generic technique for computing object-to-object collisions. Here we present a collection of the most used and most useful collision-detection techniques for 3D games using the basic set of primitive geometries shown in Figure 16.7. This is by no means an all-inclusive set because there are uncountably more possible combinations and choices for primitive object types, but they become ever more specialized and less generally useful. In any case, this is an excellent foundation for understanding basic collision techniques and developing end solutions beyond this set.

These will be additionally divided into related sections, bundled by techniques and solution complexities.

Basic Collision Primitives

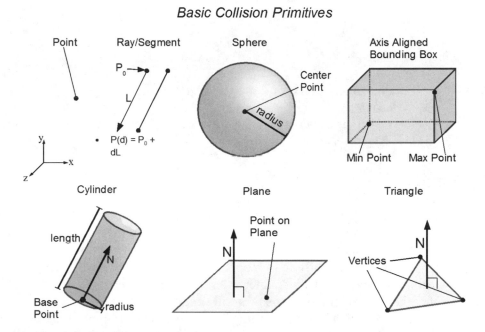

FIGURE 16.7 Collisions object types.

Foundation Collision Type Definitions

The first thing in any geometric-based algorithm is to decide on the data representation for that geometry. Some types have an obvious or common way of representation, such as a sphere with a center and radius, and others may have several options, such as axis-aligned bound boxes using min/max points or a center point and half-height and half-width, for example. Sometimes committing to one representation may make a later collision algorithm more expensive to compute. Usage will help dictate the design, and without prior knowledge of how the type will be used, developing an optimal solution is often error prone. The implementations

TABLE 16.1   Collision Object Type Table

	Point	Ray	Sphere	AABB	Cylinder	Plane	Triangle
Point	C	C	C	C	C	C	C
Ray	C	LL,A	C	C	LL,A	C,I	C,I
Sphere	C	C	C	C	C	C,I	F
AABB	C	C	C	C	C	F	A
Cylinder	C	LL,A	C	C	LL,A	A	A
Plane	C	C,I	C,I	F	A	X	A
Triangle	C	C,I	F	A	A	A	A

Legend

C = Collision detection
I = Intersection
A = Fallback test—can use AABB, Sphere, or Segment tests as approximations
LL = Rare case, uses 3D line-to-line intersection; see resources.

chosen here lend themselves to efficient performance while attempting to stay simple to understand. For a final project, the developer may choose to use an alternative representation if there is a particular advantage to do so.

To begin, let's first define some example objects. We will attempt to use classes from the previous math chapter where it makes sense.

For a test point or vertex, we will simply use the Vector class.

For an axis-aligned bounding box, we will choose a min/max point representation where the two points define the limits of the space that AABB is meant to contain.

Here is the minimal new class, AABoundingBox:

```
/**
 * Axis-Aligned Bounding Box.
 * The min and max fields are public so they can be set and read
directly.
 */
public class AABoundingBox
{
    public Vector3f max = new Vector3f();
    public Vector3f min = new Vector3f();
```

```
public AABoundingBox()
{
}

public void setMinMax( Vector3f _min, float _max )
{
    min.set( _min );
    max.set( _max );
}

public void translate( Vector3f pos )
{
max.add( pos );
min.add( pos );
}

public String toString()
{
    return min.x + " " + min.y + " " + min.z + " " + max.x + "
    " + max.y + " " + max.z;
}
}
```

The typical accessor `setMinMax()` method implements a value copy to set the min and max points. However, because the min and max points are public, they can be set directly by passing the accessor. This is intentional for maximum easy access and for the possibility of sharing points with target objects. This situation could be a problem if the user were to set them to NULL, which will cause errors in most routines because normally they would not be checking for NULL. A production class may prevent this access and additionally check for passed in NULLs for safety if the application has no need to set the min and max points directly.

There is also a convenience method for translating the box, useful for moving along with the object it is meant to contain.

And finally, the usual `toString()` method is included.

For a sphere we'll use the center and radius representation, again using `Vector3f`.

The sphere fields are public and also have accessors that perform copying as with the `AABoundingBox`. The same caveats apply.

And, of course, `toString()` is included.

```
/**
 * Bounding Sphere.
 */
```

```
public class BoundingSphere
{
    public Vector3f center = new Vector3f();
    public float radius = 1.0f;

    public Sphere()
    {
    }

    public Sphere( Vector3f c, float r )
    {
        center.set( c );
        radius = r;
    }

    public void set( Vector3f c, float r )
    {
        center.set( c );
        radius = r;
    }

    public void setCenter( Vector3f c )
    {
        center.set( c );
    }

    public void setRadius( float r )
    {
        radius = r;
    }

    public String toString()
    {
        return "Sphere < " + center + " Radius " + radius;
    }
}
```

FOUNDATION OBJECT COLLISION TESTS

This class of objects is essentially orientation-less, which greatly simplifies the testing procedures. Nevertheless, these are among the most important types because of all collision detection, they are cheapest to compute and, therefore, the most used.

Point- or Sphere-to-Sphere

Point-to-sphere is one of the simplest collision tests. Using the standard distance formula

$$d = \sqrt{(x2-x1)^2 + (y2-y1)^2 + (z2-z1)^2}$$

compute the distance between the point and the sphere center. If the distance is less than the sphere radius, there is a collision.

The main improvement to this test is to use the distance squared and the radius squared for the comparison to avoid computing the expensive square root operation. Because we are not really concerned with knowing the actual point-to-sphere distance and that the relative distance squared will generate the same collision profile as the more expensive square root distance, we can substitute the D < R test with $D^2 < R^2$. This is mathematically legal because both D and R are positive; therefore, after squaring them the inequality still holds true.

Testing two spheres is similarly done. All that needs to change is to compute the distance between the two sphere centers and compare the result to the sum of the two spheres' radii. Again, alternatively computing the squared result is a valid optimization.

Point- or AABB-to-AABB

Point- or AABB-to-AABB determination is a simple set of inequalities based on the AABB's extents and the point's components. These are by far the cheapest collision object tests and, as a result, often the most used.

```
static public boolean isCollide( AABoundingBox bb1, Vector3f
position )
{
    if ( bb1.min.x < position.x &&
        bb1.min.y < position.y  &&
        bb1.min.z < position.z  &&
        bb1.max.x > position.x  &&
        bb1.max.y > position.y  &&
        bb1.max.z > position.z )
        return true;
    else
        return false;
}
```

These four techniques are summarized in Figure 16.8.

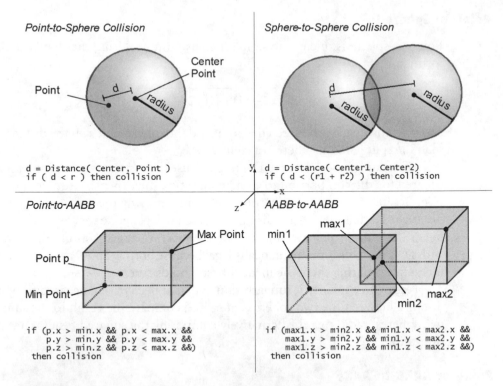

FIGURE 16.8   Point- to-AABB and -Sphere collisions.

Sphere-and-AABB

A fast approximation technique for sphere-and-AABB collision detection is to essentially replace the sphere with a temporary AABB and perform an AABB-to-AABB test where the new box is set to the size of the sphere.

Another way is to add the sphere radius to the AABB and perform the simple point-to-AABB test using the sphere center.

Both of these produce a false-positive collision in the case where the sphere is near the box's corners. The error can be fairly small, depending on the relative size of the box and sphere, and because AABBs and spheres are usually approximations to other geometry that will be used in further testing anyway, this error is often considered acceptable (see figure 16.9).

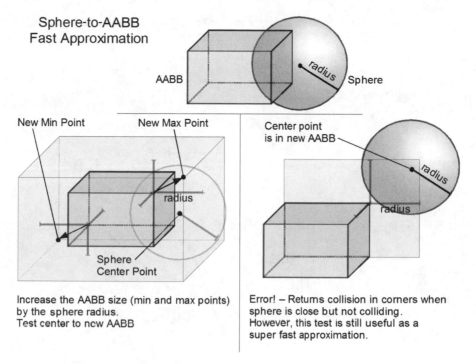

Sphere-to-AABB
Fast Approximation

AABB   Sphere

New Min Point   New Max Point

Center point
is in new AABB

radius

Sphere
Center Point

Increase the AABB size (min and max points) by the sphere radius. Test center to new AABB

Error! – Returns collision in corners when sphere is close but not colliding. However, this test is still useful as a super fast approximation.

FIGURE 16.9   Sphere-and-AABB collision.

LINEAR FEATURE COLLISIONS

This set of collision tests have in common the need to process linear features; a line, ray, or line segment are part of their solutions.

Point-to-Line/Ray

Although not strictly a collision test, finding the closest point on a line is useful for many other collision tests, such as determining nearby objects or for object selection. As we shall see, it also introduces the concept of *Vector Projection*, which is the foundation for the series of collisions of linear features as well as many other types.

Given: Line and Test Point

$$\text{Line point} = Ppt$$

$$\text{Ray direction vector} = \mathbf{N}$$

$$\text{Test point} = Tpt$$

The first step is to create a vector from P point to the test point:

$$\mathbf{V} = \text{Tpt} - \text{Ppt}$$

See Figure 16.10.

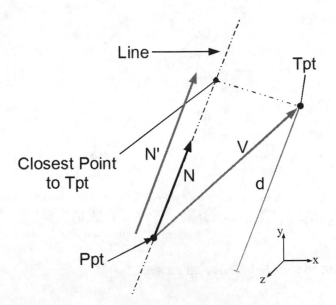

FIGURE 16.10   Closest point on a line.

The main technique in this test is the next step. Called vector projection, we will build a new vector that is equal to the projection of vector **V** onto the vector **N**. The approach we will take is to require that the line direction vector **N** be normalized prior to performing vector projection. This routine could normalize **N**, but in some cases this may be a waste of time when the line direction vector is already normalized.

In any case, **N** must be known to be unit-length to continue. If and when it is, then compute the vector projection of **V** onto **N**.

Let d = the dot product of vectors **N** and **V**, then scale vector **N** by d to create vector **N'**. It can be written as the following formula:

$$\text{Vector Projection: } \mathbf{N'} = \mathbf{N}(\mathbf{N} \text{ dot } \mathbf{V}))$$

Finally, add the new vector **N'** to the line point P to find a test point projected onto the line, or the closest point to Tpt on the line.

$$\text{Closest Point to Tpt} = \text{Ppt} + \mathbf{N'}$$

Line/Ray-to-Sphere

Ray-to-sphere, as well as the remaining linear feature collisions in this section, are simply modifications of the closest point on a line technique. Refer back to that test for more details.

Given: Line/Ray and Sphere

$$\text{Line point} = \text{Ppt}$$

$$\text{Ray direction vector} = \mathbf{N}$$

$$\text{Sphere center point} = \text{Cpt}$$

$$\text{Sphere radius} = r$$

See Figure 16.11.

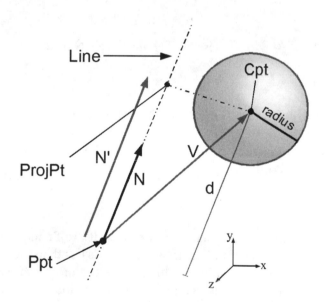

FIGURE 16.11 Ray-to-sphere collision.

First, create the vector from point P to the sphere center point.

$$\mathbf{V} = \text{Cpt} - \text{Ppt}$$

Next, compute the vector projection of $\mathbf{V}$ onto $\mathbf{N}$ as defined in Point-to-Line/Ray.

Let $d =$ the dot product of vectors $\mathbf{N}$ and $\mathbf{V}$, then scale vector $\mathbf{N}$ by d to create $\mathbf{N}'$.

The difference between computing ray-to-sphere and line-to-sphere lies in this step.

Because d is the scalar projection of **V** along **N**, if d is negative, that means that the sphere is behind the line point Ppt with respect to the direction vector **N**. In that case, the ray would not collide with the sphere, so a quick check of $d < 0$ before continuing can reject failed ray collision. Otherwise, the sphere is in front of the ray and still can be a possible collision, and the rest of the test will need to be completed.

For a line, no extra test is needed, because by definition a line is meant to go on to infinity in both directions.

For Ray

$$d = \mathbf{N} \text{ dot } \mathbf{V}$$

if $(d < 0)$ // if d is negative no collision

{ return false; }

else $\mathbf{N'} = (\mathbf{N})d$; // scale **N** by d

For Line

Vector Projection: $\mathbf{N'} = \mathbf{N}(\mathbf{N} \text{ dot } \mathbf{V}))$

Now, add the vector **N'** to point P to find the sphere center projected onto the line and call it ProjPt.

$$\text{ProjPt} = \text{Ppt} + \mathbf{N'}$$

Finally, compute the distance between point ProjPt and sphere center Cpt and compare it to the sphere radius. If the distance is less than the radius, there is collision. As with sphere-to-sphere collision, the distance squared can be computed and compared to the radius square as an optimization.

if (distance(ProjPt, Cpt) < r) { return true; } //collision

Alternate:

if (distanceSquared(ProjPt, Cpt) < r*r) { return true; }
//alternate test using more efficient distance squared.

Point-to-Cylinder

Point-to-cylinder is nearly the same as the previous test, with the exception that cylinder has a base point and length. Unlike the line/ray, this means that the body of the cylinder is a line segment, and the base and length must be tested for rejecting projected points beyond those points on the line.

Given Cylinder and Test Point:

$$\text{Cylinder base point} = \text{Bpt}$$

$$\text{Cylinder normal} = \text{N}$$

$$\text{Cylinder radius} = \text{r}$$

$$\text{Cylinder length} = \text{L}$$

$$\text{Test point} = \text{Tpt}$$

See Figure 16.12.

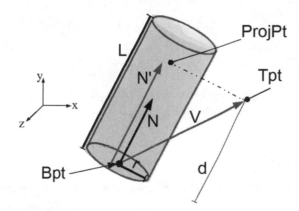

FIGURE 16.12   Point-to-cylinder collision.

First, create the vector from base point to the test point:

$$\mathbf{V} = \text{Tpt} - \text{Bpt}$$

Next, let d = the dot product of vectors $\mathbf{N}$ and $\mathbf{V}$, and compare d against 0 and the cylinder length to determine if the test point falls within the bottom and top of the cylinder. When $\mathbf{N}$ is normalized, as was required for these algorithms in the beginning of this section, the value of d is equal to the distance along vector $\mathbf{N}$ of vector $\mathbf{V}$'s projection. Because of this fact, d can be used to compare against the cylinder length for rejecting test points beyond the end of the cylinder.

$$d = \mathbf{N} \text{ dot } \mathbf{V} : \text{if } (\ d < 0 \ || \ d > \text{L} \ ) \ \{ \text{ return false; } \} \ //\text{no collision}$$

If we make it this far, then scale **N** by *d*. (This completes the vector projection of **V** onto **N**, **N'**=**N**(**N** dot **V**).)

$$\mathbf{N'} = D(\mathbf{N})$$

Now, add the new vector **N'** to the base point to find a test point projected onto the cylinder (closest point on line):

$$ProjPt = Bpt + \mathbf{N'}$$

Finally, compute the distance between point ProjPt and the test point Tpt and compare it to the cylinder radius. If the distance is less than the radius, there is collision. As with sphere-to-sphere collision, the distance squared can be computed and compared to the radius square as an optimization.

if (Distance(ProjPt, Tpt) < r) { return true; } //collision

Alternate:

if (distanceSquared(ProjPt, Tpt) < r*r) { return true;}
//alternate test using more efficient distance squared.

Sphere-to-Cylinder

Sphere-to-cylinder is the same as point-to-cylinder with two exceptions. First, when testing for the end of the cylinder, the sphere radius must be concerned. Second, the final distance is modified to test between two spheres.

Given Cylinder and Sphere:

Cylinder base point = Bpt

Cylinder normal = N

Cylinder radius = rC

Cylinder length = L

Sphere center point = Cpt

Sphere radius = rS

See Figure 16.13.

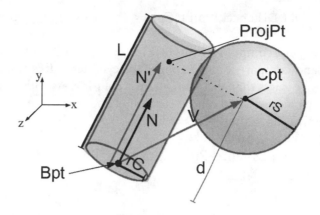

FIGURE 16.13 Sphere-to-cylinder collision.

First, create the vector from the base point to the test point:

$$\mathbf{V} = \text{Tpt} - \text{Bpt}$$

Next, let d = the dot product of vectors $\mathbf{N}$ and $\mathbf{V}$ and compare d against 0–rC and length+rC to determine if the test point falls within the bottom and top of the cylinder. By using 0–rC and length+rC we are extending the cylinder in both directions to account for the spheres radius. When the test sphere is near the ends of the cylinder it would fail to produce collisions when the center point was past the ends of the cylinder without this extra step.

$$d = \mathbf{N} \text{ dot } \mathbf{V} : \text{if } (\ d < -\text{rC} \ || \ d > \text{L+rC}\ ) \ \{ \text{ return false; } \} \ // \text{ no collision}$$

If d passes the previous test, then scale $\mathbf{N}$ by d. (This completes the vector projection of $\mathbf{V}$ onto $\mathbf{N}$, $\mathbf{N'}=\mathbf{N}(\mathbf{N} \text{ dot } \mathbf{V})$.)

$$\mathbf{N'} = D(\mathbf{N})$$

Now, add the new $\mathbf{N'}$ to the base point to find a test point projected onto the cylinder (closest point on line):

$$\text{ProjPt} = \text{Bpt} + \mathbf{N'}$$

Compute distance between ProjPt and Cpt and compare it to the sum of the radii:

$$\text{if (Distance(ProjPt, Cpt) } < \text{(rC + rS)) \{ return true \} // collision}$$

Finally, compute the distance between point ProjPt and the sphere center point Cpt and compare it to the sum of the cylinder radius and the sphere radius. If the distance is less than that sum, there is collision. As with sphere-to-sphere collision, the distance squared can be computed and compared to the radius squared as an optimization.

$$\text{if (Distance(ProjPt, Cpt) } < \text{rC+rS) \{ return true; \} // collision}$$

Alternate:

$$\text{if (distanceSquared(ProjPt, Cpt) } < \text{(rC+rS)2) \{ return true; \}}$$
$$\text{// alternate test using more efficient distance squared.}$$

Ray-to-AABB

Given: Ray and AABB:

$$\text{Line point} = \text{Ppt}$$
$$\text{Ray direction vector} = \mathbf{N}$$
$$\text{Box min point} = \text{Min}$$
$$\text{Box max point} = \text{Max}$$
$$\text{Box center} = \text{Cpt}$$
$$\text{Box radius vector} = \mathbf{R} \text{ (Max – Cpt)}$$

See Figure 16.14.

This test introduces the idea of a separating axis to our collision detection test.

The idea is to define a vector that represents an axis that separates the ray from the AABB. The final test will be whether the distance from the ray to AABB is greater than the box's "radius." Vector projection will be used similarly to the ray-to-sphere test.

First, create the vector from the line point Ppt to the box's center point:

$$\mathbf{V} = \text{Cpt} - \text{Ppt}$$

Next, compute the vector projection of $\mathbf{V}$ onto $\mathbf{N}$ as defined in Point-to-Line/Ray.

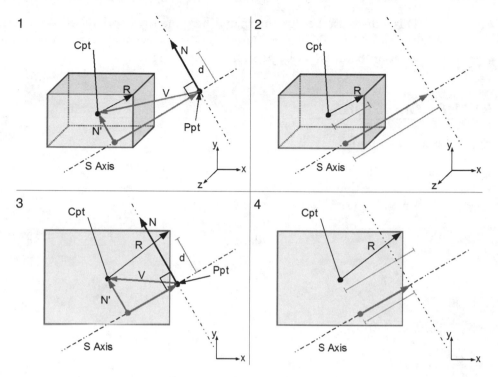

FIGURE 16.14   Ray-to-AABB collision. Frames 1 and 2 show a miss, frames 3 and 4 a hit.

Let d = the dot product of vectors **N** and **V**, then scale vector **N** by d to create **N'**.

To create the separating axis vector, simply subtract **V** from **N'**:

$$S = N' - V$$

The two distances to compare are the length of S and the length of the box's radius projected onto S, which is defined as R dot S if S were normalized. We could do it this way, but it would be more optimized to recognize that we don't need the actual distances because relative distances work similarly to the square distance optimization of sphere collision. In this case, the dot product alone gives us the solution.

if ((S dot S) < (R dot S) { return true; } // collision

This works also because no matter how the ray is oriented to the AABB, the AABB's radius as defined always produces the correct dot/distance for testing, even though it probably won't be pointing toward the ray as shown in the figure.

PLANE COLLISIONS

Closest Point-to-Plane

Similar to the linear feature collision section, we will first examine a "closest point to" technique that will be the foundation for the plane collision set.

Given Plane and Test Point:

$$Plane\ normal = N$$

$$Plane\ point = Ppt$$

$$Test\ point = Tpt$$

See Figure 16.15.

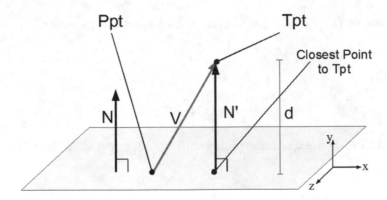

FIGURE 16.15   Closest point to the plane.

First, create the vector from plane point Ppt to the test point Tpt.

$$\mathbf{V} = Cpt - Ppt$$

Next, compute the vector projection of vector $\mathbf{V}$ onto $\mathbf{N}$.

Let d = the dot product of vectors **N** and **V**, and then scale **N** by d.

$$\mathbf{N'} = \mathbf{N}(\mathbf{N} \text{ dot } \mathbf{V}))$$

Finally, subtract **N'** from test point to find the test point projected on to the plane:

$$\text{Closest Point to Tpt: ProjPt} = \text{Tpt} - \mathbf{N'}$$

Sphere-to-Plane

Sphere-to-plane is one of the most useful tests in 3D games. It allows a volume object to test against a flat surface, which is an excellent approximation to many game collision situations. Also, when the required data is built into the game geometry and readily available, this is not only one of the cheapest collisions to compute but also one of the easiest types for which to create simply collision reaction.

Given: Plane and Test Sphere:

$$\text{Plane normal} = \text{N}$$
$$\text{Plane point} = \text{Ppt}$$
$$\text{Sphere center} = \text{Cpt}$$
$$\text{Sphere radius} = \text{R}$$

See Figure 16.16.

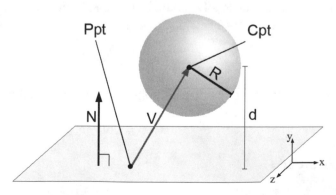

FIGURE 16.16 Sphere-to-plane test—no collision.

First, create a vector from the plane point Ppt to the sphere center point Cpt.

$$\mathbf{V} = \text{Cpt} - \text{Ppt}$$

Next, compute the dot product of vectors $\mathbf{N}$ and $\mathbf{V}$. As was explained in point-to-cylinder collision, when $\mathbf{N}$ is normalized the value of d is equal to the distance along vector $\mathbf{N}$ of vector $\mathbf{V}$'s projection. Because $\mathbf{N}$ is perpendicular to the plane, d is also the distance to the plane from the sphere center point Cpt. Because of this fact, d can be compared to the sphere radius to find possible collision. If d is greater than R, no collision occurred.

$$d = \mathbf{N} \text{ dot } \mathbf{V}$$

if ($d > $ R) { return false; } // no collision

However, if d is less than R, then collision has occurred.

If ($d < $ R) then collision has occurred.

If this is all that is desired to know for a particular routine, quitting here is fine. However, often sphere-to-plane collision tests are used to represent characters or objects colliding with world geometry, and simply detecting this is not enough. We want these objects to be moved out of collision with the plane, which is quite simple to do.

Simple Collision Reaction

To correct the sphere's position from the plane collision, the sphere center must be moved away from the plane. The direction would be along the normal, and the magnitude would be R – D. To make this displacement vector, simply create vector $\mathbf{N}'$ = scale $\mathbf{N}$ by R – D.

$$\mathbf{N}' = (\mathbf{N})R - D$$

Finally, add N' to the original sphere center and put it back into the sphere.

$$\text{Cpt}' = \text{Cpt} + \mathbf{N}'$$

See Figure 16.17.

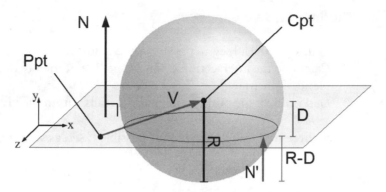

FIGURE 16.17 Sphere-to-plane test—collision occurred.

Ray/Segment-to-Triangle

The Ray/Segment-to-triangle test (see Figure 16.18) is a fundamental collision test in games using 3D geometry. Not only can it be used to represent weapons' projectile travel path against world, object, and player geometry, it can be used for picking and AI line-of-sight testing, as well as an accurate fallback test for any other bounds collision test.

Segment/ray-to-triangle is the most complex and most expensive collision test covered in this chapter. Thus, it will be broken into three stages, each containing collision tests generally useful beyond the use of this segment-to-triangle test.

Given: Line Segment and Triangle:

Triangle/Plane normal = N

Triangle/Plane point = Ppt

Line segment startpoint = P0pt

Line segment endpoint = P1pt

Line direction vector = $\mathbf{L}$ = (P1-P0)

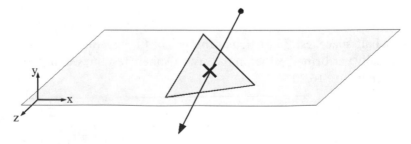

FIGURE 16.18 Line segment-to-triangle intersection.

The three steps are as follows:

1. Quickly reject all segments above and below the plane of the given triangle.
2. Calculate the intersection point of the line of the ray or segment, and the plane of the triangle.
3. Determine if the point of intersection falls within the given triangle.

These three steps can generate four possible cases, as seen in Figure 16.19.

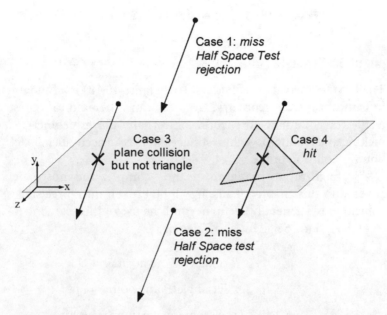

FIGURE 16.19   Line segment-to-triangle rejection cases.

3D Half-Space Test

To quickly reject segments above and below the plane we will use what is known as a half-space test. In particular this will be the general 3D half-space test and was actually performed earlier in the ray-to-sphere test but was not formalized until now. See Figure 16.20.

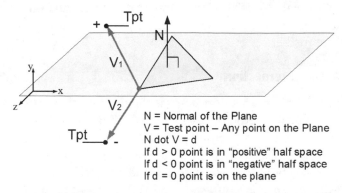

FIGURE 16.20 The 3D half-space test.

The test goes as follows:
Given: Test point and Plane:

$$N = \text{Normal of the Plane}$$

$$Ppt = \text{Any point on the Plane}$$

$$\mathbf{V} = \text{Test point}$$

Create vector from any plane point Ppt to the test point Tpt.

$$\mathbf{V} = Cpt - Ppt$$

Next, compute the dot product of vectors **N** and **V**:

$$\mathbf{N} \text{ dot } \mathbf{V} = d$$

For a half-space test we say that the test point falls on one side or the other of a given plane by the following convention:

$$\text{If } d > 0, \text{ then the test point is in "positive" half-space}$$

$$\text{If } d < 0, \text{ then the test point is in "negative" half-space}$$

$$\text{If } d = 0, \text{ then the test point is on the plane}$$

Used in the line segment-to-triangle test, we perform two 3D half-space tests, one for each of the line segments endpoints. If they are both on the same side of the plane, then the line segment does not cross the plane and there is no collision.

If the line segment's endpoints are not on the same side, then the line segment crosses the plane and there is a guaranteed intersection point. If we wish only to detect line segment-to-plane collision, we could quit now; however, for triangle, we must test further.

Segment-to-Plane Intersection

Computing the intersection point is the most costly part of this algorithm but is often unavoidable, even in cases where the final point in the triangle test fails. The process is essentially computing a ratio between the length of the line segment along the normal to the distance between the line segment start point and the plane. This ratio will be between 0.0 and 1.0, and it describes the scale of the line segment's direction vector (endpoint–start point) that would be at the point of intersection.

For example, if the ratio is 0.0, the intersection point would be at the line segment's start point. If the ratio is 1.0, then the intersection would be at the line segments' endpoint, or start point + ratio scale L (see Figure 16.22).

This can also be described and solved algebraically using the standard plane equation. We have provided the vectorial and algebraic solutions, where d is the ratio solution that must be applied back to the line segment to compute the final point.

Plane eq. $Ax + By + Cz + D = 0$,

$$\text{where } \mathbf{N}\{A,B,C\},$$
$$\text{Ppt}\{x,y,z\}$$
$$D = -(Ax + By + Cz)$$

Parametric Line eq. $P(d) = Po + dL$

$$\text{where } x = Px + dLx$$
$$y = Py + dLy$$
$$z = Pz + dLz$$

Solving both equations for d yields Figure 16.21.

$$\mathbf{d} = -\frac{(AP_x + BP_y + CP_z + D)}{(AL_x + BL_y + CL_z)} \quad \text{or} \quad -\frac{(N \cdot Po) - (N \cdot Ppt)}{(N \cdot L)}$$

FIGURE 16.21   Line-to-plane intersection equation.

Appendix ∎ **About the CD-ROM**

The companion CD-ROM for Practical Java Game Programming contains all of the figures from the book, all the examples from the text, as well as additional libraries and materials as listed. In addition, we have included the Sun J2DK. The folders contained on the CD-ROM include:

Figures: all the figures from the book by chapter

Code: examples, libraries, and materials from each chapter

Sun J2DK: the latest version of the Sun J2DK 1.4.2_04 as well as Java3D, and JOGL for Linux, MacOSX and Win32.

INSTALLATION INSTRUCTIONS

For Java:

Go into the Installs\JDK_1_4_2_04 directory and run appropriate JDK installer for your OS.

For Java3D:

Go into the Installs\Java3D directory and run appropriate Java3D installer for your OS.

For JOGL:

Copy JOGL.jar to project directory. Find appropriate JOGL binaries for your OS and copy to working or lib directory.

For more information see:
http://java.sun.com/
http://java.sun.com/products/java-media/3D/index.jsp
https://jogl.dev.java.net/

System Requirements

- Window 2000 or better, Linux or MacOSX
- Pentium 1Ghz or better
- 100M free hard drive space
- For 3D graphics examples, OpenGL 1.2 accelerated video support is required.
- For some 3D graphics examples full OpenGL 1.4 support is required

A complete listing of all files can be found in the About the CD-ROM document included on the CD-ROM itself.

Index